6-4-86

MICHIGAN STATE UNIVERSITY
LIBRARY
MAY 01 2023
WITHDRAWN

MICHIGAN STATE UNIVERSITY

OVERDUE FINES:
25¢ per day per item

RETURNING LIBRARY MATERIALS:
Place in book return to remove charge from circulation records

PU SPR 1983
ARR WTR 1984
PICKUP SPR 1984
PICKUP WTR 1985
DEC 28 '87
NOV 23 '87
NOV 30 '89
300 A331
MAY 29 1990
MAY 07 1992
MAY 28 1992
JUN 15 1992
FEB 06 1995
342
MAY 06 2008
050108

AF677882

THE CHINESE ECONOMY

The Chinese Economy

Problems and Policies

Second Edition—Revised

By JAN S. PRYBYLA

UNIVERSITY OF SOUTH CAROLINA PRESS

Copyright © University of South Carolina 1978
Copyright © University of South Carolina 1981

Published in Columbia, S.C., by the
University of South Carolina Press, 1981

Manufactured in the United States of America

Library of Congress Cataloging in Publication Data
Prybyla, Jan S
The Chinese economy.
Includes index.
1. China—Economic conditions—1949–1976.
2. China—Economic conditions—1976–
3. China—Economic policy. I. Title.
HC427.9.P74 1980 338.951 80–21979
ISBN087249–398–9
ISBN 0–87249–316–4 (pbk.)

TO

Christopher & Elizabeth

Contents

Maps

Figures

Tables

Preface

China is a giant in all respects but one. Its history spans three thousand years; its artists, men of letters, and inventors have contributed greatly to the advance of world culture and civilization; the numbers of its people are staggering (almost one-quarter of all humanity); the size of its territory is comparable to that of the world's continental powers; the industriousness, ability, gentility, as well as occasional cruelty, of its people are second to none; their fighting ability, when aroused, is awesome. In all these respects, and many more, China is a land that cannot be ignored. Every effort should be made to understand it; sympathetically, but also with rational detachment, for China has a way of ensnaring those who look at it, making them exaggerate its virtues or its faults, usually the former where Westerners are concerned. Cultural and geographical distance, no doubt, contributes to the enchantment.

The one respect in which for some centuries China has been less than a giant is economic. Developed in other ways, China entered the twentieth century in an economically pitiful condition: weak, dependent and retarded. One of the more remarkable events of the last twenty-eight years or so has been the growth of China's economy. The aim, now made explicit, is to expand and strengthen the economy so as to make China into a modern industrial power by the year 2000. It is this undertaking that I examine in this book.

My understanding of China's economy has been much aided by a visit to the People's Republic in 1974. Although the limitations of what are, after all, standard and guided tours are well known, one does gain by personal observation provided one goes intellectually prepared. I am grateful to the Pennsylvania State University and the Ford Foundation for making the visit possible.

In Shanghai I gave a lecture on the United States economy to faculty members from the divisions of political economy and international politics of Futan University, the intellectual bastion at that time of the leftist "gang of four." Elsewhere, in Canton, Suzhou, Wuxi, Nanjing, and Beijing, I had the opportunity to discuss matters of mutual professional interest with economists, educators, government and Party officials, factory managers, and people in charge of rural people's communes. While subject to the constraints de rigeur in socialist monoparty societies, these talks have been by and large useful and informative. Some of what I have learned is narrated in this book and in the various articles to which reference is made in the Suggested Readings at the end of each chapter. It is my hope that these accounts may help promote a better understanding of China's economic construction.

A few shorthand terms of Chinese communist ideology may still puzzle some readers, despite my attempt to clarify them. A useful work in this connection is *A Comprehensive Glossary of Chinese Communist Terminology* (Taipei, Taiwan: Institute of International Relations, 1978).

I am indebted to my many Chinese-American colleagues, scholars from Taiwan, Hong Kong, and Japan, Western students of China, and all those from whose perceptive work on the Chinese economy I have learned over the years. I have also drawn abundantly on China's own official published sources, some of which are listed or footnoted in the text.

Last but not least, I wish to thank Mrs. DonnaMae Weber who typed and retyped the manuscript with accuracy, efficiency, and unflagging good cheer.

JAN S. PRYBYLA
University Park, Pennsylvania
April 1978

Preface to the Revised Edition

Since the mummification of Chairman Mao and the arrest of the "gang of four," the flow of events in China has expanded and speeded up. The changes have been spectacular. The greater part of the Maoist structure of ideas and institutions has been disassembled and put in cold storage. Within the limits imposed by Marxism-Leninism and the Stalinist heritage, China became more open to its own citizens and to the outside world. A large amount of information on negative aspects of past and present economic performance has been made available for the first time as part of the campaign of denunciation directed at the fallen leaders of the left-wing faction. Further evidence of economic and social malaise was given by a brief flowering of dissident wall literature. China has embarked on the path of ambitious economic, scientific, technological, and military modernization which in the years to come will tax its resources, challenge its ingenuity, and test its internal stability. In the spring of 1980, when these words were written, there was no reasonable way to predict which of the several possible directions the economy would take or how durable and successful the venture in modernization would be.

Startling as the developments that followed the death of Mao and the fall of his allies have been, they should be seen primarily, I think, in the context of China's total socialist experience. This experience is full of sharp and wide swings of the political-social pendulum from right to left and back again. The great movements of land reform, socialization, communization, cultural revolution, and cultural counterrevolution are all parts of the pattern. The post-Mao reforms have been, so far, corrections and adjustments within the system needed for the economy to gear up for transition from extensive to intensive growth. The pendulum has been pulled back toward the right from the extreme left position to which Mao and his lieutenants had brought it during the Cultural Revolution.

In conformity with this longer term and broader perspective in which economic change in China should be seen, I have resisted the timesaving temptation of simply adding a chapter on the four modernizations to the ten chapters of the original edition. Instead, I have gone through each chapter and revised the book in the light of information that has become available since the first edition of the work appeared.

I wish once more to thank Mrs. DonnaMae Weber, who with her usual precision, efficiency, and good spirits retyped the manuscript.

J.S.P.
University Park, Pennsylvania
April 1980.

Acknowledgments

Tables 18 and 19 are reprinted from *The Spatial Economy of Communist China*, New York: Praeger (for Hoover Institution Press), 1967, by Yuan-li Wu with the permission of the publishers, Hoover Institution Press. Copyright © 1967 by the Board of Trustees of the Leland Stanford Junior University.

Parts of Tables 8, 13, 14, 15, 16, and 17 have earlier appeared in my article: "A Note on Incomes and Prices in China," *Asian Survey*, Vol. XV, No. 3, March 1975 and are reproduced here with the permission of the editors of that journal.

A part of the discussion of work incentives in Chapter 5 and parts of Tables 7, 8, 11, 12, 13, 14, 15, 16, and 17 as well as Table 10 have appeared earlier in my article "Work Incentives in the People's Republic of China," *Weltwirtschaftliches Archiv* (Review of World Economics), a journal of the Institute of World Economics, Kiel University, Germany, Vol. 112, No. 4, 1976, and are reproduced here with the permission of the editors.

I wish to thank Professor Teh-wei Hu for allowing me to use (with slight modifications) Figures 4 and 5 in Chapter 9, which had appeared in a paper presented by Professor Hu at the Allied Social Science Association meetings in San Francisco (December 1974), and which were subsequently published in his *An Economic Analysis of Cooperative Medical Services in the People's Republic of China* (Washington, D.C.: H.E.W., 1975).

THE CHINESE ECONOMY

MAP 1 China: Major Administrative Divisions

Province-level Names

Conventional	Characters	Pinyin	Pronunciation
Anhwei	安徽	Anhui	ahn - way
Chekiang	浙江	Zhejiang	juh - jee_ong
Fukien	福建	Fujian	foo - jee_en
Heilungkiang	黑龙江	Heilongjiang	hay - loong - jee_ong
Honan	河南	Henan	huh - non
Hopeh	河北	Hebei	huh - bay
Hunan	湖南	Hunan	hoo - nan
Hupeh	湖北	Hubei	hoo - bay
Inner Mongolia	内蒙古	Nei Monggol	nay - mung - goo
Kansu	甘肃	Gansu	gahn - soo
Kiangsi	江西	Jiangxi	jee_ong - she
Kiangsu	江苏	Jiangsu	jee_ong - su
Kirin	吉林	Jilin	jee - lynn
Kwangsi	广西	Guangxi	g_wong - she
Kwangtung	广东	Guangdong	g_wong - doong

Conventional	Characters	Pinyin	Pronunciation
Kweichow	贵州	Guizhou	g_way - joe
Liaoning	辽宁	Liaoning	lee_ow - ning
Ningsia	宁夏	Ningxia	ning - she_ah
Peking	北京	Beijing	bay - jing
Shanghai	上海	Shanghai	shong - hi
Shansi	山西	Shanxi	shahn - she
Shantung	山东	Shandong	shahn - doong
Shensi	陕西	Shaanxi	shun - she
Sinkiang	新疆	Xinjiang	shin - jee_ong
Szechwan	四川	Sichuan	ssu - ch_wan
Tibet	西藏	Xizang	she - dzong
Tientsin	天津	Tianjin	te_en - jin
Tsinghai	青海	Qinghai	ching - hi
Yunnan	云南	Yunnan	yu_oon - nan

ONE

Problems and Policies

PROBLEMS

One of the more lasting impressions one receives in China is of the overwhelming concern, both official and unofficial, with the country's domestic economic problem. Chinese concentration on internal issues is partly traditional: matters indigenous to the Middle Kingdom have always commanded greater attention of people and rulers alike than external ("barbarian") affairs. But the main reason is the sheer size of the economic problem and its immediacy.

In one of his early articles, written in 1919, Mao Zedong defined the problem in stark terms: "What is the greatest question in the world? The greatest question is that of getting food to eat." More elaborately, the problem is how to feed, clothe, house, furnish with simple goods and services of everyday use, and keep in good physical and mental health a very large and growing population (*Jen-k'ou,* literally "people's mouths"). The twin policy challenge is how to keep down the rate of population growth and how to increase supplies.

It is symptomatic of Mao's thought that the greatest question in the world was seen by him not as a narrowly economic question, but as a "cultural" one: a historical obstacle to be removed through mass action directed outward against the encrustations of the social environment, but also and more importantly, through peer-group pressure ("help") and self-criticism, inward against one's innermost self. The greatest question in the world required for its definitive solution nothing short of a profound transformation of man and society, man's total socialization, a merging of the individual with the mass.

As a dynasty, Maoism in China is little more than a quarter of a century old; as an organized movement, Chinese communism is sixty years old. China's history goes back three thousand years, and its weight on the present is enormous. While it would be wrong to underestimate both the resolve and the capacity of the communists to uproot old customs and habits and replace them with "newborn socialist things," it would be equally misleading to discount the staying power of tradition. The often spectacular contemporary changes and oscillations in China's society take place within a slowly changing millenial cultural mold. To understand change in China, one must first comprehend the subtleness of China's continuity. Two illustrations taken from mass campaigns, one drawn from a mass incident, and one historical allegory will illustrate the point. The movement to denounce former defense minister Lin Biao (1907–1971) was bound up with a campaign to uproot the teachings of Confucius (541–479 B.C.). More recently, the campaign to denounce the radical "gang of four" linked Mao's wife, Jiang Qing, to the Empress Lu, wife of Liu Bang, the founder of the western Han dynasty, who reigned from 206 to 195 B.C. Jiang Qing's alleged admiration for Empress Lu was taken as prima facie evidence of her intent to seize Party and state power (the "imperial seal") after the death of Mao. In authoritarian China, recourse to historical allegory—using the past to criticize the present—has always been a weapon of dissent. During the Tiananmen demonstrations in Beijing (April 1976) following the death of Zhou Enlai, some of the 100,000-strong masses chanted: "Gone for good is Qin Shihuang's feudal society. What we want is genuine Marxism-Leninism." These sentiments were interpreted by the official Chinese press agency, Xinhua, as "tricks of insinuation . . . vicious attacks on and slander of our great leader, Chairman Mao." Mao was certainly the target, though clothed in the robes of the "first emperor" founder of the Qin dynasty (221–205 B.C.), unifier of China, builder of a strong nation, scourge of the scholars, burner of books, Mao's favorite. The dynasty Qin founded was destroyed by peasant uprisings soon after his death.

A few years later as the trampled hundred flowers cautiously began to revive, the Beijing *Workers' Daily* (*Guangming Ribao*, July 17, 1979) published a historical essay by Guo Zhengzhong which related the misfortunes of Fen Zhongyan, an upright official and scholar of the northern Song dynasty, who had proposed a "new deal" to save the dynasty from the people's wrath. "The failure of the 'Qingli New Deal' was followed by the failure of Wang Anshi's reform movement. Thus, the attempts to bring about a change in the situation of long-standing poverty and weakness [the "four modernizations" of yore] were futile. The northern Song dynasty was never able to recover after this setback. Eventually it fell amid domestic troubles and foreign invasion. This is a lesson taught us by history."

POLICIES

In his 1919 article, Mao also sketched the outline of policy to be followed in solving China's problems. "What is the greatest force? The greatest force is that of the union of the popular masses. What should we not fear? We should not fear heaven. We should not fear ghosts. We should not fear the dead. We should not fear the bureaucrats. We should not fear the militarists. We should not fear the capitalists." Already at the germination stage of his political thought, Mao places the bureaucrats on the same low footing with heavenly destiny, evil spirits, ancestral bondage, warlords, and the exploiting classes. Toward the end of his life he will say: "The bureaucrat class on the one hand and the working class together with the poor and lower-middle peasants on the other are two classes sharply antagonistic to each other." Ridding China of the "three great differences"—the difference between town and country, workers and peasants, mental and physical labor—and success in the "three great revolutionary struggles"—class struggle, the struggle for production and for scientific experiment—depend on the adherence by everyone to the correct ideological line and the adoption of organizational forms and methods of struggle suitable to the task. "The correctness or incorrectness of the ideological and political line decides everything," the late Chairman Mao taught.

Ideological Line

To know precisely what the correct ideological line is at any given moment is not as easy as it sounds. There is, of course, a certain sediment of unchangeables, a theme, a leitmotiv running through the whole, but essentially the line is dialectical, derived from the principle of contradictions. It shifts, it changes, it unpredictably assumes its own opposite. "In my humble opinion," says Mao, "there is only movement in heaven and on earth." One must be nimble, one must be quick, seize the time, seize the hour, distinguish between "us" and the enemy, between Marxists and sham Marxists, and not be caught napping in the two-line struggle. To help rattled cadres find the correct line ("emancipate their minds" is the official phrase) the "pragmatists" in the post–gang-of-four leadership (people around the twice-toppled, twice-resurrected Deng Xiaoping) explained that practice is the sole criterion for testing truth, which apparently still left a lot of people puzzled and apprehensive. "Some comrades . . . are not accustomed to this, thinking that things have been 'messed up.' "[1]

The dialectical line to which all must adhere is an onslaught against immobility: the old immobility bequeathed by feudal history and the new immobilism of socialism's bureaucratic crust. The dialectical principle, with its inexhaustible fund of surprises and shifting rules of the game, serves the role that in other societies is played by competition: it works against the bureaucratization and routinization of structures, keeps officialdom off balance and the masses on edge. At a more mundane level it reflects disagreement among leaders on theory and policy as well as career rivalries and personal dislikes. At times the sinuous dialectical line produces the opposite of what is intended ("liveliness"). Wary of making a move that may be judged deviant tomorrow though correct today, cadres "cringe in fear afraid of wind and storm." "Some comrades have many worries and act slowly in implementing policies, fearing that they might be accused of being rightists. They are troubled by many taboos when they should eliminate chaos and restore order, afraid to touch this and that, and their thinking is . . . in an ossified or semiossified state." [2]

[1]*Beijing Review (Peking Review)*, July 13, 1979, p. 4.

[2]*Renmin Ribao*, May 21, 1979, in *Foreign Broadcast Information Service (FBIS)*, May 24, 1979. At a work conference organized by the Anhui Province Party Committee in January 1979, Li Jide, secretary of the Chao County Party Committee said: "For many years we felt that it was indeed difficult to be a county Party Committee secretary and a basic level cadre. What was regarded as correct one day, would be regarded as wrong the next day. You would not know what to follow. Today it is said that we have 'obsessive lingering fears' and are 'affected by pernicious influences.' Why do we have such 'obsessive lingering fears' and why are we 'affected by pernicious influences'? Do the higher authorities understand how we county Party Committee secretaries think? Those incessant political movements have made us all very nervous." Beijing Radio, January 24, 1979, in *FBIS*, January 31, 1979. "Those comrades who have been deeply influenced by the ultra-Left line and whose thinking has become ossified or semiossified oppose the discussion [of practice being the criterion of truth] denouncing it as 'de-Maoization.' " *Beijing Review*, September 28, 1979, p. 3.

With deceptive simplicity the principle states that every phenomenon contains its own contradiction, which may be benign (contradiction "among the people") or malignant (contradiction "between us and the enemy"). Benign contradictions are called "nonantagonistic"; malignant contradictions are said to be "antagonistic." In interpreting the principle it is possible to emphasize the divisive or complementary aspect of the contradiction: that which divides (the "one divides into two" version), which calls for struggle and the elimination of the incorrect component; or that which unites (the "two combine into one" version), which implies reconciliation, relative moderation, balance, and routine—a process of assimilating and culling. What constitutes a contradiction at any time and the character of the contradiction (benign, malignant) are defined by the appropriate Party authorities speaking for the masses. The appropriate Party authorities are those in power at the time the interpretation is made. On October 7, 1976, the day the leaders of the radical faction were arrested and Hua Guofeng assumed the chairmanship of the Communist Party of China, the Beijing *Guangming* daily, ignorant of the change, published a very "leftist" (and as it happened, by then "incorrect") article by Liang Xiao castigating sham Marxists, that is, those at the helm at that moment. Since then, philosophical emphasis by and large has been on the "two combine into one" aspect of the contradiction as allegedly exemplified in Mao's April 25, 1965, speech "On the Ten Major Relationships" (five of which, incidentally, deal with the economy) and in the "Four Modernizations" enunciated by Zhou Enlai in January 1975 (modernization of the army, agriculture, industry, and scientific research). The principle of contradictions is now being referred to also as the "theory of two points," which, it is said, is "a theory of emphasis": not of mutually exclusive choices, but of differing stresses. The radical gang of four has been accused, among others, of failing to understand the complementary relationship between revolution ("politics") and production. "They shouted 'revolution' as if shouting 'revolution' would make food fall from heaven."

Pursuing the correct line with all its twists and turns must be accompanied by the adoption of organizational forms and methods of struggle appropriate to the task at hand.

Organizational Forms and Methods of Struggle

"Revolution," says Mao, "is trouble-making." But the making of trouble, especially after power is seized, must not be allowed to get out of hand and disorganized. The counterweight to revolution's being trouble-making

("Great disorder in the land leads to great order") is Mao's opinion that "the Public Security Búreau is an instrument of [proletarian] dictatorship." There is nothing populist, spontaneous, or disorganized about Public Security Bureaus. "Discipline," the late Chairman stresses, "is the guarantee for the implementation of the line." Appeals for the participatory upsurge of the popular masses have always been restrained in the People's Republic by calls for the strictest of disciplines and tough organization reaching to the very roots of society. While there is (especially on the left) an ambivalence about structures and a hankering after uninhibited social contracts with the masses, the "natural Leninism," as Stuart Schram calls Maoism's organizational instinct, effectively prevents all factions from treating organization lightly. In Communist China organization—political, social, cultural, economic—has always been extremely thorough and resistant. It would be a serious misrepresentation of Maoist thought and policy to imply that Maoism condones spontaneity somehow held together by the welding power of the charismatic leader and his thought. The reservations have been not about institutional structures per se, but about the routinization of structures and their coalescing into special privilege. Despite the propensity to factionalize and pettily to personalize conflict, the organizational principle, the regimentation of people in transparent organizational boxes, has never been seriously questioned or weakened—not even during the worst turmoil of the Cultural Revolution. After the toppling of Mao's radical allies, the organizational principle reasserted itself in all its bureaucratic intricacy.

Three methods have been used to put organization to work to solve China's economic problems: orthodox administration, mass campaigns, and peer group pressure.

Orthodox administration is the day-by-day running of the economy by administrative order: planning, moving forward "link by link." This method necessitates the presence of managerial-bureaucratic hierarchies and a degree of stability. At the very least the link-by-link method produces well-behaved elites inclined to cronyism. In the eyes of some, it gives rise to an incipient ruling and exploiting class.

The solution of problems through wave-by-wave assaults, "the hurricane type of mass revolutionary movement," as Jiang Qing approvingly described the method of mass campaigns, has been employed in China frequently since the foundation of the People's Republic, and earlier in the communist liberated areas. From the standpoint of its proponents, the mass campaign is an instrument of mass participation, a counterweight to the creeping elitism of the link-by-link approach. Campaigns compel the involvement of masses of people in the affairs of the nation, combat apathy, and purge the elites. They are counted on—at least by their left-wing proponents—to bring about far-reaching changes in the structure of society and to generate technical and scientific inventions and innovations. The stringing out of mass movements, unpredictable in their timing, intensity, scope, object, and duration, gives rise to a wavelike motion full of treacherous eddies and whirlpools that swallow up the opposition and those caught napping in the two-line struggle. "I think it is a good thing to have this tidal wave. Brains which have not thought for many years may think again under its impact. At the worst, it is just a mistake," ruminated Mao in October 1966 in the midst of one of the largest political catharses in China's postwar history. Under pressure from a temporary alliance of the military (including Defense Minister Peng Dehuai and some thirty generals) and civilian cadres, Mao admitted at the 1959 Lushan conference that the Great Leap Forward mass campaign had its shortcomings: "Coal and iron could not walk by themselves and had to be transported by rolling stock. I did not anticipate this point. . . . Before August of last year I devoted my main energy to revolution. Being basically not versed in [economic] construction, I knew nothing about industrial planning." His decision to establish overnight countless backyard blast furnaces was in error: "This created a great disaster when 90 million people went ahead to smelt steel." But this great disaster is soon dismissed as relatively minor and it is praised for its educational value: "We have paid a price, blown some 'communist wind,' and enabled the people of the entire nation to learn a lesson." The modalities, not the method of mass campaigns, are at issue. Only after the defeat of the leftists has the method of mass campaigns been hesitantly shelved—for the time being. "We recognize," said the new Chairman, "that class struggle has not yet come to an end and that at the same time there is no longer any need for large scale and turbulent class struggle waged by the masses, and therefore we should not try to wage such a struggle in the future." There are to be no more tidal waves, no more cultural revolutions. But not everyone agrees. Some "comrades have been unhappy with the eradication of the pernicious influence of Lin Biao and the gang of four, and have defended their erroneous line." [3]

At the micro level of the individual citizen and the family, the method of the mass campaign has its equivalent in peer-group pressure or "public opinion," as it is sometimes called. It is the principal means of securing individual compliance with the mass line. The individual's

[3] Fuzhou, Fujian Radio, May 24, 1979, in *FBIS*, May 24, 1979.

desire to gain group approval and avoid group censure is deeply rooted in Chinese culture to the point that the notion of individuality takes on a collective meaning. One's private life is a book open to scrutiny by one's peers: formerly the family, today the city lane or block committee, neighborhood association, workshop cell, rural production team, or some other basic group unrelated by blood, organizationally linked to the center. The propensity to define privacy in bulky terms is today strengthened by the institution of public criticism and group struggle against the deviant individual, the soul-wrenching exercise of self-criticism, and the fact that everyone belongs to at least two basic groups: at the place of residence and at the place of work. Collective discipline is internalized by making private life transparent. There is no place to hide. There is no option space. There is no freedom of silence.

In the pages that follow, the economic problem in China is broken down into its main functional components of population, industry, money and banking, transportation and communications, domestic and foreign trade, and social issues (public health and education). In each case the elements of the problem are presented, followed by an examination of the policies used to deal with the challenge. The record is summarized and assessed in the final chapter.

SUGGESTED READING

Bettelheim, Charles, and Neil Burton, *China Since Mao* (New York: Monthly Review Press, 1978).

Bouc, Alain, *Mao Tse-tung: A Guide to His Thought* (New York: St. Martin's Press, 1977).

Cell, Charles P., *Revolution at Work: Mobilization Campaigns in China* (New York: Academic Press, 1977).

Chang, Parris H., *Power and Policy in China,* 2nd revised edition (University Park: Pennsylvania State University Press, 1978).

Ch'en, Jerome, *Mao Papers: Anthology and Bibliography* (New York: Oxford University Press, 1970).

Chen, Jo-hsi, *The Execution of Mayor Yin and Other Stories from the Great Proletarian Cultural Revolution* (Bloomington: Indiana University Press, 1978).

China Quarterly (London). Two articles: (1) Andrew J. Nathan, "Policy Oscillations in the People's Republic of China: A Critique," No. 68, December 1976, pp. 720–33. (2) Edwin A. Winckler, "Policy Oscillations in the Peoples Republic of China: Reply," No. 68, December 1976, pp. 734–50.

Chu, Godwin C., and Francis L. K. Hsu (eds.), *Moving a Mountain: Cultural Change in China* (Honolulu: University Press of Hawaii, 1979).

"Correct Approach to Marxism," *Beijing Review* (Beijing), November 23, 1979, pp. 9–13.

Gurley, John G., "The Past in China's Economic Present," *China Quarterly* (London), No. 65, March 1976, pp. 120–27.

———, *China's Economy and the Maoist Strategy* (New York: Monthly Review Press, 1976).

Hiniker, Paul J., *Revolutionary Ideology and Chinese Reality: Dissonance under Mao* (Beverly Hills, Calif.: Sage Publications, 1977).

Lee, Tai-ling, and Miriam London, "A Chinese Round Table on the Passing of Mao," *Freedom at Issue* (New York), No. 40, March–April 1977, pp. 3–9.

Leys, Simon, *Broken Images: Essays on Chinese Culture and Politics* (London: Allison and Busby, 1979).

Li, Honglin, "How to Look at the Two-Line Struggle in the Party," *Beijing Review*, June 1, 1979, pp. 13–15, 27.

Mao Zedong, *Selected Works*, 5 Vols. (Beijing: Foreign Languages Press, 1961–1977).

Monthly Review (New York): (1) Three articles by Paul M. Sweezy ("China: Contrasts with Capitalism"), Harry Magdoff ("China: Contrasts with the U.S.S.R."), and John G. Gurley ("The Formation of Mao's Economic Strategy, 1927–1949"), Vol. XXVII, No. 3, July–August 1975, Special Issue. (2) Paul M. Sweezy, "Theory and Practice in the Mao Period," Vol. XXVIII, No. 9, February 1977, pp. 1–12.

Munro, Donald J., *The Concept of Man in Contemporary China* (Ann Arbor: University of Michigan Press, 1977).

New China's First Quarter-Century (Peking: Foreign Languages Press, 1975).

Schram, Stuart R., *The Political Thought of Mao Tse-tung*. New and enlarged edition. (New York: Praeger, 1969).

———, *Mao Tse-tung Unrehearsed: Talks and Letters, 1966–1971* (London: Penguin, 1974). American edition: *Chairman Mao Talks to the People: Talks and Letters, 1966–1971* (New York: Pantheon Books, 1975).

Solomon, Richard, *Mao's Revolution and the Chinese Political Culture* (Los Angeles: University of California Press, 1971).

State Statistical Bureau: (1) *Ten Great Years: Statistics of the Economic and Cultural Achievements of the People's Republic of China* (Peking: Foreign Languages Press, 1960). Reprint: Western Washington State College, Program in East Asian Studies, Occasional Paper No. 5, with an Introduction by Feng-hwa Mah (Bellingham, Wash., 1974). (2) Communique on Fulfillment of China's 1978 National Economic Plan (June 27, 1979), *Beijing Review*, July 6, 1979, pp. 37–41; (3) Communique on fulfillment of 1979 Plan, *Beijing Review,* May 12, 1980, pp. 12–15, and May 19, 1980, pp. 20–24.

Wilson, Amy Auerbacher, Sidney Leonard Greenblatt, and Richard Whittingham Wilson, *Deviance and Social Control in Chinese Society* (New York: Praeger, 1977).

Wilson, Dick, *Mao Tse-tung in the Scales of History* (Cambridge: Cambridge University Press, 1977).

Witke, Roxane, *Comrade Chiang Ch'ing* (Boston: Little, Brown, 1977).

Yip, Wai-lim (ed.), *Contemporary Chinese Culture: Recent Trends*. Occasional Papers Reprint Series in Contemporary Asian Studies, University of Maryland School of Law (Baltimore, 1976).

TWO

Population

PROBLEMS

The only integrated population figures released by Communist China cover the years 1949–1956. They were published in *Statistical Bulletin (T'ung-chi Kung-tso)* No. 11, on June 14, 1957. The national population figure revealed by the census of 1953 was 582.6 million growing at 2 percent a year. The urban component at that time was 77.3 million. The 1953 survey is the only known post-Liberation census. A population count, probably for police registration purposes, was made in 1964/65, but the results were not made public. This count was referred to by Zhou Enlai in conversation with a group of American visitors in August 1972, at which time Zhou mentioned that the count had shown a population of around 700 million with a natural increase rate of just under 2 percent a year. In 1978 it was announced that "the rate of population growth in Beijing, Shanghai, Tianjin, the biggest cities in China [with an estimated combined population of about 26 million in 1977], and in Sichuan and Shandong provinces, the two most populous provinces, as well as in Hebei, Liaoning, Jiangsu, and Hubei provinces has already dropped to below 1 percent in the last few years." [1] This would mean that by 1977,

[1]*Beijing Review*, July 21, 1978, p. 4. In 1978 the natural population growth rate in

replacement-level fertility had been reached by more than half of China's people who live in these three municipalities and six provinces. A communique issued in April 1980 by the State Statistical Bureau put the population of China at 970.92 million as of the end of 1979. The rate of natural population increase at that time was said to have been 1.17 percent. [2] The objective for 1980 was to lower the rate to 1 percent. By 1985, it was said, the rate should drop to 0.5 percent. If China had succeeded in reducing her rate of natural population increase by two-fifths between 1965 and 1979, approaching replacement fertility levels, this would represent a monumental achievement for a very populous developing country. The question is, are these claims credible?

The argument in support of the claims draws on the enormous effort made by the Chinese authorities since the early 1960s to advance birth control (an effort disrupted for a while by the Cultural Revolution of 1966–69) and the modernizing changes that have occurred in Chinese society since 1949. These changes include increasing industrialization of the countryside, rising standards of health and literacy, and movement toward greater economic independence for women.

There are, however, arguments that urge caution in accepting the claims at face value. China's population statistics are not very good for at least three reasons. First there has been neglect in training professional demographers and in using those demographers who are available to collect and analyze population data. Second, the whole population problem is highly politicized. Not only are population statistics compiled by political authorities, but these authorities (especially at the commune level) are under great pressure to show positive, not to say instant, results in the birth-control campaign. [3] Third, there is some underreporting of births in rural areas and of deaths in the cities. Basic grain and private plot allocations to households are made by village-level (production team) authorities on the basis of family size as they

---

Sichuan Province (estimated total population in excess of 100 million) was reported as being 0.5 percent. *Beijing Review*, July 6, 1979, p. 20.

[2] *Beijing Review*, May 19, 1980, p. 25. Before 1949, according to P. R. C. sources, the infant mortality rate in Beijing was 117.6 per thousand. Most of the infants died of infectious diseases. By 1978 the rate had declined to 10.3 per thousand, the main causes of death being pneumonia, premature delivery, and congenital troubles. *Beijing Review*, September 29, 1979, p. 6.

[3] When the "Five-Anti" campaign was launched in 1952, the call went out to discover grafters, tax evaders, cheaters on government contracts, thieves of state property, and corruptors of state officials. Within a few days of the launching of this campaign, the head of China's secret police announced that 80 percent of his administrative personnel were corrupt in various degrees. *Renmin Ribao*, January 17, 1952.

know it. In any event, registering births at commune headquarters means the bother of a trip with little material payoff. In the cities, food and other ration coupons are issued to individuals; hence the registration of additions to the family through birth has a compelling rationale. Moreover, most births in urban areas take place in hospitals, which are more likely than rural households to comply with birth registration regulations. [4] Recent experiments in promoting birth planning may further encourage the underregistration of births. In Sichuan Province, for example, a bonus of 5 yuan a month is paid to families that pledge to have no more than one child. The bonus is equivalent to about 10 percent of an average industrial worker's monthly wage. Under this scheme families with only one child are eligible for the same housing space as a family of four. Moreover, the only child is to receive preferential treatment in school admissions and job assignments. In rural areas single children count as 1.5 persons in the allocation of private plots and are eligible for an extra grain ration. [5]

Assuming that the 1979 figure of 971 million for continental China is accurate, and assuming that the natural population increase rate of 1.17 percent is not too far from the truth, what are the implications for China?

In 1979 mainland China added 11.4 million people to its numbers, that is, more than 1,300 new mouths to feed and bodies to clothe and shelter every hour. If, as planned, the natural rate of population increase in 1980 was actually squeezed down to 1 percent (which, I think, remains highly questionable), then in 1980 an additional 9.7 million people had to be fed, clothed, and housed. While a dent has undoubtedly been made in the population problem, it remains just that: a dent. The new Chinese population figures must be viewed gingerly, not because the Chinese authorities are out to deceive the rest of the world by keeping two sets of books, but because they work from imperfect data. China's attempt to cut the rate of natural population growth by half between 1980 and 1985 (from 1 to 0.5 percent) will meet with formidable obstacles, not the least of which is the large number of people born in the 1960s who, in response to the government's urging, have postponed marriage and will now begin to bear children.

The area of China is 3.7 million square miles, about the same as that of the United States (3.6 million square miles). Over 90 percent of China's people live in the eastern half of the country. Almost all cities of more than a million inhabitants and 90 percent of urban areas with more

[4]These points are raised by Judith Banister in an unpublished paper on "Current Population Growth in China," November 1978 (Honolulu: East-West Population Institute).

[5]*New York Times*, April 24, 1979, p. A2.

than 50,000 inhabitants are located in the east. Population densities in the east begin at 130 persons to the square mile; two-thirds of the eastern half of the country has densities in excess of 260 people a square mile; one-third shows densities above 520 per square mile.

Although impressive numerically (nearly 80 million additional people between 1953 and 1978), the rate of urbanization since the early fifties has been quite modest, especiallly when compared with urbanization rates of other developing countries. In 1953 urban population represented about 13 percent ot total population; in 1979, according to Western estimates, it was not much more than 18 percent. By contrast, in Taiwan urbanization has proceeded rapidly. In 1953, 17 percent of the population lived in cities of over 100,000 inhabitants; by 1979 the proportion was 45 percent (50 percent if the count is for localities of over 20,000 inhabitants). Today around 80 percent of the working people of mainland China still make their living directly from the soil, a proportion not very different from that of the early 1950s. By contrast, in Taiwan (1978) less than one quarter of the working population was engaged in agriculture, compared with just under two-thirds in the early 1950s.

Of China's people, 95 percent are ethnic Chinese or Han. The remaining 5 percent (roughly 49 million people) consists of 55 minority peoples—or "minority nationalities" as they are officially called—most of whom live in border areas. Culturally and linguistically the minorities are distinct from the Hans. Ten of the nationalities have more than a million members each. The smallest groups each have only a few hundred people.

About one-third of the population is believed to be under twenty years of age. It is a generation that has not experienced war on the country's territory but does have childhood memories of officially sponsored civil strife and vivid recollections of the brief but violent post–Cultural Revolution mopping-up operation known as the "Strike-One-Oppose-Three" *(i-ta-sa-fan)* movement. [6] The young are literate; most have had about five years of formal education, disrupted by the Cultural Revolution of 1966–69; they are by and large committed and politically alert, also perhaps more skeptical than the immediate pre- and post-revolutionary generations. From the standpoint of the leadership the relative youthfulness of the population is both an asset and a potential liability. The asset consists in the comparatively advanced skills of the young (even though formal training suffered in the wake of the Cultural Revolution), their unquestioned patriotism, health, energy, drive, vital-

[6]The campaign, begun in 1969 and continued into 1970, was intended to "strike at counterrevolutionaries, oppose corruption and theft, speculation, waste and extravagance." It was reportedly accompanied by numerous executions.

ity, and receptivity to technical change. All are valuable resources in the task of socialist transformation and construction. At the same time, the young are thought by some Party veterans to lack revolutionary experience: they have not been sufficiently tempered by adversity, privation, and struggle—an assessment with which many young people who in the last decade were sent down to work in rural areas would probably disagree. It is alleged in some quarters that the young tend to regard the physicial and educational advantages they enjoy as a normal condition naturally due to them. The malaise often expresses itself in youthful gangsterism in the cities, a problem that apparently is not an isolated one. It merited an editorial in the *People's Daily (Renmin Ribao,* February 10, 1979) and was raised in regional broadcasts originating in places as far apart as Zhejiang and Sichuan. The Sichuan broadcast (December 1, 1978) spoke of "hooligan gangs, murder, arson, robbery, theft, vandalism, and rape." The broadcast from Hanzhou, Zhejiang Province (March 24, 1979) condemned gangs of youth who "halt traffic, damage public property, spread rumors, gamble, practice superstition, engage in hooliganism, and sell pornographic books and magazines at high prices." The possibility exists that some of these gangs trace their origin to the factional youth organizations that mushroomed during the Cultural Revolution. Shorn of ideological content and suppressed, they surface as criminal formations of discontented, disillusioned, often unemployed, urban youths.

It is necessary to repeat that the post-1953 figures relating to China's population give only a very rough idea of the magnitude of the population problem. What they say in essense is that the population is very large and growing; it is overwhelmingly rural, concentrated in the eastern part of the country, ethnically compact, and relatively young. The main issue is the addition of some 10 million people every year to an already impressive assemblage of humanity. If the population increased less rapidly, it would be easier to deal with the economic problem. The key policy question, therefore, is how to slow the rate of natural increase. After a review of China's response to this policy challenge, we shall briefly consider two other aspects of population policy: urban-rural distribution and national minorities.

POLICIES

Birth Planning

Faced with a large and growing population, policymakers have to overcome two obstacles: the first is ideological; the second, political. The ideological problem is whether a family limitation policy should be pursued. If the answer is yes, the question becomes how to implement the policy most effectively. If the answer is no, the problem of feeding, clothing, housing, and ministering to the health of the people remains and, in fact, looms even larger.

Marxist demography does not stand in the way of a family limitation policy, despite Marx's and Lenin's denunciation of the "neo-Malthusians" who, in Lenin's words, "would like to instill in the proletariat the false idea that workers can better their status under capitalism by curtailing the size of their families." A reconstruction of Marxist thinking on the subject suggests that under socialism human reproduction, like material reproduction, is to be planned in the collective interest. "True optimism [regarding the demographic and economic future of mankind]," writes the Soviet demographer Arab Ogly, "rests on the certainty that mankind is capable of subordinating spontaneous processes, including demographic ones, and will ultimately be able to adjust the 'production' of people just as, to paraphrase Engels, it will by then have adjusted the production of goods." [7] On this as on many other points of doctrine, however, Mao held views of his own which could not be readily dislodged. The late Chairman had often stated that of all the treasures in the world, people were the most precious. The Great Leap Forward (1958–1960), the first massive embodiment of Maoist development economics, was a highly labor-intensive exercise: "The more people we have," wrote *Hongqi,* the Party's theoretical journal in 1958, "the better, faster, greater, and more economical will be the results of socialist construction." The implication seemed to be that the danger of overpopulation was not imminent. Overpopulation was derivative of the structure of economic and social organization; it was not absolute. Nationalist sentiments and the rather common identification of national power with the number of nationals were also present, however discreetly, in Mao's position. The contrary argument, made by some of Mao's advisers, was that a large and rapidly increasing population made the solution of the economic problem extremely difficult, whatever the institutional setting. The importance of population—to socialism, to the country—resided in the quality of the people, not in brute numbers. The quality of the people was primarily defined by the people's health and their educational attainments, including political education. Large and growing numbers rendered qualitative improvement elusive, perhaps impossible. In the Chinese debate on the principle to be adopted in

[7]*Literaturnaya Gazeta* (Moscow), June 11, 1966.

TABLE 1 **Oscillations in Population Policy**

Period	*Pro-Natalist*	*Family Planning*	*No Clear Policy*
1949–1954	X		
1954–1958		X	
1958–1961	X		
1961–1966		X	
1966–1969			X
1969–present		X	

regard to population policy, the birth control argument was cast, most of the time, in terms of (a) planning ("the development of China's national economy in a planned and proportionate way demands that the population also grow in a planned way"), (b) the health benefits accruing to the mother and, more generally, the need to emancipate women from old prejudices and customs, and (c) the educational advantages that children derive from being members of small families.

The continuing struggle between the two opposing views is seen in the oscillation and turnabout of China's population policy since 1949. The wavering is now denied, but that does not alter the fact that it existed. In the (nonantagonistic) confrontation of pro- and anti-natalist principles of policy, the latter have carried the day. The "limited-births planning program" (*chi-hua-sheng-yu*), as the policy inaugurated in 1969 is called, was for a while after 1976 given legitimacy by being linked to the names of Mao, Zhou, and Hua: "During his lifetime, Chairman Mao showed great concern for family planning and issued a series of instructions. Premier Zhou personally directed the work of drawing up plans and laying down the relevant policies. After taking up posts in the central leading organs, Comrade Hua Guofeng himself took charge of the work on family planning." [8] The program puts greater than ever emphasis on the rural areas, makes use of both modern and traditional techniques of family planning, and—coordinated by the Party and government center—is implemented primarily by local public health authorities. Given the relatively high (as measured by the yardstick of developing countries) educational level of China's population (roughly equivalent to fifth grade) and the absence of religious obstacles to birth control, it is possible that the problem of overcoming traditional populationist attitudes on family size may be less formidable in China than in many other countries at a roughly similar stage of economic development.

[8] *Peking Review*, March 25, 1977, p. 29.

In line with a general stress on prevention in public health work, contraception is preferred to abortion. Abortions, however, are legal, available within the public health system, and free. During the period of recuperation the woman worker receives her regular wages or work points.

Modern birth control techniques include oral contraceptives (reportedly including male pills called "gossypol" made of a cottonseed derivative), IUDs, condoms, sterilization (vasectomies and tubal ligations), and abortions performed by qualified personnel. It should be noted that most of these techniques have been used in the past, but in a different social context and in a different manner. Oral contraceptives in the form of various herbs dispensed by practitioners of traditional Chinese medicine, midwives, and others were available. Male sterilization has not been unknown in China, and abortion is the world's most ancient birth control technique. The modernity of contraceptives, sterilizations, and abortions in China today consists in the legalization of the techniques, in their inclusion in the medical and public health systems and their integration in the officially approved public ethic, as well as in the emphasis on chemical and surgical intervention.

Postponement of marriage, spacing of children, and small families (*wan, xi, shao,* "late, sparse, and few," as the slogan puts it) may be regarded as more traditional techniques of family planning, although they presuppose a change of traditional attitudes on early marriage, family size, and the status of women within the family and society. A significant effort has been deployed since 1949, but especially since the Cultural Revolution, to improve the position of women by raising their educational level and increasing their participation in economic and social life on an equal basis with men. "Women," so goes the slogan, "support half the heaven." Two sets of comments should be made in this connection. First, the sharp increase in China's labor-participation ratio which seems to have occurred since the mid-1960s and which involved large numbers of women entering the labor force may have relatively little to do with the equality objective but much with static wages and rising consumer aspirations for the higher priced "secondary" (or "luxury") goods, such as bicycles, sewing machines, and simple household durables. In the setting of static money wages one way to get at these goods is by raising family disposable personal income through the entry of family members hitherto not employed or partly employed into the labor force. Second, despite marked progress made in the last thirty years to improve the status of women in Chinese society, traditional attitudes of male superiority have not been eliminated altogether, especially in the countryside. There have been complaints, for example, that women are shunted to lower paid jobs and that when they do the same jobs as the men, they are paid less. [9]

Sexual restraint outside the marriage bond may also be seen as a traditional birth control method, particularly important in China's cultural setting. The Chinese program of birth planning today combines modern and traditional techniques with, for the time being, strongly discouraging sexual relations outside marriage, encouraging postponement of marriage, and urging restraint within marriage. The Marriage Law of 1950 sets the marriageable age of 20 for men and 18 for women. Postponement is generally taken to mean that in the cities marriage should not be contracted before the age of 28 in the case of men and 25 in the case of women; in the countryside the relevant ages are 25 for men and 23 for women. Some reports indicate a combined age of 50 for married couples. Refugee reports suggest that there is a fair amount of violation of these minima in the countryside. Marriages are concluded in the old way, in the presence of both families, and are registered only when the bridegroom reaches the officially sanctioned age. A norm of two children per couple with a three-year interval seems to be the ideal. Discreetly ambitious and career-oriented young cadres rarely if ever, to my knowledge, report having more than one child. At the same time no efforts are spared to encourage young couples to use modern contraceptives, which are available free of charge and—in line with the community-service orientation of the public health system—are frequently delivered to the home by health workers together with information on their use. While other countries' experience with fertility-control programs is watched with interest, the major stress is on lessons learned from China's own experiments in this area and on self-reliance in the supply of birth-control devices.

China's birth-planning program is a good illustration of the "two combined into one" principle of "unified guidance, decentralized management." At the very top there is a Birth-Planning Leading Group under the State Council. The group's function is to formulate (on the

[9] "Marriages by purchase" including the payment by the groom's family of a "bride price" are prohibited, but according to refugees in Hong Kong, continue to be widely practiced in the Chinese countryside. A new dimension has been added by the communists' insistence on "correct" (worker, poor peasant, lower-middle peasant) social background, or "element" as it is sometimes called. A prospective bride from the correct element who is also physically fit for hard work might fetch as much as 1,000 yuan: nearly four years' earnings of a poor peasant household and twice the monthly salary of Chairman Hua. *New York Times*, December 19, 1977, pp. 1, 18.

basis of instructions received from the highest Party echelons) general guidelines for the birth-control program and to set minimum standards for its implementation. It acts as a clearinghouse for ideas and a mechanism for the coordination of the national effort. The group's recommendations are probably made directly to the State Council (the highest-known government authority in China) and through the council to the national Ministry of Health. The ministry issues general instructions to provincial health departments, health bureaus of cities and counties, and through them down the line to the thousands of health units in the communes, production brigades, and production teams in the countryside and their equivalents in the towns. It also supervises medical research in special institutes and the manufacture and distribution of birth-control devices. Local (especially provincial, municipal, and county level) public health authorities appear to have considerable latitude in implementing the general guidelines of the birth-planning program. In consultation with the relevant governmental and Party authorities (local governments, Party committees) they decide on the allocation of funds to the program at the local level, the numbers and qualifications of health personnel, the stress to be put on this or that aspect of the program, and other issues. Flexibility in implementing the program and responsiveness to local needs appear to be characteristic of the entire family-planning effort at the present time. The program, it should be noted, does not apply to China's minority nationalities.

To carry out the birth-planning program, the methods of mass mobilization and peer-group pressure are used. Four main mobilization and pressure agencies are involved: the Communist Party network, local governmental organs (formerly Revolutionary Committees) reaching down to the street and production-team levels, the public health service comprising millions of full- and part-time workers, and the mass organizations (youth league, women's federation, labor unions, and so on). Pressure to conform is exerted in various ways: through "heart-to-heart chats" between health or Party workers and young couples, in the course of which the young couples' understanding is "helped" along in the desired direction; during residential meetings of neighbors; by lectures and inquiries at the workplace; by the more formal refusal of neighborhood committees to give young people who intend to marry too early the certificate of good conduct needed to have the marriage legally registered; by setting fertility target quotas for production teams, brigades, factories, and offices; [10] through the use of the grain and

[10]Pedro Pak-tao Ng, "Planned Fertility Socialization in Kwangtung Province," *China Quarterly*, No. 78, June 1979, p. 357. Women's groups in factories frequently decide which

cotton-fabric rationing system; and by creating a general climate of opinion in which having more than two children is felt to be socially reprehensible and downright self-indulgent. Almost certainly the holding of any responsible position within the system and promotion to more desirable jobs and locations is linked to moral restraint.

Given the magnitude of the birth control campaign and the means available to the regime to elicit a fair degree of compliance, it is reasonable to assume that the birth rate has been reduced perhaps not to 1.2 percent a year as claimed, but not too far from it; 1.5 percent appears more probable. But China will have to do better than that. Even a rate of 1.2 percent means the addition of some 10 million people in a year. Eventually, and the sooner the better, the rate of natural increase will have to be pressed down to below 1 percent if living standards are to rise or even to be maintained at present spartan levels. One study of China's population-control efforts concludes that "considering the starting point and the size of the overwhelmingly rural population, China has made impressive progress in a relatively short period of time. Furthermore, she is likely to be the first developing nation of any size to reduce the growth of her population to below 1 percent per year." [11]

Urban-Rural Distribution of Population and Employment

Between 1957 and 1961 a basic change in economic policy took place in China.The Soviet-Stalinist model of development with its emphasis on imbalanced growth favoring capital-intensive heavy industry was replaced by a more balanced concept of growth emphasizing agriculture and labor-intensive industries. Externally, the policy of relying primarily on the Soviet Union and other socialist countries for trade, aid, and advice ("leaning to one side") was replaced by a more diversified policy of "leaning to all sides." But not much foreign aid was expected or received in the decade and a half that followed.While open to offers of foreign assistance (except perhaps during the Cultural Revolution of 1966–1969), China stressed self-help.

Included in the general reappraisal was the government's policy on rural migration to the cities, a phenomenon that normally accompanies economic development. Between 1953 and 1957 urban population in-

---

family will be allowed to have a child in any given year.These groups keep track of the menstrual cycles of women workers to enforce adherence to the plan. Names of workers scheduled to give birth during the year and those allowed to bear a child the year after, are posted on factory walls.

[11] *China's Experience in Population Control: The Elusive Model* (Washington, D.C., 1974), p. 45.

creased by 20 million (from 77 to 97 million). During the same time industrial development produced only 2 million new jobs in modern urban industry. The reason for the relatively modest increase in industrial job openings was that, under the Soviet-type strategy, productivity advances in modern industry, particularly in the favored heavy branches, precluded increases of employment in proportion to output. By 1957 it had become clear to at least some Chinese policymakers that imbalanced, capital-intensive, urban-anchored growth was not going to provide enough jobs in industry to absorb the natural and social increments of urban population growth. The prospect of large-scale urban unemployment, so common in other developing countries, and all the social ills that accompany it became real. The vast labor-mobilization drive known as the Great Leap Forward (1958–1960) was in part intended to mop-up unemployed and underemployed labor in both town and country. One of its unexpected side-products was a monumental, largely spontaneous migration of peasants to the cities, partly to evade the communization of life in the countryside (including the abolition of private plots, free markets, and household sideline activities), partly in response to urban industry's accelerated labor-intake at relatively attractive rates of pay because of sharp increases in industrial enterprise production plans. In 1958 alone, urban population increased by nearly 16 million, of which 10 million are thought to have resulted from migration from the countryside. Then, in 1959–1960, the bottom fell out of the Leap. A three-year depression followed, accompanied by investment and employment cutbacks. Capital imports from the Soviet Union ended; Soviet technical aid was withdrawn; there were many unfinished capital projects in the cities; farm production was down; and food shortages were widespread.

Among the various policies adopted to deal with the crisis was one designed to stop and reverse the "blind outflow" of rural labor to the cities. The essence of the policy was to make labor allocation subject to administrative decision; to eliminate all vestiges of a labor market. In the 1960s the network of administrative controls over labor mobility (a network that had been developing gradually since 1955) came to include (a) local authority permission to leave the farm, (b) permission from city authorities to stay (without such permission the migrant could not legally settle in the town or receive food and cloth ration coupons), (c) the imposition of temporary bans on labor recruitment from the countryside, and (d) massive deportations of surplus labor from the cities to the country for permanent settlement. The last, known as *xia-xiang shang-shan yun-dong* ("down to the country and up to the mountains"), became a quasi-permanent feature of China's labor allocation policy. The target population consisted of "intellectual" urban youths, i.e., graduates of junior and senior middle schools who could not be employed in the cities and, in the eyes of the regime, could be used constructively to promote economic and cultural transformation of the countryside. From 1961 through 1963 some 20 million urban dwellers (including many peasants who had migrated to the cities during the early stages of the Great Leap) were sent to the country. From 1968 through 1978 about 20 million educated urban youths were relocated. One incidental result has been a very modest increase in urban population relative to total population: from 13 percent in 1953 to 18 percent twenty-six years later.

It is argued by some people (mostly adherents of the Maoist left wing) that there are several advantages for the regime stemming from the transfer of large numbers of unemployable young "intellectuals" from the cities to the countryside:

1. Urban governments are relieved of considerable financial burdens and logistical chores involved in providing food, clothing, housing, sanitary and educational facilities, transportation, and other amenities for these extra people. In the countryside the problem is spread over a large number of administrative units and is taken care of by individual peasant families. The deportees usually live in collective households of from 20 to 30 persons which are attached to production teams or brigades of rural people's communes. Increasingly they are settled on special farms that are expected not only to be self-sufficient but also to supply the state with surplus agricultural produce and products of rural industry.

2. Since 1961 China has imported between 3 and 9 million tons of foodgrains (mainly wheat) from the West every year, and exported about a million tons of rice annually. The foodgrains import program represents a sizable charge on China's foreign exchange holdings. One explanation offered for the imports is that in view of China's relatively modest and overburdened rail transportation network, it is cheaper to feed the large coastal cities and eastern urban agglomerations by importing grain from overseas than by carting it overland from the major domestic grain-producing areas. Control over urban population growth and keeping the bulk of the people where the food is grown, at once relieve pressure on the transportation system and reduce the drain on foreign currency reserves.

3. Potential urban unemployment becomes rural underemployment. While admittedly low, the marginal productivity of the deportees

in the countryside is unlikely to be zero. There is plenty of work to be done on water conservation projects, in small local industries, in the public health field, in education, culture, rural trade, and the people's militia. Since expectations and consumption levels are kept low, the saving potential of underemployed labor is tapped and capital is formed where it is needed most.

4. Urban crime and associated social ills are reduced. If the policy works the way it should, everyone in the cities, including retirees, will have a job or will be in school. There will be no drifters; they can be weeded out as soon as they appear.

5. The transferees are expected to act as the leaven of modernization of rural attitudes, including attitudes toward birth control. Modernization through the rustication en masse of urban-educated youths is China's alternative to the more common modernization through urbanization. The city is brought to the country by millions of educated youths instead of the countryside crowding into the cities.

6. Educated young people teach the peasants modern skills and receive in return instruction in traditional farming methods based on the peasants' practical experience. They put theory into practice and learn by doing. They teach the peasants to accept and welcome change and, in turn, have their political consciousness raised by the masses of poor and lower-middle peasants. They are tempered physically and morally to become worthy successors to the revolution.

7. The permanent settlement of large numbers of young people of Han origin in minority-inhabited border areas (a) provides a reliable reservoir of manpower in the event of war (this is particularly true of regions, such as Xinjiang and Inner Mongolia, contiguous to the Soviet Union and the Mongolian People's Republic), and (b) promotes the government's policy toward minority nationalities.

The opposite argument can also be made, and has been made very insistently since the fall of the radicals in October 1976. Rustication puts the burden of assimilating millions of urban youngsters on the shoulders of the rural community, already beset by surplus labor problems, undercapitalization, a housing shortage, low income, and barely adequate food supplies. The effectiveness of the settlers in transforming traditional attitudes and generally acting as modernizers in the countryside depends to a large extent on the migrants' enthusiasm about being rusticated. The resettlement process is marked by considerable compulsion and widespread resentment. Many instances of the rusticated youths' revolutionary laxity and passivity verging on alienation have been cited by the press in the past, presumably for the purpose of teaching by negative example. After the radicals' disgrace, the pent-up resentment and frustration of the rusticated youth surged in a wave of big character posters and demonstrations in Shanghai, Beijing, and other towns.The protesters asked to be allowed to return to the cities from which they had been cast out a decade earlier; they wanted urban jobs and a chance to pursue more formal education.They described their life in the countryside as "dire" existence, full of "great misfortunes; without opportunities." The reaction of the authorities to whom the pleas were addressed was ambivalent at best. Peng Chong, mayor of Shanghai and a member of the Party's Central Committee, summed up the official position: the request was in part reasonable, in part unreasonable. It was unreasonable in that the youth already had permanent work and it was therefore inappropriate for them to return to Shanghai. People from outside Shanghai had helped modernize Shanghai, so it was only right that Shanghai people should help modernize the rest of the country. As for the reasonable part of the request, there were, no doubt, problems with resettlement, but these were matters for the local authorities to solve, not for the big-city machine. In any event, the troublemakers were a minority. [12] On past evidence the protesters run the risk of one day being branded "counterrevolutionaries" and "rightists"—fatal labels, removed only posthumously in most cases. The events of 1978–1979 show clearly that even if one assumes considerable internalization by the rusticated youths of selflessness and the ethic of public service, the lure of city lights has not been extinguished altogether, and personal career aspirations ("wanting to become an official" or perhaps just a factory hand) have not all been uprooted or collectivized. The young people's unwillingness to be torn from their homes and shipped to the backward countryside is matched by the rural authorities' distinct lack of enthusiasm about assuming the additional economic burden involved in the move. Friction between urban-educated young people and the peasants and the mistreatment of city girls by peasants and rural cadres seem to be common. All this is not conducive to the two-way learning process envisioned by the authors of the *xia-xiang* movement.

These economic and cultural problems are connected with the decision taken around 1973–1974 to settle the deportees in groups on special farms. After the gang of four were put away, the premises underlying the

[12] *New York Times*, March 16, 1979, p. A11; *The Guardian* (Manchester), March 29, 1979.

rustication movement came up for high-level reconsideration. The outcome, however, was inconclusive. The impression given was that the program would be wound down gradually, as economic circumstances permitted. Some rusticated youths who had been good workers and showed intellectual promise were to be allowed—in line with the new stress on talent—to apply for repatriation to the cities, there to pursue formal education, perhaps in newly created vocational schools. A few might be permitted to join the urban labor-force as factory and service jobs became available. But others, perhaps most, would have to stay—how long, no one could say—and others still would be persuaded to leave the cities. Presumably (but this was far from clear) the new assignments would be "softer" than most of the old ones. To defuse what was rapidly becoming an untenable situation, the newly sent-down youth were likely to be settled in rural areas not too far from the larger urban centers and the length of their field service to the people would be subject to negotiation. In a number of instances, offices and factories in the cities made direct arrangements with nearby communes for the temporary sending down of the sons and daughters of their employees and for proper treatment of the youths by the farms. In return for this, the communes were granted special "backdoor" favors by the factories and offices (e.g., preferential supply of hard-to-get materials and specialized services). The alleged ideological benefits of rustification (revolutionary tempering of the young by the peasants) are seldom mentioned.

While it is reasonable to argue that Chinese young people are by and large committed, involved, patriotic, socially conscious, receptive to the government's instructions, and responsive to peer-group pressure, the degree of their selflessness and public spiritedness should not be exaggerated. This is as much as to say that normative values espoused by the system are not necessarily identical with empirical behavior: what should be is not always or even generally what is, even though the official version of events suggests that the two are the same.The personal anguish of rusticated young people comes through in the many reports from the countryside published in the press and diffused by radio. At great risk to themselves and to their families who harbor them in the cities, millions of young people have reportedly filtered back into town, where deprived of a residence permit and basic rations they live off petty theft, the black market, and the charity of friends and relatives—frightened, denounced, and tracked down. The periodic rounding-up operations, which in addition to rusticated youths were designed to catch other "illegals" (rural beggars, demobilized soldiers) who sneaked into town when they should have been out in the fields, were known as "blowing up the red typhoon." The point made by those who oppose *xia-xiang* is that the movement not only has caused much personal and family anguish and alienation, but it also has produced (a) misemployment of educated urban youths in the countryside, (b) new crime in the cities, and (c) urban juvenile unemployment, which is not the less real for being suppressed. Hua Guofeng admitted in June 1979 that there was a serious unemployment problem. The plan for 1979 was to provide work for 7 million people in state-owned and cooperative enterprises and to subsidize the creation of work projects and service establishments in large and medium-sized cities to absorb some of the jobless. Seven million urban unemployed represented 7.4 percent of China's 1979 industrial labor force. A year earlier it was revealed that in Jinan, capital of Shandong Province, the unemployed constituted 7.5 percent of the city's total population. Most of the Jinan jobless were young illegals. Rather than blowing up yet another red typhoon, the city fathers absorbed most of the jobless youths in several work projects that included the staffing of new nurseries and kindergartens. The policy shift was significant, and apparently received the blessing of the highest state and Party authorities. [13]

Like birth control, rustication was carried out by means of mass mobilization and peer group pressure. Communist Party agencies at various levels, governmental organs of all kinds, mass organizations, and the schools were harnessed to this task. The ideological gilding that in the past attached to one's being settled permanently in the backward countryside is nowadays much tarnished, and the pressure to go and stay is not as great as it used to be. The policy is being rethought and chances are that eventually it will be dismantled. But before it is dismantled, millions of jobs will have to be created in the cities; not an easy task given the highly capital-intensive, labor-saving, developmental path that China proposes to follow in the years to come.

National Minorities

The question of national minorities is theoretically approached from the angle of class struggle: the national question is seen essentially as a class question. The official thesis has it that China is a unified multi-national

[13] It was revealed that 76 percent of the educated young people sent down by Changzhou municipality had been settled on youth farms on the outskirts of the city. "In the past our children who settled in the countryside came home for money in order to buy rations." Nanjing, Jiangsu Provincial Radio Station, February 3, 1979, in *FBIS*, February 5, 1979.

country in which all nationalities enjoy equal rights. In the past, before Liberation, many national minority groups were oppressed by the Han ruling class.The oppression was in substance the economic exploitation of workers and peasants by the bourgeoisie, which assumed the form of great-Han chauvinism and, in turn, suscitated a response in the form of minority nationalism and a frequently expressed desire of minority groups to break away from China. All this, it is argued, has changed.The people's state recognizes only antagonistic contradictions between the people (workers, former lower-middle and poor peasants, and soldiers) and those outside the people (counterrevolutionaires, rightists, unreconstructed former landlords and rich peasants, bad elements, unregenerate revisionists and die-hard capitalists), and the existence of nonantagonistic contradictions among the people. Basically, the Party's line on minority nationalities is that it is up to the masses of each nationality to decide which category (people or nonpeople) will apply and to what portion of the national group, and which contradiction (nonantagonistic or antagonistic) will be decreed as having occurred.The dictatorship of the proletariat allegedly is blind where skin color is concerned, but it is extremely sensitive to class color.

A revolt such as the one in Tibet in 1959 will bring out the troops and will be followed by years of military occupation known as the preparatory stage for transition to the status of the autonomous region. Incorrect behavior of that kind is not, as some Tibetans claim, a movement to right national and cultural wrongs. In the eyes of the Party it is living proof of the continued existence of influential class enemies in Tibet and the persistence of antagonistic contradictions in the base of Tibetan society.The solution is suppression of the incorrect aspect of the contradiction: in plain language, execution of the rebels and deportation of their children to the interior of China for political education. Some of these children might end up in national minorities institutes where they will be trained to become cadres and do missionary work upon return to their native land. On and off through the post-Liberation years, such policy had been applied to dissent and nonconformist behavior of various national minority groups, including particularly the Tibetans, Kirghiz, Kazakhs, Uighurs, and Hui.This repressive approach toward national, cultural, religious, ethnic, and linguistic diversity was especially evident during the land reform, collectivization, and communization campaigns of 1950–1952, 1955–1956, and 1958 respectively, and during the Cultural Revolution of 1966–1969. [14] The use of strong-arm methods

[14] "Under the gang of four teachers dared not use the Mongolian language in classes and large numbers of Mongolian books and reference materials were burned." Beijing Radio, January 14, 1979, in *FBIS*, January 26, 1979.

against religions and the vandalization of temples and monasteries were perhaps most widespread and intense during the turbulent years of the Cultural Revolution.

In between periods of sharp class struggle, perhaps unintentionally tinged with Han chauvinism and minority nationalism, the contradictions have been generally diagnosed as benign; and the dominant principle governing relations between minority peoples and the Hans has been that which proclaims compromise and reconciliation. As in other respects, People's China has followed here the policy of walking on two legs: in this instance, national unity with folkloric diversity. The essence of this approach is the long-range dissolution of national, cultural, and other superstructural differences through a vigorous socialist development of the economic base of all the regions of China. Since many of the areas inhabited by national minorities are economically backward, they have often been given priority treatment in resource allocation to enable them to catch up with the rest of the country. At the same time, however, because socialist consciousness in many of these regions is relatively low (the people there not only do not much like the Chinese but are unenthusiastic about communism), the policy has been not to force the pace lest benign contradictions turn malignant. Communization of property relations in the countryside, for example, has been slower in such places as Tibet than in China proper. The same caution characterized the regime's policy toward religious beliefs (called "superstitious practices") of the minority peoples, especially the Moslems. Mosques, temples, monasteries are tolerated—even exhibited to visitors—provided they are cultural relics, not functioning institutions. The rule is sometimes bent to accommodate a particularly intense united front campaign. Thus in the wake of the gang's disgrace, the united front organization known as the Chinese People's Political Consultative Conference (moribund since 1964) was revived; the Tibetan Panchen Lama (who had not been seen for fifteen years) showed up at the meeting together with two aged Roman Catholic prelates, a Protestant bishop, and the living buddha of the Chamdo monastery; and two of the remaining ten Lamaist monasteries were propped up, given a fresh coat of paint, and opened for public worship. However, the training of lamas and other religious personnel, banned for years, has never been revived. The guiding idea during periods dominated by the principle of reconciliation and compromise has been peaceful fusion of the nationalities, assimilation (some would say Sinicization). Those distrustful of the policy of merger between 922 million Hans and 49 million others, sometimes cite the wartime analogy of the rabbit pie made up of one horse to one rabbit.

Concretely, how are "two combined into one" in this matter of nationalities?

1. There is a network of institutes for minority nationalities of which the Central Institute in Beijing is the most important. The purpose of these schools is to train Party and government cadres recruited from both the minority nationalities and the Hans, but primarily the former. Upon completion of their course of study these people are sent to minority areas to propagate the knowledge of the mass line acquired in school and to become the representatives and guardians of the people's power. The institutes also run refresher courses for established cadres from minority areas.

2. The development of minority languages and dialects is officially encouraged side by side with the propagation of Mandarin with Peking pronunciation. Marxist-Leninist literature, suitably edited writings of Chairman Mao (and now, again, Liu Shaoqi), works on socialist economic construction, and literary productions on contemporary revolutionary and selected traditional themes are available in various minority languages. The importance attached to the cultivation of minority languages is that these tongues are at present the most effective and expeditious carriers of the Party's message. Local artistic creations (plays, operas) on approved themes are also encouraged.

3. Cultural and linguistic fusion is promoted by service in the People's Liberation Army.

4. Large numbers of Han settlers have been sent to minority areas. The influx of Chinese into such areas as Xinjiang and Inner Mongolia has changed the ethnic composition of those regions. For example, the Mongols today are a minority people in their own land.

SUGGESTED READING

Aird, John S., *Population Estimates for the Provinces of the People's Republic of China: 1953 to 1974.* U.S. Department of Commerce, Social and Economic Statistics (Washington, D.C.: International Population Reports, Series P-95, No. 73, February 1974).

Banister, Judith, *The Current Vital Rates and Population Size of the People's Republic of China and Its Provinces,* Ph.D. dissertation, Food Research Institute, Stanford University, 1977.

———, "Recent Population Changes in China," in *The People's Republic of China: A Handbook* (Boulder, Colo.: Westview Press, 1979).

———, *China's Pattern of Population Growth* (Stanford, Calif.: Stanford University Press, 1979).

Chen, Pai-chao, "Overurbanization, Rustication of Urban-Educated Youths and Politics of Rural Transformation," *Comparative Politics* (New York); Vol. IV, No. 3, April 1972, pp. 261–86.

China: A Geographical Sketch (Peking: Foreign Languages Press, 1974).

China's Countryside: A Vast School for Her Youth (Peking: Foreign Languages Press, 1976).

China's Experience in Population Control: The Elusive Model. Prepared for the Committee on Foreign Affairs, U.S. House of Representatives, by the Congressional Research Service, Library of Congress (Washington, D.C.: U.S. Government Printing Office, September 1974).

"China's Minority Peoples," *Beijing Review,* February 9, 1979, pp. 17–21.

Chinese Approaches to Family Planning (White Plains, N.Y.: M.E. Sharpe, Inc. 1979).

Chinese Women in the Fight for Socialism (Peking: Foreign Languages Press, 1977).

Chen, Muhua, "Controlling Population Growth in a Planned Way," *Beijing Review,* November 16, 1979, pp. 17–20. Also in the same issue: "Interview with a Specialist on Population," pp. 20–22; "Marked Results in China's Most Populous Province," pp. 22–24; and "How Tianjin's Heping District Does It," pp. 25–27.

Croll, Elizabeth, *Feminism and Socialism in China* (New York: Routledge and Kegan Paul, 1978).

Davin, B., *Woman-Work: Women and the Party in Revolutionary China* (New York: Oxford University Press, 1976).

Djerassi, Carl, "Some Observations on Current Fertility Control in China," *China Quarterly* (London), No. 5, January–March, 1975, pp. 40–62.

Dreyer, June T., "Go West Young Han: The Hsia Fang Movement to China's Minority Areas," *Pacific Affairs* (Vancouver), Vol. XLVII, No. 3., Autumn 1975, pp. 353–69.

———, *China's Forty Millions: Minority Nationalities and Integration in the People's Republic of China* (Cambridge, Mass.: Harvard University Press, 1976).

"Fundamental Change in China's Class Situation," *Beijing Review,* November 16, 1979, pp. 9–13.

Ivory, Paul E., and William R. Lavely, "Rustication, Demographic

Changes, and Development in Shanghai," *Asian Survey* (Berkeley), Vol. XVII, No. 5, May 1977, pp. 440–55.

Liu, William, "Chinese Society: Stratification, Minorities, and the Family," in Yuan-li Wu (ed.), *China: A Handbook* (New York: Praeger, 1973), pp. 669–90.

"On Class and Class Struggle," *Beijing Review,* May 19, 1980, pp. 24–26; June 2, 1980, pp. 24–26; June 23, 1980, pp. 13–16.

Orleans, Leo A., *Every Fifth Child: The Population of China* (Stanford, Calif.: Stanford University Press, 1972).

———, "China's Population: Can the Contradictions Be Resolved?" in *China: A Reassessment of the Economy.* A Compendium of Papers submitted to the Joint Economic Committee, Congress of the United States (Washington, D.C.: U.S. Government Printing Office, July 10, 1975), pp. 69–80. [This volume will be cited hereafter as *China: A Reassessment.*]

Osofsky, Stephen, "Soviet Criticism of China's National Minorities Policy," *Asian Survey* (Berkeley), Vol. XIV, No. 10, October 1974, pp. 907–17.

Parish, William L., *Birth Planning in the Chinese Countryside* (New York: American Sociological Association, 1976).

Prybyla, Jan S., "Hsia-Fang: The Economics of Rustication in China," *Pacific Affairs* (Vancouver), Vol. XLVIII, No. 2, Summer 1975, pp. 153–72.

"Religions in China," *China News Analysis* (Hong Kong), No. 1186, August 1980.

Seybolt, Peter J. (ed.), *The Rustication of Urban Youth in China: A Social Experiment* (White Plains, N.Y.: M. E. Sharpe, 1977).

Tien, H. Yuan, "The China Solution to Rapid Population Growth," Paper read at the Population Association of America (April 1980).

Wang, Naizong, "Solving China's Population Problem," *China Reconstructs* (Beijing), Vol. XXIX, No. 4, April 1980, pp. 5–7.

White, D. Gordon, "The Politics of Hsia-hsiang Youth," *China Quarterly* (London), No. 59, July–September 1974, pp. 491–517.

White, Lynn, "Population Control Policies in Urban Communist China: A Political Demography of Shanghai After 1949," in *Proceedings of the Fifth Sino-American Conference on Mainland China* (Taipei, Taiwan: Institute of International Relations, National Chengchi University, 1976), pp. 49–87.

Wolf, Margery, and Roxane Witke (eds.), *Women in Chinese Society* (Stanford, Calif.: Stanford University Press, 1975).

"The Women's Movement in China—An Interview with Luo Qiong,"

China Reconstructs (Beijing), Vol. XXVIII, No. 3, March 1979, pp. 33–36.

You, Youwen, "When a Young Man Gets into Trouble," *China Reconstructs* (Beijing), Vol, XXVIII, No. 6, June 1979, pp. 14–15.

THREE

Agriculture

The agricultural problem in China has been summed up succinctly by Mao Zedong: "The situation in China," he told a conference of Party secretaries in July 1955, "is as follows: due to the large population, there is lack of *cultivated land* . . ., *natural calamities* are frequent . . ., and *operational methods* are backward. . . . The broad masses of *peasants* . . . *still have difficulties* in many areas, and are not yet prosperous."

Since the early 1960s the policy response to the problem has been to place agriculture at the top of the regime's economic priorities. While balanced against other needs, the claims of agriculture were to receive sympathetic hearing. This was a departure from the relative neglect of agriculture during the Soviet-inspired First Five-Year Plan (1953–1957) and the very brief flirtation with the "heavy industry first" approach of 1978. In the 1950s average annual state investment in agriculture was roughly 1 billion yuan (about 7.5 percent of total state investment). In 1979 it was just over 5 billion yuan (14 percent of total state investment).

PROBLEMS AND POLICY RESPONSES

The Problem: Cultivated Land and Natural Calamities

The total land area of China is roughly 2.4 billion acres. Of this about 11 percent is cultivated land. In 1979 the sown area (i.e., that sown or transplanted with agricultural crops) exceeded the cultivated area by over 70 percent.The main reason for the sown area's being substantially larger than the cultivated area is multiple cropping and relay planting: the growing of two or three crops a year on the same land (crops are planted between the rows before earlier crops are harvested). Examples of multiple cropping are double or triple cropping of paddy rice and the sowing of late crops such as corn, millet, oats, sorghum, and tubers after the wheat harvest. Late-harvested grains (grains harvested after early rice and wheat) account for about two-thirds of China's annual grain output.The three rice harvests a year represent just under half of the country's total grain production.

The pressure of people on agricultural land is very great: sown land works out at about 0.4 acres per head of population or about half an acre per head of farm population. Little additional land is potentially suitable for farming. Most of the uncultivated land (89 percent of the total land area) consists of mountains, wasteland, desert, grassland, and urban agglomerations. A big land reclamation effort could add perhaps 1.5 percent (3.6 million acres) to the 11 percent presently cultivated, but not much more.

It should also be borne in mind that at the time of the communists' accession to power in 1949, much of China's farmland was in a deplorable state. It had been ravaged by years of war and civil strife, despoiled by invaders and domestic infighting, denuded by decades of indiscriminate timber cutting. Taking the peak prewar year as 100, grain production in 1949 was only 78.

Whatever the sociopolitical coloration of the government, China's economic system is fundamentally hydraulic: it stands and falls on the people's ability to regulate the water supply.Throughout its history China has been plagued by the twin calamities of flood and drought. Between 1949 and 1966 there were seventeen severe droughts that affected more than 200 million hectares of farmland, and ten major floods that damaged an estimated 50 million hectares. In the period of China's First Five-Year Plan (1953–1957) the loss of grain due to drought and flood was said to have been well over 50 million tons.

Three reasons for the repeated occurrence of these calamities are the great variability of precipitation ("sky water"), the uneven distribution of surface water (river flows and lakes), and the uncertain and/or insufficient provision of underground water.

In eastern China (including the south and much of the north and northeast) the mean annual precipitation averages from 20 to 30 inches in the north and northeast to 40 inches along and south of the Yangtze (Changjiang) River. In some areas of the south the mean annual rainfall averages as much as 80 inches. In western China it varies from 10 inches in Xinjiang and Inner Mongolia to 20 inches in the eastern and northeastern parts of Tibet.

The Yangtze River valley and areas to the south of the Yangtze contain a third of China's cultivated land and almost 80 percent of the country's surface water. The Yangtze River by itself accounts for 40 percent of China's total surface water flow of some 3 billion cubic meters a year, and the Pearl River in the south for another 20 percent. On the other hand, the north and northeast, with more than half the country's cultivated land, have only 7 percent of the surface water. The north's main water artery, the Yellow (Huangho) River, accounts for only 2 percent of China's total surface flow.

At the present time about half of China's cultivated land is irrigated, although the effectiveness of the irrigation varies. Depending on local conditions, an effectively irrigated area is one capable of withstanding drought for a period of between 30 and 70 days. Perhaps as much as one-quarter of the irrigated area is today irrigated effectively. The irrigated land—the largest irrigated area in the world—draws about 90 percent of the needed water from surface sources (rivers, river dams, lakes, ponds), and most of it involves silt-removing operations. About 10 percent of the water is drawn from wells. In the last fifteen years or so, however, this method of obtaining water has rapidly gained in importance. About 200,000 tube wells equipped with power pumps have been sunk each year since 1972. An equally impressive record has been registered in drainage work, much of it integrated in the irrigation system.

In the past, floods and drought caused great property damage and loss of life. The breaking of the Yellow River dikes near Zhengzhou, Hunan Province, by Nationalist troops in 1938, intended to halt Japanese advance, resulted in the death of nearly a million people and affected a total of almost 13 million people. The Yellow River flood in 1933 in Hebei, Shandong, and Henan affected almost 4 million inhabitants with a death toll of 18,000. The drought of 1928, which hit thirteen provinces, resulted in a decline of output to 20 percent of the normal level. The natural calamities of 1959–1961 were in part responsible for the abandonment of the Maoist Great Leap Forward and caused serious dislocations in the country's economy.

Responses to Problem of Cultivated Land and Natural Calamities

Every year during the slack farm season millions of Chinese are engaged in water conservation and land management work. It is without a doubt the largest operation of its kind in the history of humanity, the monumental scope and significance of which have not been fully grasped outside China's borders. By far the greater part of the work is done by hand, with the aid of only simple tools. The spectacle of millions of hands, methodically and in a highly organized manner, transforming the face of the earth is among the deeper impressions one brings out of China. There has never been much disagreement within the leadership on the need to master the land and its water supply. There have been debates, however, at times acrimonious ones, on the precise way in which this was to be done and the proximate objectives to be achieved.

Current policy dates back to the early 1960s. The main characteristics of this policy, as described in official documents, are as follows:

1. Primary emphasis is on improving the existing agricultural land through drainage and irrigation work rather than on additions of new land through reclamation. In conformity with the principle of balance (walking on two legs) reclamation is not neglected. Penal farms, army farms, the Production and Construction Corps of the People's Liberation Army, and some regular state farms all do a great deal of reclaiming of deserts, swamps, sea-covered land, and other areas. But reclamation in this sense is not the top priority. According to official Chinese sources, total irrigated area in 1979 was 3.5 times what it had been in the early post-Liberation years, reaching nearly 120 million acres. The irrigated area in the Yellow River basin quadrupled during the period.

2. Within the existing, improved agricultural land, primary emphasis is on further ameliorating and extending areas of high and stable yields. Stable high-yield areas are lands naturally suitable for agriculture because of favorable climatic and soil conditions, and equipped with effective irrigation and drainage facilities and other inputs. The policy has meant, among other things, emphasis on extending the area under effective irrigation and drainage systems rather than on maximizing the area under simple irrigation and drainage. It is thought that the acreage presently classified as producing high and stable yields (about 20–25 percent of cultivated land) can be increased to one-third of the cultivated area, provided irrigation and drainage machinery, improved seeds, chemical fertilizers, and other modern inputs are available in the required quantities, qualities, and combinations.

3. Connected with the above policies is the emphasis given to multiple cropping and crop diversification.

4. Primary stress is put on small- and medium-sized projects carried out locally by communes, brigades, and teams in a semitraditional,

labor-intensive way employing locally procured material resources. The provinces and the central government undertake the very large, mechanized, modern projects into which local systems are fitted. In contrast to the helter-skelter work of the Great Leap Forward years, the present local effort is carefully coordinated with regional and national water control plans.

5. Measures are taken to reduce the nonagricultural uses of good farmland. Burial grounds have been plowed up, and pressure is put on families to opt for cremation rather than burial. Whole villages have been moved from valleys onto hillsides, where they occupy less valuable agricultural land. Irrigation and drainage systems eventually are to be put underground in order to save on land presently taken up by ditches, canals, and reservoirs. Urban sprawl and the construction of factory complexes on good farmland are controlled.

6. A network of meteorological stations and a system of typhoon and flood warnings have been developed. Weather predictions and alerts are communicated to the farms by radio.

But the agricultural record is not all positive. "In the past twenty years the policy for the development of agriculture has been vacillating and unstable. There have been violations of economic law and natural law in dealing with some problems. . . . The practice was often to focus attention on one endeavor, abuse administrative orders, give blind commands, and demand uniformity in everything." [1] Specifically criticized has been the one-sided emphasis (now attributed to the influence of the gang of four) put on expanding the output of grain—"promoting a single-product economy"—and the consequent neglect of animal husbandry, fisheries, sideline production, cash crops, and forestry. Since the reemergence of Deng Xiaoping in July 1977, Chinese media have revealed that far-reaching ecological damage had been done in the past by the massive drive to grow more grain: "taking grain as the key link and ensuring all-round destruction." Thus in Heilongjiang Province the indiscriminate cutting down of forests and the plowing up of vast tracts of barren land in the Sanjian Plain have led to erosion and depletion of the soil: the province's rich black earth is being eroded at the rate of 1 centimeter a year, and the organic content of the soil is declining each year at between 4 and 6 percent. Heilongjiang's forestry resources have been reduced by 30 to 40 percent compared with the early 1950s, or roughly by 17 million acres. [2] In Yunnan, large areas of rare tropical

[1]Beijing Radio, Xinhua Report on Shaanxi Cadre Meeting, February 4, 1979, in *FBIS*, February 6, 1979.

[2]*Guangming Ribao* (Beijing), May 18, 1979, in *FBIS*, May 23, 1979.

forests were burned and the soil put to the plow. Once the fertilizer provided by the remaining vegetation was gone, grain production fell sharply. In Inner Mongolia plowing up grasslands turned 967,000 acres of good pastureland into desert, while 1,934,000 acres of land have been invaded by sand. Since the beginning of the Cultural Revolution in 1966, the number of livestock in this Autonomous Region declined by half. "This is a calamitous destruction of pastoral wealth. For the sake of apparent immediate utility, damage that will last for centuries has been caused." [3] In Hubei Province there were 1,056 lakes in 1949, each with a surface of 161 acres; today there are only 500 such lakes left. The others were converted into grain fields. "Indiscriminate catching [of fish] reached an appalling degree." [4] According to the *People's Daily* (October 18, 1978), the number of fish caught in the late 1970s did not reach the level of twenty years earlier. Despite great efforts expended over three decades to control silting on the Yellow River, the problem persists, and vast quantities of loess (some 1.6 billion tons a year) are carried off by the river. In the one-sided pursuit of "taking grain as the key link," the cultivation of sugar beets and oil-bearing plants was reportedly neglected. Oil-bearing plants, for example, are grown on only 6 percent of the sown area and are in short supply; edible oil is rationed at 4 catties (2 kg or 4.4 lb) per person per year. Interestingly, the criticism leveled against excessive preoccupation with expanding the output of grain is not accepted by all. The Party Committee of the late Chairman's home province—Hunan—defiantly made it known that there is still plenty of barren upland land there and lots of water that can be used in the grain production drive. "The province was right," they said, "in attaching importance to grain in the past. It is, therefore, necessary to persistently apply certain effective methods in developing grain production and continue to have a firm grasp on grain production." [5]

China's grain output in 1979 was 332 million metric tons, and the

[3]*Renmin Ribao* (Beijing), January 23, 1979, p. 2; Hohhot, Nei Monggol Regional Radio Station, January 26, 1979, in *FBIS*, February 2, 1979. Because of the destruction of grasslands and inadequate winter fodder reserves, in the winter of 1977–78 more than 3 million head of cattle out of Xilin Gol (Nei Monggol) League's 7 million head of cattle "died outright." The report continues: "Statistics show that the number of cattle which die in this manner annually is no lower than the number of animals delivered to the state by herdsmen." "Places which used to be favorable to both men and cattle and which had a bountiful supply of water and grass, have been turned into barren lands without a single blade of grass for grazing sheep. Only sand and wind remain." Beijing Radio, July 29, 1979, in *FBIS*, August 3, 1979.

[4]*Beijing Review*, April 27, 1979, p. 8.

[5]Changsha, Hunan Provincial Radio Station, January 28, 1979, in *FBIS*, January 31, 1979.

objective is to produce 400 million tons by 1985. Much of the increase is to come from rising output per acre, but the reclamation of some 13 million hectares of what is described as wasteland is also on the agenda. From 1949 through 1977 China reclaimed 17 million hectares of land, or roughly 0.6 million hectares a year. To reach the 1985 target, the annual addition from 1978 through 1985 will have to be more than 2.5 times bigger. The policymakers' preoccupation with grain is, of course, understandable. Per capita grain (domestic output plus imports) in 1979—which, we are told, "surpassed the highest level of the past"—was still only 350 kilograms per head. Assuming that two-fifths of this goes for animal feed and industrial uses, the 1979 food grain availability works out to roughly 210 kilograms per person. State regulations in China set the minimum consumption of grain at 150 kilograms per head per year. Thus the margin between minimum and actual is quite narrow. Consumption of 210 kilograms of grain per head per year is tolerable provided the diet also contains vegetables, oil, sugar, fish, and meat in sufficient quantities. It is precisely on this score that the past policy of imbalance is criticized.

Mao's 1955 reference to backward operational methods was intended to cover technology and the social organization of agriculture. We shall discuss these two aspects of the operational problem and the policy responses to them in turn.

Problems of Operational Methods: Technology

Technology may be defined as the "systematic application of scientific or other organized knowledge to practical tasks." [6] The systematic application of scientific knowledge to practical tasks constitutes "modern" technology. The application to practical tasks of other knowledge, especially knowledge of accepted, proven, and largely manual ways of doing things, inherited from long experience and handed down from father to son, constitutes "traditional" technology. Technology is embodied in capital goods, current material inputs, and nonmaterial processes (know-how).

CAPITAL Productive capital, both traditional (e.g., draft animals) and modern (e.g., tractors), is in short supply. The greater part of the work in the fields is still being done by hand. "You might say there's very little

[6]John Kenneth Galbraith, *The New Industrial State* (New York: Signet Books, New American Library, 1968), p. 24.

'farming' in China. Most everything there is gardened—as it is in Japan. The Chinese use incredible amounts of skillful hand labor.''[7]

In 1978 the number of draft animals in China was in the neighborhood of 100 million, up from 60 million in 1949; expressed in 15 standard horsepower units, there were 500,000 large and medium-sized tractors, compared with 400 or so in 1949. Power-driven drainage and irrigation machines totaled 65.6 million horsepower, compared with 100,000 thirty years earlier. This is no mean achievement for a country that has had to rely on itself for the great bulk of capital formation.

Two qualifications should be appended. First, 1949 was a very bad year. Chinese communist authorities like to use it as a starting date for comparisons, but the procedure is not quite legitimate. It was a year of extraordinary destruction and desolation at the end of several decades of foreign war, civil strife, and chaos. Second, the quality of much of the equipment produced after 1949 leaves room for improvement, there is a shortage of spare parts and maintenance personnel, and a fair amount of nonchalance about the fact that equipment should come in integrated sets. A tractor needs attachments; otherwise one is obliged to hook the old plow onto the tractor and have a peasant run after it, which is what has happened in some instances (these are known locally as ''sweat tractors''). ''Some of the farm machines,'' says the Communique on the Fulfillment of the Economic Plan for 1978, ''were of poor quality, maintenance work fell short of demand, and the rate of use was not high. The rate of availability of tractors in good condition was only 70 per cent on the average.''[8] Many machines delivered to the farms were lemons. The Guangzhou (Canton) Tractor Plant, built in 1966, had produced by the end of 1978 a total of 7,000 tractors, not a single one of which could be used.[9] ''The peasants complained: 'We sold our live oxen to buy iron oxen [tractors], but what we got were dead oxen.' ''[10] The shortage of repair and maintenance personnel may have to be tackled through consolidation: the merging of the many machine repair workshops located in communes and within subdivisions of communes (production brigades and even some production teams), and the standardization of models (at present there are 1,500 different kinds of

[7]Sterling Wortman, vice-president of the Rockefeller Foundation, head of U.S. agricultural team visiting the People's Republic of China, August–September 1974. *RF Illustrated* (New York), Vol. II, March 1975, p. 4.

[8]*Beijing Review*, July 6, 1979, p. 39.

[9]*Renmin Ribao*, January 7, 1979, p. 3, in *China News Analysis (CNA)*, (Hong Kong), No. 1149, March 2, 1979, p. 6.

[10]''Minister Apologizes to Peasants,'' *Beijing Review*, September 8, 1978, p. 21.

tractors and implements made by numerous local workshops, each item made à la carte, so to speak, with little thought given to the interchangeability of parts). Local authorities are being encouraged to transfer educated urban youths out of manure collecting into machine operating and repairing.

The consolidation of rural workshops and the concurrent upgrading of technology in the consolidated plants are bound to be difficult and controversial.The solution will call for a fine sense of proportion and a measure of ideological consensus if a potentially disruptive rush into the old neo-Stalinist extreme of large, capital-intensive, and urban-based plants is to be avoided.What seems to be needed is to correct ever so slightly the existing proportion between large agricultural machines produced in centrally run factories and less complex, medium-sized and small machines and implements suited to local topographical and soil conditions, made on the bespoke tailor principle by counties, communes, and the larger production brigades. For years the production of light, garden-type, "walking" tractors had been stressed. Between 1965 and 1973 the production of all tractors rose sixfold; that of walking tractors thirty-twofold. In 1978 the number of such hand tractors was 1.4 million.These machines can be hitched to a two- or four-wheeled platform and serve as an improvised mini-truck. Many of them are on the roads of east China bringing vegetables and other produce into the cities. But, since the announcement of the modernization plans, the temper has changed. Rather than taking pride in the ingenuity of the masses who turn a garden tractor into a truck, it is now argued that this is done because the supply of trucks to the farms has lagged well behind needs. The proportion of large and medium-sized tractors in the total tractor stock is to be increased in the coming years. For a start, between 1977 and 1978 the output of regular tractors went up by over 14 percent, while the production of garden tractors rose by just over 1 percent. Mechanical pumps are fairly evenly divided between electrical and internal-combustion pumps. One-fifth of the mechanical pumps in operation are used for irrigation; two-fifths are used in drainage. A large proportion of the pumps is produced by rural industry at the country and commune levels as well as by labor-intensive urban workshops.

In 1955 the Chinese set for themselves the objective of "basic" mechanization of agriculture by 1980.This target was reaffirmed in the Draft Ten-Year Economic Modernization Plan, 1976–1985. "Basic" is apparently taken to mean that 70 percent of the major processes in agriculture, forestry, animal husbandry, sideline production, and fishery are to be mechanized, the proportion rising to 85 percent by 1985.

Agricultural mechanization has always been a controversial issue with China's communist leaders. Not only was there the question of whether mechanization should precede or follow collectivization (this was answered by Mao's massive collectivization and communization of 1955 and 1958), but some leaders asked how much sense wholesale mechanization made in an economy in which 800 million peasants were packed into a cultivable area of 100 million hectares.

By 1979 the mechanization objective had been trimmed. The pace was to be moderated and the scope widened to cover operations other than grain cultivation. State-financed mechanization was to be pushed in a number of carefully chosen key or "base" areas, especially in the northeast (for crop production) and around the three municipalities of Beijing, Shanghai, and Tianjin. These bases would serve as models for other places. Each province would be encouraged to set up at least one fully mechanized county by 1980–1981. In addition to the currently practiced purchase and ownership of farm machinery by communes and production brigades, state-run and -owned tractor stations would be reestablished and would rent machinery to the farms. [11] The notion of basic mechanization still covers semimechanization, as it did when Mao was alive, but the official enthusiasm about it is not as great as it used to be; "for instance, while developing tractor production [local areas] also pay great attention to improving animal-drawn implements. While more and more trucks are used in agriculture, the number of animal-drawn and hand-pushed rubber-tired carts has also steadily increased." [12]

CURRENT MATERIAL INPUTS We shall consider here only natural and chemical fertilizers, pesticides, and seed improvements.

Before 1949 the use of chemical fertilizers in China was negligible. Agriculture depended for plant nutrients almost entirely on traditional (natural) fertilizers, the collection and transportation of which absorbed a significant portion of rural manpower—perhaps as much as 50 percent. In 1957, at the end of the First Five-Year Plan, China produced about 160,000 tons of chemical fertilizer (nutrient weight). In 1978 the figure was 8.7 million tons. In addition, about 2 million tons were imported in 1978. The industry developed at a fast pace in the 1960s and early 1970s, but production stagnated from 1973 through 1976. Despite the enormous strides made in the production and application of chemical fertilizers

[11] State tractor stations were done away with in the late 1960s.

[12] "China's Agricultural Mechanization," *China Reconstructs*, February–March 1977, p. 15.

over the years, natural fertilizers still constitute the bulk of China's fertilizer consumption, and their collection, preparation, and distribution continue to command large amounts of farm labor.

Beginning in the mid-1960s much stress was put on the development of small chemical fertilizer plants run by local authorities. By the mid-1970s more than half of China's chemical fertilizer production came from such plants—some 1,400 scattered all over the country—most of them producing nitrogenous fertilizer. On the positive side of this development was the handy availability of chemical fertilizers to farms and a lesser burden on transport and storage, hence smaller loss and deterioration of quality during both operations. The negative features included the comparatively low nutrient value of the fertilizer and the high cost of production in what were often makeshift plants.There is talk of "rationalization," and the implication is that at least some of the local plants (those operating at a substantial loss) will be closed down.

While developing labor-intensive chemical fertilizer factories at the local (mainly county) level, China contracted in Western Europe and Japan for the purchase of thirteen large synthetic ammonia-urea complexes of a very high order of technical sophistication.When in full-capacity operation these plants alone are expected to produce a volume equal to China's total nitrogen output in 1973. Consequently the share of small plants in chemical fertilizer output is expected to fall markedly by 1981 or thereabouts when all the giant complexes are in full operation.

In the past losses from pests and plant diseases were heavy. Control was mostly traditional, concentrated on the manual removal of diseased plants, driving ducks which feed on insects across paddy fields and other such methods. [13] These same methods are used today. Before 1949 the use of chemical pesticides was extremely limited.The bulk of China's pesticide production consists of insecticides that are produced in several hundred factories located in various parts of the country. Insecticide production in the early 1960s was in the neighborhood of 100,000 tons (standard weight). In 1978 insecticide output was 533,000 tons. It is possible that in the late 1970s about half of China's cultivated area was under pesticide control. Biological pest control is stressed; for example, predatory insects and insect pathogens are widely employed to control cotton aphids. In 1979 ladybugs were used to control cotton aphids on

[13]Henry J. Groen and James A. Kilpatrick, "China's Agricultural Production," in *Chinese Economy Post-Mao* (Washington, D.C.: U.S. Government Printing Office, 1978), Vol. I, p. 635.

one-third of Hebei Province's cotton acreage. The state has funded the construction of several plants for breeding beneficial insects and producing bacterial insecticides. [14]

An important problem facing China is the development of improved varieties of seeds and strains. While substantial progress has been made, especially in rice, where a high-yielding (6 to 7 tons per hectare) dwarf rice variety has been developed by the Chinese themselves, the overall picture is more clouded. There remains much room for improvement in corn, where as of the mid-1970s high-protein high-lysine types were unknown in China. The problem is linked to the political uncertainties that over the years have surrounded the agricultural research and educational system.

NONMATERIAL PROCESSES Agricultural research, education, and extension work constitute a particular, nonmaterial input into farming, one which results in improved material inputs and in the rise of farm output and productivity. Generally speaking, agricultural research in China has been oriented toward short-term results in raising yields through the application of relatively simple processes. This trend became particularly prominent during the Cultural Revolution (1966–1969) and remained so for some years since. Until 1976 production-oriented research was cast into a left ideological mold in which longer-term, basic research became suspect because it was believed to contain the seeds of elitism and because it was allegedly divorced from the daily labor of the masses, being carried out in predominantly urban environments by highly trained personnel. Some scientific institutes were physically dismantled and sent down into the countryside together with the scientists. At a minimum, a rotation system was instituted in accordance with which, at any given time, about a third of a research institute's staff would work in the fields alongside the peasants.

A marked expansion has taken place since 1965 in commune agricultural extension programs and demonstration-experimental plots. There are longer-term costs involved in this approach. "The research base is narrow, the labs are badly equipped. There's no work on the more sophisticated approaches to disease resistance or plant physiology. In the great push to increase production, research efforts have virtually ground to a halt. . . . Most of the highly trained people are in their sixties and too few young people, it seems, are being trained. . . . There's also some urgency about collecting and storing genetic material.

[14]Beijing Radio, May 18, 1979, in *FBIS*, May 18, 1979.

The Chinese must get their plant germplasm into storage banks," reported the Rockefeller Foundation-sponsored team of U.S. agricultural experts in 1974. The ability of China to restore balance in this area and to make progress in basic agricultural research was considered by the team to have been China's most serious long-range agricultural problem. The problem, as we shall see, is not limited to the development and propagation of nonmaterial agricultural inputs. The question of the weights to be applied respectively to the narrowly practical and the broadly theoretical, to the shorter- and longer-term interests of the economy, to "learning by doing" and "book knowledge," reappears on and off in the debates about the appropriate policy responses to the problems facing China in education and public health (Chapter 9).

Responses to the Problem of Technology

Typically, the agriculture of an underdeveloped country will use traditional technology: draft animals, wooden or cast-iron plows, hoes, picks, flails, spades, waterwheels, windmills, farmyard manure and nightsoil, inherited patterns of crop rotation, bacterial pest control, unimproved varieties of seed, and so on. Incremental changes in traditional technology (small improvements in the existing tools and procedures) can help raise output and productivity and make physical labor less backbreaking, but there is a limit to what can be done by taking the road of semimodernization. There seems to be a traditional production possibility frontier that can be crossed only by injecting modern science-based technology into agriculture. For the most part such technology is generated outside agriculture and has to be imported from industry, much of it from foreign industry. In Marxist terminology, the crossing of the traditional production possibility frontier represents the transformation of quantitative into qualitative change. The process is known more generally as the intersectoral transformation of agriculture: the introduction into farming of modern capital goods, current inputs, scientific procedures, and flexible mental attitudes. Technological transformation goes hand in hand with a profound change in outlook.

China's response to the problem of agricultural technology since the early 1950s shows several sharp swings from right to left and back again. During the First Five-Year Plan (1953–1957) the emphasis was on industry-based modernization. Then, for a while, during Mao's Great Leap Forward (1958–1960) the expertise of the educated and specialized was shunted aside and faith was put in technological improvements made by the peasants. From 1961 through 1965 a compromise solution was sought, combining the two approaches: incremental improvement of traditional capital, current inputs, and processes; and modernization of capital, inputs, and processes. Conceptually, the first emphasizes "redness"—the creative genius of the politically conscious masses of poor and lower-middle peasants that allegedly flourishes in the heat of class struggle; the second puts stress on the professional expertise of a formally trained elite corps of scientists, engineers, and technicians, and deemphasizes class color. As Deng Xiaoping put it, "It doesn't matter whether the cat is black or white, so long as it catches mice." The compromise of 1961–1965 came to an abrupt end with the Cultural Revolution (1966–1969). During that cataclysmic event the preoccupation was more than ever with redness, class struggle, and brainstorms by the aroused masses. In the uneasy, factionalized, power-grabbing period from 1970 till the death of Mao in September 1976 and the elimination of his left wing protegés (Jiang Qing, Yao Wenyuan, Wang Hongwen, and Zhang Chunqiao) the following October, an unstable equilibrium between the two approaches to technology was reached. The peasants concentrated on small improvements and innovations linked to local conditions. Before being generalized, such inventions were reviewed by various "three-in-one" panels of peasants, cadres, and technical experts. Because of unfortunate past experience with the fruits of peasant ingenuity, the opinion of experts was listened to more attentively during that period than it had been during the heady years of the Leap Forward and the Cultural Revolution. Even so, with radical influence strong in governmental and Party circles, the experts had to be circumspect lest they be branded "rightist."

After the dissolution of the radical cabal, emphasis shifted very rapidly toward scientific and technical expertise, and longer-range intersectoral transformation projects. In a gesture of united-front reconciliation, non-Party intellectuals of bourgeois and other unapproved backgrounds were welcomed back into the fold and urged to devote all their time to helping shift dramatically agriculture's production possibility frontier. There were to be no more interruptions from stints of manual labor in the countryside; every effort was to be made to put the experts back in jobs for which they were trained rather than having them pick up garbage in the cities. "There is no need," said the Beijing *Guangming Ribao* (January 23,1979), "to criticize capitalism or revisionism or to shout slogans such as 'Without closing the road to capitalism, it will be impossible to advance to socialism.' What we should say now is: 'Without equipping agriculture with advanced technology, it will be impossible to modernize farming.' " References to the Dazhai brigade of Shanxi Province—which used to be cited as a model of unstinting labor and all-round self-reliance using simple tools and still simpler technology—were quietly dropped. At a work conference sponsored by the Central Committee and held in the winter of 1978, the participants concluded that "Dazhai stressed 'hard work' but did not attach importance to science; [stressed] politics, but not production. Five hundred million peasants cannot follow the way of the 80 households [of Dazhai]." Finally, in 1980, the Dazhai model was dismissed as an outright fraud. Such achievements as Dazhai had made were due to huge government subsidies plus statistical cheating by the people's models. [15]

Agricultural mechanization and chemicalization are to be pursued vigorously with stress on larger machines and bigger, more modern chemical fertilizer factories. The stock of large and medium-sized tractors was to rise by 70 percent between 1976 and 1980; that of walking tractors by 36 percent; and the stock of medium-sized and large tractor-drawn tools was to more than double. During the period, the power capacity of irrigation and drainage machinery was to increase by almost a third and the irrigated area by over 30 percent, to cover some 145 million acres by 1985. Chemical fertilizer output was scheduled to go up by almost three-fifths. Sixty-five large and medium-sized water conservancy projects and eleven aquatic products projects were to be completed "as quickly as possible." Foreign agro-technology, both in the form of equipment and processes was to be imported. There are a number of obstacles to the achievement of these objectives. These include a shortage of rolled steel, the competing demand for steel by the armaments industry, a tight fuel supply situation, and a shortage of well-trained technical personnel.

A big problem apparently is the inefficient use often made of modern inputs by local bureaucracies and farm managements. The problem was reportedly raised in a political context at a Politbureau meeting in the winter of 1978 in connection with the criticism of a leftist Politbureau member, Ji Dengkui, who had publicized the thesis that in China one-twentieth of the world's soil feeds one-quarter of the world's population. "You said that one-quarter of the population was fed. Were they fat or thin? You prattled that output of chemical fertilizers was 19 times greater than before liberation, total motive power for agriculture was 83 times more than before liberation, and rural electricity output increased 157.7

[15] *Dong Xiang* (communist periodical in Hong Kong), No. 4, January 16, 1979, in *FBIS*, January 23, 1979; "No Deification of Dazhai," *Beijing Review*, August 11, 1980, p.5.

times. However, agricultural production increased only 1.5 times compared with the pre-liberation period. What is there to brag about?"[16] Improvement in the returns to agricultural investment and labor will presumably be sought through institutional changes designed to upgrade agricultural planning and farm management.

The pragmatic, post–gang-of-four drift of China's economic policy is unlikely to sweep away those components of the Maoist legacy that prove themselves in the light of practice to be viable and suitable for China's specific conditions and level of development. Thus, in the past, changes in traditional attitudes and techniques were brought about not primarily by bringing peasants to the cities or sending traveling agricultural extension teams to the countryside, but by permanently installing in the countryside a vast network of semimodern industries producing a wide range of consumer and capital goods and current farm inputs. In 1978 the output value of the 1.4 million commune- and brigade-run workshops came to 49 billion yuan with investments totaling nearly 10 billion yuan. Much of the cement, chemical fertilizer, irrigation and drainage equipment, electric power, clothing, and processed food production in China originates in these rural workshops, which also do a lot of repair and maintenance work. The capital equipment of rural industry is quantitatively and qualitatively modest, but the degree of labor intensity should not be exaggerated. For many if not most of the workers in these rural establishments, this is the first exposure to industrial technology. The introduction to the modern industrial world is made on the spot, without migration to the cities. The policy of rural industrialization will probably not be reversed, but it will almost certainly be modified to conform to the drive for technological and scientific modernization. The possibility is real that in the pursuit of economies of scale rural workshops (including the 1,600 agricultural machinery plants) will be consolidated and some might even be closed down. But the operation is unlikely to be either hasty or drastic, so long as the post-gang alliance of political forces and their "line" remain undisturbed. However, the post-Maoist leadership's open, if not unopposed, devotion to modernization will probably imply some deemphasis of the rural-based, labor-intensive, skill-deficient approach to the technological problem; a shift in priorities, away from self-reliant peasant innovation, toward specialized expertise. There is an as yet loosely formulated idea of creating agro-industrial-commercial complexes in the countryside. "Modernization raises the question: What shall we do with the man-

[16] Ibid.

power freed through modernizing farming? We can't transfer the surplus labor force into the cities and into urban industry because these areas are already densely populated. The way out lies in developing a diversified economy in the countryside and exploiting local natural resources through more industrial enterprises in the communes." [17]

Problems of Operational Methods: Social Organization

Mao's reference to the backwardness of China's operational methods was made on the eve of collectivization. The system of small-scale private farming created by the land reform of 1950 was, in Mao's eyes, irreconcilable with (a) technical progress in agriculture, especially in the area of water conservation, (b) socialized and semisocialized industry, and (c) ideological purity. As on other matters, Mao's conviction that the social relations of production in agriculture needed to be changed drastically was not shared by many other communist leaders, but it prevailed. By the latter part of 1957 Mao became convinced that the degree of socialization represented by agricultural collectivization was not sufficient from the standpoints of technological progress and ideology. In the latter part of 1958 the newly collectivized agriculture was communized. The 740,000 agricultural producers' cooperatives (collective farms), each with roughly 160 households, were merged into 24,000 rural people's communes, averaging over 5,000 households each. Although the internal organization of the communes has undergone many changes since 1958, the communes and their subdivisions remain (but perhaps not for long) the fundamental form of rural organization in China.

Responses to the Problem of Social Organization

In Marxist theory at the very heart of the dialectical process is lodged the contradiction between material productive forces (broadly, technology) and social relations of production (the institutional-organizational framework, including property structures, within which technology develops). Of the two, technology appears to be the independent variable,

[17] "China's Agriculture and Its Future," *China Reconstructs,* August 1979, p. 24. In 1978 commune- and brigade-run industrial enterprises "provided 2.6 billion yuan in direct aid to agriculture" equivalent to 60 percent of the 1978 state investment in capital construction in agriculture. "A considerable portion of future investment will have to be provided by commune- and brigade-run enterprises." In mid-1979 there were 28 million peasants employed in these enterprises, or almost 10 percent of the rural labor force of 300 million. *Beijing Review,* September 28, 1979, p. 5.

the initiator of historical change. The social envelope within which technology unfolds, the institutions of economic society, appear in the Marxist schema to be the dependent variable. Theoretically, institutional change follows changes in the material productive forces (technology). Institutional arrangements, especially property structures, which inhibit the development of technology may have to be uprooted violently through land reform, collectivization, communization, or nationalization, but the uprooting comes in response to, not in advance of, technical change. [18]

Despite the leading role ascribed by theory to technology, both Stalin and Mao attached enormous importance to the other side of the contradiction: the institutional-organization system. Stalin's massive collectivization of the 1930s was repeated in China in 1955–1956 and pushed farther in 1958. Stalin explained his collectivization with the dogmatic assertion that collectivization was timely because the Soviet Union had the most mechanized agriculture in the world, which was not true then and is not true now. Mao's reason for headlong collectivization and later communization of the peasantry was anchored in a particular interpretation of the dialectical process. To Mao, the social relations of production (especially property structures) seem to be the independent variable of the contradiction. A change in the social environment will, Mao believed, generate rapid technical progress by releasing the enormous inventive and innovative energy of the masses of poor and lower-middle peasants. Modernizations will come on the crest of the revolutionary wave. The emphasis is on destroying the institutional shackles of the will. Correctly inspired collective willpower is the core of the economic base. All one need do is liberate it. While containing elements of idealism (as Mao's opponents were quick to point out), the position is also Leninist in the importance that it attaches to the power of organization.

There is an interesting dichotomy to the handling of the mechanization-socialization problem. A very elaborate system of transitional institutions had been worked out to ease the peasants into the fully socialized setting. There were mutual-aid teams, both seasonal and permanent, and lower-level cooperatives. The idea seemed to have been not to rush things, to correlate step-by-step improvements in traditional technology with slowly rising but still quite rudimentary forms of social-

[18]Some students of Marxism, it is fair to report, interpret the relation between productive forces and the social relations of production as a chicken and egg problem. In their view the premature transition to socialism occurs because politics takes command for Lenin's or Mao's reasons.

ization. Then, suddenly, without warning, the whole works was cordoned off and collectivized, only to be communized two years later.

The rapid collectivization of agriculture in 1955–1956 did not produce the spectacular release of technology expected of it. There is evidence that, at least in the short run, the opposite was true. After a partial and short-lived retreat from the "little great leap" in socialization (autumn 1956 to summer 1957), a truly big leap in the transformation of the institutional structure of agriculture was taken in 1958.

Insistence on the leading dynamic role of the social relations of production, the leaps in agricultural policy, and the intentional recurrent destabilization of the political situation in the countryside during the Maoist era were severely taken to task after Mao's death. "Comrades attending [the Gansu Province Party Committee Work Conference] maintained that over the past 20 years and more, there have been continuous political movements in Gansu. Cadres and masses have been perpetually involved in these movements, and human relations have been so tense, it was impossible for anyone to have the time or energy for production and construction." [19] The need now, it is said, is for unity and stability in the countryside. The "five stabilities" that are counted on to help promote modernization are stability in politics (ideological line), policy, system (economic-social organization), cadres, and labor force. There are, however, still those who yearn for the old Maoist turbulence, the "whatever faction" as they are sometimes called, those who argue that "whatever Chairman Mao said must be carried out." To which Deng Xiaoping replied: "Some people say we must do what Chairman Mao said. Actually, there are too many things which Chairman Mao did not say. . . . Practice is developing. We must study the new situation and solve new problems." [20] The debate goes on, and morbid fear that the line will change again is much in evidence. "Is it possible that another struggle against the 'right deviation' will be launched some years later when agricultural production has improved?" [21] The answer is almost certainly yes.

In terms of the number of people involved, cultivated acreage, and

[19]Beijing Radio, February 6, 1979, in *FBIS*, February 6, 1979.

[20]*Dong Xiang*, No. 4, January 16, 1979, in *FBIS*, January 23, 1979. "We must repudiate religious concepts concerning the 'savior,' criticize feudal and divine rights of kings as well as paternalistic notions." "Remove Obstacles to Realization of the Four Modernizations," *Renmin Ribao*, May 1, 1979, in *FBIS*, May 30, 1979.

[21]*Renmin Ribao*, editorial, January 26, 1979, in *FBIS*, January 31, 1979. "Some cadres say that because Lin Biao and the gang of four confused right and wrong, they are not able, even now, to understand what is socialism, what is capitalism, and what is right and wrong. They hold that they would rather give up than make a mistake in correcting other people's errors. . . . Some cadres say that they feel muddleheaded now. . . . Some persons

output of major products, the people's communes are the most important form of agricultural organization in China today. In addition to the communes there are a number of state farms modeled on the Soviet prototype.They are located mostly in north, northeast, and northwest China, where soil and other natural conditions are less than optimal. Most of them appear to be highly subsidized. They own almost a quarter of all tractors and a higher proportion of specialized farm machinery. Farms run by the People's Liberation Army (PLA) for its own use also exist.These are a species of state farms. Penal farms are located in the more inhospitable regions of the country.They are peopled by political prisoners and common-law criminals and are, in essence, concentration camps from which few, if any, ever return.They have been euphemistically referred to as facilities for education through labor, or "New Life Farms." There are also 200 state-run forest farms. Until 1979 most state farms operated at a financial loss.

RURAL PEOPLE'S COMMUNES The system has five constituent units: communes, production brigades, production teams, work groups, and individual peasant households. [22]

In 1974 there were more than 50,000 communes (up from 24,000 at the time of their formation in 1958, but fewer than in the early 1960s). An average commune had 15 production brigades, 100 production teams, about 3,350 households, and roughly 14,720 members.The average arable land area was just over 5,000 acres. It should be remembered, however, that considerable variations existed in the size of communes, both in membership and in land holdings. I have visited a suburban grain commune with 17,000 households, over 80,000 persons, and more than 40,000 acres of land. (Suburban communes are as a rule larger and better off than rural communes.)

In 1974 there were about 750,000 production brigades with, on the average, 7 production teams to a brigade; that is, roughly 220 households or 980 people, and 336 acres of arable land.

The number of production teams was thought to have been about 5 million, with an average of 33 households (145 people) per team and 49 acres of arable land.

Below the production teams are smaller formations known as "work

---

say that they do not dare take action because they are not sure what is going on. . . . They look fore and aft, and fear this and that." *Liaoning Ribao* article broadcast by Liaoning Provincial Radio Station, Shenyang, May 23, 1979, in *FBIS,* May 31, 1979.

[22]The numerical data in the text below are drawn from the excellent study of the commune system by F. W. Crook in *China: A Reassessment of the Economy* (Washington, D.C.: U.S. Government Printing Office, 1975), pp. 366–410.

groups."They seem to be of two kinds: crop field-work groups and "diversification" groups that deal with collective sideline occupations—fishery, forestry, and others. The number of such groups within the team varies widely, as does the number of workers within each group. They appear, however, to be quite small, consisting of between six and twelve workers (which could mean a couple of households). Although this origin is emphatically denied by the authorities, the work groups trace their origin back to the post-Leap depression years, when production responsibility (fulfilling quotas for delivery of produce to the state under contract) was devolved onto individual peasant households. The system was then known as "Three Freedoms and One Contract": freedom for the households to cultivate private plots, to trade on free markets, and to make basic production and income distribution decisions; and the households' obligation ("one contract") to deliver to the state stipulated (contracted for) quantities of grain and other produce. Later, when farm production recovered, the system was denounced as "revisionist" and was linked to the then (now no longer) disgraced former head of state Liu Shaoqi. Devolution of detailed production decisions and income distribution responsibilities to lower levels is a sure sign that the agricultural situation is troubled. After the Cultural Revolution some provinces quietly slipped in a system called "Five Things Fixed and One Reward," which had been tried earlier in some places. Under the system each production team was divided into several work groups, each of which had a fixed number of people, worked a fixed plot of land, and was given a fixed production quota, with fixed rates of payment to the members (work points) and fixed targets for production costs. These "five things fixed" were determined by the production team on the basis of instructions received by the team from higher authorities, and presumably in consultation with the work group. For exceeding the planned output the groups received a bonus from the team. They could also be punished financially for not fulfilling their assigned tasks. At least theoretically, under the system the production team continued to own the means of production, to work out the production plan in accordance with output and state produce purchasing instructions handed down from above, to assign tasks to the groups, and to distribute income (both basic grain rations and "economic income"). These functions, especially income distribution, were not to be transferred down to the groups. Yet that is apparently what happened in many places. The system was sharply criticized by the radicals in 1976, and quite a few work groups were disbanded. In response to the "urgent desire of the masses," but perhaps mostly "to reverse the chaotic situation of management'' in the countryside, the system was reintroduced and given official blessing in 1978. Some comrades, however, were worried because they suspected that the ''Five Fixes and One Reward'' might result in the dissolution of the production teams and ''going it alone.'' These people measure progress in the building of socialism by the level at which key decisions are made. The production responsibility system, in their view, pushes China in the opposite—revisionist, capitalist—direction. [23] The apprehension felt by these unreconstructed radical elements cannot be but sharpened by Party resolutions that urge ''assigning certain odd jobs to individual households and persons.'' In a number of places production teams were simply disbanded and the groups or individual households took over. A poster that appeared on ''democracy wall'' in February 1979 demanded the abolition of the people's communes and the reinstatement of village committees that existed before 1958. [24]

Rural households in 1974 were believed to number 167 million, with an average of 4.4 persons and 1.9 ''labor powers'' (working members) per household.

Although communes differ widely with respect to size, location, natural endowments, income, and the number of production brigades, teams, and work groups each has at its command, the general principles governing their internal organization and relations with outside authorities (counties, provinces, and the central government) are uniform and have remained fairly stable since 1970. Except for a few across-the-board changes, the principles have not changed a great deal since 1963. These principles cover property rights, division of functions within the commune organizations, and extracommune relations. However, there is increasing talk that a basic change in the principles underlying the commune form of organization is in the offing.

Property Rights. Within the commune system assets are owned at four levels: three social (commune, brigade, team) and one private (households). The theoretical long-range objective is to ''raise the level of ownership'' so that eventually all assets, save the most personal, will be communally owned. In the meantime by far the greater part of the

[23]Haikou, Hainan Island Regional Radio Station, May 21, 1979, in *FBIS*, May 25, 1979. The Soviet counterpart of the Chinese work group is the semiautonomous (sometimes mechanized) *zveno* or link.

[24]Nei Monggol Regional Radio Station, Hohhot, January 26, 1979 report on Regional Party Committee Work Conference, in *FBIS*, February 2, 1979. Kyodo, Tokyo, February 2, 1979, in *FBIS*, February 5, 1979.

assets within the system are owned and managed by the production teams, although after 1969 ownership by communes had risen fast, mainly because of the rapid expansion of commune-owned industries.

In theory, the production team has far-reaching property rights in and responsibilities toward the land it cultivates, the labor power it acquires from its member households, the manual and semimechanized farm tools and the draft animals it uses, and the water-management works it has built to serve the land within its jurisdiction. It also possesses extensive property rights over those portions of its output not earmarked under the mandatory state plan for delivery to state authorities at state-fixed prices and for payment of the agricultural tax. In principle the team's land, labor, capital, and the nonearmarked output cannot be commandeered arbitrarily by other divisions of the organization (the brigades or commune), although these other divisions have in practice many means of putting pressure on the team to do their bidding (e.g., through the supply of consumer and producer goods, productive inputs, and services needed by the team). In principle, for example, the team has to be compensated for the labor hired by the commune to do commune-wide water conservation work and, after fulfillment of its delivery and tax obligations to the state, it has considerable discretion (subject to limits placed by the Party branch at the brigade level) to determine the distribution of the remaining income among the various uses it deems appropriate.

Production brigades exercise property rights over those assets that exceed the financial possibilities and technical capabilities and needs of the production teams; for example, some orchards, timberlands, fish ponds, swine-breeding facilities, a rising portion of farm machinery and mechanized equipment, and some rural industries such as grain, fiber, and edible oil and fodder-processing plants, as well as farm machinery and equipment repair works. More advanced brigades own and operate a wider range of industries. F.W. Crook mentions food-processing plants producing bean curd and noodles; weaving shops making gunny sacks, straw mats, hemp rope, and other items; kilns making bricks, tiles, and lime; paper manufacturing plants; and hydroelectric power stations. [25] Brigades also own or have an equity stake in some reservoirs and other water-control facilities, health stations, elementary school buildings, branch stores of the supply and marketing cooperatives, and branch

[25]F. W. Crook, "The Commune System in the People's Republic of China, 1963–74," in *China: A Reassessment*, pp. 391–92. The following description of the formal organization of the commune system draws on this study and partly on official literature and personal observations.

offices of the credit cooperatives. In conformity with the long-term objective of raising the level of ownership within the commune system, production brigades have in the years 1966–1976 extended the range of assets under their control.

The commune's property rights cover the following:

1. A relatively small portion of the commune system's farmland: mainly, land devoted to experimental and demonstration plots (agricultural extension work); orchards, also of the "model" kind; animal husbandry farms; the larger and more advanced sort of fisheries, including fish farms; and forestry farms.

2. Rural industries beyond the financial and technical capacities of production brigades and teams: grain-processing mills, mechanized and semimechanized farm implement factories and repair-maintenance workshops, increasingly, tractor stations, hydroelectric power generation stations, chemical fertilizer factories, small coal mines, iron works, pumping equipment factories, sawmills, stone quarries, brick and tile kilns, shipyards using locally procured materials, and a variety of light industries including shoes, light bulbs, clothes, and some export items (clay figurines, jewelry, straw products, porcelain).

3. Fixed assets (or a portion of them) relating to such services as public health (commune clinics), education (high school buildings), storage, marketing (stores, fairgrounds), credit (credit cooperatives), and communications (wired broadcasting service).

4. Commune-wide water management works, including power equipment, reservoirs, dams, dikes, and ditches.

Most peasant households own the house they live in and have de facto property rights to the household ("private") plots allocated to them by the production team to which they belong. The plots average about 60 square feet per family and are apportioned according to the number of people in the household (an average of 0.015 acre per commune member). These dimensions represent about 5–7 percent of the team's arable land. The plots strictly speaking are not private; the land belongs to the team, but the team hands it over to member families with extensive rights of use. Produce from private plots and from household sideline (handicraft) activities, as well as the poultry and pigs raised by households and the fruit trees on the plots, are the property of the households. Most of the produce is consumed by the family. Any surplus may be sold to other households or the collective on rural markets (village fairs), or to supply and marketing cooperative branch stores at the brigade level. The greater part of China's production of hogs, poultry, rabbits, and vegetables comes from household subsidiary plots, as does most pig-supplied manure. [26]

In practice the neat four-tiered property division was not always respected. Property rights of the different levels but especially of the two lower ones—the production teams and rural households—were routinely violated, particularly during and after the Cultural Revolution. The problem, however, cannot be ascribed to factionalism. It is built into the system and merely becomes worse when the radicals are in power. The problem is twofold: (1) The system, by definition, favors centralization of authority. The basic assumption, despite occasional protestations to the contrary, is that the center (the top) knows better than the rest of humanity what is good for everyone. "Mass democratic consultations" notwithstanding, the system is built like a pyramid, and the apex invariably lords it over the base. (2) There are really two systemic pyramids: the government and the Party. Of the two, the Party is the more important and influential by far. Hence there is a second, built-in interference, from the higher Party pyramid to the lower governmental one, which affects each and every hierarchical level.

"The right of a production team to control the use of its own collective property disappeared." [27] Brigades under pressure from commune authorities, communes under pressure from counties, counties under pressure from prefectures, and so on up, commandeered without compensation team labor for various land melioration and industrial projects, requisitioned land, used team members' houses as office space, borrowed funds for industrial, educational, and public health uses and failed to pay back the monies borrowed. For example, "the [Jinshan] commune [Wuxian County, Jiangsu Province] today still owes its production teams 73,000 yuan for three years of work performed by 10,000 team members on a canal project, 110,000 yuan including the money it borrowed for its industrial enterprises and the amount it had to pay for the land requisitioned for its own use, and 10,000 yuan to compensate for the peasants' houses that were occupied by the commune's afforestation teams. This total debt of 193,000 yuan means that each team has to shoulder an extra burden of 950 yuan . . . [not to mention] the frequent requisition of their labor power by the county." The county, at one point, demanded that every brigade have its own primary and middle school. "This had rather serious consequences. Weitang Commune spent

[26] There are 300 million pigs in China, most of them privately owned by peasant households. The pigs live on low-cost feed such as corn stalks, vegetable waste, cotton leaves, rice husks, and the by-products of grain processing.

[27] *China Reconstructs*, August 1979, p. 32.

130,000 yuan in four years expanding its schools, 30 percent of which was paid by the production teams. During that period 64 teachers were added, also paid from team funds over and above state subsidies and tuitions. Some of the schools were actually operating below capacity. . . . Now these schools have been merged to save funds." [28] Some localities implemented "indigenous local practices" that included raising grain procurement quotas at short notice and simultaneously lowering the price for the products purchased. Counties and communes supplied the peasants with "expensive but shoddy products from some ill-managed factories." On top of all these government channel violations came abuses perpetrated by Party authorities. To cite but two examples, in Anhui Province a commune Party secretary ordered the uprooting of hemp planted by a production team. "Destroying chicken coops, beheading chickens, uprooting ginger crops and pulling up tobacco plants all became 'revolutionary activities' "; in Zhejiang Province a commune Party Committee plowed away the soybeans of a production brigade because "they did not follow the Party's instructions." [29]

The right of the household to its private plot, sideline production, and access to village fairs was also disregarded, especially after 1965. Following the demise of the radical leaders, this became known as "violations of the individual's right person." These violations were aided and abetted not only by the general principle that what is up and to the left is more correct than what is down and to the right, but by what can only be described as "lawlessness": the absence of well-defined and observed criminal and legal codes. Of course, the existence of such codes will not in itself guarantee that the individual's rights are respected, especially if the Party, whoever may be in charge, remains de facto, if not de jure, above the law. But at least it can help restrain to a degree the arbitrariness in everyday life, although, as the experience of Stalin's Russia shows, not by very much. In any event, limits were imposed on individual commune members' holding of hogs, chickens, ducks, and

[28] *Beijing Review,* April 20, 1979, pp. 19–20. In Hunan Province in 1978 "leading departments at various levels returned to production teams 100 million yuan which they had taken from them over previous years in violation of the Party's rural economic policies." Beijing Radio, May 16, 1979, in *FBIS,* May 18, 1979.

[29] *Beijing Review,* April 20, 1979, p. 19; Beijing Radio, January 20, 1979, in *FBIS,* January 22, 1979; Beijing Radio, January 24, 1979, in *FBIS,* January 31, 1979. Various Party officials at above production brigade levels in Yingxian County, Shanxi Province, commandeered team labor and practically all the trucks in the county during the spring plowing to build 50 houses for themselves and their families. The houses were built on good farmland. Some 20 people were engaged in building each house. *Beijing Review,* July 27, 1979, p. 5.

sheep; under prodding from brigade Party branches, team leaderships instructed households what was to be grown on the private plots; production teams swapped barren land for fertile household plots; odd pieces of land around the peasants' houses were counted as part of the household plot; and people who engaged in sideline activity and trading on village fairs were denounced as capitalists, speculators, bad elements, and much more. In a tight supply situation these measures merely drove private activities underground. [30] "We must refrain from labeling people, beating them with sticks, and grabbing them by their pigtails." [31]

In view of the taut, hierarchical, administrative command structure of the system and in light of the post-gang revelations about widespread violations of the four-level property scheme, the formal property rights, functions, and extra-commune relations described here must be seen in a perspective more critical than that which would be suggested by a simple enumeration of the principles that are supposed to govern those rights, functions, and relations.

Functions. An enumeration of the property rights formally vested in the various divisions of the commune has already given some insight into the functions of the different divisions. Here we shall elaborate on this theme.

The representative and managerial organs of the commune are regarded as the basic units of state power and state administration in the countryside. Each commune has a People's Congress consisting of representatives elected by the members. The commune People's Congresses are supposed to be elected every two years by commune members eighteen years of age and older. They are the rural grassroots units of state power which culminates with the National People's Congress (NPC), which in theory is to be elected every five years, and the NPC's Standing Committee.The commune people's congresses elect the di-

[30]Work Conference of Inner Mongolian Regional Party Committee, Nei Monggol, Hohhot Regional Radio, January 26, 1979, in *FBIS*, February 2, 1979. "As a Chinese saying goes, 'A river rises when its tributaries swell.' . . . It is necessary to give full play to the initiative of the 800 million peasants, who are likened to so many tributaries, in order to ensure the supply of meat, vegetables and other necessities to the cities . . . Lin Biao and the gang of four . . . counterposed the 'river' against the 'tributaries.' They said that 'only when the river is full to overflowing will there be water in the tributaries,' but turned a blind eye to the fact that 'when the tributaries dry up, the river inevitably becomes shallow." *Beijing Review*, October 26, 1979, p. 4.

[31]Third Enlarged Plenum of the Fourth Guangxi Regional Party Committee, Guangxi, Nanning Regional Radio Station, January 19, 1979, in *FBIS*, January 22, 1979.

rector, deputy director, and members of the commune's administrative committee, which is in essence the basic unit of government in rural areas.[32] A third and extremely influential organ of power within the commune is the commune Communist Party Committee headed by the commune Party secretary. The committee oversees the work of the administrative committee, transmits the Party's line from on high (the county, province, and central Party organizations), "helps" in the election of the appropriate nominees to the commune's administrative organs, and is generally in charge of policy at the commune level. Commune officials normally perform two functions: one within the administrative committee and another within the Party committee. Key departments within the administrative committee (e.g., militia affairs) are normally held by the commune Party secretary or his deputy. Administrative and Party offices are located in one place within the commune, normally in a market town or in a complex of buildings that may include the commune's cooperative store, a branch of the People's Bank or a credit cooperative, maybe a machinery repair station, the tax office, a grain depot, and so on. In addition to this administrative and Party work, commune officials are required to participate in physical labor during 200 days in the year. Most commune officials are classified as state (rather than cooperative sector) employees and are paid regular salaries in line with their civil service grades. However, for physical labor done in the fields they are rewarded like other peasants with work points proportionate to their labor input.

Commune authorities (congress, administrative committee, Party committee) receive instructions from higher state and Party organs, interpret these instructions in light of local conditions, transmit the instructions to lower units (brigades and teams), coordinate and supervise the execution of the orders, and report back up the ladder. Among the more important instructions is the state plan for the delivery by the commune (in fact, by the commune's constituent units, particularly the teams and work groups) of certain agricultural commodities such as grain, edible oilseeds, and cotton—known as "first category" goods—at state-fixed prices, and the agricultural tax obligation. The purchase by the state of first category goods falls into two parts: prescribed purchases and unified purchases. Grain and edible oilseeds are covered by

[32]Revolutionary Committees introduced by the Cultural Revolution to replace local governments were abolished in 1978–79. "Our electoral work turned out to have been mere formality for a long time. . . . Candidates for delegates were nominated in the name of 'democratic consultation.' As a matter of fact, they were selected and decided on by a few individuals." *Renmin Ribao,* May 22, 1979, p. 3.

prescribed purchases where the state fixes the quantity of these goods to be purchased from each province, county, commune, production brigade, and production team. A production team, once it has fulfilled its assigned obligation to the state, may sell any surplus grain or edible oilseeds to the state at state-fixed prices of 50 percent or more above the basic compulsory delivery prices, or it may sell the surplus at a rural fair at free market prices. Cotton is subject to unified purchases by the state, which means that apart from the amount reserved for each individual's own use as specified by the state, the production teams must sell all their cotton to the state at a state-fixed price. Anyone with cotton left over from the amount allocated for his personal use may sell it at the rural fair. [33]

The plan, in the drafting of which the commune authorities are supposed to be involved through ongoing consultations, also covers general output instructions and projections for the purchase by the state of various "second category" (or "nonstaple") goods. Unlike first category goods, these commodities are normally not rationed; they include mainly poultry, pigs, and eggs. The purchase of second category goods (especially pigs and eggs) is subject to a procurement quota system. Peasants who raise pigs and hens are obliged to deliver a certain proportion (specified by each locality) of their pigs and eggs to the state; the rest is left for consumption by the family or disposal at the rural fair. When pork and eggs are in plentiful supply, the procurement quotas cease to operate.

The commune works with the state purchasing station located at commune headquarters to fulfill the compulsory delivery plan for first category goods and with the state's tax office to collect the agricultural tax. Through the commune-run supply and marketing cooperative commune authorities purchase for the state second category goods from teams, brigades, and households either directly or at rural fairs over which the commune exercises supervision. The supply and marketing cooperatives also channel consumer and producer goods obtained from within the commune or from outside to the commune's constituent units.

After the fall of the radicals, the system of prescribed purchases, unified purchases, and procurement quotas for first and second category goods introduced at the beginning of the First Five-Year Plan (1953–1957) was criticized by some economists, among them Xue Muqiao: "In some places, when the amount of prescribed purchases and the

[33]Xue Muqiao, "A Study in the Planned Management of the Socialist Economy," *Beijing Review*, October 26, 1979, p. 15.

procurement quotas are too high, the peasants who grow the crops cannot eat their fill and those who raise pigs do not have pork on their tables.Their flagging enthusiasm for production impaired the growth of agricultural production, which in turn made the shortage of supplies in the cities even more acute.'' The solution proposed by these economists was to ''bring about an equilibrium between supply and demand by means of the law of value,'' i.e., to replace prescribed, unified, and procurement quota purchasing, sales to final consumers at below equilibrium prices, physical rationing, and state subsidies, by market price rationing. ''We must learn the law of value in regulating agricultural production. But will this give rise to price hikes in farm produce? This is likely, but such price hikes are reasonable.'' [34] The big practical question is whether the freeing of agricultural prices would be politically reasonable, i.e., whether it would lead to riots in the cities.

In conjunction with the state, the commune provides banking and credit facilities for its constituent units.This is normally done through either a commune-level branch of the Agricultural Bank or through commune-run but state-controlled credit cooperatives.These institutions nowadays make mainly production-type loans to communes, brigades, and teams as well as some consumption and sideline production loans to households.

As we have seen, the commune operates rural industries, including machine maintenance, repair, and sometimes manufacturing plants and tractor stations. It is heavily involved in water management work. In fact, it would not be an exaggeration to say that the construction of irrigation and drainage systems requiring the mobilization of large numbers of peasants during the slack farming season is the basic rationale for the commune. In this important sphere of activity the communes have been highly successful.The commune also provides agricultural extension services.

Communes operate high schools and are in charge of public health work and the cooperative medical service within their area.Through their military affairs department, commune-level administrative committees in conjunction with the commune Party committee run the people's militia regiments or battalions, which, in addition to performing public security functions, act as fire brigades, relief workers during

[34]Xue Muqiao, *ibid.,* p. 16. Xue recognizes, however, that ''at present, it is still impossible for us to abolish unified purchasing and procurement of many major farm products. But we must be aware that this is not a normal procedure in the planned management of the national economy.'' In 1974 such views would have been considered ultra-rightist and those who expressed them would have been rectified in the severest manner.

disasters, and model detachments on difficult water conservation or other commune-wide projects. The longer-range purpose of the militia is to act as an auxiliary of the People's Liberation Army in the event of war—to "drown the invader in a sea of humanity."

Commune authorities are responsible for the construction and maintenance of local roads (even railroads) within the commune system and are involved in wired broadcasting activities.

Production brigades have Member Congresses, which elect Brigade Administrative Committees, headed by the brigade chief. Paralleling this organ is the brigade Party branch headed by the Party branch secretary. As at the commune level, the brigade Party branch is involved in every facet of brigade activity and exercises an influential role in the management of the brigade. Brigade cadres are obligated to put in 300 days of the year in physical labor and are remunerated according to the work-point system that applies to the laboring rural masses. Higher brigade cadres, however, are regarded as state employees and are paid regular salaries (for their administrative duties) applicable to their not very elevated civil service grade.

The brigade receives the state plan from commune authorities and apportions it among its constituent teams, making certain that the plan is executed with respect to first and second category goods, taxes, and production assignments.

Brigades are involved in much water management work as well as in road building. They run certain industrial undertakings, operate some orchards, fish ponds, primary schools, and health stations, and administer the rural cooperative medical service. They have militia companies or platoons that perform functions similar to those of commune-level militia regiments and battalions. Increasingly, commune-level supply and marketing cooperatives have branch stores within production brigades, and credit cooperatives also operate branches at this level.

The brigade is essentially a link in the commune system's chain of command and the Party's basic organizational unit. It remains primarily—with a few well-publicized exceptions—a unit of administration and labor mobilization rather than a unit of production.

Of all the institutions in rural China the one of most direct importance to the individual and his family is the production team. While the family is tolerated, indeed catered to by the regime, in the countryside it is the team that is the officially recognized, legitimate social unit. The team corresponds (very broadly and not invariably) to the traditional village; it may be described, more accurately perhaps, as a small collective farm

It has a Members' Congress, which elects the Team (Managerial) Committee consisting of a team leader, his deputy, an accountant, a work points recorder, a militia platoon commander, and sometimes a repairman who takes care of the team's tools and equipment. (In some better off or larger teams there may be a makeshift maintenance and repair workshop for hand and semimechanized tools.) By now there are probably Party cells within most teams. Team officials get paid according to the work point system.

The team performs two basic functions: in normal times it is the unit of farm production and the unit of income distribution. It carries out the state procurement plan in regard to first category goods (grain, oilseeds, cotton), meets its tax obligations, and makes contractual arrangements for the sale of second category goods with the state's commercial departments, normally through brigade and commune channels. As we have seen, when the going gets rough the team delegates its production powers to smaller work groups or even, on occasion, to individual households under what is known as the "production responsibility system." The idea behind this is that, despite what ideology may say, the small work group knows better than even the team how a particular piece of land should be cultivated, tended, and harvested. The work groups are obliged to turn over the grain they produce to their supervisory production teams to be weighed, registered, and stored, but they are allowed to handle "surplus" grain themselves (i.e., grain that the team leadership determines is over and above the groups' contractual obligation to the team). The team decides—with the aid of general criteria communicated to it from above—on the division of income into three shares: the state's, the collective's (team), and the individual members'. (The state's share is predetermined by the team's compulsory delivery and tax obligations.) With respect to the income distribution function, the production team is China's basic rural agent of labor motivation. (The actual methods of remuneration of labor are discussed below, in the section dealing with peasant incomes.) In times of economic stress, however, as was mentioned earlier, the income distribution function has been delegated to lower levels: the work group or even the individual family. This tendency is viewed with considerable alarm by some sections of the Party leadership because, as they see it, it amounts to an informal dissolution of the collective farm system. "For the work groups to distribute the harvest themselves violates the principle of having the production team handle products, income, and distribution in a unified way. . . . This makes it impossible to fulfill the state's grain procurement quotas and set aside collective grain reserves [since the hungry groups will tend to "distribute all"]." [35] The team theoretically is responsible for its own physical and financial management; it takes care of its land, labor and equipment, and draws up its profit and loss accounts. Some production teams engage in subsidiary production activities, such as making straw products and renting carts out for the transportation of goods.Team members frequently work part-time in brigade or commune workshops and on brigade or commune water management projects—sometimes willingly, other times under duress. But the overwhelming preoccupation of China's production teams is with the growing of grain. There is usually a paramedic ("barefoot doctor") and one or two health workers at the team level; like the barefoot doctors, they work part-time in the team's fields.

The basic function of rural households is to supply labor to work groups, teams, brigades, and communes. Households, as we have seen, also raise pigs and poultry and grow vegetables and fruits on their household plots; they make simple handicraft products for sale at rural fairs or through a supply and marketing cooperative. Members of households frequently work part-time or full-time in a county industry in the nearby town. All these activities, however, are not allowed to interfere with the household's basic obligation of supplying manpower to the team collective.

Extra-Commune Relations. Some indication of the commune system's relations with state authorities outside the system has been given in the discussion of commune, brigade, team, work group, and household functions. Only a few details need be sketched in.

The relations of the commune system with the state are of three kinds: command-and-obey, contractual, and consultative. The first arises in connection with the state plan, especially as this concerns the delivery of first category goods at state-fixed prices and the commune system's tax obligations.This type of relationship is essentially hierarchical, administrative, and manadatory, although even here consultation does take place before the orders are issued. Another illustration of this type of relationship is the control exercised by the state over commune and brigade activities (including their finances) through the commune and brigade offices of the People's Bank, the Agricultural Bank, and credit cooperatives. Commune accounts are kept at the bank,

[35]Letter from Comrade Chen Renji of the General Office of Ledong County Party Committee, Hainan Island, *Hainan Ribao,* May 24, 1979, in *FBIS,* May 25, 1979.

which acts not merely as agent for its customers but (and above all) as controller, supervisor, and monitor. Brigade and team accounts are also kept at the bank or at the credit cooperative, which, despite its cooperative locally managed status, is closely supervised by the state and works in accordance with the state's banking regulations. The important "guiding" role of the Party organization is yet another example of vertical relations.

The second type of relationship is more horizontally inclined; it arises in connection with the sale by the commune and its constituent units of second category goods to state commercial departments and other kinds of contractual relations, for instance, cooperation among communes on joint projects, such as water management, construction of hydroelectric power stations, and of chemical fertilizer plants. But, and this is important, the contracts derive from the plan, not the plan from the contracts.

The third type of relationship, consultation, occurs in the process of formulating the state plan. The commune is not only asked to feed higher state authorities with statistics and other information, but is associated in the process in a more active way. Given the importance attached to agriculture in China, state authorities may be presumed to be reluctant to issue plans that harm farm production, weaken incentives, or lower productivity. One would imagine, therefore, that they would be inclined to listen to what the basic rural units have to say about proper farming.

Despite the contractual and consultative trappings introduced into China's administrative command system at the time of the Cultural Revolution, the dominant command-and-obey type relationship between communes and other state authorities had not been substantively modified. The size of the country, the comparatively backward state of communications, and factional feuding at the top did give lower echelon units the opportunity to avoid executing some central directives that were not in the units' micro interest and to play hide-and-seek with the planners. But the bulk of information flows remained of the command-and-obey, vertical kind. In any kind of central administrative planning the rights of self-determination of lower units, however generously spelled out, are bound to come in conflict with both the philosophical premises of the system and its everyday practice. The hierarchical relationship is never really in question. What is questioned, especially when times are hard, is the extent to which the order-giver should listen to the order-receivers. In the disastrous post–Great Leap agricultural situation and again in the wake of the Cultural Revolution, the stress was on contractual relations between the basic producing units and their superiors, on consultation, and on less interference by Party functionaries in economic planning (at the very time that the Party's apparatus was being strengthened). But "contractual relationship" still meant that the contracts were based on centrally predetermined production and delivery quotas. Contracts were not to be the expression of lateral, freely concluded market-type arrangements: planned balances of the economy determined the contracts, not the other way round. The state was ready to negotiate with communes about the purchase of some sideline products, but the "negotiable prices" that emerged were to be under "state leadership." Village markets were again all right. Local state and Party authorities, however, were asked to keep a sharp lookout for speculators, shady dealers, and other capitalist elements, to prevent prices from rising to "undersirable" (i.e., market-clearing) levels, and generally to aim for "control without lifelessness and liveliness without chaos."

If the theoretical blueprint of the commune system were followed in practice, there would be a number of advantages to this form of rural social organization in China. The commune seems to be capable of mobilizing resources, especially labor, for flood- and drought-prevention work or, when needed, for disaster relief. In very rapid order, a commune is capable of supplying thousands of people to strengthen or repair dikes, to dig ditches, reservoirs, and canals, and to perform other water management jobs—something that was either not possible or more difficult under earlier systems of rural organization.

Another potential advantage is flexibility. Despite the large size of the rural people's communes, important production and income distribution decisions are supposed to be made by what often amounts to the traditional village community (the production team), but they are to be taken within a definite set of ideological postulates. The divorce between inputs of effort by individual peasants and remuneration should not be under the circumstances as great as it is where the accounting unit (e.g., collective farm) is larger. The various functions are (at least in the blueprint) distributed among organizational levels according to where they fit best and where they would be performed most rationally and effectively. It makes sense for the commune to own and operate the heavier machines, and for brigades (sometimes even teams) to own and operate tractors and other light machinery.

A third advantage of the commune is its ability to cater quickly to a variety of local needs. The majority of communes in China are fairly self-sufficient, albeit at a low level of material welfare: a great part of the capital investment, many social and cultural amenities, and a good part of consumer goods are generated locally by each commune. The central state provides only some very large infrastructural investments, and the state at the provincial level fills in gaps in medium-sized projects serving several communes or counties. The demands on state resources are thus minimized and the state is in a position to allocate resources under its command to projects of high national priority, which as a rule tend to be technically more sophisticated, complex, and costly.

The theoretical advantages of the commune system of social organization, however, have not always been allowed to manifest themselves in practice. In a tight resource supply situation, with enormous pressures being put on lower-level cadres by superior authorities to fulfill and overfulfill often unrealistic production targets, the general tendency has been to ignore the carefully elaborated theoretical division of rights and functions and to act in a rough and arbitrary fashion. It transpires, for example, that much—if not most—of the team labor conscripted for commune and county-wide water conservation work was either unpaid or underpaid; in short it was quite simply a *corvée*. So one of the major advantages of the commune system—the ability to mobilize large amounts of labor for flood and drought prevention and disaster relief—was, in execution, something less than could be expected. In fact, indiscriminate conscription of team labor for such work, and the financial burden on the teams that was involved in the operation, no doubt disrupted the orderly process of production in the villages. Also, the system spawns a large bureaucracy at every level; layer upon layer of privileged, often arrogant, sometimes ignorant, always jittery Party and state functionaries at loggerheads with the peasants and with one another. From the perspective of the center the danger is that local self-sufficiency, however rudimentary, will strengthen the centrifugal forces traditionally present in Chinese society, promote the creation of "independent kingdoms," spur "localism" and "departmentalism," and encourage the "mountain stronghold mentality." All of these are problems inherent in any administrative command system. The institution of the commune, some argue, tends to strengthen these systemic propensities. Under such an arrangement there is also bound to be some sacrifice of the benefits that accrue from an interregional specialization of functions. After the removal of the radicals the virtues of commune self-sufficiency, while still mentioned, distinctly took second place to calls for commune specialization.

In the wake of the post-Mao revelations about the abuse of the "grain only" policy, the subversion of the farm incentives system by egalitarian exercises in income distribution, and serious structural defects in the official three-level commune organization (commune, brigade, team), the whole concept of the rural people's commune was put in question. The institution of the commune became increasingly linked to the deteriorating reputation of Mao as an economist and provider of the people's needs, and its origins were (at first obscurely, later directly) traced to the disastrous years of Mao's Great Leap Forward. As the decade of the seventies drew to a close, pressures mounted for a thorough reappraisal—open and formal—of the theoretical underpinnings and practical implementation of the commune idea. In documents published by the Communist Party of China in October 1979, the Party leadership asserted that during the rule of Mao millions of Chinese went hungry because of the late Chairman's mistakes and the political instability that marked his regime after 1958. Specifically selected for criticism and serious reexamination was the institution of the people's communes.

Peasants Still Have Difficulties: Problems and Responses

Two subjects will be examined: living standards of peasants and systems of income distribution in the countryside.

LIVING STANDARDS The standard of living in the countryside is low and precarious compared with the cities, and there appear to be quite marked differences in income among state farms, communes, brigades, teams, and households, and (despite a significant narrowing) among geographical areas. Families at the bottom of the social and economic ladders are the so-called Five-Black Categories: counterrevolutionaries, rightists, bad elements, former landlords, and former rich peasants—many of whom live in a kind of exile in their own villages, "under the supervision of the masses," as the official euphemism has it. The Five-Black, it is often said, represent at most 5 percent of the population, or about 45 million people, but their number is probably greater. Anyone at any time can slip into one of the Five-Blacks, for example, by acting like a rich peasant in the estimation of the cadre-prompted masses. Following the removal from power of the gang of four, the sharply antagonistic policy toward the Five Blacks and their children was to have been moderated in line with the more general emphasis on reconciliation and the combining of two into one. People were thenceforth to be judged by their own political conduct rather than to be forever cursed because of incorrect social lineage. The change in policy was not without qualification. "Counterrevolutionaries and enemy agents, criminals and political degenerates who seriously disrupt socialist public order, and new exploiters such as grafters, embezzlers, and speculators [still exist]. Remnants of the gang of four and of the old exploiting classes, including the few unreformed landlords and rich peasants who persist in their reactionary stands and carry on antisocialist activities in the political and economic spheres [are still around]," according to Hua Guofeng. [36] The contradiction between them and the people was to be resolved by means of proletarian dictatorship, but this time "strictly within the socialist legal system." There are also many families of approved class background, however, that suffer from low incomes because of advanced age, disability, or an insufficient number of able-bodied workers (labor powers) in the household. Unlike the Five-Black, such families are protected by the "Five Guarantees," which nowadays comprise free or subsidized allocations of grain, cooking oil, firewood, medical care, and pocket money (about 3 yuan a month, or $1.80, in the better-off communes). Such help is paid out of the welfare fund of the production team or brigade to which the household in difficulties belongs.

The Commune System. Communes and brigades get their revenue from the sale or renting of products turned out by the land and industries under their jurisdiction and from the sale of services.The buyers are the state, units of the commune system, and other communes.The major services consist of renting out tractors and farm machinery to production teams, renting timberlands, supplying electricity to units of the commune (including individual households), machinery repair, storage, product processing (e.g., milling), primary education (households pay primary school fees to brigades), transportation, provision of medical services under the cooperative medical service (annual membership fee paid by peasants who join the system plus nominal payments for visits to brigade clinics and operations), veterinary services, and so on.

The principal source of revenue for production teams is the sale of agricultural produce, especially grain, to the state agencies. Grain (but also other commodities, e.g., fats and oils, cotton) are sold to the state at two sets of state-determined prices: a quota price for compulsory deliveries, and a higher, above quota price.These prices have been raised a number of times since 1953, the year in which grain purchasing and marketing were nationalized. In 1975 the purchase prices of the principal products acquired by the state from production teams were said to have

[36]Hua Guofeng, "Report on the Work of the Government," *Beijing Review,* July 6, 1979, p. 9.

been more than 90 percent higher than in 1950, but apparently this was not high enough because in 1979 the procurement price for compulsory grain sales to the state was increased by 20 percent. At the same time prices of grain and grain products sold to the mass of consumers have been kept relatively steady. In other words, the government subsidizes the price of grain to the urban consumer, and this subsidy is likely to be quite sizable. The below equilibrium retail prices of rice and bread are backed by urban rationing. State retail prices of nonstaple foods (pork, beef, mutton, poultry, eggs, vegetables, aquatic products, and milk, among others), however, have been raised on occasion. A round of sharp price increases for such items was mandated on November 1, 1979. Compared with 1978, state prices at retail for the various foods were raised as follows: pork, 33 percent; eggs, 32 percent; aquatic products, 33 percent; beef and mutton, 33 percent. The prices of vegetables were to be "slightly raised or not raised," presumably depending on season and local supply and demand, and milk prices were to be "appropriately readjusted under strict control." In most socialist countries of Eastern Europe such sharp overnight hikes in food prices would have resulted, no doubt, in riots and defenestrations of Party officials. The price increases were made so as to lessen the burden of subsidies on the state budget, and they were in line with the opinion of Xue Muqiao and other economists that China "must learn to use the law of value in regulating agricultural production."

Official spokesmen used to stress that the compulsory delivery quota was arrived at after thorough discussion with the producers and that it was fixed in such a way as not to burden the producers "unreasonably." (The preceding year's harvest was normally to be used as a guide in setting the current year's quota.) The produce so acquired by the state is used for central inventories, feeding the cities, export, and other centrally determined uses. It represents nowadays something less than 40 percent of the production teams' total annual output. The teams are also encouraged—perhaps pressured would be a better term—to deliver to state agencies grain, oilseeds, cotton, and other goods over and above the quota at prices roughly 50 percent above the basic quota prices for equivalent products. Such sales entitle the team to receive priority in the allocation by the state of chemical fertilizer, fodder grain, tractors, and other current and capital inputs. The teams also enter into contracts with provincial, municipal, and lower-level government commercial departments for the supply (under contract) of a wide variety of goods (e.g., vegetables and fruit) at prices arrived at by mutual agreement within certain centrally determined limits.

Widespread abuses of the compulsory and above quota procurement system have been reported after the death of Mao. The quotas were often set too high compared with the output potential of the farms; they were changed at short notice; and the prices at which the produce was procured were altered arbitrarily by the procurement agencies, no doubt with the connivance of higher-up authorities.

The production team also derives income from payments received for delivery of various "nonstaple" farm produce and sideline products, and payment for services rendered to other units of the commune by team members. Income from these activities may be in cash or kind. The last would include such items as insecticides, pesticides, farm tools and other inputs, as well as manufactured consumer goods, including medicines. The prices of chemical fertilizer, pesticides, and diesel oil supplied to the commune system in 1975 were said to have been one-third to two-thirds lower than in 1950. The factory prices and the market prices of farm machinery, chemical fertilizers, insecticides, plastics, and other manufactured goods for farm use were to be cut by 10 to 15 percent in 1979 and 1980 "on the basis of reduced cost of production." Prices of medicines—including those dispensed by commune clinics, brigade health stations, and team barefoot doctors—have been reduced several times since 1949. On August 1, 1969, they were cut by 37 percent and are now only about one-fifth of what they were in the early post–1949 years. Preventive vaccines and drugs for children and some oral contraceptives are supplied free of charge. Prices of medicines are the same throughout the country. Payments for deliveries of goods and services by teams, brigades, and communes are supposed to be made promptly. In 1979 the state purchase price for quota deliveries of grain was raised by 20 percent (another 50 percent on top of the 20 percent for above quota sales). At the same time state purchase prices for eighteen main farm and sideline products (including cotton, oil-bearing crops, and pigs) were increased by 24.8 percent on the average. The price increases of 1979 were part of a package of policies designed to improve agriculture's terms of trade with industry and to better the financial position of farms and peasants. [37]

[37]The 18 major categories of agricultural products for which state purchase prices had been raised after March 1979 included the following (when available, the increase in purchase price compared with 1978 is given in parentheses): grain (20 percent for quota deliveries; and 50 percent rise on top of the 20 percent for above quota deliveries); fats and oils (25 percent for quota; 50 percent for purchases above the quota); cotton (15 percent quota; 30 percent rise for purchases above the purchase quota); pigs (26 percent); other 14 products (20 percent–50 percent). *Beijing Review,* November 9, 1979, p. 5.

Since the demise of the radicals, but especially from November 1978 through March 1979 (an interlude sometimes called the "Beijing Spring") an unprecedented amount of information on rural living standards came to light. Scattered though the data are, they point to widespread poverty verging in some instances on destitution. In the first edition of this book, based in part on income data obtained during my 1974 visit to China, I suggested that the average monthly basic (workpoint) income of a working member in the best commune was 42 yuan, while the equivalent income in the poorest commune was 10.50 yuan (or roughly, at the exchange rate then, \$21.00 and \$5.25). I assumed, on the basis of earlier studies, that there was an income differential of 1:4 between the poorest and best communes. There was probably, I argued, a significant clustering of peasants in below average to poor communes, and there were considerable variations in income among individual households within the same team, among teams, among communes, and among regions. Over the longer run, however, there seems to have been a trend toward less inequality in the distribution of income within the teams. Granted that expenditures on housing and utilities in the countryside were minimal, health and education services were provided at nominal rates, and the prices of basic necessities were low compared with average earnings, the equivalent of a little better than five dollars per head per a month (17 cents per day) in cash and kind from communal activities—which is what the majority of people in China were getting—was not far from subsistence. Calculations based on my 1974 visit to China suggested that a single person working in modern industry, who lived in a factory dormitory and ate in the factory canteen, would spend about 16 yuan a month on housing, food, health, and transportation. Allowing for lower costs of these items in the countryside and the doubling up of family members under one roof, a person might just get by on 10.50 yuan a month. His clothing and any other consumer necessities, however, would have to be purchased with money obtained from private plot and household subsidiary activities. In such a setting the apparently quite common saying: "For grain rely on the collective; for cash rely on yourself," took on a new relevance and urgency. It also helped explain why, in violation of administrative control over labor allocation, team members kept wandering off to nearby townships in search of more attractive earning possibilities. The peasants, indeed, were still not prosperous.

At the end of January 1979 several thousand peasants poured into Beijing to protest their living conditions. According to eyewitness reports, many were "sick, on crutches, dressed in rags and tatters, wretchedly poverty stricken.'' [38] Numbers of them were arrested. For a time, several hundred regularly demonstrated in the center of the city in front of Zhongnanhai, the residence of Hua Guofeng and other Party and state leaders. A dissident publication (later suppressed), *Enquiry,* published an eyewitness report of what came to be known as ''democracy wall'' in Xidan Street, Beijing, describing a destitute peasant woman at the entrance to the Zhongnanhai residence, who tried to sell one of her two children because, she said, she could not feed them anymore. At the same time, in front of a ministry, another woman hung signs around the necks of her two children offering them for sale. [39] An essay by a tenth-grade student in Shanghai about a peasant woman beggar and her baby in Nanjing Road, became a cause célèbre and a test of how far one could legitimately go in emancipating one's mind (which is why, the student explained, he had written the essay in the first place).The presence of ''a handful'' of beggars was admitted by Wu Duo, deputy director of the Political Education Department of the Shanghai Teachers' University, who was called in by the Shanghai Municipal Party Committee to help clarify the educational aspect of the problem. ''The cause of such a phenomenon is not entirely the product of the socialist system.'' After being reeducated, the student wrote: ''We cannot just notice the sad, pleading eyes of one or a few beggars, but overlook the happy smiling faces of the broad masses of the people.'' [40]

With a few exceptions, Table 2 shows figures pertaining to per capita (not per worker) income from work for the collective (i.e., income that excludes earnings from private plot and household subsidiary activities, except where noted). These figures appeared in the Chinese press over a period of time during which ''truth in reporting'' was the order of the day.

I think it is safe to presume that the examples cited in the provincial and national media did not describe the worst places. What emerges is a rather disturbing picture of the apparent inability of the commune organization to provide members with incomes that would make ends meet. In commenting on the Anhui situation (daily per capita incomes as low as 8 fen—roughly 5 cents a day) ''comrade Chen Pingyuan, secretary of the Fengyang County Party Committee said: 'Fengyang County has been building socialism for thirty years, but many people in the rural areas still do not have enough to eat and are poorly clothed.' '' In a

[38]Agence France Presse (AFP), Beijing, in *FBIS*, January 25, 1979.

[39]AFP, Beijing, February 2, 1979, in *FBIS*, February 5, 1979.

[40]*Jiefang Ribao*, May 17, 1979 article broadcast by Beijing Radio on May 17, 1975, in *FBIS*, May 21, 1979.

classic understatement, *Fujian Ribao,* commenting on the situation in the Jukou commune, said that "judging by the current incomes of the peasants, a few production teams are not yet enjoying abundance and some are rather poor. The peasants there can only maintain basic living standards." In terms of the statistical code language in common use, "a few" signifies "many," and "some" stands for "a lot." [41]

Let us assume that the average daily per capita income of peasants from collective work in 1978 was 0.21 yuan a day (13 cents).This, according to official sources, was about 14 percent above what it had been in 1977. In 1979 the per capita income of commune members derived from work for the collective was 0.23 yuan (14 cents) a day.

Information on income from household private plots and related family subsidiary activities is hard to come by; not as hard as it used to be when the radicals were running things, but still difficult enough. Also in the better-off communes (those in the suburbs of large cities or equipped with fairly well developed rural industries) part-time work by some family members in factories is an important source of supplementary income. [42] Whether employed in urban state industry or rural communal workshops, the peasants are likely to earn wages that, for the same type of job, are below those of regular workers, and they are not likely to receive from the factory the social security benefits reserved for regular unionized labor. If only private plots and sideline activities are considered (not commune workshop or urban part-time or temporary factory employment), then it would appear that on the better-off communes such noncollective income accounts for 35 to 40 percent of total household income. [43] On below average to poor communes the proportion of "private" to total income is much greater. In all communes, except the very rich ones, proceeds from sales of produce from private plots to the state and on village markets represent a significant part of household cash income.

The disgraced former defense minister Lin Biao is quoted as having said that in China "the state is rich and the people are poor." Ban Yunqu, a member of the exceptionally prosperous Zhiaoli production

[41]In the past "an obvious decrease in grain production was labeled as 'having more grain than can be consumed.' " Beijing Radio reporting an Anhui Provincial Party Committee Work Conference, January 24, 1979, in *FBIS,* January 31, 1979.

[42]From the standpoint of urban planners these "experienced rural laborers" (including many relatives of urban cadres) who float into urban factory employment are "unplanned surplus laborers." Anhui Provincial Radio Station, Hefei, May 24, 1979, in *FBIS* May 30, 1979.

[43]Beijing Radio, May 17, 1979, in *FBIS,* May 18, 1979.

TABLE 2 Reported per Capita Income of Peasants from Collective Work, 1978

Economic Unit	Location	Income (yuan) Per month	Income (yuan) Per day	Source
Commune (commune members)	Nationwide	6.16	0.21	*Beijing Review*, April 21, 1980 p. 17
Paijiang No. 12 Production team	Xinan Commune, Xiapu County, Fujian Province	18.33	0.61	*Fujian Ribao*, 1.21.79 (*FBIS*, 1.23.79)
"More than 20 production teams"	Joukou Commune, Jianyang County, Fujian Province	10.83	0.36[a]	*Fujian Ribao*, 1.21.79 (*FBIS*, 1.23.79)
Xingshisi production brigade	Gannan County, Heilongjiang Province	33.33[b] [20.00]	1.11[b] [0.67]	*Renmin Ribao*, 1.20.79 (*FBIS*, 1.23.79)
Yuguan Commune (per commune member)	Archeng County, Heilongjiang Province	19.50	0.65	Heilongjiang Provincial Broadcasting Station Harbin, 1.21.79 (*FBIS*, 1.24.79)
Luan County				
—"rural areas"		5.41	0.18	
—"many places" (per worker)	Anhui Province	9–12	0.30–0.40	Beijing Radio, 1.24.79 (*FBIS*, 1.31.79)
—"a few places" (per worker)		2.50	0.08	
Wugui production brigade	Xindu County, Sichuan Province	10.05	0.34	*Beijing Review*, 4.20.79, p. 27
"Five Cassias Village" (production brigade)	Tianyuan County, Sichuan Province	11.08[c]	0.37	*China Reconstructs*, August 1979, p. 26
Kuyuan County	Ningxia Province	2.42	0.08	*Renmin Riboo*, 11.26.78

[a]This income was reached only after the commune abolished "its erroneous decision on limiting the size of peasants' incomes," which it had made in the past.

[b]This figure is based on total family income (i.e., from collective and household sideline and private-plot activities) of 2,000 yuan a year. I assume the average family to be composed of five members—probably too low a figure. A conservative estimate would put the proportion of income derived from noncollective activities at 40 percent. This would bring income per head from collective work to the figures shown in brackets.

[c]4.32 yuan in cash (ca. 39 percent), "the rest in food."

team in Zhejiang Province, says: "You know how fast bamboo shoots push up after a rain; that's the way our life is improving these days." Ban exaggerates. There is more truth in the late Chairman's statement that "the peasants still have difficulties." "Living standards for the vast majority of Chinese peasants remain low." [44]

State Farms. State farms are state-sector enterprises. They are generally larger than the average commune and specialize in a particular crop or livestock production. They practice extensive cultivation and are more mechanized than the communes. Usually located in the north, northeast, and northwest of the country, they often engage in large land reclamation projects and use a regular wage system of remuneration. In 1979 there were about 2,000 state farms, covering more than 4 million hectares (9.7 million acres) of land, and employing 5 million workers. Of these 2,000 farms, 400 were "advanced," that is, operating without subsidies and producing 10 tons of grain per worker per year, with 50 to 70 percent of the grain produced being "marketable" grain (i.e., delivered to the state). The other 1,600 state farms were operating at a financial loss and marketed only 30 percent of the grain they produced.

SYSTEMS OF RURAL INCOME DISTRIBUTION State farm workers receive part of their remuneration in kind, and the rest in the form of regular wage payments according to a system that is not very different from that prevailing in state industry. (The industrial wage system is described in Chapter 5.) Capital is granted from the state budget not from indigenously generated sources. Since 1977 there has been some talk of accustoming state farms to borrowing capital from the banking system rather than getting it free from the state treasury.

By far the greater number of (commune-based) peasants are paid according to a system of work days or work points which was originally adopted from the Soviets, but which has been modified over time to suit both the Maoist interpretation of Marxism-Leninism and the Chinese way of doing things. As we have seen, the organizational unit in charge of income distribution is the production team, less commonly, the brigade. The team's total annual income in cash and kind is distributed in the following manner.

1. Payment of agricultural tax. The tax is supposed to be levied on the "set yield" of the land, not on the actual yield in a given year. The set

[44] Ibid.

yield is determined for each locality on the basis of such factors as soil conditions, rainfall, and amount of fertilizer used. What emerges is roughly set yield equals normal yield. The set yield and the tax rate on that yield were to remain unchanged for several years, and the amount of tax was to be fixed once every five years, not to vary from year to year. The intent was to provide incentive to peasants to raise actual yields and so reduce their tax burden. In the early 1950s the agricultural tax was about 10 percent of the actual yield. By the early 1970s, because of increased output, the rate of tax on actual yield had fallen, it was claimed, to around 5 percent in many places. The tax assessment is expressed in weight of grain per *mou* and converted into value terms at the grain purchase price current at the local state procurement station. In the event of crop failures due to natural disasters, the agricultural tax may be reduced or altogether removed, and the affected farm unit may become eligible for relief in grain and cash. The tax may be paid in cash or grain. However, if paid in grains, as it most often is, the unit price of such "tax grain" is 3 to 8 percent below the posted purchase price of grain at the county wholesale station. [45]

In the post-Mao years it was revealed that, in fact, the tax had been quite erratic and exacting. Apparently it was not fixed for five years in advance, but was changed at will by local authorities. The reports also implied that the tax was often burdensome; probably fixed on actual rather than the set yield, or else the set yield was estimated in ways prejudicial to the farms' actual production potential. In 1979 the need for a stable and properly computed agricultural tax was emphasized by the highest authorities. In addition, in grain growing areas all low-yield and grain-deficient production teams with per capita grain allocations under the minimum taxable level were to be exempt from the agricultural tax. The minimum taxable level was to be determined by each province, municipality, and autonomous region, and was to be reviewed and approved by the State Council.

2. Payment of industrial and commercial tax. (This applies only where the brigade is the basic accounting unit.) Income derived by the communes and brigades from their industrial and commercial establishments is subject to tax. Before 1979 a one- to two-year tax holiday was usually granted to newly established enterprises of this kind. In 1979 the holiday was lengthened to two to three years, except for enterprises producing cigarettes, alcoholic beverages, cotton yarn, and some other products. Income from such items is taxed at high

[45]H. V. Henle, *Report on China's Agriculture* (Rome: F.A.O., 1974), p. 196.

rates. The minimum taxable income of commune- and brigade-run enterprises was also raised from 600 yuan per year to 3,000 yuan. In frontier regions and minority nationality (autonomous) counties, all commune and brigade enterprises were exempted from tax for a period of five years beginning in 1979.[46]

3. Having met its planned, above plan, and contractual obligations to the state, the team covers its current production costs.

4. It then sets aside a portion of its income for capital and welfare funds. These funds cover some of the team's capital and social-cultural expenditures (the idea is to cover as many of these as possible), but other units of the commune, as well as higher echelons of the state administration and the banking system, may occasionally chip in with grants, subsidies, and loans, especially in areas where capital investment, welfare, and other services provided by the different levels overlap and interlock (e.g., the rural medical service, where referral of serious cases is made by the team's health workers up the ladder to the commune or county hospital). Services rendered to members of the team or to the team as a group by higher echelons will normally be charged against the team's welfare, capital, or current account. As we have seen, the financial help provided to the team by its parent bodies was often outweighed by charges against the team's revenue made by brigades and communes for capital expenditures and services established by these echelons in response to orders from above, and from which team members benefited marginally if at all.

5. After paying the agricultural tax, covering current expenses, subtracting sums for capital (including inventory) formation, and welfare, the team distributes the remaining income among its members in two ways: 70 percent of the remaining income is distributed among all members on a straight per capita basis (90 percent during the reign of the radicals): the other 30 percent (10 percent under the radicals) is shared out according to the work points system.

Different ways of implementing the work points system have been used over the years. I shall consider three of the most commonly used methods of calculating work points: (1) the piece-work system; (2) the equal-shares system; and (3) the work-grade system, which comes in two variants, (a) fixed and (b) flexible.

1. Piece-Work System. The first way is the system as it should be

[46]Beijing Radio, February 4, 1979, in *FBIS*, February 5, 1979.

according to its Soviet inventors. In theory, each job on the farm is assigned a given number of norm work points. For example, [47] cutting stalks of ripe grain in the field and bringing the stalks to the threshing machine earns 3 work points per 100 catties (110 lbs.). Threshing earns 1.2 points per 100 catties. Mending river dikes with clay earns 15 points per work day in one team, 70 points in another. Occupations such as ditch digging, carpentry, and maintenance work tend to have their norms expressed in points tied to time. Team households are required to deliver to the team 60 to 70 percent of the household human and animal manure. Payment for this manure is in cash or work points. The number of points earned by each worker is entered daily in a register by work points assessment cadres (often rusticated urban educated youths). Before 1966 and again after 1977 a team member who exceeded the work norm assigned to him was rewarded by bonus work points. Underfulfillment of the norm entails a reduction in the work points attributed to the worker that particular day. Planning authorities have complained that bonus distribution since 1978 has been indiscriminate. What apparently is often done by harassed team leaderships is to set aside a part of the harvest as a bonus fund (at the expense of the accumulation funds) and to distribute the fund equally among all the team's "labor powers" without heed to differences in individual production performance.

The norms are set for each job by the team's leadership in consultation with the membership and in accordance with general guidelines promulgated by the government. The total number of work points earned by the team members during any given agricultural year is divided into the produce (in yuan) available for distribution as members' income from the collective. This gives the yuan value of a work point for that year. Each member then receives his remuneration in cash and kind according to the yuan value of the work points accumulated by him during the year. A basic grain ration for each member is guaranteed. Payments are made to individual members of the team, not to heads of households.

The mechanics of the system are Soviet. The peasant is the residual claimant on the farm's residual income; that is, the last claimant. The material condition of a residual claimant however, will depend on the size and stability of the previous claimants' shares. In Russia these shares were very sizable and erratic, so that over most of the Stalinist period, little was left for distribution to collective farm members.

[47]Borrowed from Andrew Nathan, "Paying the Chinese Farmer," *Far Eastern Economic Review* (Hong Kong), February 27, 1964, pp. 457–58.

In China, at least since 1961, the idea had been to arrive at something approaching an optimal and "just" allocation of resources among the claims of the state, the collective, and the individual, and between farm capital formation and distribution. The line in these matters is known as the principle of "Three-Way Attention" to state, collective, and individual interests. The state's interest is expressed in the form of the agricultural tax and produce procurement. The interest of the collective expresses itself in the public accumulation funds. Individual interests of the collective's members are expressed in the amount of income distributed as payment for labor. Under a government regulation promulgated in 1961, not less than 50 percent of total income must be distributed to members each year, not less than 10 percent must go to capital accumulation, [48] and at least 2 percent into the welfare fund. The state, it is often pointed out for the benefit of overzealous cadres, "should not in any way overbuy grain from the teams." If it does, or if it raises the agricultural tax too much, it will "dampen the production enthusiasm of the peasant masses," i.e., undermine the individual members' interest in collective labor and send them scurrying off to their private plots and household subsidiary activities.

It is also important, the Party reminds its cadres, to handle the relation between on-farm accumulation and distribution properly, and to avoid the errors of dogmatism (too much accumulation) and revisionist economism (too much distribution). The fact that Party authorities constantly have to remind the cadres not to buy too much from the farms and not to accumulate too much on the farms suggests that a bias in favor of furthering the state and collective (team) interest at the expense of the individual (team members) is built into the system. The local cadres are very careful to read the state's intent accurately. If they keep pressing for higher purchase quotas and more on-farm investment, it is not because they read the signals wrong, but because large procurements and high rates and amounts of accumulation are prized by the system, if not always in so many words. Where there is a conflict between the interests of the state and of the collective or the individual, the safest thing for a cadre to do is to promote the state interest.

What constitutes too much accumulation, distribution, or procurement is not determined by high-powered economic analysis and fine marginal measurement. In each case a largely intuitive appraisal is made

[48]According to H. V. Henle, *Report on China's Agriculture* (Rome: F.A.O., 1974), in the early 1960s accumulation rates as low as 2 to 5 percent were not only tolerated but centrally recommended. Capital accumulation, it was argued, must not be seen by the peasant masses as something abstract, even hostile to their welfare.

of the peasants' degree of political consciousness—the producers' willingness to postpone current consumption without a significant drop in their input of effort. What the traffic will bear is then compared with some notion of the state's needs in terms of grain supplies to feed the cities, cash crops, exports, and reserves, as well as with a rather rough estimate of the capital needs of the teams, brigades, and communes in the near future.

2. Equal-Shares System. The trouble with the work points system as just outlined is that it is complicated and time consuming. There are thousands of jobs on a farm, each job has many subdivisions, each of which should be assigned a work points norm. The system demands a fairly high degree of arithmetical skill, close and honest supervision and recording of work points, and much legwork by the work points recorders. It tends to breed tensions between cadres and rank-and-file team members and to generate disputes within the membership over the accuracy and equity of work points allotted to different individuals. The system, in short, is cumbersome. Moreover, since labor is a residual claimant on the farm's income (i.e., it gets whatever is left over) the labor cost component of the farm's production costs cannot be calculated in advance. This makes cost accounting problematical. To lighten the burden, an alternative, simpler work points system has been devised. The number of work points earned by the team during the year in fulfilling a given number of jobs is estimated globally. This is then distributed equally among those members who actually worked; the others get nothing. Because of its disincentive effects, this method is discouraged by superior authorities.

3. Work-grade System. A fairly widespread way of calculating work points is the work-grade method. Members of a production team are assigned to fixed work grades according to the team's estimation of their "labor power." Thus, an able-bodied adult male may be assigned grade 1, which carries with it 10 work points for a working day, while an elderly man might be assigned a grade 3 or 4, which earns him only 4 work points for a day. Exactly how democratic the process of assigning members to work grades actually is becomes a matter of some practical concern to members. It very probably depends on locality, the personality of members and the team leadership, and the more general "political time of day." Assignment to given work grades may range in democratic procedures from individual decision by the team's leader (backed by higher-up authorities) to decisions made by the whole team membership in general meeting. F.W. Crook is of the opinion that the system has worked, by and large, in an egalitarian direction, that is, that assignments have tried

to minimize individual work points (and hence income) differences. Bernstein notes that rusticated urban youths on occasion may have been discriminated against in being assigned to the lower work grades by resentful peasants. [49]

The *fixed variant* of the work-grade system means simply that once assigned, the peasant receives the number of work points attached to the grade, irrespective of his actual performance. The *flexible variant* is one in which actual performance of a peasant assigned to a grade is evaluated after the job either by the team's management or, less commonly, by general meetings of members.

Egalitarian schemes of income distribution in the countryside, including mass meetings of teams or, in some cases, brigades, to determine who is to get how much, have been roundly denounced since 1978. The old "Liuist" policy of letting individual peasant households get rich, provided they do so by raising their output and productivity, was revived under the second political reincarnation of Deng Xiaoping. When the gang of four (and their protector, Mao) were in charge "there were many cases in which peasants in the better-off villages were deliberately held to a poor standard of living to narrow the income gap among peasants in certain areas. The result was disastrous." [50] The politicization of rewards has also been criticized: "In the past . . . work points were given according to one's rank and political attitude, not according to one's work." [51]

Agricultural Output

We examined the fluctuating policy responses of China's communist government and Party to the problems cited by Mao with a minimum resort to production figures. The reason, of course, is that despite some recent improvements the available Chinese figures are few and far between and they are not terribly good. Western estimates—especially

[49]F. W. Crook, "The Commune System of the People's Republic of China, 1963–74," in *China: A Reassessment*, p. 401; Thomas P. Bernstein, "Urban Youths in the Countryside: Problems of Adaptation and Remedies," *China Quarterly*, No. 69, March 1977, pp. 89–90. In 1979 "peasants have been asked to monitor levels of pay to ensure that egalitarian policies of recent years are not revived." Beijing Radio, May 16, 1979, in *FBIS*, May 18, 1979.

[50]Beijing Radio, May 17, 1979, in *FBIS*, May 18, 1979.

[51]Xizang (Tibet) Regional Broadcasting Station, Lhasa, February 3, 1979, in *FBIS*, February 5, 1979.

those turned out by agencies of the United States government—while abundant, are not very reliable either. The compulsion to quantify, however, is strong, and if used with care, the figures can be illuminating. In this section a few general orders of magnitude are given for broad informational purposes, with the usual warnings.

Table 3 brings together some basic indicators of agricultural performance between 1952, when reconstruction of the economy had been completed, and 1978. The figures for 1952, 1957, 1977, and 1978 are from the Chinese themselves. Figures for 1965, 1970, 1975, and 1976 are U.S. government estimates.

Grain production between 1952 and 1978 rose at an average annual rate of 3.4 percent, while the output of cotton grew at the rate of 2.7 percent per year. During the same twenty-six-year period population grew at an average annual rate of 2.5 percent. Thus the annual rates of increase in grain and cotton output per head were 0.9 and 0.2 percent—a very modest improvement. If net imports are added to domestic production, total grain supply per person in 1978 was 47 kilograms better than twenty-six years earlier. In other words the margin between adequate supplies and disaster remains narrow, and the cost of importing grain is quite onerous. Grain yield, which in 1952 was 1,375 kilograms per hectare, was estimated (by the U.S. Department of Agriculture) at 1,984 kilograms per hectare in 1978, an average annual increase of 1.7 percent. Thus yield increases accounted for half the annual growth rate of grain output over the period. Between 1952 and 1978 the yield of cotton doubled from 234 kilograms to 469 kilograms per hectare. Grain, vegetable oil, and cotton fabric rationing to urban residents exists to this day. The rations are differentiated according to age, type of work, and presumably locality. (In the past the rationing was also determined by class status.)

Official China is given to hyperbole both in claiming present successes and denouncing mistakes made in the past by factional rivals now under lock and key. Not long ago the Cultural Revolution was depicted as a gigantic happening that released China's material productive forces by revolutionizing the political consciousness of the masses. [52] In 1974 it was explained that China's socialist economic history really began only in 1966. Now, and for how much longer no one can tell, the Cultural Revolution is described as a costly economic flop and a time of madness.

[52]According to Agence France Presse, which claims to have it from "a well-informed Chinese source," 400,000 persons were killed during the Cultural Revolution and an additional 100 million were directly or indirectly victimized by political measures. *FBIS*, February 3, 1979.

TABLE 3. **Agricultural Performance**

	1952	*1957*	*1965*	*1970*	*1975*	*1976*	*1977*	*1978*	*1979*
I. Production (million metric tons):									
Grain	161	191	194	243	284	285	283	305	332
Cotton	1.3	1.6	1.6	2.0	2.4	2.3	2.0	2.2	2.2
Raw sugar	0.5	0.8	1.4	1.6	1.8	1.8	1.6	1.8	
Oil-bearing crops	3.7	3.8					4.0	5.2	6.4
Sugarcane	7.1	10.4					17.8	21.1	21.5
Beetroot	0.5	1.5					2.5	2.7	3.1
Jute, ambary hemp	0.4	0.5					0.9	1.1	1.1
Silk cocoons	0.1	0.1					0.2	0.2	0.3
Tea	0.1	0.1					0.3	0.3	0.3
Aquatic products	1.7	3.1					4.7	4.7	
II. Livestock (million head, year end):									
Large animals	79	84					94	94	95
Sheep and goats	67	98					161	170	183
Hogs	93	146					292	301	320
III. Production, trade, and grain supply (million metric tons):									
Domestic production	161	191	194	243	284	285	283	305	332
Net imports	-0.26	-1.47	4.78	3.22	1.73	0.91	6.44	8.43	
Supply	161	190	199	246	286	286	289	313	
IV. Grain imports (million metric tons):	0	0	5.9	4.6	3.5	2.1	6.9	9.4	
V. Population (millions, year end):	576.0	646.9					945.2	958.1	970.9
VI. Grain production and supply per capita (kilograms):									
Production	280	295					299	318	342
Supply	280	293					305	327	
Net foodgrain supply (60%)	168	176					183	196	
VII. Net foodgrain supply index									
1952 = 100	100	105					109	117	
1957 = 100	95	100					104	111	

SOURCES: State Statistical Bureau, *Ten Great Years* (Beijing, 1960); Communique on Fulfillment of China's 1978 National Economic Plan (June 27, 1979) *Beijing Review,* July 6, 1979, p. 38; Communique on Fulfillment of China's 1979 National Economic Plan, *Beijing Review,* May 12, 1980, p. 14; CIA, *China: A Statistical Compendium* (July 1979), p. 607.

Neither explanation will do. As usual, the facts of the matter lie somewhere in between. The Cultural Revolution did introduce a number of institutional innovations that were not without merit. Arrogant elites were badly shaken, doors that had been locked for years were set ajar for the masses to rampage through, and the poor received a hearing. Production did not suffer as badly as is now made out. Between 1965 and 1975 agricultural production is believed to have grown at an average annual rate of 4 percent. During the most turbulent years of the Cultural Revolution (1965–1970), agricultural output is thought to have risen at an average annual rate of 5 percent. True, much of that growth was of the "extensive" type, achieved through the brute addition of factors. The stress was on a slowly changing mix of semitraditional and modern farm techniques and on self-reliance. Contracts concluded for the purchase abroad of thirteen huge chemical fertilizer combines, however, belie the impression of a largely do-it-yourself, backyard-type chemical fertilizer production. In 1965 only 2.1 million tons of chemical fertilizers (nutrient content) were produced, and another 640,000 tons were imported. In 1976, when the radicals were thrown out, production was 5.8 million tons and imports 1 million tons.

From 1965 through 1976 the grain yield rose by about 20 percent and the yield of cotton by 40 percent. Every year over 100 million people moved between 15 and 25 billion cubic meters of earth in the world's greatest land melioration program.

It is also true, however, that there has been mismanagement, some of it due to the bickering of leaders at the top, some inherent in the system itself. The gigantic land improvement effort has produced not just more grain but ecological damage as well. The food situation remains precarious despite the enormous expenditure of human effort and ingenuity. As the decade of the 1970s moved toward its close, the broad masses of peasants in China still had difficulties and were not yet prosperous by any means. Technical operational methods, while still backward, had made progress. The commune system was yet to find an organizational form that would be satisfactory at once to the state, the collective, and the individual farmer. The question of incentive systems adequate to the task ahead remained to be solved. There was retreat, probably tactical, from centralization, but Party and state functionaries still told the peasants how to go about the business of farming: "In places where seeds cannot germinate or seedlings are withering because of lack of water, it is necessary to go all out to find water."[53] The plague of natural

[53]Heilongjiang Provincial Party and Revolutionary Committee instructions to peasants on combating drought, Heilongjiang Provincial Broadcasting Station, Harbin, May 28, 1979, in *FBIS*, May 30, 1979.

calamities—of drought and floods and earthquakes—had not been banished, but steps had been taken to contain its destructive power. There was less fear of heaven, but still much dread of the ruthlessness and unpredictability with which those at the helm changed the meaning and direction of the dialectical line and slapped fatal labels on people who were not agile enough to adjust to the change in time.

SUGGESTED READING

Bennett, Gordon, *Huadong: Story of a Chinese People's Commune* (Boulder, Colo.: Westview Press, 1978).

Berner, Boel, *China's Science through Visitors' Eyes* (Lund, Sweden: Research Policy Program, University of Lund, June 1975).

Blecher, Marc, "Income Distribution in Small Rural Chinese Communities," *China Quarterly* (London), No. 68, December 1976, pp. 797–816.

Chiu, Li, and Chieh-yun Tien, *Inside a People's Commune* (Peking: Foreign Languages Press, 1974).

"Country Fair," *China Reconstructs* (Beijing), Vol. XXVIII, No. 10, October 1979, pp. 28–32.

Crook, F. W., "Chinese Communist Agricultural Incentive Systems and the Labor Productive Contracts to Households," *Asian Survey* (Berkeley), Vol. 13, No. 5, May 1973, pp. 470–81.

———, "The Commune System in the People's Republic of China, 1963–74," in *China: A Reassessment,* pp. 366–410.

Dawson, Owen, *Communist China's Agriculture* (New York: Praeger, 1970).

Greer, Charles, *Water Management in the Yellow River Basin of China* (Austin: University of Texas Press, 1979).

Hallford, S. S., "Mechanization in the PRC," *Current Scene* (Hong Kong), Vol. XIV, No. 5, May 1976, pp. 1–12.

Henle, H. V., *Report on China's Agriculture* (Rome: Food and Agriculture Organization of the United Nations, 1974). Withdrawn from circulation at China's request.

"How Chiaoli Production Team Distributes Its Income," *China Reconstructs* (Peking), Vol. XXI, No. 9, September 1972, pp. 26–29.

Hsu, Robert C., "Agricultural Mechanization in China: Policies, Problems, and Prospects," *Asian Survey* (Berkeley), Vol. XIX, No. 5, May 1979, pp. 436–49.

"Inquiry into Guidelines for Agriculture." *Beijing Review,* January 28, 1980, pp. 20–26.

Jing Hua, "A Glimpse of Rural Life," *Beijing Review,* April 14, 1980, pp. 17–26.

Khan, A. R., "Taxation, Procurement, and Collective Incentives in Chinese Agriculture," *World Development* (Oxford), Vol. VI, No. 6, 1978, pp. 827–36.

Kuo, T. C., *The Technical Transformation of Agriculture in Communist China* (New York: Praeger, 1972).

Leeming, Frank, "Progress towards Triple Cropping in China," *Asian Survey* (Berkeley), Vol. XIX, No. 5, May 1979, pp. 436–49.

Lippit, Victor, *Land Reform and Economic Development in China* (White Plains, N.Y.: M.E. Sharpe, Inc., 1975).

Liu, Chenlie, "How a Farm Family Get Its Income," *China Reconstructs* (Beijing) November 1979, pp. 40–41.

London, Miriam, and Ivan D. London, "Hunger in China: The Failure of a Dream?" *Worldview* (New York), Vol. XXII, No. 10, October 1979, pp. 44–49.

Lou, Fu, "A 'Dragon' of Farming, Industry, and Commerce," *Beijing Review,* August 4, 1980, pp. 17–25.

Morehouse, Ward, "Notes on Hua-Tung Commune," *China Quarterly* (London), No. 67, September 1976, pp. 582–96.

Myrdal, Jan, *Report from a Chinese Village* (New York: New American Library, Signet Books, 1966).

Nickum, James E. (ed.), *Water Management and Organization in China* (White Plains, N.Y.: M. E. Sharpe, 1979).

Parish, W. L., "Communist Agricultural Organization. China: Team, Brigade, or Commune?" *Problems of Communism* (Washington, D.C.), Vol. XXV, No. 2, March–April 1976, pp. 51–65.

———, and Martin King, *Village and Family in Contemporary China* (Chicago: University of Chicago Press, 1978).

Perkins, Dwight H., "Constraints Influencing China's Agricultural Performance," in *China: A Reassessment,* pp. 350–65.

———, "A Conference on Agriculture," *China Quarterly* (London), No. 67, September 1976, pp. 596–610.

Plant Studies in the People's Republic of China: A Trip Report of the American Plant Studies Delegation (Washington, D.C.: Committee on Scholarly Communication with the People's Republic of China, National Academy of Sciences, 1975).

Printz, Peggy, and Paul Steinle, *Commune: Life in Rural China* (New York: Dodd, Mead and Co., 1977).

"Public Ownership of the Means of Production in China," *Peking Review* (Peking), No. 51, December 22, 1972, pp. 5–7.

Shen, T. H., "Agriculture in Communist China: Its Organization, Planning, Technology, Production, and Trade," *Issues and Studies* (Taipei, Taiwan), Vol. XI, No. 4, April 1975, pp. 29–59.

Sigurdson, Jon, "Rural Industrialization in China: Approaches and Results," *World Development* (New York), China issue, No. 7–8, 1975, pp. 527–38.

"The Socialist New Countryside." Nine articles from PRC sources. *Chinese Sociology and Anthroplogy* (White Plains, N.Y.), Vol. IX, No. 1, Fall 1976.

Stavis, Benedict, *The Politics of Agricultural Mechanization in China* (Ithaca, N.Y.: Cornell University Press, 1978).

Strong, Anna Louise, *The Rise of the Chinese People's Communes* (Peking: New World Press, 1964).

Tachai: Standard Bearer in China's Agriculture (Peking: Foreign Languages Press, 1972).

Ullerich, Curtis, *Rural Employment and Manpower Problems in China* (White Plains, N.Y.: M. E. Sharpe, 1978).

United States, Central Intelligence Agency, *People's Republic of China: Atlas* (Washington, D.C.: U.S. Government Printing Office, November 1971), pp. 52–59.

United States, Department of Agriculture, *Agriculture in the United States and the People's Republic of China,* Foreign Economic Report No. 94 (Washington, D.C.: February 1974).

"What Do We Mean by . . . 'Take Grain as the Key Link and Ensure All-Round Development'?" *China Reconstructs* (Peking), Vol. XXIV, No. 1, January 1975, p. 7.

Whyte, Martin K., "Inequality and Stratification in China," *China Quarterly* (London), No. 64, December 1975, pp. 684–711.

Wu, Chou, *Report from Tungting—A People's Commune on Taihu Lake* (Peking: Foreign Language Press, 1975).

Xu, Zhigang, and Zhou Jinghua, "Economic Policies in Rural Areas," *Beijing Review*, April 20, 1979, pp. 15–25.

FOUR

Industry I

An unchanging objective of the communist regime has been to turn China into a modern industrial country in the shortest possible time. This broad goal, on which there has always been consensus among the leaders, can be interpreted in different ways for purposes of policy. There can be and has been disagreement on the way in which the industrialization objective could be reached. As with other points at issue, the industrialization debate has tended to be cast in dialectical opposites and has assumed an ideological (correct versus incorrect) form.

PROBLEMS

The industrial problem in China may be broken down into a number of subproblems, some of them inherited from pre-1949 days, some acquired since 1949. In this section we shall briefly examine several of these. In a subsequent section (which is continued in Chapter 5) the regime's policy responses will be considered.

Intersectoral and Intrasectoral Priorities

The question to be resolved concerns the relative standing of industry on the regime's scale of priorities, the relative position of light and heavy industries within the industrial sector, and the comparative emphasis to be given to this or that line of production within the light and heavy industry subsectors. A related question is the implication for other economic sectors of any given ranking of priorities. If, for example, the planners put heavy industry at the top of the list, would this entail neglect or exploitation of agriculture?

Property Structure

The question here concerns the degree of socialization, its pace, and the extent of foreign ownership.

Considering the degree of socialization, the range of theoretical alternatives is from private ownership (circumscribed by the government's fiscal, monetary, and other policies), through various cooperative and state-private property arrangements, to outright ownership of industry by the state. Except for the early post-1949 period of reconstruction (politically known as the period of "New Democracy"), the first alternative was not seriously entertained. To the communist leaders industrialization meant socialized industrialization.

However, the postreconstruction time schedule of socialization was at issue. The alternatives ranged from instant to very gradual socialization. That the latter was at one time considered is indicated by the variety of intermediate property blueprints that had been drawn for the express purpose of slowly easing the capitalists into the socialized matrix. Linked to timing was the question of whether and to what extent the former owners of industrial assets should be compensated by the state. In any event, the question was not difficult to answer, but it was the subject of controversy. The problem was brutally resolved during the Cultural Revolution (1966–1969), and then partially reversed in 1978–1979.

The third question concerns the extent to which foreigners—private interests as well as governments—are to be permitted to share in the ownership of industries in China. Again, except for a brief period before the Korean War and after 1977, equity participation in Chinese industry by private foreign interests was most of the time not a realistic option. To the communist leaders industrialization meant ownership of Chinese industry by the Chinese. From 1949 to 1955, however, participation by a friendly foreign government—the Soviet—was, a reality. It took the form of the "joint stock companies" that operated in a number of sensitive sectors of China's modern industry (e.g., petroleum exploration and extraction, rare metals and minerals, and civil aviation).

Centralization and Decentralization

More significant perhaps than the structure of legal titles to property (private, cooperative, state-private, state) is the extent of operative rights over assets granted to the actual users of the assets, including notably the state industrial enterprises. Is the user granted broad autonomy in the matter of acquisition, use, and disposal of assets? What important decisions on these and other questions are reserved for superior authorities of the state, and what is the meaning of "state"? Is it provincial or national authority, for example? Also, which pressure group (e.g., the army, the bureaucratic establishment, the Party's left or right wings) constitutes the state or influences it most at any given moment? These are delicate and complex questions of the distribution of economic power. They call for an examination of the industrial macro and micro structures, including the organization, principles, and methodology of industrial planning.

Plant Size and Technological Options

An important problem facing China's communist policymakers has been plant size and technological choices. Broadly, the question is what weights to assign to the development of large-scale, capital- and skill-intensive, technologically advanced, modern industry and to small- and medium-scale, relatively labor-intensive, technologically less sophisticated, traditional industry. The options need not be mutually exclusive. There are, as a matter of fact, many possible intermediate solutions: intermediate as regards plant sizes, capital and skill intensity, and technologies. Given China's factor endowment (abundant manpower, comparatively limited capital) and, over much of the post–1949 period, the absence of readily available foreign sources of technology, the final choice will tend to be to an extent a function of "historical necessity," that is, partly out of the hands and beyond the will of policymakers. Still, historical necessity may be interpreted in different ways by planners equipped with different ideological lenses, and attempts may be and have been made in China and elsewhere to bend history to the leadership's will. The question was posed with renewed urgency after the fall of the radicals in 1976 and the announcement of a ten-year economic modernization plan for China.

Decision on plant size and technology will normally have repercussions on the spatial distribution of industry.

Spatial Distribution

The communists inherited a modern industry that was not only small in terms of output value and employment, but was technologically retarded and geographically highly concentrated. With few exceptions, modern industrial plants in both light and heavy industries were located in coastal areas, principally in a few large cities.

According to Y. L. Wu, the five cities of Shanghai, Tianjin, Quingdao, Beijing, and Nanjing at the end of World War II accounted for 90.7 percent of industry's motive power, 78.8 percent of industrial employment, and 80.2 percent of all factories. If Wuhan, Chongqing, and Guangzhou are added, the quasi-totality of industrial motive power, industrial employment, and factories was to be found in China's eight cities. As late as 1954 the provinces of Hebei, Liaoning, Shandong, Jiangsu, Zhejiang, Guangdong, and Fujian, and the cities of Shanghai, Tianjin, and Beijing accounted for 70 percent of the gross value of industrial output. [1]

The communist regime regarded the spatial distribution of industry that it inherited undesirable for several reasons. First, from a military strategic standpoint the high concentration of industry in coastal regions represented an obvious danger. Second, the location of modern industry was irrational from the standpoint of domestic distribution of fuels and raw materials and markets for the finished products. Third, and closely connected with this, was the fact that the existing spatial characteristics of Chinese modern industry were the result in large measure of China's political history of the nineteenth and early twentieth centuries. In the formation of this history foreign intervention in behalf of foreign political and economic interests played an important part. A redistribution of industrial capacity followed naturally from the communist regime's emphasis on China's national interest. This included, among others, the development of hitherto retarded regions in the interior of the country.

Incentives

Incentives are prods to economic units designed to make these units go about the system's business as expeditiously and efficiently as possible.

[1]Yuan-li Wu, *The Spatial Economy of Communist China* (Published for the Hoover Institute by Praeger, New York, 1967), pp. 8–11.

Economic incentives may be classified in a number of ways: positive and negative, collective and individual, competitive and cooperative, material and moral. The problem is to strike an optimal balance between each pair of relations and among them all, a balance that is consistent with the achievement of the system's economic objectives and with the country's philosophical, ethical, and political goals. Alternatively, the problem may be seen as that of eliminating one of the contradictions in each pair and establishing a homogeneous, mutually reinforcing set of incentives; for example, a system of positive, collective, cooperative, moral prods resting on a common outlook.

One of the issues considered under this heading is the industrial wage structure including basic, bonus, and social wages, wage levels, wage differentials, and allied subjects. The problem is of the utmost concern to China's communist leaders and fundamental to the philosophical assumptions on which contemporary Chinese society rests. A propensity of the Chinese communist system to resort to mass administrative mobilization and peer-group pressure has already been noted. In Chapter 5 we will explore how these methods are applied to industry and how they mesh with other means of eliciting workers' response to and compliance with the system's goals.

Relative and Absolute Size of Industry

The communists took over an overwhelmingly rural country. In the 1930s the contribution of modern industry and handicrafts to national income was about 10 percent; the share of modern industry alone was much less: not much more than 3 percent. By 1949 industry's share was somewhat larger because of the accelerated development of manufacturing and mining by the Japanese in Manchuria in the late 1930s and early 1940s, and the Nationalists in some areas under their control. Because of wartime destruction and the stripping of Manchurian industry by the Soviets at the end of World War II, however, the increase in industry's share of national income was probably quite modest by 1949.

In 1955 there were an estimated 262 million peasants in China's labor force. In that year the number of employees in industry was at most 8 million, plus slightly over a million workers engaged in basic construction.

Many industries that form the backbone of the modern economy did not exist or existed only in the most rudimentary form before 1949. The output of other key industries ranged from small to insignificant. In 1952, after completion of reconstruction, China produced only 1.3 million tons of steel, 66 million tons of coal, 436,000 tons of crude petroleum, 7.3 billion kilowatt-hours of electricity, 181,000 tons of chemical fertilizer, and 3.8 million meters of cotton cloth.

POLICIES

Intersectoral and Intrasectoral Priorities

"In the national economic plan priority is given to agriculture, light industry, and heavy industry in that order." [2] "If we consider the national economy as a whole, it is agriculture, in the final analysis, that determines the scope and tempo of industrial development. . . . Practical experience has enabled the cadres to realize that 'more' agriculture leads to 'more' light industry, and 'more' agriculture and light industry lead to 'more' heavy industry, while 'more' heavy industry makes for 'much more' agriculture and light industry. This is the dialectics of the growth of agriculture, light industry, and heavy industry." [3]

AGRICULTURE AND INDUSTRY This ranking of intersectoral priorities dates back to 1961 and was reaffirmed in 1978 by the new leadership of Hua Guofeng and Deng Xiaoping. It was arrived at after bitter disputes among the leaders and the near disaster of the Great Leap Forward (1958–1960). Until 1957 China's intersectoral priorities were Soviet-Stalinist, placing emphasis on investment in industry (particularly heavy industry) with a concurrent neglect of agriculture. In China this neglect stopped short of exploitation; the masses of peasants in China were never treated with the calculated brutality that Stalin directed at Russia's collective peasantry. Still, the stress on capital formation in industry was unequivocal and, in China's specific context, politically and economically untenable over the long run.

The Great Leap Forward, despite the massive and spectacular if ultimately fairly useless work done in agriculture, was in its emphasis on industrial production a Maoist adaptation of Stalin's industrialization policy. Whereas from 1953 to 1957 (First Five-Year Plan) the average annual rate of growth of industrial production was 14 percent, in the two Leap years 1958 and 1959, it was 29 percent, plummeting, to –19 percent

[2] *China Reconstructs*, Vol. XXII, No. 7, July 1973, p. 20.

[3] "Relationship between Agriculture, Light Industry, and Heavy Industry—Summary of a Discussion among Cadres in Kwangtung Province," *Peking Review*, No. 34, August 25, 1972, p. 9.

in the post-Leap recession of 1961–1962. Total industrial employment in 1958 alone rose by almost 17 million compared with 2 million from 1953 through 1957.

Because of the thoughtlessness that marked economic management during the Leap and the withdrawal of technical and other assistance by the Soviets in 1960, much of the industrial capacity brought into being during the early Leap years could not be utilized without important alterations, and a good deal of it was unfinished by the time the Soviet experts left with their blueprints. The damage done to the land by the highly organized but largely uncoordinated mass movements of 1958 and 1959, however, was probably greater than that done to industry through sharply raised output targets and the speeding-up of work. The "agriculture first" policy inaugurated in 1961 was a pragmatic corrective to the earlier policy that favored industry, rather than the establishment of a new and opposite bias against industry. The policy was balanced in the sense that the rate and scope of nonagricultural growth were to be determined by the output of agriculture.

The reaffirmation of agriculture's leading position after the departure of the radicals was also a corrective to what the postgang leaders saw as the sabotage of agriculture by the radical left during and for some years after the Cultural Revolution; this despite the fact that throughout the period 1961–1976 agriculture was formally the number one sector. While the radicals, it was now said, paid lip service to agriculture, they actually nearly ruined it by their wrongheaded incentives policies, which they rammed down the peasants' throats. And thus, even though agriculture had been held in high official esteem since 1961, nineteen years later a regional Party committee reflected that "agriculture and animal husbandry are very weak links in the national economy." [4]

Light and Heavy Industries The relative stress put on the development of light and heavy industries is not as clear as the first sentence in this section suggests. There seems to be a continuous shifting at the margin, of investment and other resource allocation priorities from one to the other, depending on time and the decision-making discretion of the governmental authority involved. In times of recession, such as the one following the Great Leap and in 1976, light industry producing consumer goods tends to be favored, if only to keep citizens' tempers down to politically manageable levels. Local, including provin-

[4]Work Conference of Inner Mongolian Regional Party Committee, Nei Monggol Regional Broadcasting Station, Hohhot, January 26, 1979, in *FBIS*, February 2, 1979.

cial and municipal, authorities are inclined to favor investment in certain profitable branches of light industry.

On the other hand, the needs of national defense, the requirements of agriculture, and the policy of developing light industry call for capital equipment that only heavy industry can furnish. "Building a modern industry, modern agriculture, and strong national defense requires advanced equipment from heavy industry. To develop heavy industry, however, requires a great amount of funds. In China today, one of the main sources of these funds is the accumulation of light industry [i.e., light industry's relatively wide profit margins, which feed the state's accumulation funds]. Light industry needs comparatively less funds, goes into production faster, and the period of capital turnover is shorter. Therefore, while giving priority to developing heavy industry, China is also actively developing light industry." [5] This general argument has been maintained after October 1976, and was at first linked to Mao's 1956 theses on the "Ten Major Relationships." [6]

SUBSECTORAL PRIORITIES The priorities to be given to different subsectors of industry are, no doubt, the subject of an ongoing debate among different segments of the leadership, between the center and the provinces, and between the military and civilians. Visual impressions gained in Chinese cities and some parts of the countryside suggest that light industry has done comparatively well under the present dispensation. Basic consumer goods are available in what appear to be adequate quantities and are of satisfactory quality. The retail distribution of the products of light industry seems to be superior to that of other communist countries. But visual impressions tend to be narrowly focused and, given the system, not very representative of the whole where foreign viewers are concerned. "In commercial enterprises," writes *Nanfang Ribao*, official organ of the prosperous Guangdong Province, "poor management, bad service, overstocking of commodities, and rotting and deterioration of products are very serious. . . . The common situation of industrial enterprises in our province is poor quality of products, high consumption [of raw materials], excessive waste, low profits, and great losses." [7]

In the early post-Leap years the general line was that within the

[5] *China Reconstructs*, Vol. XXII, No. 8, August 1973, p. 21.

[6] Chung Chin, "China's Road to Industrialization," *Peking Review*, No. 14, April 1, 1977, pp. 12–15.

[7] Guangdong Provincial Broadcasting Station, Guangzhou, May 25, 1979, in *FBIS*, May 25, 1979.

producer-goods sector, those industries should be stressed which directly helped agriculture. This would include steel, of course, and petrochemicals, and power—especially coal, electricity, and petroleum—as well as certain branches of the machine-building industry. Today the argument in support of these industries is made often in the language of national security needs, but the "back agriculture" argument remains basic.

Light industry in China now, and probably for some years to come, stresses simple things: food processing (much of it done in commune-run plants), textiles for the standard clothing worn by everyone, and consumer durables ranging from Thermos bottles (which serve a combined culinary and heating function) to sewing machines, bicycles, and watches for those with larger incomes. From the beginning of the Cultural Revolution until the demise of the radicals ten years later, the general guideline in the matter of consumer goods was to avoid excess. Community standards then in force demanded the suppression of conspicuous consumption by those who—like some upper-echelon cadres—could afford the display. An enormous educational effort was expended from nursery school on up to keep personal aspirations for both material goods and professional honors in check. The public display of private wealth, however modest and whether tangible or intangible, was socially reprehensible. The injunction extended to the external appearance of public buildings and factories. Apparently many cadres (beginning with the top radicals who laid down the ethic) in everyday life ignored this "theoretical vandalism," as it is now called. Among numerous examples cited by the press after the fall of the gang, was the case of the deputy director of the foreign trade bureau in Jilin Province, who in twenty days spent 26,000 yuan entertaining seven people who had come to Jilin to make on-the-spot investigations of the province's export potential. This local gang of eight consumed—if the figures are believed—1 ton of famous wines, 60,000 choice cigarettes (375 cigarettes per person per day!), and 12 kilograms of top-quality tea. The sum of 26,000 yuan represented a month's wages for 500 young industrial workers, or one year's earnings of 100 able-bodied peasants. [8]

[8]*Beijing Review*, June 15, 1979, p. 8. Higher cadres "constantly worry and fear the lack of security measures to protect them. They live like hermits, are closely guarded, and can scarcely be reached by ordinary cadres and the masses. When they go out they have a large entourage in tow to keep the masses at a distance of several *li*. When they go to the theater they ask for special boxes. When they eat out they want reserved tables. When they preside over a meeting they place their lecterns far away from the masses." *Renmin Ribao*, January 22, 1979, in *FBIS*, February 2, 1979.

The excessive language used to drive home the lesson of revolutionary asceticism has been interpreted by some—including the post-gang leaders—to mean the glorification of poverty: making poverty an absolute virtue and the defining characteristic of socialism and communism. "Life has to be hard and material welfare ignored. . . . Revolution ordained that everyone should be poor." [9] While there is some truth to this rendering of the Maoist message, it is not the whole truth by far. The essence of the Maoist argument seems to be to ration out the available consumer goods and white- and blue-collar jobs evenly at the source by lowering the horizon of expectations rather than by trimming demand for these things on the market through price, physical rationing, or selective "credentialism." Reduction of demand through price and rationing coupons is certainly used, but in the Maoist order it is secondary to the basic trimming of wants at the source. The attempt has met with both open and passive resistance. A good deal of the labor productivity problem with which China is now trying to come to grips has its origin in this massive effort expended over the years to instill asceticism in the people and make them reject the notion of rising material aspirations. Together with a number of other Maoist positions, this interpretation of economic development was rejected by the post-Mao leadership. To harbor thoughts of material advancement became again a legitimate state. Standardized clothing of an unimaginative cut was no longer considered indispensable to socialist construction, and for people to become materially better off (through labor) at different rates was again sanctioned.

While there can be little doubt about the strategic reorientation and shift of priorities from industry to agriculture and from heavy to light industries in the wake of the Great Leap Forward, this change does not appear to have been accompanied by a parallel reorientation of intersectoral and interindustry wage differentials. Such differentials are normally used to induce labor mobility in the directions favored by the planners. The failure to implement a reform of intersectoral and interindustry wage differentials, which would reflect the changed strategic orientation, has been interpreted at times to mean that nothing much changed. A more cautious conclusion would be that the new planners' preference function was implemented to a considerable extent by methods different from those used in the past. After 1960 labor mobility

[9] *Beijing Review*, June 15, 1979, p. 14, and January 19, 1979, p. 5. Nikita Khrushchev once put it more bluntly: Communism to Mao, he said, meant "a lot of hungry people sitting around an empty table in perfect equality."

in the desired sectoral and industrial directions became increasingly a function of administrative order rather than wage policy.

Property Structure

DEGREE OF SOCIALIZATION At the present time most productive assets in China, including land, are owned socially, meaning that they are owned by the state or by cooperative organizations. As Chapter 3 notes, the most important cooperative organization is the rural people's commune and its subdivisions. In urban areas the cooperative sector consists of so-called neighborhood, street, or block industries, which are essentially artisanal and service enterprises.

State assets are theoretically held in behalf of the whole people. Cooperative assets are held for the members of the particular cooperative organization. By far the greater part of the assets owned by cooperative organizations comes from three sources: original capital contributed by members; the cooperatives' accumulation from current production; and, marginally, purchase from the state sector. In other words, the cooperatives are expected to take care of their capital needs out of their own initial and current resources as far as they can. They "should not ask the state for help." On the other hand, assets held by state enterprises have been allocated to those units in the form of free, nonreturnable grants out of the state budget. In late 1979, however, it was decided that investment in capital construction would be made by loans from the People's Construction Bank of China rather than by budgetary grants. The new method was to be tried out in the light and textile industries and tourism in Beijing, Shanghai, and Guangdong Province. The loan transactions were to be handled by contracts concluded between the bank and the borrowers. These contracts were to stipulate legal and economic responsibilities of both sides, including compensation for economic losses. Borrowers were obliged to repay the principal and interest by the designated date. For heavy industry enterprises the period was not to exceed fifteen years; not more than five years for smaller projects. A borrower who completed a project on or ahead of schedule and repaid the principal and interest ahead of time, was to be permitted to retain the monies accrued from profit and other sources (which normally would have had to be turned over to the state) for the rest of the period stipulated in the contract. These monies could be used for production development and workers' and employees' welfare (e.g., housing). If the sums borrowed were not repaid on time, the enterprise was required to repay the amount out of its working capital and improvement funds. Interest on the unpaid balance was to be doubled. According to *Beijing Review* (December 7, 1979), "This change conforms to the principle of doing economic work according to economic law." It was expected to cut down on unreasonable requests for government investment funds and for approval of unnecessary projects.

In the rest of the economy, since the early 1950s and as late as 1980, profits earned by state-sector units are remitted to the state's central fiscal bodies, often by way of intermediary state supervisory and managing authorities, which retain portions of the remittance. There is also some residual private property in the means of production. Its most important manifestation is the rural household plot (Chapter 3). Dwelling houses in the countryside are, as a rule, owned by the families that live in them. Some houses in the cities are privately owned. Since early 1979 the construction of dwellings by individuals with state assistance—previously banned in the cities—has been encouraged.

Most modern, capital-intensive industry of varying size is in the state sector. A good part of the more traditional, labor-intensive, semimechanized industry—especially the smaller workshops—is owned by cooperative organizations, both urban and rural. Urban cooperative enterprises comprise neighborhood, street, and block workshops, which sometimes act as subcontractors for larger plants, but more generally concentrate on basic maintenance and repair services to the population. In the municipality of Shanghai, which comprises the city proper and a number of semirural suburbs, in 1971 there were 9,900 industrial establishments. Of these, 3,200 were owned by the state and 6,700 by urban and rural collectives. Of the collectively owned industrial enterprises, 3,800 were under people's communes and production brigades. These commune- and brigade-owned establishments employed 10 percent of Shanghai's industrial workers. The urban cooperative enterprises employed another 10 percent of the municipality's total industrial work force. [10] At the end of 1978 some 20.5 million people were employed in urban collectively owned enterprises, compared with 75.5 million in state enterprises. Collective enterprises are supposed to operate on the principles of economic accounting (i.e., they are responsible for their own profits and losses); they are not guaranteed a regular supply of fuel and raw materials from the state's material-technical

[10] Charles Bettelheim, *Cultural Revolution and Industrial Organization in China* (New York: Monthly Review Press, 1974), pp. 45–46.

supply network; wages are normally lower than in comparable state factories; and there are fewer, if any, fringe benefits. Once they reach a certain size and/or capital intensity, a certain number of workers, and a certain level of technical sophistication, and have larger than local marketing operations, cooperative industrial ventures are, as a rule, transferred to the state sector at the appropriate state level of ownership, supervision, and management, but there is much flexibility in the way the rule is interpreted.

There seems to be a measure of official ambivalence about urban cooperative enterprises. They are regarded in some quarters as being of low status and carrying little prestige compared with state-sector firms, and there is a corresponding push to have them upgraded to state ownership. This trend has been criticized in the central press, which now urges the establishment of many more urban cooperative undertakings to relieve juvenile unemployment and to increase the variety and availability of consumer goods and services in the cities. "Not very long ago, some people thought erroneously that these [cooperative] enterprises were 'capitalist loopholes,' and had to be stopped by hook or by crook. What we should do today is to enlarge these 'loopholes' into gates. In other words we should set up more collectively owned enterprises. . . . As far as hand work is concerned, I think collective ownership may possibly be superior to ownership by the whole people. . . . It is not Marxist to regard ownership by the whole people as invariably superior to collective ownership." [11]

TIME SCHEDULE OF SOCIALIZATION In order to ease the transition from private capitalist to socialist property relations, the government of the People's Republic of China had in readiness a set of transitional property structures. The expectation was, at least in the very early post-liberation years, that these arrangements would evolve quite gradually into full socialist institutions. This, however, was not to be the case.

The two most important transitional property constructs in industry and retail trade were "elementary state capitalism" and "advanced state capitalism" (or joint state-private property). Elementary state capitalism—under which the owner of the factory or shop sold the greater part of his output to and received most of his key materials from

[11]Xue Muqiao (adviser to State Planning Commission and director of the Economic Research Institute of the Commission), "Noted Economist on Employment," *Beijing Review*, August 17, 1979, p. 15.

state agencies at state-fixed prices, but remained in charge of his assets as de jure owner—was liquidiated in 1951–1952 in the course of two mass campaigns: the "Three-Anti" and the "Five-Anti." In advanced state capitalism the assets of the former private owners became private shares in a joint state-private business, following inventory taking and revaluation of the assets decided on by the state. The private partner thenceforth received dividends on his shares out of the net income of the jointly owned enterprise. The state's capital contribution to the joint venture consisted most of the time of a certain portion of the revalued private assets. The state thereupon became entitled to the portion of the net income represented by its shares. The former owners were normally retained as managers working alongside state-appointed managers. The most important policy decisions, however, were made not by them but by the state appointees.

In a more advanced version of state capitalism, the jointly owned businesses were amalgamated by trades or branches of industry in various localities and grouped under specialized corporations or trusts. The dividend to the private partner was replaced by payment to him of a fixed interest rate on his share of the business. He no longer had even a nominal ownership claim to any assets and became, in effect, a junior state employee in what used to be his business. State capitalism of this more advanced kind persisted in some service branches of the economy (e.g., some retail shops and restaurants) until the Cultural Revolution (1966–1969), when it was liquidated. A similar fate met the transitional property arrangements in the urban handicraft sector.

In 1966 fixed interest payments were terminated, the bank accounts of the "national capitalists" were seized, and personal effects, such as jewelry, were confiscated. Those who had occupied admininstrative posts under Party supervision before the Cultural Revolution, were assigned to manual jobs and their pay was cut. They were not entitled to sick leave, medical insurance, retirement pensions, or death benefits. Their children were tainted with inherited class incorrectness and found it difficult to pursue higher education or land a decent urban job. The former national capitalists were often made to share their living quarters with worker families, or their homes were taken away from them. These measures were criticized after the reintroduction of united-front tactics in 1978. All bank deposits were to be returned along with the interest due on them; other property was also to be given back. Homes of the former bourgeoisie were to be vacated and returned to the original owners or their families. High salaries were to be paid again together with the amount held back since 1966. "Proper adjustments" were to be made in work assignments. Social security privileges (medical insurance, sick pay, retirement pensions, death benefits) were to be restored and the stigma of wrong class background removed from the children of the former bourgeoisie. The fixed interest due since 1966 was to be computed and paid in full. There was, of course, left-wing opposition to these measures. "It cannot be presumed that the party's policy toward the national bourgeoisie will be implemented smoothly, without encountering any obstacles." [12]

The socialization of industry, retail trade, and the handicrafts proceeded by leaps, with little heed to the elaborate structure of intermediate institutions that had been drafted earlier, presumbly in anticipation of a lengthy passage to socialism. For all practical purposes the socialization of modern industry was accomplished by 1952 (despite the vestigial persistence of advanced state capitalism until 1966), and by 1960 the handicrafts, too, had been fully socialized.

FOREIGN EQUITY PARTICIPATION By 1955 practically all foreign equity participation in Chinese industry had been ended and the situation did not change until 1979, when the restriction was considerably eased. To promote advanced technology imports a law on joint ventures was adopted. The law provides that foreign participation in a joint venture must be at least 25 percent, but no upper limit to the foreign share is set. Even though, according to Vice-Premier Li Xiannan, "the proportion of investment by foreign companies can be higher than 50 percent and the duration may be 10 years, 20 years, or even longer," the implication of the law is that foreign participation will tend to be kept to less than 50 percent and the duration of the venture is not spelled out. A two- to three-year tax holiday for foreign investors is granted provided they supply China with equipment and technology that is "truly up to advanced world standards and appropriate to China's needs"—two conditions that may not always be compatible. Foreign stockholders who reinvest their share of the profits in China can apply for restitution of a part of the income tax paid. Net profits may be remitted abroad through the Bank of China. Foreign personnel living in China will be subject to income tax (which Chinese nationals do not pay) and will be allowed to repatriate their after-tax earnings abroad. Under the law, the chairman of a joint venture's board of directors is appointed by the Chinese, the vice-chairman by the foreign partner. Managers can be selected from either side. The law remains vague on the extent of the

[12]Beijing Radio, January 25, 1979 in *FBIS*, January 29, 1979.

foreign partner's control over personnel matters, especially dismissals, and on such important questions as protection of minority interests, the corporate tax rate, and accounting procedures. Joint ventures are to be supervised by two bodies: the Foreign Investment Control Commission, which is to pass judgment on whether to approve or reject any proposed joint venture, and the China International Trust Investment Company, charged with coordinating foreign investments and the uses of imported technology. Only practice will show how workable the scheme is. Much will, of course, depend on the preservation of internal political stability, specifically on the survival of the relatively moderate line pursued since October 1976.

Centralization and Decentralization

Although the legal structure of property is important, operational control over assets and the extent of that control granted to the actual holder of the assets are economically more significant. Legally, we have seen, almost all industry in China is socially owned, and most of it is owned by the state.

In this section we shall examine three subjects: (1) the meaning of state; (2) the industrial macro-structure (including the organization of industry and the principles and procedures of planning); and (3) the industrial micro-structure (essentially, decision-making within an enterprise).

THE STATE The state is the rambling administrative network that stretches from the Council of State at the top and center, down and outward to the managerial level of the individual industrial enterprise or the rural people's commune. Property rights granting the holders various degrees of operational control over assets are vested in the several state authorities below the Council of State, including the producing enterprise. A system that gives lower-level state authorities (especially the firm) extensive rights over the acquisition, use, and disposal of the means of production may be described as a decentralized system. When the rights of such authorities are severely circumscribed, as they are in the Soviet Union, the system is centralized. The granting or withholding of broad rights over productive assets is usually correlated with the granting or withholding of other decision-making powers, such as marketing and pricing decisions, but the correlation is rarely perfect. Even where property rights in the means of production are decentralized, the central organs often arrogate to themselves the right to fix key prices and wage rates, control the allocation of materials and labor, and take strategic decisions regarding the volume, assortment, and distribution of output.

Over most of the Five-Year Plan (1953–1957), the Chinese industrial system was centralized on the Soviet model. Property rights of governmental units below the central state (national) ministries—of which there were some eighty—were very limited, as were the lower units' other discretionary powers. The situation changed in 1957 when important operational rights, including some decisions on the acquisition, use, and disposal of assets, were transferred from the top- to lower-level governmental units. The aim was to make the former system less rigid and to remove from the shoulders of central planners and their immediate subordinates, the ministries, burdens that they were not well equipped to carry. The 1957 reform reduced the number of central ministries by about two-thirds and, with a few exceptions (e.g., defense-related industry), removed from the survivors the bulk of responsibility for detailed planning and supervision within their areas of competence. In 1976 the number of central economic ministries was probably about twenty. The functions of these ministries with regard to industries within their jurisdiction were more aggregated and more concerned with broad strategic variables than they had been before.

The trend begun in 1957 was reinforced, but in a confused and unworkable way, during the Great Leap Forward. Decentralization proceeded by default, so to speak, because of the disruption in the normal operation of central planning authorities. One of the Leap's fatal problems was that it never quite abandoned the Stalinist preoccupation with output maximization, while trying to combine that goal with maximization of employment and the pursuit of certain, rather far-reaching egalitarian social goals within a decentralized and progressively less coordinated administrative structure.

Some of these incompatibilities were corrected in the course of the post-Leap years. The postulate of decentralization was not abandoned, but an end was put to the lack of coordination that marked the outburst of 1958 and 1959. The authority of the center was reaffirmed after 1962, but not to the degree that prevailed before 1957. Anarchic and centrifugal tendencies were curbed and the need to harmonize local initiative with the national interest was made clear.

The Cultural Revolution (1966–1969) reemphasized the decentralization postulate by its insistence on "power seizures," "bombarding the headquarters," rusticating the bureaucrats, and more generally by its occasional open defiance of central authority. Between the end of the

Cultural Revolution and the ascendancy to power of Hua Guofeng (early 1970–October 1976) the question of centralization versus decentralization of the state apparatus was subjected to contradictory pulls; it became enmeshed in intra-Party maneuverings and was used for factional infighting. The eclipse of the leftist leaders in October 1976 shifted emphasis once again toward centralism: "Chairman Mao pointed out that throughout the country there were quite a number of people who throve on anarchy. To solve this problem it was imperative to strengthen collective leadership and oppose decentralism. . . . Chairman Mao put the stress on the strict observance of discipline under democratic centralism."[13] The post-1976 harping on the need for centralized collective leadership, strengthened discipline, Leninist organization, and vigilance against the emergence of "independent kingdoms and feudal lords" hints at more than just the bureaucratic proclivities of Mao's successors. It came in the context of a troubled situation in many provinces—a renewed pulling apart. Later, when a modicum of political stability had been restored, the drift toward economic centralization was strengthened by attempts to implement long-term planning again, and by the decision to import large amounts of advanced technology. The ambitious import program stretching to 1985 and beyond called for central coordinating organs and was geared to the establishment of very large firms, which presumably would be under central state control. As of mid-1979 the number of ministries, commissions, and special agencies under the State Council had risen to 42: 33 ministries (26 of them economic), 7 commissions (including the State Planning Commission and the State Economic Commission), and 2 special agencies (the People's Bank of China and the All-China Federation of Supply and Marketing Cooperatives).

The propensity for industrial branches and even individual enterprises to seek a modicum of plan fulfillment security by vertical integration (a systemic propensity due to a chronically tight input supply situation) came up for particularly heavy criticism after 1976, and the critics focused on the economic costs of such a procedure rather than its political threats to central authority. "China's industries have been placed under the management of various localities and departments. The drawbacks are many: there is the overlapping of administrative organs,

[13] Committee for Editing and Publishing Chairman Mao Tse-tung's Works, The Central Committee of the Communist Party of China, "Introducing Volume V of the 'Selected Works of Mao Tse-tung,'" *Peking Review*, No. 17, April 22, 1977, pp. 19–20. There were signs in mid-1980 that this committee—headed by Hua—was in the process of being discredited.

offices are overstaffed, and factories are often run without consideration for the results. Very often there are several factories in one place turning out the same product, each having its own way of operation independent of the others. This has led to waste of raw materials and manpower. Sometimes the same factory has workshops for casting, forging, and repairing. This tendency is not confined to the big complexes; the small factories have been developing in this direction as well." [14] In an experiment limited thus far to several small sewing machine plants in Beijing, a few television factories in Shanghai, and some machine-building and textile plants elsewhere, the individual enterprises were merged and specialized, their product was standardized, and they were placed under a single reorganized management sworn to apply strict economic accounting and vested with marginally greater latitude of decision-making. The idea was to break down a multitude of vertical integrations practiced by small plants and to increase the benefits flowing from size, specialization, and standardization of product by setting up umbrellalike companies charged with coordinating production and management. [15] The movement pointed in the direction of recent Soviet experiments with merged industrial entities known as *proizvodstvennye ob'edineniia*.

The issue of what powers should be delegated to lower state authorities, to what extent these delegated powers should be circumscribed by Party authority at every level, the exact duties and responsibilities of the periphery toward the center and the other way round—in short the whole "chessboard" concept of economic planning and management—remains in a fluid state. Western economists are not agreed whether to regard China's system as a relatively centralized one or not. It is plausible to approach the decentralization measures taken at various times from a dialectical perspective; decentralization enables the center better to control what it is desirous of controlling than would be the case under a formally more centralized arrangement. The dismantling of some institutional means of central control and supervision has not been accompanied by the removal of the less visible bonds that hold China's society together. Among these is a cultural unity going back thousands of years. Moreover, cellular organization has always been tight and most of the time responsive to Party guidance from on high.

[14]*Beijing Review*, June 15, 1979, p. 5.

[15]"Most of our tractor, machine tool, and diesel engine plants have their own foundries, forges, repair works, and workshops for manufacturing tools. This has weakened our technological strength, labor productivity, and equipment use." Beijing Radio, May 26, 1979, in *FBIS*, May 29, 1979.

INDUSTRIAL MACRO-STRUCTURE China's system of industrial organization, its simultaneous use of centralized and decentralized means and procedures, may be examined under two topics: (1) organizational structure of planning, supervision, and control, and (2) planning principles and methodology.

Organizational Structure. The structure of industrial organization is shown in simplified form in Figure 1. Sectoral and subsectoral ministries prepare output, assortment, and other general indicators for their respective industrial branches, within broad constraints imposed by the State Planning Commission. Provincial and municipal subsectoral production-line offices and specialized agencies are the immediate (decentralized) state supervisors of provincial and municipal industrial enterprises. Production-line offices coordinate the activities of enterprises producing the same product (e.g., iron, steel, textiles, chemicals, and electric power). The number of plants supervised by each office ranges from a dozen to several hundred. Specialized agencies are subdivisions of the production-line offices. They are in charge of specific products (e.g., tractors and medical drugs) of the specialized plants under their jurisdiction.

Centrally run enterprises and enterprises in the decentralized state sector are, to my knowledge, subject to no rigid and detailed criteria for inclusion in either category. The decision to include an enterprise in the centralized state sector appears to be taken on a variety of practical grounds with the aid of some general conceptual guidelines. Such guidelines were contained in a 1969 directive, which stipulated that an enterprise should be centrally financed and supervised if this is justified by its (a) size in terms of employment and/or output, [16] (b) technological level, (c) importance for national defense, (d) dependence on imports of capital equipment from abroad and importance for exports, (e) strategic position in the national economy as a producer of key capital goods (the Leninist notion of "strategic heights" of the economy), and, partly as a

[16] What organizationally constitutes a large, medium-sized, or small enterprise in terms of employment is interpreted flexibly. It depends on several things, including the sector of industry within which the enterprise operates and its geographical location. In Shanghai, for example, a large enterprise in the textile branch means that one employs over 3,000 workers. In the same municipality an enterprise of the mechanical engineering branch is considered large if it employs over 1,000 workers. In 1971 large enterprises accounted for 30 percent of industrial output in value terms; medium-sized enterprises for 26 percent; and small enterprises for 44 percent. Bettelheim, op. cit., pp. 46–47. The 1969 directive cited by H. V. Henle, op. cit., p. 77.

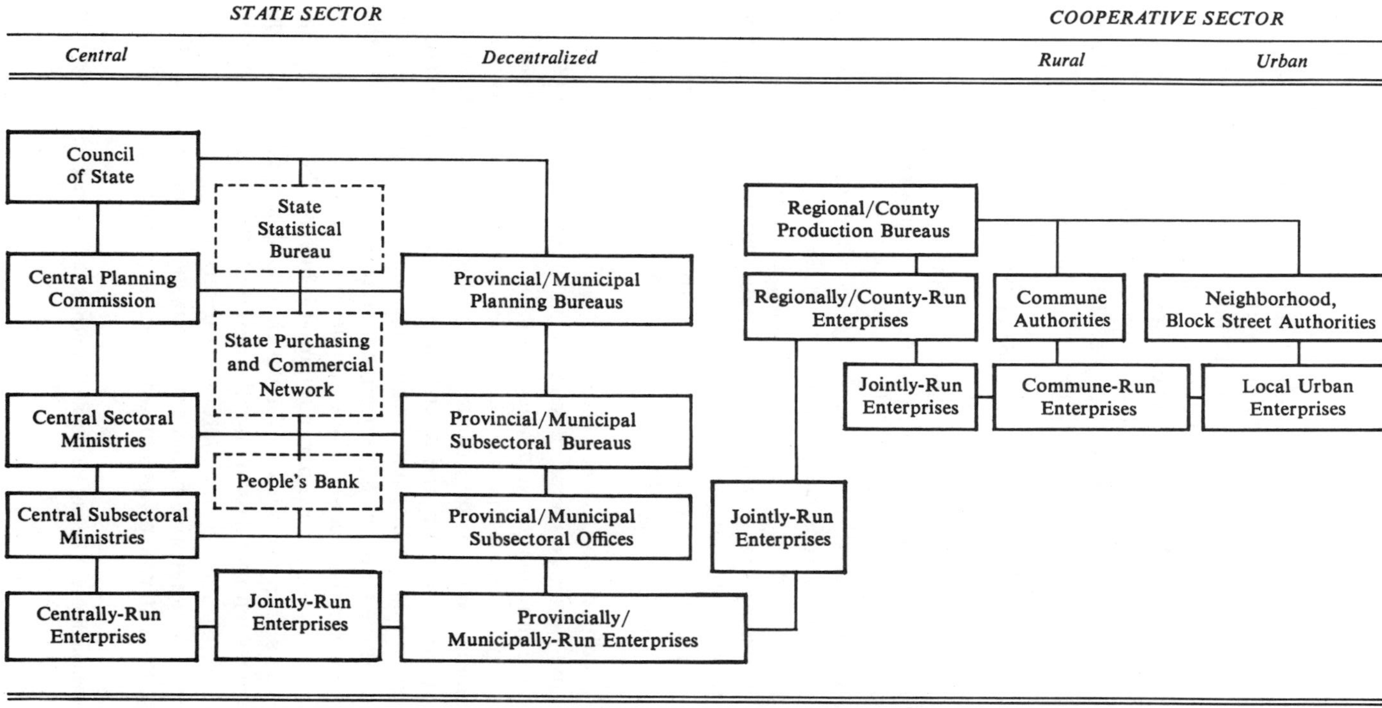

FIGURE 1. *Industrial organization.*

consequence of all these, (f) dependence on investment allocations from the central state budget. In 1957 almost half the value of output of Shanghai's industry originated in central state enterprises, whereas in 1970 the proportion was only 7 percent. The remainder came from locally administered and owned state and cooperative establishments.

There reportedly has been a trend, especially between 1970 and 1974, for some large enterprises to move toward dual rather than exclusively central state control. For example, the Anshan Iron and Steel Corporation before 1970 was solely under the Ministry of Metallurgy. Since that time it has been under the shared responsibility of the Ministry and Liaoning Province, which has not visibly diminished Beijing's control over this large establishment. [17]

This sending down (or in other cases sending up) of enterprises is quite common. It indicates, again, that there are no rigid boundaries between the centralized and decentralized state sectors. Such shifting of enterprises occurs also within the decentralized state sector. When it is felt, for a variety of reasons, that an enterprise (say under county authorities) has outgrown the ability of those authorities to direct it (because, for example, it now serves a clientele scattered over a larger area than the county), the enterprise may be transferred to regional or perhaps provincial state authorities. Similarly, downward transfers within the decentralized state sector occur, as presumably do joint controls.

Similar fluidity exists between the decentralized state sector and the commune and urban cooperative sectors. Commune workshops, for example, once they mature technologically, or when they seem to require capital investments that are clearly beyond the capacity of commune accumulation funds to provide, or for other reasons that will be judged on their economic and social merits, may be transferred to county or even higher state authorities and become integrated in the state plan. Movement of decentralized state enterprises into the cooperative sector also occurs. For example, the decentralized (or even central) state may enter into partnership with lower-echelon cooperative bodies to set up an industry for which a special need is felt, and withdraw from such association once the new industry is able to stand on its own and repay the original state investment.

Control of an enterprise by a central ministry means, among other things, that the enterprise's production plan is set and most of its raw

[17] Audrey Donnithorne, "Recent Economic Developments," *China Quarterly*, No. 60, December 1974, pp. 773–74.

materials are allocated by the supervisory ministry, and that enterprise profits are remitted directly to the central fiscal authorities. The province or municipality within which the enterprise is located not only receives a copy of the plan, but the planned activites of centrally controlled industrial units also form an organic part of the provincial or municipal plans.

In the case of joint control or control by a decentralized state authority, some portion of the transmitted profit will be retained by the provincial, municipal, or other authority involved. The output of jointly run enterprises may be distributed by the center or by its partner (province, municipality, or whatever). Apprentice labor in such cases will usually, but not invariably, be assigned to the enterprise by the provincial, municipal, or other decentralized state partner. The pricing of output will depend on the importance of the commodity within the national economy. Some goods are priced by the center (the State Price Commission or a ministry in consultation with the Commission); other goods, primarily goods of local significance, are priced by lower-level authorities. Such pricing will be done within centrally established parameters.

A further complication arises in connection with an enterprise's political structure. The criteria for political control are not always the same as those for economic-administrative control. For example, the Dalien Locomotive and Carriage Plant is under the economic-administrative control of the (central) Ministry of Communications, but the plant's Party committee is subordinated to the Dalien Municipal Party committee, which is also responsible (through the plant Party committee) for political movements and some labor questions within the plant.

Bearing in mind the fluidity of intersectoral distinctions, rural cooperative sector (commune and brigade) industrial enterprises conform to the following general criteria laid down in the early 1960s: [18] (a) they are agro-oriented, producing consumer goods (e.g., food processing using local produce), or producer goods (simple agricultural machinery, current inputs such as chemical fertilizers of relatively low nutrient content, and electric power for water control purposes); (b) they engage in the extraction of locally available raw materials, such as coal and iron ore, and in the initial processing of such materials—most important, they should not, as a rule, compete with central state enterprises for resources, whether raw materials, fuels, or skilled labor; (c) they turn out simple consumer goods for local consumption (e.g., clothing, blan-

[18] H. V. Henle, *Report on China's Agriculture* (Rome: F.A.O., 1974), p. 79. See also, above, Chapter 3.

kets, shoes, furniture, and kitchen utensils); (d) they produce industrial components for centrally run and decentralized state enterprises, as well as spare parts that are in short supply; and (e) they manufacture other kinds of goods and provide maintenance and repair services, the production and supply of which can be undertaken locally and are judged to be socially desirable. The key is self-reliance, simplicity, and sturdiness of design and a modest degree of capitalization and technique. This should not be interpreted to mean that commune-run enterprises are just another name for traditional cottage industries. Their capital endowment, while sparse and technologically simple, is not rudimentary. Generally it is used in a labor-intensive way. Moreover, the amount of equipment is increasing and the technology used is improving by on-the-spot, innovative accretions.

The purpose of the commune-run industrial sector is (a) to initiate or accelerate the development of backward areas; (b) to absorb seasonally or permanently surplus farm labor; (c) to introduce the peasants to industrial techniques and modes of thought; (d) to utilize local raw material deposits that would be inconvenient or uneconomical for the central, provincial, or even county state bodies to exploit, and to put to use materials (e.g., scrap metal) discarded by the larger industries; (e) to turn out simple goods of mass consumption, thus immediately benefiting the welfare of rural inhabitants in even the most remote places; (f) to help relieve bottlenecks in the supply of industrial componenets and spare parts; and (g) to raise the gross income of communes and brigades. [19] Such enterprises require little initial capital outlay; the recoupment period is comparatively short, thus easing inflationary pressures; labor inputs can be varied according to the needs of farming and water conservation work without seriously affecting the quantity and quality of the plants' output; and distribution of the product is uncomplicated, since in most cases it is limited to the immediate area of the commune.

Urban cooperative sector industrial enterprises are artisan-type undertakings in urban agglomerations, as well as service establishments (e.g., tailors, barbers, and shoemakers). They, too, often produce industrial components and spare parts mostly for the local market. They are, as a rule, initiated by local residents (especially housewives) and employ a large proportion of women. They rely on locally secured, mainly waste materials.

The proliferation of commune-type and small to medium urban

[19]In most cases the better-off communes are those that have well-developed workshops and plants, "an undertaking more profitable than farming." In some suburban communes, revenues from industrial and sideline production constitute 75–90 percent of the communes' total income.

cooperative and state (muncipal) establishments (which began in 1958 and which has been vigorously and less haphazardly promoted since the Cultural Revolution of 1966–1969) seems by and large to have benefited the economy and enhanced social welfare. Such industries are not the product of refined economic calculation. They do, however, make sense in the context of a nonmarket, administratively directed economy and that economy's particular factor endowment. Administrative channels of communication are shortened and declogged, the disguised saving potential of the rural masses is tapped, and capital is formed where it is needed most (in the countryside). The perennial command economies' problem of spare parts shortages is lessened and local initiative in economic matters is not stifled.

On the other hand, these do-it-yourself industries are notoriously wasteful in their use of resources, including fuel; they do not always confine themselves to locally procured materials; and they often produce an inferior product. As I had occasion to witness, industrial safety in such workshops is poor and the accident rate must be very high. Some of them have taken up valuable agricultural land and, while often recycling waste materials from larger factories, they are pollutants in their own right. Commenting on industry in general, but small and medium-sized plants (including rural ones) in particular, a *Renmin Ribao* editorial (May 10, 1979) stated; "some of [the enterprises] are not operating normally, some turn out poor quality products with little variety, and some produce high cost goods with little profit or even at a loss. The overwhelming majority of enterprises in China today belong to this category."

After the ascent of the modernizers to power in 1976–1977, it became fashionable to stress industry's problems, whereas formerly only the achievements, some of them fictional, were made public. That there is much inefficiency and waste, and that these get worse as one climbs down the industrial ladder, cannot be denied. But the problems must be seen in the perspective of the generally painful and prolonged process of industrialization practically from scratch. Some of the troubles are technical-engineering and can be remedied with relative ease. Others are organizational, inherent in the system of economic management that the Chinese adopted from the Soviets and adapted to their own ends, and here the solutions are more elusive and politically difficult. But by and large, despite the problems, the effort has been heroic and the accomplishment meritorious.

Planning Principles and Methodology. Economic planning in China, while seen as an essential component of socialist society, is not enveloped in the mystique with which Stalin and his followers surrounded it in the U.S.S.R. The five major *principles* of Chinese planning are politics, the whole and its parts, flexibility, consultation, and proportionate development.

1. Politics. Economic planning must take account of—indeed must give prominence to—the political objectives and social goals of the Communist Party and the People's Republic of China. These have been laid down in the Party's and government's resolutions on the General Line for Economic Construction and interpreted in several planning directives. An important corollary is that maximizing behavior on the part of all economic units cannot be based only on narrow economic-financial criteria, but should at all times be infused with the system's moral and political philosophy. An enterprise, for example, may strive to maximize its profits, provided the surplus called profit is a measure of social utility as defined in the line and interpreted in the directives. Utility maximizing by individuals is legitimate on the condition that the utility function explicitly includes the rules of correct private and group behavior, again as laid down in the line and directives. Growth may be maximized, but not at the expense of other overriding goals. Material incentives, as we shall see, are necessary, but they should not be the exclusive stimulus to productive effort. Chinese economic calculation is always political, but the precise weight and meaning attached to politics or "political consciousness" depends on the times, more precisely on the type of people who are at the helm. In times of radical dominance (1958–1960, 1966–1969, and off and on until October 1976) politics all but took over and was given a very narrow, dogmatic, yet highly volatile meaning. In times of relative moderation, there is more willingness to pay heed to "objective economic laws," encase the political element in organizational boxes and keep it as much as possible from disrupting planning, management, and economic construction in general. In such times, he who works well, overfulfills his quota, produces profits, raises his productivity, and reduces materials intensity is prima facie politically conscious. But after years of left-wing ascendancy the cadres are uncertain: "Some comrades have themselves bound up in knots, not daring to say or do anything not written down in books or documents or not said and sanctioned by leaders. They just mechanically copy or pass on whatever comes to them." [20] The phenomenon, called "formalism," is also known more earthily as "sitting on the privy and producing nothing."

[20] *Renmin Ribao*, January 4, 1979.

One of the changes in the relation between politics and economics was sanctioned by the Third Plenary Session of the Eleventh Central Committee of the Communist Party of China held in December 1978. The Session put forward five basic principles that were to guide the Party in carrying out China's Four Modernizations: (a) the Party's work was to shift to socialist economic modernization; (b) the process of "emancipating minds" (i.e., shifting from a left-wing to a right-of-center ideological position) was to be pursued; (c) "the machine" was to be "set in motion" (i.e., work was to begin on much needed administrative, economic, and criminal legislation; the institutions of China's economy, shattered by the Cultural Revolution were to be rebuilt and restructured); (d) truth was to be sought from facts (not from left-wing interpretations of the late Chairman's selected sayings); and (e) there was to be "uniting as one and looking forward" (i.e., a shift toward predominantly a "two combine into one" approach to contradictions within and outside the Party—which covered a united-front approach toward bourgeois intellectuals and national minorities—and looking forward to reconciliation rather then backward for grudges and score settling). As soon as these comparatively pragmatic principles of policy were announced, the left counterattacked. While it is all right to seek the Four Modernizations in the five ways just outlined, it is equally important, they said, to adhere to the "Four Basic Principles," to uphold (a) the socialist road, (b) the dictatorship of the proletariat, (c) the leadership of the Party, and (d) Marxism-Leninism-Mao Zedong Thought; all of which sounds like a throwback to the days of Jiang Qing. The combination, it was stressed, of economics (four modernizations in the five ways) and politics (the four principles) would give rise to a "Chinese-style modernization," rather than to blind copying from foreigners. The four principles were described by some in leftist language, as "four magic weapons for achieving the four modernizations, and four magic stays of our country and our society. They give strength to prop up the sky." However (not without good reason) "some comrades [thought] that once the four fundamental principles are put forward, emancipating the mind is no longer allowed." [21] "Some comrades even have doubts whether the decisions of the central authorities [taken at the Thrid Plenum] are in accordance with Marxism-Leninism-Mao Zedong Thought." This gave rise to "the ideological trend of skepticism

[21] The left-wing sentiment is found in an article published by *Hongqi*, No. 5, May 4, 1979, pp. 11–15, in *FBIS*, May 22, 1979; the right-wing sentiment is found in *Jiefangjun Bao* (Liberation Army Daily), May 21, 1979, in *FBIS*, May 22, 1979. Cf. also, "Carrying Out the Four Modernizations is the Biggest Politics," *Renmin Ribao* editorial, April 11, 1979 in *Beijing Review*, April 27, 1979, pp. 10–13.

about the Party's principles and policies.'' [22] Or as *Renmin Ribao* (May 5, 1979) put it in what was surely the understatement of the year: ''At the moment there is a tiny incipient trend of skepticism towards socialism'' in China. [23]

2. The Whole and Its Parts. A guiding principle of economic planning is the chessboard concept to which I have already referred. While decentralization, including the formation of nearly self-sufficient units (both geographical and functional) was at various times encouraged, self-sufficiency was at all times to be moderated by the larger interest of the republic as a whole. To assure that the parts do not fall into the trap of autarkic kingdoms, three guidelines must be adhered to: (a) the formal structure of economic management must be uniform all over the country; (b) industrial economic units must strictly adhere to the line and directives in exercising their decision-making powers; and (c) the plan targets, once set, cannot be changed by the autonomous decision of the unit for which they are set. However, much reliance for unified planning was at all times placed on unified political consciousness—the same conditioned political reflex shared by all strata of society. After the fall of the radical leadership in October 1976 emphasis began to shift, not without resolute opposition, toward central coordination through highly structured organizational means and enunciated rules and regulations, rather than through superstructural, ''born again'' happenings. The chessboard was once again seen as an *apparat*, a closely fitted system of economic institutions bound by certain objective laws, rather than as a ouija board propped up by magic stays and held together by a shared faith that was constantly renewed and strengthened by ritualistic immersions in a flood of the Master's words. While lip service continued to be paid to regional and functional self-reliance, there was less insistence on it and increasing criticism of it on economic grounds. Self-reliance, it was said, stressed hard work instead of lighter work achievable through modernization, it chopped up the chessboard, and was costly by causing duplication of effort, lack of standardization, and loss of the potential benefits of specialization. How much recentralization there would be and how much autonomy would be accorded to individual enterprises remained open questions to which, in time, answers were to be given by

[22]Fujian Provincial Broadcasting Station, Fuzhou, May 24, 1979, in *FBIS*, May 24, 1979.

[23]Cited by *Beijing Review*, May 18, 1979, p. 10. ''Have the Party's economic policies 'overstepped the limits,' or are there 'forbidden areas' in the minds of some comrades? Have the Party's economic policies 'drifted away from the correct orientation,' or do some comrades not understand the laws of socialist economy?'' *Renmin Ribao*, May 19, 1979, in *FBIS*, May 21, 1979.

practice: "Any management systems and methods (such as centralized or decentralized management, the enterprises have or do not have the right to decide for themselves)—all must be tested in practice. If they impede the development of the productive forces, they must be reformed no matter in which book they appeared and no matter who had approved them." [24]

3.Flexibility. Planning norms (targets) should not be rigid.They must be sufficiently broad to allow for needed changes and adjustments in the course of the execution of the plan. Enterprises are normally granted a 10 percent contingency margin in the use and disposal of production factors.The hallowed Soviet principle of "taut planning" or "strained balances" (high output norms with low input allocations—or asking more than can reasonably be delivered) is rejected.The plan's goals should also be tailored to the organizing ability of the cadres.The implementation of the principle of flexible planning is facilitated by Chinese nonchalance when it comes to arithmetical precision in social matters. Despite this, and the general adherence to the principle of flexibility by all leadership factions, far-reaching violations of the principle occurred during both radical and moderate periods.

4. Consultation.The final plan must be the outcome of genuine and sustained consultation (one is almost tempted to say "bargaining") among the various levels of the planning hierarchy.The error of "commandism" or arbitrary "planning from above," must be avoided as much as its opposite, unapproved "spontaneousness." Horizontal consultation between lower-level planning bodies is not excluded outright. Consultation must be carried out in an "open door" way—it must involve in some way the mass rank-and-file.

Trangressions against the principle of consultation occur in practice all the time simply because (whether the right or the left is in power) the economic system (like its political counterpart) remains inherently hierarchical and authoritarian.There is no built-in mechanism in the system that requires genuine consultation, that is, equal-to-equal discussion. Each echelon of authority is accountable for what it does primarily to a superior authority, not to parallel units or to subordinate levels.When the left wing stirs up the masses, the apparent control of bureaucrats from below soon turns into a forest of competing upward hierarchies, each vertically responsible to its own factional leaders and its contact men in Beijing.

5. Proportionate Development. A principle much neglected during

[24]*Beijing Review*, June 15, 1979, p. 17.

1958–60 and the Cultural Revolution (1966–69 and after) was that outlined in the 1950s by the then minister of commerce Chen Yun, and earlier—with equal practical disregard—by Stalin. The economic plan, the principle states, should be arranged according to the conditions and resources of the "four balances": (1) balance of expenditures and revenues of the state budget; (2) balance in the issuance and withdrawals of bank credits; (3) balance of supply and demand of materials; and (4) balance of receipts and foreign exchange payments. A comprehensive balance should be achieved among these four. In the absence of a market mechanism, to bring about the four balances and reconcile them in one comprehensive balance calls for a well-developed, sophisticated, and smoothly functioning planning methodology. It is to the consideration of such a methodology that we now turn.

The *methodology* of industrial planning in China can be discussed under three headings: time horizons, planning procedures, and pricing policies.

1. Time Horizons. Planning in China normally unfolds within three time periods: ten years or longer (perspective planning), five years (long-range planning), and one year (short-term planning). Theoretically, work on the five-year plan should begin about a year-and-a-half before, and the plan should be ready at the beginning of the five-year period. This schedule appears to have been observed mostly in the breach. The First Five-Year Plan was not published until 1955. The Second Five-Year Plan (1958–1962) was disrupted by the Great Leap Forward and the Sino-Soviet break, and was declared to be completed in three years. The Third Five-Year Plan did not materialize until 1966 (instead of 1961 or 1963). It was almost immediately thrown into disarray by the Cultural Revolution. The Fourth Five-Year Plan was inaugurated on time in 1971, but no details were published. The Fifth Plan also came on time (1976), but in view of the important events of that year (death of Mao, change of leadership, rout of the radicals), it was stillborn.

A year earlier (1975) Zhou Enlai outlined a ten-year modernization plan covering the years 1976–1985. This was buried, together with its first component five-year plan, during the struggle for succession to Mao, and did not reemerge until March 1978, when presumably it had already run for over two years. The ten-year plan was accompanied by general projections until the year 2000. Because the damage inflicted on the economy by the succession fight turned out to be severe ("a hundred broken things are waiting to be put right''), and the objectives of the plan were much too ambitious and poorly coordinated, the plan was redrafted. It reemerged toward the end of 1978 split into three subperiods (1978–1980, 1981–1985, 1986–2000) and considerably toned down. The first three years were to be devoted to picking up the pieces. The name given to this portion of the plan was reminiscent of that attached to the 1961–1965 period of recuperation from the nefarious effects of Mao's Great Leap Forward. The plan was said to be one of Readjustment (of objectives), Restructuring (of economic planning), and Consolidation (of enterprise management).

The perspective (ten years and more) plans sketch out in very broad brush strokes the direction that the leadership wishes the economy to follow. Such plans are, in essence, statements of bulky objectives regarding output, sectoral growth rates, trade, and the development of resource bases. One hopes that the objectives are internally consistent; they evidently were not in the ten-year plan 1976–1985.

The five-year plan contains general indicators of the basic proportions envisioned for the economy: projected output of major products, basic inputs, breakdown between investment and consumption, import and export projections, and the desired sectoral structure of the economy. This part of planning is the responsibility of top planners in the State Planning Commission who, in light of the top regime's political goals and on the basis of statistical information available to them from the field, submit their project for review to Party-government organs including provincial and municipal organs. Having been approved and modified by the Party-government apparatus, the broad plan framework is firmed-up by the inclusion in it of more detail under four headings: (a) a set of input-output relationships or ''material balances'' (which are, in effect, disaggregated input-output tables for particular sectors and industries, and presuppose a knowledge of the technical relationships [technical coefficients] between and among the inputs and outputs)—at the national level the material balances cover between 600 and 800 key products, compared with over 1,000 in the U.S.S.R.; (b) a set of national value balances, including national income, investment, consumption, the wages fund, savings, costs, some prices, and the state budget; [25] (c) a labor balance, including skilled scarce manpower allocation and training; and (d) sectoral plans.

[25]This is the "financial plan" that expresses the basic physical proportions under material balances in yuan terms that are hoped to be consistent with the physical relationships to which they apply.

There is considerable question in my mind about the actual state of the planning art in contemporary China. During the radical period after 1966 planning methodology was neglected, when it was not actively trampled on, and the tools of physical and, especially, financial planning were allowed to rust. Many of the leading economic theoreticians were imprisoned and, after their ten-year confinement, were outdated and outpaced by events. The description of planning methodology given here is therefore a somewhat idealized version. Chinese economic planning is, to put it mildly, in a bit of disrepair at present. The Chinese have an enormous appetite for knowledge and an equally formidable capacity to learn; but the process of readjustment, restructuring, and consolidation is likely to take longer than the projected three years.

2. Planning Procedures. There are four levels of planning: national, provincial/municipal, *xien* (county), and enterprise. The preparation of ten-year plans involves primarily the top (national) level; five-year plans, the first two levels. The working out of the annual plans engages all four levels, especially the bottom two.

Insofar as one can reconstruct the existing procedures from scattered, often conflicting, sometimes embellished information, the annual planning process unfolds ideally in the way outlined below.

The general plan indices for the given year prepared by the center under the four major headings noted above (which, as we have seen, are the result of discussion within the national and provincial/municipal organs) are communicated to lower-level authorities. In the case of centrally run industries, the plan goes to the central ministries and subministries involved, where it undergoes a process of disaggregation, finally landing in the enterprises.

Where the plan applies to industries run by provincial or municipal authorities, it is sent down to the appropriate provincial or municipal planning bureaus and subsequently to the various subsectoral organs (bureaus, production-line offices, and specialized agencies) where it is broken down until finally it ends up in the respective enterprises. Provincial and municipal planning authorities do have some latitude within the basic ratios set by the center, but they are not allowed to violate those ratios.

Lower level, especially *xien,* authorities are given latitude to make decisions within the basic ratios communicated to them, but they are not allowed to violate those ratios as broken down for their guidance by provincial and municipal authorities. Their compliance with the guidelines is assured by higher-echelon budgetary control. The *xien* and other local level authorities are permitted to accumulate small funds for investments outside the state plan, technical improvements, and so on.

Enterprises, too, have decision-making discretion within the plan indices communicated to them by their supervisory organs (*xien*, province/municipality, and central state ministries).This discretion is mainly operational.Two examples of such discretion will illustrate what is involved. First, Chinese enterprises are expected to find their own suppliers and buyers. The function of the production-line offices, specialized agencies, and commercial bureaus of the province, or in the case of *xien*-run enterprises of the appropriate *xien* offices, is to help enterprises in this task.They put buyers and sellers in contact. Second, direct interenterprise contracting is permitted.The supply contracts frequently set out in detail those specifications that are not explicitly defined in the plan.The function of superior state authorities is to act as broker and supervise the fulfillment of the contract by the parties.The contracting parties do not have the right to alter the contract on their own initiative. Subcontracting by enterprises is also permitted and widely used, on the same general conditions as apply to interenterprise contracts.

The annual indices, when initially handed down through centralized and decentralized state channels, are "preliminary" or "advisory." Upon receipt of such indices at the enterprise level, from 1966 until October 1976 three steps were taken: (a) the preliminary norms were "discussed by the masses of workers, cadres, and technicians," especially as they related to plant capacity, labor skills, technical innovations, availability of inputs relative to the proposed output, and so on; (b) factory management personnel, technicians, and workers made on-the-spot studies and investigations of user needs by making field trips to retail stores and/or plants that received the final or intermediate product; and (c) commercial departments of the state (provincial, regional, *xien*) dispatched their personnel to the factories, where they informed managements, technicians, and workers of what they perceived to be marketing needs.

The results of these various discussions, studies, investigations, meetings, and telephone conferences were then pooled and discussed once more by the factory collective. Following this, a concretized proposal based on the original indices but modified (usually upward) was forwarded to the relevant supervisory agencies.The proposals were examined and coordinated by superior agencies, discussed with enterprise heads in a series of meetings at provincial, municipal, and county levels, reconciled, and drafted into the final plan. In conformity with the principle of flexibility, enough leeway was supposed to be left in the final plan to take care of unforeseen developments.The bulk of the final plan was cast in the form of interenterprise contracts.

After 1976 this system of mass consultation and the see-saw process of plan formulation came in for a good deal of criticism both veiled and direct. The democratic component of the process, it was said, had not been observed in everyday practice in the spirit in which it had been formulated. Rather, it took the form of factional bickering at the enterprise level and the involvement of some workers, especially the young, in the resolution of managerial questions, a task for which they were not equipped. Managerial authority was diluted and labor discipline dissolved.

In the future (how long, no one can tell) there is to be less mass consultation of the populist unstructured kind, and more well-defined power vested in enterprise directors and their ministerial superiors. Managers are to manage in line with instructions from above, engineers tend to their engines, and workers work. Involvement of the rank-and-file is to be through organizational channels, approved and supervised by the Party, not by pasting posters over machines, malingering on the job, or staying at home. While exploring other possibilities, the system, if given a chance, is likely to return initially to its Soviet origins. In 1974 the then existing planning arrangement was praised to us as a smoothly functioning example of socialist participatory democratic centralism. After 1976 large chunks of it were described as "selling dog meat as mutton." With all those people traveling to and from conferences, making investigations away from their workbenches, telephoning, and exchanging experiences, the system was also blamed for creating high costs of economic information flows. The modified post-1976 Soviet-type system (which perhaps is transitional) is unlikely to improve matters on this score. In the absence of markets there have to be organized meetings of bureaucrats. The meetings will still be there, only now attended by different people and more socially segregated than they were under the left regime. Between January and April 1979, in Inner Mongolia, 88 meetings were held with the approval of the regional authorities. The meetings lasted 675 days, and occupied the energies of 6,776 people. Each meeting lasted from five to ten days or more. Only a narrow range of subjects was discussed at each meeting. [26]

3. Pricing Policy. Chinese communist pricing policy adheres to the following general guidelines:

a. Industrial wholesale prices (and agricultural state procurement

[26]Nei Monggol Regional Broadcasting Station, Hohot, May 28, 1979, in *FBIS*, May 30, 1979.

prices) are not expected to play an autonomous guiding function in the economy, i.e., they should not be the main basis for decisions made by producing units. Their function is to act as backup "value" instruments to quantitative orders. Industrial (and agricultural) enterprises do not possess price-fixing rights. Prices are determined outside the enterprises by the competent central or decentralized state authorities, not through the interaction of suppliers and users in the market. All such interactions are brokeraged and monitored by nonenterprise state organs. The maximization of income of each producing unit in Mao's time was not an overriding consideration in determining the level and structure of the unit's productive activity, but it has become more important since 1977.

b. Although retail prices to consumers do play a limited equilibrating function and do influence consumer purchasing decisions, both the general level of such prices and relative consumer prices are set by the central or decentralized state authorities in ways that reflect the state's social preferences (its political line). In regard to the pricing of consumer goods, the guideline for setting the general level of prices is financial macro-equilibrium, i.e., the need for the general level of consumer goods prices to be such that the sum total of prices absorbs the disposable income available to consumers.

In regard to the prices of individual consumer goods three basic rules are followed. First, goods adjudged by the state to be "essential" (e.g., food grains and medicines) will have very low prices attached to them; where necessary (e.g., textile fabrics, food grains, and cooking oil) the low price will be backed by physical rationing, or—as in the case of families with insufficient labor powers or families of revolutionary martyrs—the goods will be distributed free of charge in certain specified quantities.

Physical rationing is not limited to basic items such as grain, cooking oil, and cotton cloth; at various times meat, sugar, and—depending on time and place—200–300 other commodities in short supply have been subject to rationing. The food ration applies to restaurants; for example, rationing coupons must be presented to obtain a meal. The grain ration varies according to age and occupation from roughly 13 kilograms to 25 kilograms per month. In 1978 in Peking 20 percent of the grain ration was in coarse grains (sorghum, millet); in Shenyang coarse grains accounted for 70 percent of the ration. In 1976 the cotton cloth ration was reportedly 4.5–5.3 linear meters for the year. There is apparently a lively gray-to-black market for clothing coupons, especially in cotton-growing areas. The monthly edible oil ration was 200 grams per person in 1977 and meat quotas ranged from 0.5 to 1 kilogram per household per month. Pork rationing was started in July 1976 and reportedly abandoned four years later, at least in the capital. [27]

Essential goods are sold at average cost in the particular branch of industry, or below cost. In the latter case they are sold to consumers at a state-subsidized price or taken out of the price mechanism altogether. If the state considers it desirable, the price of essential consumer goods may be lowered even though the costs of production remain unchanged or have risen (as during a poor harvest year).

Second, goods adjudged by the state as falling within the category of "everyday necessities" (e.g., coal for heating) are priced above average cost. In this case, the retail price includes a profit margin, or "surplus for society," as the Chinese used to prefer to call it. The price will, as a rule, be reduced when the average cost of producing these items falls. The price reduction will normally be made with a time lag, at times a considerable one. In the meantime, the gain from the larger profit margin is appropriated by the state treasury.

Third, in the case of goods considered by the state to cater to "secondary" consumer needs, the retail price will be set well above average branch cost. The size of the profit margin will depend in each case on the planners' decision with respect to the quantity of such goods which the planning authorities want to see produced during any given planning period. [28] The retail price in these cases is set with an eye to clearing the predetermined volume of supply off the shelves. The consumer has what is described as "free choice," to buy or not to buy the goods at the given prices, but the level of such prices relative to average money earnings tends to discourage "excessive" purchases. For exam-

[27] Li Chen, "The World of Ration Coupons," *Chung-kung yen-chiu (Studies on Chinese Communism)*, Taipei, Vol. X, No. 7, 1976, pp. 43–61; idem, "The Relation between Household Registration and the Food Rationing System," ibid., Vol. X, No. 8, 1976, pp. 50–72; Ch'en Po-wen, "The Planned Marketing System in Mainland China," *Fei-ch'ing yueh-pao* (Chinese Communist Affairs Monthly), Taipei, Vol. XX, No. 6, 1977, pp. 15–20; C. and J. Broyelle, "Comment vivent ces Chinois ?" *L'Express*, Paris, January 23–29, 1978, pp. 64, 66–68, 71–73; "Living Conditions on the Mainland," *What's Happening on the Chinese Mainland*, Taipei, Vol. 4, No. 20, 1977, pp. 1–4; Ting Shan, "A Discussion of Canton Ration Cards," *North to South*, Hong Kong, Nos. 70, 71, 1974; *Beijing Review*, July 26, 1980, pp. 5–6.

[28] The difference between cost of production and the final selling price is referred to by the Chinese as "surplus for society" or "state's net income." In fact, certainly in the case of nonessential consumer goods, this surplus (profit) contains a sales or "turnover" tax element. The profit is essentially monopoly profit, appropriated in its entirety by the monopolist—the state.

ple, bicycles (an important means of private transportation) retail in China at between 120 and 170 yuan (more on the black market), representing roughly two or three month's wages for an average worker in modern industry. Nonrationed silk, wool, and other fabrics are also priced well above the (ration-backed) price of cotton fabric. Decreases in the average cost of producing nonessential goods may, but as a rule are not, passed on to the consumer in full or in part.

It should be noted that the borderlines between essential goods and everyday necessities, and between the necessities and secondary goods are not frozen. Over the years, more and more goods have come to be regarded as essential by the planners, but they are not necessarily subsidized. Bicycles, for example, are increasingly seen as everyday necessities, but there has been no marked effect on their pricing.

Such a price policy involves selective reductions in consumer goods prices carried out infrequently.The selectivity benefits primarily the poorer sections of the population (the distribution of real income is less unequal than the distribution of money income), and the infrequency of the price adjustments benefits the state accumulation and other (e.g., agricultural price support) funds. Selective wage adjustments, as we shall see, have been infrequent in the past and concentrated on the lower end of the wage scale.

Such a policy also results in overt price stability.The stability of industrial wholesale, agricultural procurement, and consumer retail prices is thought to be an essential ingredient of physical planning. From the standpoint of the planning authorities, stable prices are useful devices for the control and evaluation of plan performance.The existence of overt price stability, much strained in recent years, does not, imply the absence of suppressed inflation which manifests itself in lines outside stores, cutting corners on quality, and black markets. All three phenomena have been present in China with varying degrees of severity over time.

Finally, the cost of production which forms the basis of industrial wholesale prices is the average cost prevailing in the particular branch of industry in which the product is made.The cost is also "planned" in the sense that it takes into account anticipated reductions in unit cost resulting from technological advances. It is also probably weighted by the respective output value contributions of the various enterprises composing the branch and takes account of regional cost variations. In addition to average, branch, planned, weighted, regionally differentiated prime cost of production (which includes the cost of materials, fuels, direct and indirect labor, and depreciation), the profit margin (if any), and, in the case of nonessential consumer goods, profit-cum-hidden-tax margin, the final price includes average transportation charges.

In the mechanics of its economic accounting the Chinese pricing system is based on the pre-1967 Soviet prototype. The main difference consists in the kind of goods that are classified as essential, everyday necessities, and nonessential. While remarkable for its stability, the system posseses all the disadvantages of its Soviet predecesor. It is possible that these various drawbacks (including notably the absence of a charge on capital) are felt somewhat less in China both because the Chinese economy is less complex than the Soviet economy, and economic policy is implemented in most years with more flexibility in China.

After the purge of the radicals, industry, farming, and other undertakings were urged to strictly practice economic accounting (Chinese equivalent of Soviet *khozraschet*), reduce costs, and operate at a profit. Under the regime of the gang of four, it was alleged, any attempt by enterprise managements to lower costs and increase profits was called "fanaticism for value," "capitalist production under the guidance of output value and profit in command." Now that "the gang of four has been overthrown, we can boldly talk about profits." [29] But talking boldly about profits will not help when profits are not a synthetic multidimensional success indicator of enterprise performance. The price and wage structure of China, I believe, does not even remotely mirror relative scarcities and utilities within the system. Except for ad hoc tinkering here and there, the structure of wages remained practically unaltered for twenty years, while clearly the underlying labor supply and demand conditions underwent enormous changes. Because prices in China are not in any sense efficiency prices, the profits based on these prices tell nothing about allocative optimality. To instruct enterprises to follow economic accounting in quest of efficiency is deceiving when the prices in which this accounting is conducted are defective indicators of opportunity costs. One of the prerequisites for improving enterprise management in China is a general reform of prices and wages, one that would make prices into carriers of information about the usefulness of goods to users and the cost of producing such goods. Very few administrative command economies have so far been willing to undertake such a thorough reform. "Adjusting [i.e., reforming] prices," says Xue Muqiao, "is a very complicated task that cannot be accomplished for the time being" (*Renmin Ribao*, 6–10–1980).

[29] *Guangming Ribao*, Beijing, December 26, 1977, in *FBIS*, January 10, 1978.

INDUSTRIAL MICRO-STRUCTURE From 1966 until mid-1979 the former Soviet-inspired system of enterprise management was changed in a more collectivist direction. From the province down to the individual industrial enterprise or rural people's commune, each unit possessed a revolutionary committee headed by a chairman and vice-chairman and a Party committee. The revolutionary committees were organs of administration while the Party committees concerned themselves with the political life of each unit, but were not averse to intervening directly in purely managerial matters.

One student of the managerial system that issued from the Cultural Revolution, described it in the following terms: the "revolutionary committees [at the enterprise level] are very heterogeneous: some act as standing management committees, some have only two fulltime members, while the rest pursue their normal functions, some manage themselves, some act as a board and appoint a managing director who accounts to them periodically. In large enterprises, there are subcommittees. In each, one cadre has responsibility for looking after day-to-day affairs. Another rule seems to be that all committee members and directors must, in addition to their management function, exercise one major (manual) production function in the enterprise, as engineer, welder, blacksmith, adjuster, etc. No exclusively managerial stratum is tolerated. The committee is also responsible vis-à-vis the higher state bodies for the plan fulfilment." [30] The Cultural Revolution (1966–1969) attempted to democratize the management of enterprises by reducing the powers of the enterprise director and the perquisites of the office. The revolutionary committees that replaced the directorial structure were supposed to include politically correct managerial cadres, technicians, and "representatives of the masses." Party committees at the enterprise level were to be composed of the old, the young, and the middle aged. In fact, for a while after the Cultural Revolution the army ran everything, and to this day it is active in the economy.

The revolutionary committee, once regarded as one of the "new-born socialist things" that distinguished Chinese from other (especially the Soviet) versions of socialism, is now a thing of the past. After June 1979, revolutionary committees were described as "provisional institutions which appeared during the Cultural Revolution" and were no longer able to meet the needs of the new period of socialist modernization. They were formally abolished by decisions of the Fifth National People's Congress (1978) and the Standing Committee of the Congress (1979).

[30]H. V. Henle, op. cit., p. 47.

The committees as they allegedly functioned (rather than the idealized picture drawn of them by their left-wing architects), apparently contributed to serious erosion of the managerial function at the enterprise level and helped undermine labor discipline. During the regime of the revolutionary committees, worker absenteeism became rampant, on-the-job performance was less than exemplary, attention to the quantity and quality of output was minimal, and the need for industrial safety rarely crossed anybody's mind. Managers and key technical personnel were being reeducated in May 7th schools and through manual labor. Whatever the class benefits of this moving around, it was pushed—it was later alleged—to the point where managerial professionalism simply went under. The revolutionary committee became the instrument par excellence of factional struggle. It paralyzed initiative by scattering about the right to make key decisions, branding all disciplinary action as a right-deviation, and by allowing anarchy gradually to take over at all levels of the firm. Workers were told that they were the masters of their workplaces. Since they sensed that this was not quite so, they took what advantage they could of the power struggle in the Party, and arrogated to themselves fringe benefits that made everyday life a little less hectic—a sort of compensation for stationary money wages. Professor Thomas Robinson, who visited a particular factory just before the gang's fall, was told proudly that "in the old ["Liuist"] days we the workers had to punch in and punch out. All that is now done away with." The punch clock, it was said later, was apparently replaced by a visitors' book. When they did turn up for work, workers often quite simply did less work. Lifelong employment is practically guaranteed in China (a phenomenon now criticized—at least in its abused form—as the "iron rice bowl"), and in the atmosphere of factional uncertainty, what manager would dare fire a loafer? Supervision, it was alleged, became lax; the supervisors themselves were politically and professionally supervised by elusive guardians of the ambiguous "correct" politics.

One must, of course, allow for pathos and artistic embroidering. The enterprise picture during the Cultural Revolution and the struggle for succession may not have been bright from the standpoint of organizational efficiency, but it was later painted in perhaps darker colors than it actually had been, in order to make things look bad for the defeated faction and to saddle the defrocked with the entire blame. One thing remains clear: the old pre-Cultural Revolution ("Liuist") system of enterprise management is being rebuilt piece by piece, although not without considerable active and passive opposition from some workers, managers, and unreconstructed leftists, who "wear a pair of new shoes but travel along a beaten track.'' From the standpoint of some workers (especially the young products of the Cultural Revolution), the organizational tightening-up and the delineation of authority and seniority is not good news when compared with the relaxed working pace of the past and the factionalized populism of the factory floor that had prevailed under the regime of dog-eat-dog. The managers, at least a goodly proportion of them, are frightened lest the power they are now asked to exercise comes to haunt them when the political wind again changes direction. Restoring directorial prerogatives and reviving the trade unions as supervisors of worker compliance with managerial orders, putting emphasis on seniority and experience rather than on political consciousness acquired in street brawls, requiring strict cost accounting, and so on are only the beginnings of an arduous and complex repair work to the whole system of incentives that had become unstuck during the Cultural Revolution and the struggle for succession. The small fringe privileges that the workers acquired by default during times of political turbulence were paralleled on a larger scale by cadre privileges and other elite ''unilateral transfers of property'' from the state to individuals (theft). The new stress on rules, regulations, certified performance, costing, structures, and Leninist discipline is almost sure to lead to new distortions as the ''correct'' cadres overcome their fear and begin throwing their weight about to gain advantages for themselves and their relations. Some readers of *Renmin Ribao* doubted that the problem could ever be solved. Cadres, they wrote, were always ''local emperors and even the Party's Central Committee could do nothing about them, let alone the press.'' [31] The problems of enterprise management and worker productivity were, in the wake of the Cultural Revolution, problems of morale, of deep-seated skepticism, and of disbelief in the basic honesty and permanence of the new order. There were as many victims of the cleaning-up operation as there were beneficiaries, and this made the building of a consensus on industry's micro structure extremely delicate and elusive.

The not so new, organizationally defined ''democracy'' at the enterprise level (which is to compensate for the factionalized populism of yore) consists, for the time being, of (a) an enterprise Party committee elected every two years by Party members within the enterprise (the election being essentially of the Soviet-type) headed by a Party secretary assisted by deputy secretaries and several members; (b) a working or administrative committee (managerial board) headed by the enter-

[31]*Renmin Ribao*, May 30, 1979, in *FBIS*, May 31, 1979.

prise director assisted by deputy directors and responsible technical-administrative cadres; (c) in some places a "workers' (or people's) supervision group" under the leadership of the Party committee representing workers and staff members. This group (which in the case of retail stores may include representatives of the public and of suppliers) holds regular meetings and acts as a structured grassroots surveillance organ within the enterprise. (d) Also in some other places there are "congresses of workers and staff" held a couple of times a year and consisting of representatives "elected for a term of two years from among those who are good ideologically and in vocational work, have close ties with the masses and are honest and upright in their ways." [32] Between the sessions of such congresses, the day-to-day work is conducted by a trade union working committee made up of model, veteran, and service workers, technicians, and cadres from the enterprise's workshop trade union organizations, some of whom work for the committee full time. Workshop directors are supposed to be elected under the watchful eye of the plant's Party committee. All this is quite old-fashioned, orthodox, and Soviet. [33] The new leaders have expressed cautious interest in Yugoslav-type workers' councils, but as of this time the interest was tentative and theoretical.

In addition to giving workers a feeling or perhaps illusion of participation in the newly restructured hierarchical enterprise setup, there is the urgent need to upgrade managerial and technical professionalism which had fallen victim of the decade of cultural exercises. The managerial paralysis about which there has been so much complaint after the fall of the gang is explainable in part by the fact that many chairmen and vice-chairmen of the former enterprise revolutionary committees were children of the Cultural Revolution with all that this connoted in technical and professional deficiency. After 1976, when not demoted, these people simply did not know what was expected of them in functional terms, while recoiling from what was demanded of them politically by the new masters in Beijing.

While trying to solve the morale and efficiency problems, the post-gang leaders bruited about the idea (earlier taken up by the Soviets) of leaving a portion of enterprise profits at the enterprises for disposal, within reason, by enterprise managements. With these retained profits, enterprises could set up three major funds: one for material incentives

[32] *Beijing Review*, June 8, 1979, p. 17.

[33] In another classical understatement, *Renmin Ribao* (editorial, May 5, 1979) put the matter this way: "It must be admitted that our socialist democratic system is not yet perfect."

(bonuses) to "advanced workers," including managerial, technical, and clerical staffs; one for social-cultural purposes (especially for the construction of badly needed worker housing); and one for enterprise investments ("production development") outside the state plan. Payments into and out of the funds would be made by the director in accordance with norms handed down by superior supervisory, and planning authorities, and with the approval of the enterprise Party committee. Of course, the incentive effect of the funds would depend on the availability of materials for investments outside the plan, availability of consumer goods on which bonuses could be spent, and the precise manner in which the funds were allocated. [34]

As the 1970s came to a close, the trend of the debate on the role of industrial enterprises in the overall system of central administrative planning was in the direction of giving enterprises more say in decision-making and insisting that ministries and other supervisory agencies make greater use of economic levers of control. All this has a familiar ring to those acquainted with the Soviet economic debates of the early to mid-1960s. "The kind of management mentality that regards the enterprise as an appendage of any administrative organ or as a bead on an abacus that can only be moved at the external command of the upper level, is incompatible with the needs of realizing the four modernizations." [35] The Soviet reforms never came to very much, and a decade and a half after Liberman the Soviet economic system was as centralized and administrative as it had always been. Whether China can find the right combination of central control and enterprise initiative, administration and the market, remains to be seen, but so far the track record of socialist economic reforms is not very encouraging. Vesting enterprises

[34]On January 17, 1979, *Renmin Ribao* complained of the ineffective way in which payments into enterprise incentive funds were made in the metallurgical industry of Hubei Province. In 1978 the Wuhan Iron and Steel Works made above-plan profits amounting to 60 million yuan. Under the existing rules the Works could keep 10 percent of that amount. Instead, however, all the plants under the Hubei Metallurgical Bureau were thrown into the bag with the Wuhan Works. Many of the other plants made losses, so that in the end only 40 million yuan of profits was left and only 4 million yuan could be paid into enterprise incentive funds. Half of this amount was then distributed among all the metallurgical plants in the province (regardless of whether they had made profits or losses), and the Wuhan Works ended up with only 1 million yuan (instead of 6 million) in retained profits. *FBIS*, January 23, 1979. On the relative significance of profit-sharing and price reform, *see* Xue Muqiao, "Some Opinions on Reforming the Economic System," *Renmin Ribao,* June 10, 1980, in *FBIS*, June 25, 1980.

[35]Resolution of the Central Committee of the Communist Party of China, "Promote Economic Democracy," *Guangming Ribao*, January 13, 1979, in *FBIS*, January 22, 1979.

and other basic units of the economy with far-reaching allocative (including income distribution) decisions is sooner or later equated with "blind spontaneousness" which the system holds in horror and promptly suppresses because in its eyes it represents competing nodes of power and a threat to the Party's absolute supremacy.

SUGGESTED READING

Andors, Stephen, *China's Industrial Revolution: Politics, Planning and Management, 1949 to the Present* (New York: Pantheon, 1977).

Bonavia, David, "Inflation," *China Trade Report* (Hong Kong), January 1980, pp. 5–6.

Brugger, W., *Democracy and Organization in the Chinese Industrial Enterprise, 1948–1953* (Cambridge, England: Contemporary China Institute, 1976).

Chang, Y. F., "Several Problems of Commodity Pricing under the Socialist Systen," *Jingji Yanjiu* (Economic Research), (Beijing), No. 7, 1967, in *Chinese Economic Studies* (White Plains, N.Y.: International Arts and Sciences Press), Winter 1969–70, pp. 146–76.

Chen, N. R., "The Theory of Price Formation in Communist China," *China Quartely* (London), July–September 1966, pp. 35–53.

Chou, S. H., "Prices in Communist China," *Journal of Asian Studies* (Ann Arbor: Mich.), Vol. XXV, No. 4, August 1966, pp. 645–63.

Donnithorne, Audrey, *China's Economic System* (New York: Praeger, 1967), Chapters 6–9.

Henle, H. V., *Report on China's Agriculture* (Rome: Food and Agricultural Organization of the United Nations, 1974), pp. 73–81.

Kuan, Ta-tung, *The Socialist Transformation of Capitalist Industry and Commerce in China* (Peking: Foreign Languages Press, 1960).

Lardy, Nicholas, R., "Centralization and Decentralization in China's Financial Management," *China Quarterly* (London), No. 61, March 1975, pp. 25–60.

Lau, Lawrence J., "Economic Development and Industrialization," in Yuan-li Wu (ed.), *China: A Handbook* (New York: Praeger 1973), pp. 533–78.

Liu, Guonguang, and Zhao Renwei, "Socialist Economic Planning and the Market," *Beijing Review* (Beijing), No. 31, August 3, 1979, pp. 8–12.

Perkins, Dwight H., "Price Stability and Development in Mainland

China," *Journal of Political Economy* (Chicago), Vol. LXXII, No. 4, August 1964, pp. 360–75.

———, *Market Control and Planning in Communist China* (Cambridge, Mass.: Harvard University Press, 1966).

Prybyla, Jan S., "Role and Determination of Prices in Mainland China," in *Proceedings of the Fifth Sino-American Conference on Mainland China* (Taipei, Taiwan: Institute of International Relations, 1976), pp. 503–37.

———, "Patterns of Industrial Development in China: 1965–76 and 1976–78," in Jürgen Domes (ed.) *Chinese Politics After Mao* (Cardiff: University College Cardiff Press, 1979), pp. 109–27.

Rawski, Thomas G., "China's Industrial System," in *China: A Reassessment*, pp. 175–98.

Robinson, Joan, *Economic Management, China 1972* (London: Anglo-Chinese Educational Institute, March 1973, pp. 2–7 (Industry); pp. 21–23 (Prices); pp. 33–34 (Industrial Management); pp. 35–36 (Neighborhood Factories).

Schell, Orville, *In the People's Republic of China: An American's First-Hand View of Living and Working in China* (New York: Vintage, 1978).

Swamy, S., "Retail Price Index in the People's Republic of China," *Review of Economics and Statistics*, Vol. LI, No. 3, August 1969, pp. 309–19.

Tsakok, I., "Inflation Control in the People's Republic of China, 1949–1974," *World Development* (Oxford), Vol. 7, 1979, pp. 865–875.

United States, *Joint Publications Research Service* (JPRS), (Washington, D.C.),"Analysis of Prices in Communist China," August 8, 1962, *No.* 14771.

Why China Has No Inflation (Peking: Foreign Languages Press, 1976).

FIVE

Industry II

POLICIES *(continued)*

Plant Size and Technological Options

The choice of plant size and technology has been discussed by implication in Chapter 4, in the section dealing with centralization and decentralization of China's industrial structure. Here we need only add a few explicit comments.

In arriving at decisions regarding the technologies (and by extension, plant sizes) to be adopted, three determinants will normally be at work: (1) The feasibility of borrowing advanced technology from abroad, i.e., (a) the willingness of technologically more advanced countries to export their technology in the form of complete installations, blueprints, or advice, and (b) the ability of the importing country to pay for the imports and absorb them once delivered. (2) Factor proportions (hence costs), especially the domestic supply of labor of varying skills relative to capital, but also the availability and geographical dispersion of fuels and raw materials. [1] (3) The system's social welfare function, by which is

[1]Connected with this is the constraint of factor combinations in various industries and the possibility (or lack of it) of substitution between factors. In many modern industries factor

meant the preferences in social, political, and cultural matters of the system's effective decision-makers (e.g., in market-type economies, the preferences of consumers, business units, organized labor, and the government expressed in the market through money votes, or other means; in centrally planned "command" economies, the preferences of the system's political leaders, or, less accurately, "planners' preferences").

China's initial (1950–1957) choice of capital- and skill-intensive techniques concentrated in producer goods industries may be explained in terms of what, until the early 1950s, was thought to have been the ready, not to say potentially generous, availability of such technology from the Soviet Union on financial terms that China could expect to meet. As earlier in the Soviet Union, the comparatively small but advanced steel, machine building, and power sectors concentrated in the industrially established coastal areas and Manchuria were expected to trigger more general development and outweigh any inconveniences flowing from China's peculiar factor proportions (large pool of unskilled labor and acute shortage of capital). By 1957 it must have become abundantly clear to China's policymakers that Soviet economic aid was falling short of expectations and that alternative sources of borrowing (i.e., from the developed capitalist countries) were excluded by political considerations.

It should be remarked that the First Five-Year Plan's choice of technology and plant size typical of the centralized state sector was never as unqualified as the prototype Stalinist choice in the U.S.S.R. had been. In the 1950s half the gross output of industry in China came from the decentralized state sector's small and medium plants using labor-intensive, semitraditional technology. Moreover, a 1951 government decision supported the development of local industry side-by-side with technologically advanced, large-scale plants under central control. But the trend was unmistakably in the direction of the latter.

In 1958 the emphasis shifted to local industry at any cost, on any scale, but especially miniscale. The Great Leap Forward's choice of technology and plant size was discredited in part because of the particular sectoral option that dominated it. Because of the peculiar optimal capital-labor proportions (emphasizing capital) that characterize the steelmaking process and the relatively narrow room for factor substitution, because the steel industry is sensitive to economies of scale, and

combinations tend to be fixed. Steel, for example, can be, but should not be produced in tiny backyard furnaces using rudimentary techniques.

because a workable product cannot be made from shoddy materials, the Leap's backyard furnaces fed by backyard iron ore, coal, and household pots and pans were a fiasco. Perhaps as much as one-third of the steel made during the Great Leap was unusable. Unusable, also, were many of the mass inventions and innovations that, according to the Leap's philosophy, were to take the place of expert research branded as elitist. The whole adventure was typical of the Chinese-Maoist propensity to overcorrect what were deemed to be current policy mistakes.

Balance was first introduced into the choice of size and technology in 1961 and, despite loud disputes and verbal acrobatics, has been adhered to ever since. An important development in 1964 was the formalization of an always present penchant for a closer association of technological theory and practice. The reform concerned industrial design and stipulated that the designer must be present at the site where his design was being erected, and he was fully responsible for the engineering stage of his design. This stress on the combination of theory and practice, the preference for applied research and for being on the spot, were generalized and given even greater prominence by the Cultural Revolution (1966–1969).

Until 1977, China's policy stressed both technologically advanced urban-based, large-scale industries and intermediate, labor-intensive technologies in the greater part of the decentralized state and cooperative sectors, particularly in the agricultural- and consumer-oriented industries at, but mainly below, the provincial supervisory level. As we have noted earlier, labor intensity is not synonymous—as it tended to be during the Leap—with indigenous (traditional) production methods. Fairly sophisticated capital equipment can be seen in many county-, commune-, and school-run plants, but wherever possible (i.e., wherever the substitutability of factors allows it), the equipment is used in a labor-intensive way. Still, one suspects that there must be underemployment of labor in quite a number of the local plants, and machines are frequently seen standing idle. The local plants are generally small but, unlike what happened during the Leap, they are now integrated in a network of feeder industries. Under the slogan of "socialist cooperation" more advanced technological know-how is diffused and adopted by the smaller units whenever feasible. What is feasible and when it is feasible has until now been determined by rule of thumb, largely without the benefit of an elaborate economic theory. [2] Such a system generated

[2]Although information is sparse on this point, the frequent reference in official literature to the advantages of comparatively low initial capital outlays and the relatively short pay-off periods in connection with small and medium (local) industry, suggests that investment choices, especially as they concern alternative technical processes, are based on recoupment

technological innovation (mainly improvements on traditional techniques) at the grassroots through the interaction of worker and expert suggestions that are tested and evaluated within and outside the plant.

There is evidence that in choosing among industrial investment options, provincial- and lower-level state authorities were always to a degree guided by the relative profitabilities of the different branches, production lines, and plant sizes. The stress put by decentralized state authorities on the development of "nonessential" consumer goods industries that produce goods of local significance (which, by virtue of this, are frequently priced by the local authorities at good profit-yielding levels) suggests that resorting to the profit motive as an investment criterion is not alien to China's decentralized state planners despite years of left-wing disparagement of profits. [3]

The three-stage plan to modernize China by the year 2000 has brought with it renewed emphasis on sophisticated technologies imported from the West and Japan, on capital and skill intensity, and on large-scale operations. Selective borrowing of advanced foreign technologies has gone on all the time, even during the Cultural Revolution, but since the fall of the radicals the scope has been expanded and the pace stepped up. Under the combined slogan of "leaning to all sides" (i.e., selectively learning and trading with all and sundry—socialist and capitalist alike, preferably the latter) and the "four modernizations" (modernization of agriculture, industry, science-technology, and national defense) central state sector industries as well as industries run jointly by the center and the provinces or municipalities, import what are judged to be applicable foreign technologies in the form of complete plants, patents, blueprints, technical advice, professional seminars given by exporters, and so on. There is no shortage of offers from the West. The main limitations appear to be price and China's own best judgment as to the applicability of any given foreign technique to specific conditions, present level of development, and social objectives. China's capacity to absorb imported up-to-date technology has been weakened markedly by the damage inflicted on education by the Cultural Revolution: there is a shortage of highly skilled managerial, scientific, and technical-engineering personnel, and there are problems with

---

period coefficients that are compared with some recoupment period norm. Recoupment period coefficients were used for many years by Soviet planners until displaced (in the 1960s) by the more advanced "coefficients of relative effectiveness." These are reciprocals of the recoupment period coefficients. They are compared with a norm of relative effectiveness, which is, or should be, a market-clearing interest rate.

[3]Audrey Donnithorne, "China's Cellular Economy: Trends since the Cultural Revolution," *China Quarterly,* No. 52, October–December 1972, p. 617.

planning the imports in such a way that the new technologies are not islands unto themselves but parts of a consistent mutually reinforcing pattern.There are also deficiencies in the infrastructure and problems with the construction industry which make the absorption of advanced technology problematical.The new leadership appears determined to overcome these difficulties.The sights are set high and the post-Mao temper is unmistakably modern and urban.While the do-it-yourself approach to technology has not been scrapped, since 1977 it has been relegated to a supporting role. "What should be done with old equipment after new machines have been imported?" The obsolete machines discarded by key enterprises should be sold, it is argued, to county-level factories, and the machines of county-level factories should be sold to commune-run workshops. [4] In other words, the technology of small and medium-sized industrial undertakings is to be upgraded and presumably subjected to a more careful professional evaluation.Toward the end of 1979 articles appeared pleading the case of such undertakings and warning against the dangers of single-minded "gigantism" and the fetish of foreign technology.

Spatial Distribution

According to Y. L. Wu, "the stated goals of Communist China's locational policy are: (1) to correct the 'irrational' pattern of pre-Communist spatial economy; (2) to establish new economic and industrial centers closer to raw materials and consumer markets; (3) to strike a proper balance between intraregional self-sufficiency and interregional specialization; (4) to enhance national security, the evaluation of which has changed with an increasing appreciation of the rising vulnerability of inland provinces to modern long-range weapons systems; (5) to allow for requirements in international geopolitics; and (6) to develop medium and small cities in the interior rather than large cities on the coast." [5] These six stated goals can be summed up in a single desideratum: geographical dispersal of industry away from the (more developed) coastal areas.The overall goal of dispersal has not been pursued consistently.Table 4 shows the shifts in locational policy between 1949 and 1980.

Despite the oscillations in locational policy, the actual movement over the years has been in the direction of the ostensible goal. For the

[4]*Beijing Review,* July 27, 1979, pp. 17–18.

[5]Yuan-li Wu, *The Spatial Economy of Communist China* (New York: Praeger, 1967), p. 200.

whole period 1949–1980, the growth of industrial production in the interior has been more rapid than in the industrially established coastal areas. This difference in output growth rates probably increased for a while after the Cultural Revolution. Although in evaluating the differential the low initial output base of the inland areas must be taken into account, a significant contributor to the fast rise of industrial production in the interior has been investment by the state in new plant and possibly the infusion of better skilled, urban-educated manpower. Long-established industrial enterprises in the coastal areas were instructed to set up subsidiaries in the interior. This was done by transferring machinery and skilled personnel to the subsidiary enterprises and helping them out until they became selfsupporting.

The initial three years (1978–1980) of the modernization program appeared to put much stress on consolidation and tapping the potential of the established industrial centers. The subsequent five years, too, seem to be destined to favor "key" projects in well-grounded, experienced industrial areas. Thus, without neglecting industrialization of the less-developed regions, it is likely that for some years to come the already advanced coastal provinces will get a new lease on life and will benefit from the projected massive technology imports.

At the beginning of the communist era in China, the coastal provinces were industrially so far ahead of the rest of the country that, despite years of catching up by the less-developed regions, there is still a marked imbalance between the industrial endowment of coastal and inland areas. Despite the post-Mao shift in locational policy, however, the hinterland is undergoing industrialization, most often by the creation

TABLE 4 **Changing Emphasis in China's Locational Policy**

	State Investment Emphasis	
Period	*Undeveloped Regions*	*Developed Regions*
1953–57[a]	X	
1958–60	X	X
1961–65[b]		X
1966–76	X	
1977–80		X

[a]During the period of the First Five-Year Plan, 55 percent of industrial investment was allotted to inland, less developed areas, and almost 75 percent of investment in new industrial plants.

[b]Numerous small plants hastily created during the Great Leap Forward were closed down during the early years of this period. The emphasis was on consolidation of the existing, mostly long-established, centers of industry.

of numerous small and medium-sized, somewhat modernized traditional plants (workshops) in rural areas; small and medium-sized urban centers are springing up everywhere; regions that formerly had no heavy industry (such as steel and iron), but possessed the raw materials needed by heavy industry, now operate such industrial facilities. The Ningxia-Hui Autonomous Region, Inner Mongolia, and Xinjiang, among others, are examples of rapid and significant industrialization of once industrially backward regions. Still, just before the Cultural Revolution (around 1965), the nine long-established industrial centers accounted for 60 percent of total industrial capacity, while the 57 medium industrial centers (many of them created since 1949) had only 30 percent of capacity. To this day Shanghai retains its unquestionably dominant position on China's industrial landscape. An important corollary of the dispersion of industry since 1949 has been the reduction in regional income differentials. It is probably true that today this differential, while important, is the narrowest in China's history.

Incentives

DEFINITIONS Material work incentives are the granting to a person or group of persons the capacity to acquire consumer goods and services. Such capacity may be given in the form of money, or it may be in kind. In the former case the recipient clearly has more options than in cases where material incentives are received in kind.

Moral incentives are psychic rewards: honor rolls, titles, citations, testimonials, and other pats on the back. They may, but need not, be tied to material recompense. Their effectiveness depends on the recipient's outlook and attitude toward the society and groups to which he belongs.

Individual incentives are external stimuli directed principally at the individual's or household's self-interest. But individually directed incentives may also make their appeal to a person's sense of social responsibility, professional ethic, and so on. Group (or collective) incentives benefit the individual indirectly through the performance of the group as a unit. Personal interest (material and/or moral) is tied to the interest of the collective.

Competitive incentives set one unit (individual or group) against another, as in a race. Cooperative incentives emphasize and reward solidarity, mass participation, mutual help, and exchange of experience.

All the above are exogenous prods. Endogenous (or ideological) incentives consist in the worker's inner satisfaction drawn from a job well done, irrespective of external recognition—the "instinct of workmanship" as some have called it. In socialist societies endogenous ideological incentives concern the worker's satisfaction from a job well done for the community.

Disincentives are material or moral punishments directed at the individual or the group.

THEORY The behavioral theory underlying the use of various kinds of work incentives and disincentives during the periods of transition from capitalism to socialism and from socialism to communism may be reconstructed as follows.

Under the capitalist mode, man's nature is quiescent, i.e., it requires exogenous prods or impulses to impel it to productive activity. The quiescence is presumably due to man's alienation from himself and society—that self-estrangement Marx speaks of in his *Economic and Philosophical Manuscripts*. The exogenous impulses under capitalism assume the form of individual material incentives and disincentives. These propel man to seek maximum satisfaction for himself alone. Quiescence is transformed into productive activity by the individual material incentives' and disincentives' setting in motion man's rational selfishness, his self-interest. The pursuit of egoistic objectives, in turn, contributes to man's further alienation from himself and society. In the Marxist lore of capitalism, disincentives (hunger and misery) play an increasingly important role in the capitalist system as it heads for self-destruction.

Under the socialist mode, natural quiescence is not fully eradicated. The influence of the old mode on man's attitude toward work remains strong at the beginning of the socialist stage but, under proper management, diminishes over time. For some time under socialism, therefore, men have to be impelled to work by means of material appeals to their self-interest. As part of the process of socialist education, however, the use of individual material incentives becomes gradually less important. Simultaneously, resorting to group material incentives (rewards accruing to the individual from the performance of the group of which he is a member) becomes more significant. Atomistic competition among individual people is deemphasized and progressively replaced by competition among collectivities. As the socialist stage matures, individual and group material incentives based on competition yield to moral incentives both individual and collective, the importance of the latter rising over time. The competitive element of moral incentives is gradually deemphasized. Disincentives, which at the beginning of the socialist period took on a distinctly individual and material form, become increasingly socialized and moralized: from loss of pay for deviant behavior to loss of face in front of the group. Presumably, over the long run, resorting to any kind of disincentives becomes unnecessary.

As socialism matures into communism, exogenous impulses wither away. Individual, competitive, material incentives are dumped first. Group, competitive, material incentives disappear next. Individual and then collective competitive, moral prods diminish and fade away. For a while longer all that remains of exogenous prods are collective, cooperative incentives such as mass participation in decision-making, mass evaluation of work performance, exchange of technical information among collectives, and the advanced pulling up of the backward. Even these become unnecessary when at the end of the road man's nature is totally collectivized and internally energized.The individual merges in the group and is indistinguishable from it. He expresses himself through the group, is completely other-minded, and works only for the group. His former quiescence and need for external stimuli to action turn into endogenous fervor ("mass enthusiasm") propelling him to exert himself unstintingly for the community. In Marx's words, communism is "the real appropriation of the human essence by and for man; . . . the complete return of man to himself as a *social* (i.e., human) being—a return become conscious and accomplished within the entire wealth of previous development." [6] On the basis of this theory, the development and transformation of incentives during the passage from capitalism to communism is shown in Table 5.

In Maoist perspective, the progression of incentives under socialism given in Table 5 is correct. Incorrect or revisionist development, such as the Maoists thought had occurred in the Soviet Union and Yugoslavia, would show a stagnation of exogenous incentives at levels 1 and 2, or a backsliding from levels 4 and 5 to levels 1 and 2. Some backsliding, the Maoists believed, had occurred in China during the "Liuist" period 1961–1965. After 1966 the whole array of socialist incentives was deployed, the main thrust until 1976 having been in the direction of levels 6 and 7.

If one ignores for the moment the distinction between competitive and cooperative incentives, the use of work incentives in China in the period 1949 through 1980 developed as shown in Table 6.

[6]Karl Marx, *Economic and Philosophical Manuscripts of 1844*. Translated by Martin Milligan. Edited by D. J. Struik (New York: International Publishers, 1964), p. 135.

TABLE 5 **Development and Transformation of Work Incentives (Marxist Historical Progression)**

Level	Source	Type of Incentive	Capitalism	Socialism	Communism
7	Endogenous	Endogenous fervor ("mass enthusiasm")			
6		Group cooperative moral incentives			
5		Group competitive moral incentives			
4	Exogenous	Group moral disincentives			
3		Individual competitive moral incentives			
2		Individual competitive material incentives			
1		Individual material disincentives			

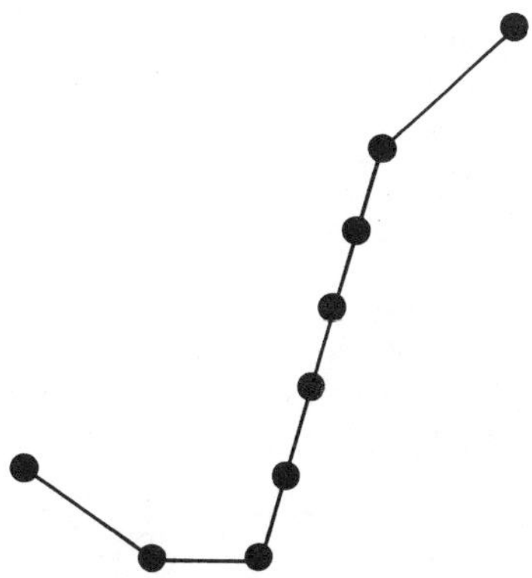

FUNCTIONS To impel men to engage in productive activity involves four things: (a) movement of people into the labor force (labor participation ratio); (b) movement of workers to desired geographical, sectoral, industrial, and plant locations (horizontal mobility); (c) movement of workers up and down the occupational skill ladder within the enterprise (vertical mobility); and (d) satisfactory performance of the assigned duties (quality, productivity). In the first case incentives are used to utilize as fully as possible the existing actual and potential pool of capabilities. In the second case they are used to induce the desired spatial, intersectoral, interindustry, interfirm allocation of those capabilities. In the third case incentives are employed to encourage the acquisition and upgrading of skills. In the fourth case they are used to elicit given quantitative and qualitative norms of performance.

As has been noted earlier, in China today the whole array of competitive and cooperative, material and nonmaterial inducements is directed at individuals and groups to achieve a high labor-participation ratio; the planned interregional, intersectoral, interindustry, and interenterprise allocation of labor; skill improvement; and quality level. Until Mao's death, the ostensible long-run trend had been in the direction of moral, collective, cooperative incentives that eventually were counted on to generate endogenous mass fervor and, by virtue of this fact, make external stimuli superfluous. There is considerable skepticism about the

TABLE 6 **Work Incentives in China**

Period	Material	Moral	Individual	Collective
1949–52	X		X	
1953–57	X		X	
1958–60		X		X
1961–65	X		X	
1966–70[a]		X		X
1970–76[b]	←X→		←X→	
1976–77[c]	←X		←X	
1978–80	X		X	

[a]Once the "Liuist" opposition to socialized moral incentives had been overcome during the Cultural Revolution.

[b]→Dominant trend. ←Subsidiary trend noticeable after 1971.

[c]←Dominant trend.

practicality and effectiveness of the trend and the goal among members of the present leadership. After 1977 differentiated material incentives directed at individuals and groups came back into vogue.

A workable generalization would be that a high labor participation ratio, probably the highest in the communist world, is obtained by a combination of a low-wage policy, administrative assignment, and peer-group pressure.The policy of low wages had been used by Stalin in the U.S.S.R; in order to make ends meet within the household, both husband and wife normally had to work.The same is true in present-day China. In addition, school children are made to participate in productive labor as an integral part of their formal education, and retirees are often assigned to various jobs in the neighborhood.The right not to work is inoperative in practice. Inactivity earns social opprobrium, and social opprobrium has dire consequences for those who opt for leisure over work. How much idling there is on the job is difficult to say, but visual evidence points to a purposeful but very relaxed pace in both city and country.

Horizontal mobility since the Cultural Revolution has been mainly a function of administrative order. Regional, intersectoral, interindustry, and interplant wage differentials do exist, but their allocative role appears to be secondary to administrative distribution of the work force.The major responsibility for directing labor to planned employment rests with provincial and municipal labor bureaus.They and their subordinate offices are also responsible for the recruitment of people into the labor force—upon graduation from school, for example. A useful distinction is between nationwide mass horizontal movement, such as the large-scale transfer of people from urban to rural areas (*xia fang*) and the horizontal movement of individual workers.

Vertical mobility relies more on wage differentials within the enterprise, although there are exceptions.The persistence of direct material inducements to improve one's skills and of material reward differentials used to be deplored by the purists among the Maoists, recruited mostly from among the extreme leftists, [7] but it was defended by others in the name of the socialist distributive principle " from each according to his ability, to each according to his work, and more pay to him who works more." The result for a time was a two-legged compromise. "In applying the principle 'from each according to his ability, to each according to his work,' China opposes equalitarianism yet prevents great disparities.There are pay differentials between heavy and light, complex and simple work, but these should not be too large." [8]

Satisfactory performance of the assigned duties means fulfillment or overfulfillment by the individual or the group of the work norm specified in the production plan. The norm will usually make explicit a number of dimensions sought: quantity, quality, safety, economy, and productivity.

Before the Cultural Revolution overfulfillment of the norm was frequently rewarded by extra pay. During the Revolution and until 1977, over-quota performance was expected as a matter of socialist consciousness and solidarity. A good deal of the labor trouble in 1974–1977 was traceable to the abolition (or at least the severe limitation) of bonus payments and the general downgrading of individual material incentives.

The official stance, if not at once the practice, changed sharply after October 1976. Egalitarian schemes of income distribution and insistence on group moral incentives, the lack of competitiveness among workers and of competition among enterprises, were jettisoned together and denounced as ultraleft deviations peddled by the gang of four. The switch from the neo-Maoist (largely egalitarian and nonmaterial) system of rewards to differentiated material incentives had to be explained, of course, in ideological terms: "While political and ideological work helps improve the people's understanding of things, the distribution principle 'to each according to his work' solves the practical problem of material life . . . . The higher the level of a laborer's ideological consciousness is

[7]E.g., Yao Wenyuan, "On the Social Basis of the Lin Piao Anti-Party Clique," *Hongqi*, March 1975. English-language text in *Background on China*, Chinese Information Service, New York, B-75-09, March 25, 1975.

[8]"Wages and Prices in China," *China Reconstructs*, Vol. XXIV, No. 4, April 1974, p. 40.

and the better his life becomes, the more ardently will he love socialism and the more consciously will he plunge into his work.This will help raise labor productivity greatly." [9] The reasoning is not very different from that used to justify similar policies during the Liu Shaoqi administration of the early- to mid-sixties. But left dissent has not been silenced. In the midst of official jubilation about the reinstituted policy of "more pay for more work, less pay for less work, no pay for no work," and the admission that no shame attaches to people's trying to improve their material lot, Shanghai Radio warned on a sharply dissonant note that "spiritual encouragement [must be] the leading factor and material incentives the secondary factor."[10] Left noises from Shanghai can be ominous. "While implementing the principle 'to each according to his work,' we have encountered all kinds of resistance," complained *Renmin Ribao* (May 31, 1979). "Some people dislike the system and describe it as 'getting together to keep an eye on money.' "

Material Incentives and Disincentives Material incentives and disincentives in industry consist of the wage and salary system for production workers and employees (managerial, technical, clerical personnel).[11] The structure of the system has been adopted by the Chinese from the Soviets. Despite many modifications since its installation in the 1950s, the wage and salary mechanism resembles its Soviet prototype to this day in the more formal mode of its operation. It departs from the Soviet system, however, in a number of significant ways, which can best be described as the spirit in which it operates.The departures consist mostly in the repeated attempt to socialize, moralize, cooperativize, and equalize the wage and salary system as part of an effort to remake human nature.This effort had Mao's full approval and was enthusiastically endorsed by the Party's left wing. Others, more concerned with immediate production results and the possibly adverse longer range effects of such efforts at human engineering on the modernization of the economy have tended to interpret the moral, cooperative, egalitarian Marxist message much more cautiously and conservatively. Whenever they got a chance (1961–65 and again after 1976), they rolled back the ideologically prescribed progression of incentives and brought the system of rewards back down to level 2 or even level 1 (Table 5).

As originally adopted, until the Cultural Revolution and again since 1977, the industrial material reward and punishment system comprised

[9] *Peking Review*, February 17, 1978, p. 8.

[10] Shanghai Radio citing *Jiefang Ribao*, April 22, 1979, in *FBIS*, May 18, 1979.

[11] It goes without saying that the effectiveness of the wage and salary incentive system hinges on the availability of consumer goods.

three elements: basic wages, supplementary or bonus wages, and the social wage.The system is shown in Figure 2. Separate basic and bonus wage scales existed (and exist to this day) for production workers and employees.

Production Workers' Basic Wages. In a given plant there is a system of labor grades for production workers.These labor grades normally range from 1 to 8. Grade 1 defines the least skilled work qualifications (but not apprentice labor); grade 8, the highest skill requirements (roughly equivalent to foreman grade). [12] Labor grades have work coefficients attached to them.The coefficient attaching to labor grade 1 is always 1 (base coefficient). Coefficients attaching to higher labor grades are multiples of the base coefficient. Labor grade 1 has a wage in yuan attached to it. Since the Cultural Revolution this has been predominantly a time-based wage. [13] After 1976 piece rates were rehabilitated on a selective basis. While time rates remained most common, piece work was reintroduced in certain branches, for example, in the loading and unloading of ships. "In the present circumstances when wages are low, payment by piece serves as a premium and a socialist incentive that has no negligible function in improving the life of the masses." [14] The wage

[12]If the Soviet example is adhered to, the requirements for each labor grade will be described in detail in a wages manual issued by the appropriate central authority.The description would include type of work, knowledge required, and examples of work. After the Cultural Revolution and until October 1976, under "knowledge required," formal credentials were deemphasized. In the Soviet Union a six-grade system for industrial production workers seems to be in general use.

[13]Piece rates were favored in the 1950s, but apparently were never implemented on the scale they exhibited under Stalin in the U.S.S.R. In China piece-rate payments never covered more than 45 percent of the industrial labor force. In the Soviet Union during some years, as much as 75 percent of the industrial labor force worked on the piece-rate system. "Even if material incentives cannot be abolished completely, a piece-work wage system is no longer needed." *Economic Research* (Beijing), No. 1, 1959, p. 53.Time rates have assumed more importance in the U.S.S.R., too, since the mid-1960s.The reasons for the shift away from piece-rates there include more widespread mechanization and automation and greater quality consciousness.The reasons for the withering away of the piece-rate system in China include the following considerations: (1) piece rates give rise to conflict between management and workers over work norms, (2) workers' fears lest overfulfillment of piece-rate norms lead to a permanent upward revision of the norms, hence a decrease in pay, and (3) technical difficulties involved in establishing and altering norms. China did not have the trained personnel to do this. P. Schran, "Institutional Continuity and Motivational Change: The Chinese Industrial Wage System, 1950–1973," *Asian Survey,* November 1974, p. 1025. To this day, labor grade calculations, skill definitions, and work quotas are "unscientific," and therefore prone to abuse by workers and management. *Gongren Ribao* (Beijing), May 22, 180, pp. 1, 3, in *FBIS,* June 25, 1980.

[14]*Renmin Ribao,* November 22, 1978, p. 2.

FIGURE 2. *Industrial material reward system.*

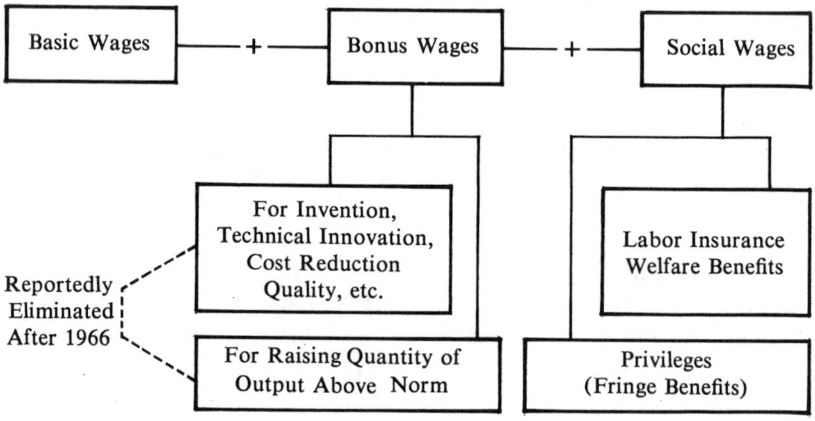

rates for higher labor grades are the wage for labor grade 1 times the appropriate coefficient (i.e., the coefficient attaching to each successive labor grade). The weekly or monthly wage for each labor grade can be obtained by multiplying the hourly wage by the number of hours constituting a working week or month. Apprentice labor is paid at rates well below the grade 1 of regular workers. A first-year apprentice in a modern heavy industry factory might get as little as 22 yuan ($14) a month. Also, pay scales of people working in small-scale urban cooperative industry (for the most part housewives) are lower than those of state industry. On the average such workers make 20–25 yuan a month.

Some examples of an eight-grade system of basic wages for industrial production workers in China are given in Table 7. In order not to clutter up the table, the coefficients have been omitted after the first example (Beijing No. 1 Machine Tools Plant).

After remaining stationary for years, basic wages were raised across the board on October 1, 1977. [15] The increase applied to 64 percent of

[15]General wage increases were given in 1956 and 1963. Between 1952 and 1957 the average money wage of industrial workers rose by 7.4 percent per year. Between 1957 and 1971 the average wage dropped by 10 percent due mainly to the policy (a) freezing the top wages, (b) not replacing those who retired at top wages with new people who would be paid the same wage, and (c) raising the lowest wages. The 10 percent loss was made up by the increase of lower level wages after 1971. Taking 1952 = 100, the index of average industrial money wages in 1977 was around 160–170. Christopher Howe, "Wages, Prices and the Standard of Living of Urban Workers in the PRC," *China Business Review,* July–August 1978, p. 11.

industrial workers, workers and staff in the commercial and service trades, teachers, scientific, technical, medical, literary, and art workers, and government functionaries. About 46 percent of the workers and employees received increases in the wage rates applicable to their particular labor grade. Another 18 percent were moved up the labor grade ladder because "they had been classified too low for their jobs." Generally, the wage increase was of the order of 10 percent. Thus, in order to update the information presented in Table 7, the basic wage figures should be raised by about 10 percent, and the same applies to the data in Tables 8 through 13. While the raises were said to benefit primarily those earning less than 90 yuan a month, workers with many years of experience (i.e., with seniority and presumably better pay) were also included. Views of coworkers were apparently sought in deciding whose wages should be raised, but the final determination was made by Party committees.

Another round of wage increases took place in 1978. At that time 2 percent of workers and government employees (compared with 46 percent the year before) received wage increases. A third round was announced in November 1979, covering 40 percent of workers and government employees. In 1979 wage adjustment coincided with stiff price increases for a number of nonstaple foods, including pork, beef, mutton, poultry, eggs, milk, vegetables, and fish.

The multiples of the grade 1 coefficient and the basic wage in yuan attaching to labor grade 1 (hence, the whole wage scale) will vary according to (a) the degree of inherent difficulty of the job, (b) the environment within which the job is performed (e.g., hot work, underground work, work involving health hazards or demanding above average physical effort), (c) the location of the plant, and (d) the position of the job and the industrial sector of which it is a part on the planners' scale of priorities. Regional wage differences for the same work reflect the estimated relative arduousness of climatic and other conditions in different areas of the country, the position of the given locality on the planners' scale of developmental priorities, and cost of living differences. (Incidentally, the size of the food ration for the same category of workers varies from place to place, presumably reflecting regional cost of living differences.) [16]

Wage differences according to the position of the job and the indus-

[16] A Hong Kong source (early 1970s) speculated that China was divided into 12 cost-of-living regions. A bowl of noodles (2 ounces) was said to cost 8 cents in Suzhou (Jiangsu Province), 10 to 12 cents in Shanghai, 14 to 16 cents in Canton and 20 cents in remote small towns of Guangdong Province.

TABLE 7 **Basic Wage Scales for Industrial Production Workers, 1959–1973**

		Enterprise (year)				
Labor Grade	*Coeffi-cient*	*Beijing No. 1 Machine Tools Plant (1973)*	*Anshan Iron & Steel Company (1959)*	*Rough Rolling Mill, Anshan Iron & Steel Co. (1972)*	*Anshan Iron & Steel Company (1973)*	*Shenyang No. 1 Machine Tools Plant (1972)*
1	[1.00]	34.00	34.50	34.50	34.00	33.00
2	[1.18]	40.10	40.74	40.00	n.a.	38.90
3	[1.40]	47.50	48.11	48.13	n.a.	45.80
4	[1.62]	55.00	56.82	56.82	n.a.	54.00
5	[1.80]	61.10	67.10	67.10	n.a.	63.60
6	[2.27]	77.10	79.25	79.25	n.a.	74.90
7	[2.67]	90.90	93.59	84.50	n.a.	88.20
8	[3.15]	107.10	110.40	110.00	114.00	104.00
Ratio (Max.: Min.)		3.15	3.2	3.2	3.4	3.2

SOURCE: Carl Riskin, "Workers' Incentives in Chinese Industry," in *China: A Reassessment,* pp. 216–17.

trial sector on the planners' indifference map include the following considerations: desired size of plant, preferred technological option (capital versus labor intensity), importance to the national economy and exports, producer versus consumer goods, and material production versus services output. All these variations presumably are used to assist administrative measures aimed at promoting labor mobility in the socially desired directions, both horizontal and vertical. After 1976 the renewed emphasis on formally certified qualifications led to the establishment of a system—how widespread, it is difficult to say—of vocational and professional examinations. The results of these examinations were to be taken into consideration by those responsible for the assignment of labor to different employments and locations. [17]

At various times attempts have been made to include qualitative standards in the wage norms. Before the Cultural Revolution three quality ratings were incorporated in each of the eight wage grades. Thus

[17]The system included in some places examinations for secretaries and directors of small plants who, after attending vocational classes sponsored by the relevant supervisory bureau, took the exams to see what they could do. "Their average was over 90 percent"—which says something either about the examiners (propensity to minimize trouble for themselves in a fluid ideological situation by giving everybody a high grade and keeping the grade spread narrow) or about the exceptional ability of the leading cadres of small industry. Beijing Radio reporting on an experiment in Zhejiang Province, May 21, 1979, in *FBIS,* May 24, 1979.

a worker in, say, grade 5 would receive the full wage attaching to that grade only if he fulfilled both the quantitative norm and achieved an A quality rating. Quality output rated B would entail a reduction of between 6 and 8 percent of the basic wage. Work rated C quality was returned and no payment was made to the worker until at least B-level quality standard was reached. The system lent itself particularly well to individual piece work. Since the fall of the gang the problem of quality control has been given a great deal of attention. A *People's Daily* editorial of August, 17, 1977, urged a "quality first" approach to production: "Quality must come first. Quantity is important, but quality must be taken as a precondition. . . . Grasping quantity at the expense of quality, pursuing output value alone to the neglect of the eight technical and economic targets specified by the state . . . [is] erroneous." Similar behests have been sounded since the installation of the socialist system in China, and they are not very different from the daily lectures on the need to eliminate shoddy quality given by Soviet planners for the last fifty years. The problem is rooted in the system of administrative command which, despite slight modifications, stresses a gross quantitative approach to economic growth in a taut input supply setting. In such a setting, the most rational way of fulfilling output plans (from the producer's perspective) is by cutting corners on the quality of the product, and verbal exhortations and fines are unlikely to change it. A number of pre-Cultural Revolution quality-control mechanisms have been restored since 1976. The reinstated quality-control procedures had been eliminated at the height of the Cultural Revolution as part of a leftist drive to rid the economy of "superfluous rules and regulations" that, it was argued, had been introduced by revisionist so-called experts to fool the masses.

The most skilled production worker in the plants gets more than three times the wage of the unskilled worker (see Table 8). Hoffman [18] reports that the ratio of 1:3 is a rough middle-range ratio in Chinese industry. As a general but fairly elastic rule, industries that put great strain on the workers (mainly heavy industries) have exhibited wage differentials greater than 1:3 (Hoffman cites a Qingdao heavy industry plant with a hard work differential of 1:3.6), while in light industries the ratios were generally below 1:3. My own observations in China (February 1974) yield a spread of less than 1:3, the differential being greatest in the heavy industry plants (Table 8). The average monthly wage of

[18] Charles Hoffmann, *The Chinese Worker* (Albany: State University of New York Press, 1974), p. 98.

TABLE 8 **Basic Monthly Wages of Production Workers in Modern Industry, 1974–1978**

	Wage (yuan)			
Enterprise	*Minimum*	*Maximum*	*Ratio*	*Average*
Shanghai Machine Tools Plant No. 1 (6,000 employees)	42	124	2.95	68
Nanjing Petrochemical Plant (3,800 employees)	35	97	2.77	53
Suzhou Silk Factory (1,600 employees)	30	n.a.[a]	n.a.	50
Suzhou Embroidery Research Institute (200 employees)	54	94	1.74	n.a.
Beijing Arts and Crafts Work-	35	n.a.	n.a.	60
shop (1,300 employees)[b]	(40)	(102)	2.55	n.a.
Shanghai Diesel Engine Factory (1975)	40	129	3.23	65
Shanghai Port Working Area No. 30 (1975)	40	90	2.25	65
Northwest Textile Factory, Xian, Shaanxi (1977)	32	104	3.25	n.a.
Guangzhou Automobile Parts Factory, Guangdong (1978)	39	106	2.71	n.a.

SOURCE: Jan S. Prybyla, "A Note on Incomes and Prices in China," *Asian Survey,* Vol. XV, No. 3 (March 1975), pp. 262–78. Christopher Howe, "Wages, Prices and the Standard of Living of Urban Workers in the PRC," *China Business Review,* July–August 1978, pp. 10, 15.

[a]n.a. = not available.

[b]Data in parentheses are from James Tobin. "The Economy of China: A Tourist's View," *Challenge,* March–April 1973, p. 29. Professor Tobin visited this workshop in 1972.

production workers in modern industry in 1974 was in the neighborhood of 55 yuan ($27.50); rising to very roughly 60 yuan by 1979. [19] Hong Kong sources indicate that minimum and maximum production workers' wages (1974) were as given in Table 9.

The absolute amount of wages in each labor grade has typically been higher in heavy industry than in light. After the Cultural Revolution the difference was presumably less than it had been in the mid-1950s. Since

[19]The average monthly wage of skilled workers in Daqing oilfield (a model enterprise) in 1978 was 60 yuan a month. Beijing Radio, January 27, 1979, in *FBIS,* February 6, 1979. During his visit to China in the summer of 1979, Professor Jürgen Domes compiled the following figures based on visits to nine factories: average monthly wage for male workers—61.34 yuan; for female workers—54.35 yuan. In six of these nine factories the presence of "temporary" workers was openly admitted. Their share in the workforce was between 4.5 percent in a ceramics factory in Foshan (Guangdong) and 34.7 percent in a tobacco factory on the outskirts of Changsha (Hunan). Private communication to the author from J. Domes.

TABLE 9 **Basic Monthly Wages of Production Workers by Management Category, 1974**[a]

	Wage (yuan)		
Industry	*Minimum*	*Maximum*	*Ratio*
Industries under central state management	39	107	2.73
Industries under provincial management	37	97	2.62
Industries under county management	34	83	2.44
Industries under the management of authorities below the county level	30	77	2.57

SOURCE: "Ranks and Wages," *China News Analysis*, No. 966 (July 12, 1974), p. 6.

[a]No account is taken of regional variations within each industrial management category.

women workers dominate light industry employment, there is de facto wage inequality between men and women. The difference, it is argued, merely reflects the difficulty of heavy as against light industrial work. Wages in centrally and provincially managed industries are as a rule higher than wages in industries managed by counties and lower-level authorities (Table 9).

In the 1960s the Soviet Union reduced the number of labor grades in industry from eight (sometimes ten or more) to six, and at the same time it proceeded to narrow the spread between the lowest and highest paid production workers, primarily by upgrading the pay of the lower paid workers. (In fact, the reduction in the number of labor grades was merely a legal recognition of a widely practiced fact. In their competition for scarce labor, enterprise managements reclassified workers in ways designed to eliminate the first two grades; thus, a worker with hardly any skills would be recruited into grade 3 and classified as semiskilled.)

The Chinese have not eliminated any labor grades since the 1950s. They have, however, on two occasions before October 1977 (1963, 1972–1973), moved workers in the lower wage grades, en masse, up by one or two grades. This was presumably a cost-of-living adjustment measure as well as a temporary compression of the occupational wage gap. The temporary nature of the compression is suggested by the fact that (unlike what happened in the Soviet Union) the lowest grades were not eliminated; they were emptied of occupants, until new recruits could replenish the lower ranks. [20] It is ironic that the basic wage span for industrial production workers is greater in China than in the Soviet Union (where it is typically 1:2), although it is the Chinese who accuse

[20]Peter Schran, "Institutional Continuity and Motivational Change: The Chinese Industrial Wage System, 1950–1973," *Asian Survey*, Vol. XIV, No. 11, November 1974, pp. 1019, 1027.

the Soviets of sliding into bourgeois income gaps. Present wage spans in China, however, are narrower than those that existed under Stalin's rule at a lower level of the U.S.S.R.'s economic development—a level more comparable to China's present state of development. Moreover, the Soviet total wage differential (inclusive of selective bonuses) is certainly greater than the 1:2 ratio indicated by the basic wage scale. Around 1955–1956 the differentials between grades were standardized in China—approximately 18 percent in heavy industry and construction and roughly 17 percent in light industry. A comparison of minimum, maximum, and average wages in various plants points to a clustering of workers in the lower wage grades. Hoffman [21] suggests that a high proportion of low-skill workers has tended to be more typical of the newer (e.g., chemicals) than the long-established (e.g., textiles) industries.

The October 1977 and later basic wage adjustments did not by themselves widen the wage spread. However, as I shall argue more forcefully when we come to the bonus wage, total wage differentials are likely to become wider in the future, always assuming that the current modernization drive survives the political traps that inevitably will be laid for it by a left opposition that refuses to be brought to its knees. That wage differentials may have to be stretched because the present ones act by and large as a damper on labor productivity, has been suggested by *Renmin Ribao* (May 5, 1978): "The wage spread may be readjusted rationally." In line with the renewed attention paid to professionalism, exceptionally talented people will be promoted rapidly and will not necessarily climb the wage ladder rung by rung. There is the possibility that, given the enormous investments projected for urban-based plant and equipment (which presumably will result in significant gains in labor productivity in such plants), the urban-rural income gap, wide as it is, will become greater.

Small industries in people's communes often use work points. State farm workers work under different labor grade classifications, as do members of the PLA's Production and Construction Corps.

Employees' Basic Wages. The term *employees* covers managerial, technical, and clerical personnel, as well as people working in the state or Party administration, teachers, medical personnel, and cultural workers. Employees' wages are subject to separate labor grade schedules, a practice taken over from the Soviets. There are many such schedules. They are much more complex than the standard eight-grade

[21]Hoffman, op. cit., pp. 99–100.

schedules for production workers. The national civil service schedule reportedly contains twenty-five grades or thereabouts (not counting service personnel). The system, especially as it applies to cadre grading, is not talked about very much. Table 10 gives information on the system of grading government workers; it is based on data from people who have lived and worked in China. It should be noted that each labor grade may have as many as eleven regional variants to reflect differentials in living costs. Table 11 gives data (dating from the mid-1950s) on the governmental salary structure in a relatively well-off provincial authority. This information apparently was drawn from "private sources." Although the data go back to the mid-1950s (1955 or 1956, when the wage scales in the state administration were reformed), they are still relevant insofar as employee basic wage schedules have not changed greatly since 1956, even though the highest salaries were reportedly trimmed during the Cultural Revolution and salary adjustments were made in 1977 and later. Note that the basic salary of the highest paid administrative official in Canton (chairman of the late Provincial Revolutionary Committee) is slightly more than 8 times the basic wage of the least skilled worker in the province's modern industry and about 12 times the basic wage of the lowest grade government clerk. Assuming average per capita income from collective work in a poor commune in Guangdong Province to be 12 yuan a month (a little better than in other places), the highest salary in Canton is 25.8 times greater.

Technical personnel in industry (engineers and technicians) are classified in 13 grades at the national level. The grades assume different values in enterprises of different sizes; usually three enterprise sizes are recognized: large, medium, and small, although (as we have seen in Chapter 4) what constitutes large, medium, and small is interpreted flexibly. On the basis of various samples obtained by travelers in China, I would put the lowest salary at 50 yuan a month and the highest at 200 yuan or a differential of 1:4. At two plants I visited in 1974 the average technician's monthly salary was given as 80 and 90 yuan. Higher grade 1 salaries have been reported. [22] It is conceivable that there is a small number of top-level scientists, engineers, and technicians in the defense

[22]M. Meissner, "The Shenyang Transformer Factory—A Profile," *China Quarterly*, No. 52, 1972, p. 731, reports technicians' salaries of 230 yuan a month. Schran, op. cit., p. 1021, shows salaries of chief engineers and directors of rank 1 enterprises (in 1955) to have been as much as 230 yuan. Deputy chief engineers, chief designers, and chief mechanical engineers in such top-ranking enterprises were at that time getting up to 195 yuan per month. The lowest industrial employee monthly wage (servants, mail clerks, etc.) was 36 yuan. Howe, "Wages, Prices . . . ," op. cit., p. 11, reports top technical-staff salaries in Beijing of 340 yuan a month in 1978 (with the lowest being 46 yuan).

TABLE 10 **Labor Grades of Employees of the State Administration About 1974**

Job Description	Grades 1	2	3	4	5	6	7	8	9	10	11	12	13	14	15	16	17	18	19	20	21	22	23	24	25	26	27	28	29	30
Chairman of the C.P.C. (Mao) (+vice-chairmen of the PRC?)[a]	■																													
Prime Minister (Zhou) and vice-premiers		■	■																											
Cabinet ministers and people in similar posts				■	■	■	■	■																						
Heads and deputy heads of provincial revolutionary comm.					■	■	■	■	■																					
Bureau and committee chiefs and deputies in the central govt.						■	■	■	■	■																				
Bureau and committee chiefs in provincial governments								■	■	■	■	■																		
Department heads and deputy heads of ministries										■	■	■	■	■																
Heads and deputy heads of counties													■	■	■	■	■													
Section chiefs and deputies in the central government														■	■	■	■	■												
Department heads and deputies in provincial governments															■	■	■	■	■											
Section chiefs and deputies in provincial governments																■	■	■	■	■										
Section chiefs and deputies in counties																	■	■	■	■	■									
Ordinary clerks[b]																		■	■	■	■	■	■	■	■	■				
Service personnel																									■	■	■	■	■	■

SOURCE: "Ranks and Wages," *China News Analysis*, No. 966 (July 12, 1974), pp. 4–5.

[a]The monthly salary attaching to this grade has been variously reported as 400 yuan to 540 yuan.

[b]The lowest monthly salary of grade 26 has been reported to be 30 yuan in 1978.

TABLE 11. **Basic Monthly Salaries of Government Employees in Canton, Mid-1950s**

Job Description	*Work Grade*	*Salary (yuan)*
Chairman of Guangdong Province Revolutionary Committee	8	310
Head of a bureau	(8–12)[a]	200–210
Head of a department	(14–19)[a]	160–174
Head of a section	17	128–130
	18	120
Clerks (lowest grade)	26	35

SOURCE: "Ranks and Wages," op. cit., p. 6.

[a]Presumed grade range based on Table 10. Add roughly 10–15 percent to obtain approximate 1980 data.

sector, for example, who are under separate or modified schedules and earn substantially higher salaries.

By and large, the difference between minimum production workers' wages (grade 1) and the highest technical personnel salaries (grade 1 on the technical scale) is 1:5, perhaps a little more.There appears to be a considerable overlap between above average workers' and technicians' salaries as given in Table 12.Thus, the higher paid production workers receive basic monthly wages substantially above the salaries of beginning and middle technicians.The ratio of the highest paid production worker (grade 8) to the highest paid technician (grade 1) is roughly 1:1.7.These differentials are relatively modest by international standards. Compared with the technical personnel of the work place, the higher paid workers in China are not badly off in terms of status as reflected by pay. According to Schran [23] the rule appears to be that the wages received by grade 8 production workers should rank between the lowest and the next lowest grade applicable to technicians (e.g., between grade 13 and grade 12).The lowest wages of engineers are higher than the highest wages paid to technicians.

Schran maintains that in 1956 the lowest basic wage of office employees exceeded the lowest basic wage of production workers and that the differential between the highest and lowest basic wages (production workers and employees) within an enterprise did not exceed seven. Hoffman [24] reports that in a sample of industrial enterprises the spread was 1:6 (least skilled production worker to top manager), but that in

[23]Schran, op. cit., p. 1022.
[24]Hoffmann, op. cit., p. 103.

TABLE 12 **Overlap between Industrial Workers' Basic Wages and Technicians' Basic Salaries, 1972[a]**

	Workers' Job Grades							
Personnel	*1*	*2*	*3*	*4*	*5*	*6*	*7*	*8*
Rough Rolling Mill, Anshan Iron & Steel Co.	34.50	40.00	48.13	56.82	67.10	79.25	84.50	110.00
Shenyang No. 1 Machine Tools Plant	33.00	38.90	45.80	54.00	63.60	74.90	88.20	104.00
		Technicians' Salary Scale						
		13						1
Technicians' salary		50.00		overlap		80.00	90.00	175.00+

SOURCE: Workers, Table 6. Technicians, Meissner, op. cit.
[a]In yuan per month.

most enterprises surveyed the difference was not as large. Table 13 contains data on technical personnel wages in two plants that I visited in 1974. This is supplemented by information collected by other visitors to China in the early 1970s.

Administrative personnel in colleges and universities are reportedly divided into 25 grades, whereas teachers are ranked into 12 grades. In my conversations with university people, four academic ranks were recognized: teachers, lecturers, associate professors, and professors. It was emphasized that professorial ranks were being phased out so that some day all university and college instructors would be known only as teachers. More important, the relatively high salaries of full professors were not to be continued after the retirement of the people who received them (most of the full professors are quite elderly). In any event, university professors had been shorn of power by repeated rectification campaigns, and their status and influence (until 1977) had been brutally diminished by the Cultural Revolution. Table 14 gives ranges for university and middle school salaries. They were obtained during my visit to the institutions listed.

Professor James Tobin reports that average wages of all staff in a Shanghai hospital (1972) were 67 yuan per month. The average monthly salary of doctors was 87 yuan. Some physicians and surgeons were making as much as 200 to 300 yuan per month. [25]

[25]Tobin, op. cit., p. 29.

TABLE 13 **Basic Monthly Wages of Technical and Managerial-Administrative Personnel in Modern Industry**

		Wage (yuan)		*Ratio*	
Personnel	*Year*	*Minimum*	*Maximum*	*(max.: min.)*	*Average*
Nanjing Petrochemical Plant	1974				
Technical Personnel (380 persons)		50	150	3.00	80
Managerial and administrative personnel		40	140	3.50	n.a.[a]
Suzhou Silk Factory	1974	—90—		n.a.	n.a.
Anshan Rolling Mill	1972	58	154	2.66	n.a.
Tangshan Kailan Coal Mine: Mine No. 1179	1972	n.a.	145	n.a.	n.a.
Beijing No. 1 Machine Tools Plant	1972	90	120(?)	. . .	n.a.
Beijing Metal Wire Factory	1972				
Technical personnel		n.a.	189	n.a.	n.a.
Managerial personnel		n.a.	164	n.a.	n.a.
Shanghai No. 1 Cotton Mill	1972	80	>200	. . .	150

SOURCES: Nanjing Petrochemical Plant and Suzhou Silk Mill: J. S. Prybyla, "A Note on Incomes and Prices in China," *Asian Survey,* Vol. XV, No. 3, March 1975, p. 266. Other: Peter Schran, op. cit., p. 1030.

[a]n.a. = not available.

Retail Prices of Consumer Goods. The incentive effect of basic money wages must be deduced from the prices of consumer goods on the assumption that the goods are actually available at the posted prices. It will be recalled that Chinese consumer goods pricing policy distinguishes between essential goods, everyday necessities, and secondary goods. It should also be remembered that the borderlines between these three categories of goods are not frozen. From personal observations and reports by other travelers in China, I have compiled Tables 15, 16, and 17, which give samples of retail prices—primarily, though not exclusively, in Beijing, Shanghai, and Canton. [26] Strong inflationary pressures have been acknowledged after 1976. In 1979 retail prices, as officially admitted, rose 6 percent. Unofficial reports spoke of a price rise nearer 25 percent. Suppressed inflation, manifesting itself in shortages and disguised price hikes is much in evidence.

[26]Most of the material in these tables was first published in my "Work Incentives in the People's Republic of China," *Weltwirtschaftliches Archiv,* Vol. CXII, No. 4, 1976, pp. 784–86.

TABLE 14 **Basic Monthly Wages of University and Middle School Personnel, 1974**

	Wage (yuan)			
Personnel	*Minimum*	*Maximum*	*Ratio*	*Average*
Nanjing University				
Professors and associate professors (90)	200	300	1.50	n.a.[a]
Lecturers (274)	70	130	1.86	n.a.
Teachers (1,051)	53	70	1.32	n.a.
Nanjing Normal (Teachers') College				
Professors	n.a.	300	n.a.	n.a.
Lecturers (1727)[b]	n.a.	100+	n.a.	n.a.
Teachers	50+	n.a.	n.a.	n.a.
Suzhou Middle School (Jiangsu)				
Teachers and administrative personnel (200)[c]	50	140	2.80	60

[a]n.a. = not available.
[b]Figure in parentheses includes administrative personnel.
[c]Figure in parentheses is for teaching staff only.

Bonus Wage. Bonuses and other reward supplements to the basic wage were commonly used in China from the 1950s until 1966; then again, hesitantly at first, after 1972.Various bonus mechanisms were employed in the 1950s and early 1960s.They added not more than 12 percent (the legal upper limit) to the basic wage of the recipients—probably much less.Their net effect was to increase income inequality. Bonus payments were fullly rehabilitated in 1977.

The general characteristics of the new system toward the end of the 1970s were as follows. First, as compared with the "Liuist" period (1961–65) the system was probably less complex and the bonuses more modest. In fact, many Western observers believed them to have been too low (roughly 10 percent of the wages fund for production workers) to have had any significant incentive impact. A Party secretary from a Beijing factory wrote to *Beijing Ribao* (February 4, 1979) that the introduction of bonuses created new problems and new contradictions. For example, boiler-room workers shut off the heating system because they said their bonuses were too low.The shop floor was so cold that the workers had to keep their hands in their pockets. "This had a direct effect on production." On the other hand there have been complaints that the bonuses were too high and that they were sloshed around indiscriminately. In fact, "some units by distributing bonuses have gone

TABLE 15 **Retail Prices of Selected "Essential" Consumer Goods and Services in Cities, 1974–76* (Continued)**

Commodity	*Unit*	*Officially Reported Price (yuan)*	*Observed Price Range (yuan)*
Rice, husked (rationed)	0.5 kg	0.14	0.14–0.18
Wheat flour, medium grade (rationed)	0.5 kg	0.18	0.17–0.20
Beef (unrationed)	0.5 kg	0.60	0.60–2.00
Pork (rationed)	0.5 kg	0.90[a]	0.90–1.80[b]
Chicken (unrationed)	0.5 kg	1.25 [1.00]	1.00–1.80
Potatoes (unrationed)	0.5 kg		0.06–1.00
Eggs (unrationed)	0.5 kg	0.90 [0.90]	
Vegetables, unspecified (unrationed)	0.5 kg	0.088[c]	0.08–0.20[d]
Soy sauce (rationed)	0.5 kg	0.27	
Fresh fish (unrationed)	0.5 kg	0.50	0.50–2.00
Vegetable oil (rationed)	0.5 kg	[0.80]	0.55–1.00
Fur hat (with ear flaps—Liberation Army style)	unit		4.00–6.80 and up
Rent, urban apartment, 23 sq. m. (utilities excluded)	month		1.50–5.45[e]
Rent as percentage of average worker's pay in Beijing		(3–5%)	(up to 15%)[f]
Fees in primary and middle schools	6 months	2.50–5.00[g]	

SOURCE: Officially reported price, "Wages and Prices in China," *China Reconstructs*, April 1974, p. 41; October 1979, p. 32; and visitors' notes. Observed price range, personal observations, and reports by travelers in China.

*Bracketed figures represent May 1979 prices. As of November 1, 1979 state retail prices of several food products increased compared to the official 1978 prices.

Product	*Percentage Price Increase*
Beef	33
Pork	33
Chicken	"appropriate adjustment"
Eggs	32
Vegetables	"appropriate adjustment"
Fish	33

Rent, charges for water and electricity, transportation fares, and tuition fees were to remain unchanged.

[a]In large (over 1 million inhabitants) and medium-sized cities.

[b]Probably reflecting to an extent differences in quality as well as the fact that hog prices are set by local authorities. Most pigs in China are raised privately, as part of commune household agricultural sideline activities.

[c]Average price on the Beijing retail market in 1972. Cf. "Wages and Prices in China," op. cit.

[d]The range possibly reflects the varying composition of the "vegetables" basket, seasonal variations, and regional differences, including the fact that vegetable prices are set locally. Most vegetables in China are produced on the private plots of commune farmers.

[e]The 5.45 yuan a month is rent for a 23 sq. m. apartment in the Chaoyang workers' residential development in Shanghai (1974), occupied by a family of five. Prybyla, "A Note on Income and Prices in China," op. cit., p. 274. Most rural (commune) households own their homes and pay no rent.

[f]The monthly expenditure of typical Shanghai families on housing and fuel in the last several years has been reported as having been about 20 percent of the family budget.

[g]The fees are normally remitted for "households in difficulties" provided such households qualify for remission under existing economic and political ("class origin") rules.

from profit to loss." Commodities (such as vacuum bottles, handbags, and cloth shoes), one report said, were being given away under all sorts of names; the giveaways came to 50–60 yuan or more per person at year's end, and enterprises were competing with one another, to see who would give the higher bonus. "If each staff member and worker gets a bonus of 20–30 yuan, the total cost would be more than 1 billion yuan, a frightening figure. . . . We must shout at the top of our voices to tell units wantonously giving away cash bonuses and real objects to stop!"[27] Second, compared with the "Liuist" period, differentiated bonuses were not, as a rule, paid directly to individuals but to enterprise workshops and work teams.They were awarded for the fullfillment of norms set by the state plan—for example, the norms for volume of output, consumption of raw and semi-finished materials, quality, and so on. These awards were made monthly by the enterprise management. Every workshop then held an "appraisal session" (attended by the Party branch secretary and his deputy, the workshop director and his deputy, the workshop statistician, and team leaders) at which workers in each team were reviewed. Every member of a team that had fulfilled its state norms and had been awarded a bonus received an equal bonus provided he had fulfilled his norm for, say, attendance.

The system was severely criticized for its excessive simplicity and egalitarianism. Basically the problem seems to have been this: given the low absolute level of basic wages, enterprise managements tended to view bonuses as a simple wage supplement to be distributed evenly among all workers and employees (a procedure that had the additional merit of protecting the enterprise managements from possible future accusations of right-deviationism, elitism, and revisionism). By paying equal amounts to workers who were more productive, who did nothing

[27]*Renmin Ribao*, January 25, 1979, in *FBIS*, January 26, 1979.

TABLE 16 **Retail Prices of Selected "Everyday Necessities," 1974–76**

Commodity	*Price Range*[a] *(yuan)*
Charcoal (100 kg)	2.20–5.00
Coal (100 kg)	2.40–4.20
Kerosene (0.5 kg)	0.30–0.40
Soap (bar)	0.20–0.90
Cooking pot	1.00–5.00
Frying pan	1.50–2.00
Haircut (men, including shampoo)	0.25–0.50
Light bulb (25 watt)	0.38
Pencil	0.04–0.08
Movies (1 ticket)	0.10–0.25
Cigarettes (Chinese) (20)	0.27–0.54
Political comic book	0.01
People's Daily	0.05
Canvas shoes (plastic soles): men's	4.00–5.50
women's	3.00
Polyester shirt (men) simple	4.30

SOURCE: Personal observations and reports by travelers in China.
[a]Part of the price differences for any given commodity may be due to quality and regional factors.

extra, or who quite simply did not turn up for work, the intended incentive effect of bonuses was, of course, lost. "The way bonuses were issued at the end of the year by our enterprise units was like 'giving everybody a free meal.' " Enterprise managements simply added a certain percentage to everyone's basic (tariff) wage and called it a bonus. "Even those units the management of which was a mess and which not only failed to turn in profits to the state but made financial losses, also issued bonuses to their workers. Egalitarianism was practised as a general rule in distributing bonuses by enterprise units." [28] In some localities and units "lavish" cash prizes and materials were given away in the name of issuing year-end awards. "Tremendous sums of money" were allegedly spent in this way without much result. The procedure caused "financial strain on the state and affected the market" (i.e., fueled suppressed inflation).

In addition to the charm of simplicity, concern with the low absolute wage level, and insurance against future political risks, the managements' propensity to treat bonuses as equally shared wage supplements

[28]*Renmin Ribao* reprint of article from *Caimao Zhanxian Bao* on the bonus system, May 18, 1979, in *FBIS*, May 21, 1979.

TABLE 17 **Retail Prices of Selected "Secondary" Goods and Equivalent in Industrial Working Hours, 1974—76**

Commodity	Price Range[a] (yuan)	For Purchase by an Industrial Production Worker with average pay (55 yuan per month)	minimum pay (35 yuan per month)
		required working hours[b]	
Bicycle	120.00–170.00	436–618	686–971
Foot-powered sewing machine	200.00	727	1,143
Television set (black & white, ca. 9″ screen)	300.00	1,091	1,714
Radio set (upright)	80.00–120.00	291–436	457–686
Transistor radio	30.00–106.00	109–385	171–606
Thermos bottle (large)	7.00	25	40
Clock	10.00–20.00	36–73	57–114
Camera	20.00–450.00	73–1,636	114–2,571
Bed (double)	70.00–190.00	255–691	400–1,086
Mattress (double)	40.00–45.00	145–164	229–257
Wrist watch (without band)	20.00–918.00[c]	73–3,338	114–5,246
Fur hat (good fur, with flaps)	120.00–200.00	436–727	686–1,143
Leather shoes—men's (good quality)	25.00–30.00	91–109	143–171
Full-length winter coat (ladies')	153.00	556	874
Woolen trousers (men's)	23.00–27.00	84–98	131–154
Trousers (men's, light fabric, for summer wear)	7.00–13.00	25–47	40–74

SOURCE: Personal observations and reports by travelers in China.

[a]Note that part of the price differences for any given commodity may be due to quality and regional factors.

[b]Assuming a month of 25 working days, each day consisting of 8 working hours, i.e., a total working month of 200 hours. To the nearest hour.

[c]918 yuan = price of a Rolex.

was also caused by the inadequacies of the price system. "When the price is reasonable, in other words when it accords with the law of value created by extra work, the bonus can be explicitly determined according to the approximate extra profit. This being the case, the taking of a certain portion of extra profit and using it as bonuses should be simple and feasible. However, there are many questions about price, the gradual solution of which will take a fairly long time." [29] As we saw earlier, enterprise incentive funds are of little use if the profits from which they are formed are based on defective (non scarcity) prices. Additionally there was need to reexamine the work norms set by the plan for individual workers, teams, and workshops. Some of these apparently were so low that "extra work" meant nothing. There was need to "strengthen the management of fixed work quotas so as to reflect fairly correctly the extra work done by the workers." Above all, "we should lead the masses to understand that the idea of egalitarianism is backward, reactionary, and harmful." [30] Egalitarianism was a favorite idea of the Maoist creed.

On the other hand there are voices from the wings warning of the dire consequences that await those who harbor the idea of the "omnipotence of bonuses": the error of some leading comrades who once considered bonus "revisionist stuff" but now grasp the mistaken idea of "more bonus, more work; less bonus, less work; no bonus, no work." [31]

Social Wage. As was mentioned earlier (Figure 2), the social wage has two main components: labor insurance/welfare benefits and privileges (fringe benefits). The dividing line is not always well defined.

The first component of the social wage (which we may call the social wage proper) includes retirement, accident, disability, and maternity benefits, and child care, education, and medical coverage. (The last two items are discussed in Chapter 9.) As a general principle the social wage is not paid according to labor contribution but on the basis of need as perceived by the authorities. The psychological impact of the social wage on people who traditionally had been neglected by society tends to be more important than the monetary value of the benefits. In the 1950s labor protection, medical insurance, and educational services represented about 15 percent of the aggregate wages fund. In 1978 state expenditures on labor insurance and other social benefits came to 10 percent of the total wages bill. In 1957, of the 40 million nonagricultural workers, only 11.5 million were covered by labor insurance and 6.6 million by free medical care.

The social wage benefits primarily workers employed in modern state sector industry. Except for medical care, workers in neighborhood industries are not covered. To what extent the coverage applies to work-

[29] Ibid.
[30] Ibid.
[31] *Beijing Review*, April 20, 1979, p. 5.

ers in commerce and in the service trades is not certain. Workers in modern industry, especially those employed by centrally or provincially/municipally managed enterprises, get the "best break." The best break means retirement at 60 for men and 55 for women at 70 percent of the formerly earned wage, calculated on the number of years worked (miners can retire at 55); free medical care or at a nominal registration fee (0.10 yuan per visit to a clinic in Shanghai); 56 days' maternity leave; full pay during two months of certified illness; full pay during periods of disability caused by job-related injury; free physical checkups once a year; and (at least on paper) strict application by management of the rules of occupational safety.

My impression was that occupational safety was a serious problem, an impression amply borne out by articles published in the Chinese press after 1976. During my visits to a number of large modern and small local plants, I noticed that there was an almost universal lack of safety glasses and other elementary protective equipment. The problem got worse as one moved from the modern sector to school and commune-type industrial workshops. "During the period of construction many factories, mines, and other enterprises paid attention only to production and rarely considered safety or facilities to prevent dust and noxious substances." The problem now is "serious" and "the infection rate is high." In Qingdao Municipality, for example, of more than 400 newly built, expanded, and rebuilt production and construction projects in 1975–1977, only 12 percent met the criteria for public health required for the designing of industrial enterprises. In addition there were more than 900 other projects that were either not approved or secretly built, and almost all of them lacked safety features and dust and noxious substance prevention facilities. [32]

Education, while not free, is heavily subsidized. In Nanjing household expenditure per child per semester is 5 yuan for middle school and 3 yuan for grade school. Books and stationery are extra and cost roughly 2 yuan per child per semester. The education of a child in Shanghai costs about 6 yuan per semester including books and stationery. Nurseries and kindergartens are available, especially in the larger industrial plants. It appears to be a fairly widespread practice to board young children (even as young as eighteen months' old) during the week and pick them up on weekends, but the tradition of babysitting grandmothers remains more common. In the Chaoyang workers' residential development in

[32]Beijing Radio, May 20, 1979, in *FBIS*, May 23, 1979. Also Beijing Radio, May 23, 1979, in *FBIS*, May 25, 1979 ("Strengthen Labor Protection and Improve Safety in Production").

Shanghai the cost of keeping a child in nursery school is 2 yuan a month (including meals), the state contributing another 7 yuan. University education (if one can get in) is free. Students receive stipends that are comparable to the wage of an apprentice in modern industry (less than 30 yuan a month), or free board plus a modest monthly allowance.

The second component of the social wage consists of fringe benefits of all kinds. In China's current perspective, fringe benefits may be divided into legitimate communal consumption items and reprehensible, but still quite common, advantages flowing from one's location on the power pyramid. To argue that some people in the leadership press for the elimination of power-based incomes is correct. To claim that such incomes do not exist, or that they are not actively (if discreetly) sought by many officeholders, or that they are viewed as illegitimate by all members of the Party and state bureaucracies would be quite erroneous.

Legitimate communal consumption items include factory mess halls where meals can be had at reasonable prices, dormitories for single workers, shared recreational facilities, local transportation subsidies, allowances for haircuts and extra nutrition when working under comparatively difficult conditions, and overtime and extra night-shift pay. Many of these had been reduced or suspended (e.g., overtime pay) during the Cultural Revolution. I was told that the monthly cost of three meals a day in the canteen of the Shanghai Machine Tools Plant was 13 yuan (1974). At the Nanjing Petrochemical Plant the cost of bedding down in a room 18 square meters in area, five workers to a room, was 0.15 yuan a month. Subsidized housing in general may be considered as part of a wage earner's social income. As shown in Table 15, rents and utility rates are generally moderate compared with earnings. In Nanjing (1974) the rent of an apartment 16 square meters in area was typically 5 yuan per month, electricity included. Living space is limited and most apartments are overcrowded. The rent for 23 square meters of space may be shared by as many as six people at least two of whom work full time and two others receive some kind of pension. The most common procedure is to consolidate all the family members' separate earnings into a single household budget.

Power advantages persist even though they are routinely decried and occasionally tracked down. The Cultural Revolution made the exercise of power more precarious and the enjoyment of the attendant benefits more perilous than ever, but it did not eliminate the advantages of power. In fact, it was later alleged, the asceticism preached by the radicals was a sham, and abuse of monoparty privilege was more blatant and widespread than ever before. The wife of the late Chairman and one of the leaders of the radical faction, Jiang Qing, was, it turns out, all along "a parasite and a vampire." She and her three friends, Yao Wenuyan, Wang Hongwen, and Zhang Chungqiao, did nothing to stop such apparently widespread phenomena in the new China as "wild ambitions . . . speculation and commercial machinations . . . beating, smashing, and looting . . . embezzling of public property and violation of social law and order." On the contrary, it is charged, they took to all this "like flies taking to filth." [33] Wang Hongwen, who was personally elevated by Mao to a high station, "embezzled and stole like mad," and "led a decadent life" on the proceeds. [34] Mao's wife "indulged herself all the time in gluttony and pleasure-seeking and in doing mischief." [35] But these violations of socialist morality were not limited to the top brass.They were, and apparently continue to be, a common feature of Party life. "Some cadres now pursue special privileges and sinister trends and utter lies and empty words. Problems of laziness, slackness, and softness exist in some leadership groups.The masses are very discontented with this situation." [36] Addressing a Beijing rally attended by several thousand unhappy people in Tiananmen Square, a worker drew applause when he said: "We had wiped out capitalists, landowners, and rich peasants, but now we have a new rich class. . . . There are bureaucrats who can eat what they want, go where they want, take their children abroad while many people's stomachs are empty. . . . At least in the time of feudalism if you had a complaint you could go to the magistrate's office and they would listen. Now, if you call a Communist office on the phone, the answer always is 'He's not there, or he's busy'." [37]

Despite admonitions that power is delegated to officials by the masses and is exercised on behalf of the people, the lowest grade cadre has an enormous edge over any single member of the citizenry. Acknowledging the existence of special privileges is not denying the effort made during Mao's lifetime to humble certain power-holders, repeatedly and without warning, in order to integrate them with the masses. Nevertheless, upper-echelon cadres are not only clad in finer fabric, but they are also provided with better residences, vacation resorts, chauffeured

[33] *Guangming Ribao* (Beijing), January 26, 1977, in *Survey of People's Republic of China Press (SPRCP),* No. 6298, March 14, 1977, p. 13; and *Renmin Ribao,* February 17, 1977, in *SPRCP,* No. 6313, April 4, 1977, p. 8.

[34] *Peking Review,* May 6, 1977, pp. 37–38.

[35] *Guangming Ribao,* March 26, 1977, in *SPRCP,* No. 6318, April 13, 1977, p. 51.

[36] Hefei, Provincial Broadcasting Station, Anhui, May 21, 1979, in *FBIS,* May 23, 1979.

[37] *New York Times,* September 14, 1979, p. A3.

limousines, air transportation, and reserved "soft-seat" places in railway coaches. Post-Cultural Revolution campaigns against cadres' children entering the universities "through the backdoor" and evading downward transfer to the countryside point to the continued presence of influence-peddling in both high and low places. Like the enterprise quest for self-sufficiency through vertical integration this, too, is a built-in systemic problem that reemerges as soon as it is suppressed.

COMPETITION The push to replace competitive individual incentives and disincentives (e.g., the threat of being fired from one's job for not performing well) by cooperative group incentives has raised the problem of the role of competition in promoting worker productivity and enterprise efficiency. In almost all socialist systems (Yugoslavia being a possible exception) workers are assured lifelong employment and state enterprises, like old soldiers elsewhere, they never die, they are simply bailed out. Stalin's Stakhanovite movements of the thirties and forties and the wave upon wave of centrally inspired socialist emulation campaigns in which enterprise *x* challenges enterprise *y*, were meant to fill the incentive gap left by guaranteed employment and firm longevity. (The problem is not improved by the arrangement whereby socialist producing enterprises produce, say, shoes or special steels, but do not have to sell them.) With regard to enterprise performance the result has been a "stagnant situation." "They said that a very important reason for the 'stagnant situation' in some enterprise management ranks was that there were no rivals." "The emperor's daughter," they said, "is not worried about getting married." [38] With respect to individual workers the problem is known as the "iron rice bowl," or "eating from the common pot." [39] "In China enterprises which operate below capacity or have to stop production for the time being, do not sack workers [as in capitalist countries under 'free competition' do].They always work out plans to restore and develop production under the guidance of the state plan." [40] The arrangement, while cosy, has its drawbacks. In Kaifeng, Henan Province, for example, of 400 large factories, 110 were at one point operating below capacity or had ceased operations altogether, while keeping everyone on the payroll. "Unbreakable rice bowls exist because there is a common pot.This practice is very harmful. . . . We

[38] *Renmin Ribao,* May 19, 1979 (based on a *Jiefangjun Bao* report), in *FBIS*, May 21, 1979.

[39] In presocialist society, it is said, "breaking the rice bowl" meant that a person was dismissed from his post.

[40] *Beijing Review,* May 25, 1979, p. 9.

must break the unbreakable rice bowls. The first thing we must do is to get rid of the common pot."[41] Easier said than done. In Hungary much of the ambitious modernization reform aimed at raising enterprise efficiency and worker competition by breaking the goulash bowl was undone by worker and management resistance and threats of defenestrating Party officials who would dare remove the common pot. Welfare state arrangements, like collectively bargained wages, are not downwardly flexible.

MORAL INCENTIVES AND DISINCENTIVES Moral incentives are psychic rewards. They make their appeal to professional pride, sense of responsibility, empathy, and the cooperative spirit. According to Mao, moral incentives are superior to material ones. More important, moral incentives directed at an emerging, or (in Marxist terms) reemerging, collective consciousness are more desirable than those that address themselves to a person's self-esteem. Noncompetitive moral group incentives are in this view the best of all, the nearest thing to the final communist goal of an all-embracing endogenous labor enthusiasm.

Individual competitive moral incentives include nonpecuniary honors accruing to a worker or employee, such things as the mention of this name on the plant's honor role, a certificate of appreciation, or a medal. Such rewards do, of course, merge with material incentives; for example, sending model workers to regional conferences or even to Beijing to shake hands with Chairman Hua, or whoever may be in charge at the time.

Group competitive moral incentives usually take the form of emulation drives in which factories, departments, shifts, or groups within the plant vie with one another in the fulfillment and overfulfillment of assigned tasks. I have seen charts and tables on factory walls in Suzhou and elsewhere advertising the performance of the plants' various production groups, each group's accomplishments identified by variously colored flags and by a number of red stars.

The stress since the Cultural Revolution and until Mao's death had been on expanding the scope and deepening the impact of cooperative moral incentives, especially collective ones. Individuals and groups were urged to help one another not only in production but in improving attitudes toward labor. Indeed, some statements in the press conveyed the impression that achieving the correct proletarian-revolutionary work style was more important than raising the volume of output. After

[41] *Jilin Ribao* article, Jilin Provincial Broadcasting Station, Changchun, May 19, 1979, in *FBIS*, May 22, 1979.

October 1976 this attitude was criticized as a deviation from the line, an error peddled by the gang of four: the noxious "fetish of consciousness."

A great deal of time and effort is expended in China on rectifying individual and group conduct, on forcing thought and action into those grooves defined by the Party as correct, socialist, and revolutionary. The transformation of man from an individual to a collective being through massive behavioral engineering and psychological management had, by and large, taken precedence over statistically measurable growth of output. Socialist cooperation in raising production and bringing about attitudinal change is reinforced by mass participation in mass movements, meetings, and other forms of collective interaction. The purpose is to promote group solidarity and to combat individual alienation. Whether the relentless pressure put on individuals to take part in endless group events (many of which are highly orchestrated, convoluted, and ritualized) will over the longer run curtail or augment alienation remains an open question. Signs of combat fatigue in the ranks of the masses have been apparent all along. They came into the open on several occasions: in 1957, for example, and again twenty years later.

The Maoist blueprint for a new society, including Mao's vision of China's future economic system, hinges on the emergence of the new socialist man, the most important of all the "socialist newborn things" (which have been severely put to the test in the post-Mao era). Without that selfless, collectivized person, wholly dedicated to the service of the people, ignoring the sugar-coated bullets of material reward and nonmaterial privilege, firm and resolute in proletarian class stand, the Maoist model has no chance. In this perspective the new man is necessary because, dissolved in the mass, he controls himself by an internalized ethic of work, is satisfied with a job well done for the community, and does not expect to be rewarded or differentiated by material recompense that would set him apart from others. All this eliminates the need for supervisory bureaucracies that are the bane of socialist systems, obviates the danger of new elites rising on the ashes of the old, and makes capital accumulation a cinch, because without compulsion (taxes, high prices, low wages) consumption is reduced and productivity is increased. The invisible hand of the market, which in the classical economic schema promotes social harmony through the pleasure-maximizing behavior of freely competing individual economic men, is replaced by the invisible hand of collective consciousness, the dissolution of the individual and his complete socialization. In the new socialist man's absence, Mao's vision runs the risk of turning into bureaucratic state capitalism *à la russe,* with quaint local colorations and Chinese cultural infusions. It may conceivably—to the horror of the left purists—go beyond and cross the discreet frontier between administrative command and Yugoslav-type market socialism.

So far, despite some progress in putting together this robot (a good deal of it stemming from private fear), the process of creation has not much advanced. The new socialist man may be as much an abstraction as the economic man of nineteenth-century English classical economics. Under Deng Xiaoping, the somewhat more reluctant Hua Guofeng, and people like them, the probability that the new socialist man would survive early infancy was not good. In the post-Mao years statements urging the masses to emulate individual heroes like the "iron man" of Daqing were made primarily in the name of increased production, that is, for a specific (neo-Stakhanovite) economic purpose rather than on general principles of socialist consciousness. Symptomatically, some of the former heroes of consciousness, like the model peasant of Dazhai, Chen Yongqui, quickly fell into disfavor with the new forces-of-production-oriented policymakers. The spirit of self-denial (meaning low personal consumption) and hard work exhibited by the resurrected models was seen, in the context of the post-Mao modernization drive, as a necessary if temporary means of capital accumulation at high rates, rather than as character-forming in its own right.

The hero Lei Feng, brought to life for the third or fourth time, was offered in the late 1970s to all young people as an example of discipline and submission to orders of the duly constituted Party authorities. By means of a subtle shift of emphasis—which became less subtle as the years went by—the image of the new Chinese socialist man began to resemble the composite picture of a model Soviet worker in Stalin's days. The four gangsters, it was argued in a dialectical switch, regarded the broad masses as "lambs" and "muddle-headed fools with no political consciousness." [42]

Relative and Absolute Size of Industry

Industrialization has progressed substantially if erratically since the communist takeover in 1949. The absence of official statistical series makes it difficult to quantify this progress. The data given below are for the most part Western estimates based on scattered and incomplete Chinese statistical pronouncements. As the decade of the seventies came to a close there were signs that the long-standing reluctance of the

[42] *Guangming Ribao,* March 6, 1977, in *SPRCP,* No. 6299, March 15, 1977, p. 39.

Chinese authorities to release meaningful data concerning the industrialization effort would not be as obsessive in the future as it had been in the past. For one thing, foreigners who were being asked to advance billions of dollars, yen, marks, and francs to help China's modernization were not prepared to do so merely on China's say so.They asked to see the accounts.The argument that foreign bankers, businessmen, and governments should be flattered by China's new willingness to borrow from them on a long-term basis, did not wash any more by 1980. Chinese offers to do business were accepted enthusiastically, but increasingly with hard-nosed realism and requests for reciprocity.

Industrial production is believed to have grown at an average annual rate of 11 percent between 1952 and 1978 and at 10 percent per annum on the average between 1965 and 1978. [43] The faster growing subsectors were producer goods, especially machinery. Consumer goods output grew at an average annual rate (1953–1978) of about 8 percent (or roughly 6 percent per capita). Eckstein estimated that in 1970 industrial output (including construction) accounted for just under 40 percent of China's national income (compared with about a quarter in 1956). [44] The progressive industrialization of the country is reflected in the commodity composition of China's exports. In 1952 industrial products represented 18 percent of China's total commodity exports; by 1978 this proportion had risen to roughly 50 percent. [45]

There have been important increases in the production of a number of goods, for example, crude oil, chemical fertilizer, and finished steel. Crude oil output was about 400,000 metric tons in 1952 and about 1.5 million tons at the end of the First Five-Year Plan in 1957.The 1979 output was 106 million tons. Chemical fertilizer output (standard weight) was estimated at almost 60 million metric tons in 1979 compared to 194,000 tons in 1952. Crude steel production was over 34 million tons in 1979; it had been 1.4 million tons in 1952; the figures for finished steel were 24 million tons in 1979 and 1 million tons in 1952. Although coal production has risen significantly over the years (coal is China's primary energy source) from 66.5 million metric tons in 1952 to 635 million tons in 1979, the growth rate has been erratic, reflecting political pulls and pressures on the industry, and the technical level of mining and pro-

[43]Industrial output in Taiwan from 1952 through 1978 grew at an average annual rate of 16 percent.

[44]Alexander Eckstein, "Economic Growth and Change in China: A Twenty-Year Perspective," *China Quarterly,* No. 54, April–June 1973, p. 236.

[45]Industrial goods constituted 8 percent of Taiwan's commodity exports in 1952 and about 88 percent in 1978.

cessing operations remains low. Electric power output rose from 7.26 billion kilowatt hours in 1952 to 282 billion kilowatt hours in 1979. Despite what is numerically an impressive performance in all these fields, coal, electricity, and steel (together with transportation, as we shall see later) constitute bottlenecks in the economy, and production methods remain comparatively backward and wasteful.The problem, as we have noted, is technical not only in an engineering sense of the term. At issue also are techniques of enterprise management and of macro planning. A solution to the first problem (upgrading of enterprise management) can, indeed, help tap the "hidden potential" of existing firms, lower production costs, raise labor and capital productivity, and cut down on what the Chinese themselves recognize is an irrational, wasteful employment of natural resources. But such a solution is at best a paliative. Its longer range success is contingent, among other things, on installing a fairly reliable mechanism for measuring opportunity costs so that financial outcomes are roughly indicative of the degree of enterprise efficiency.This is as much as to say that the economy's macro planning must be concurrently restructured, an undertaking fraught with far-reaching systemic implications and one on which other reforms of administrative command systems have foundered.There exists, to be sure, an enormous store of accumulated theoretical modeling and practical experience in this field, but the final solution remains politically delicate and elusive. How far down the road of systemic departures from Mao's and Stalin's prescriptions the new Chinese leadership is willing and, more important, able to go remains at this stage uncertain. In the more relaxed political climate of the immediate post-Mao era, the talk had been bold and ideas on reform outran the practical possibilities of their implementation.There are bound to be disappointments and reverses in China's projected experimentation whether the path of development is more or less authoritarian. At the very least, the will to give it a try was there at the turn of the seventies and, unlike what had earlier happened in Eastern Europe, the Chinese had no compelling need to look over their shoulders to gauge the reaction of their Soviet neighbor to what they proposed to do with their system.

Despite the stress on light industry since the early 1960s, progress in the production of some basic consumer items such as cotton cloth has been fairly sluggish.Western estimates suggest that the output of cotton cloth between 1952 and 1978 had just about tripled, while population increased by a little more than two-thirds. Per capita consumption of cotton cloth rose from 6.7 linear meters in 1972 to an estimated 10 meters in 1978, not an overly generous allotment.There have been, however, impressive gains in the output of some secondary consumer goods such as bicycles (annual output in 1979 of about 10 million units compared with 80,000 in 1952) and sewing machines. Part of the annual output of these commodities is exported.

SUGGESTED READING

Bernardo, Robert M., *Popular Management and Pay in China* (Quezon City: University of the Philippines Press, 1977).

Chao, Kang, *Capital Formation in Mainland China, 1952–1956* (Berkeley: University of California Press, 1974).

Chen, Nai-Ruenn, "Industrial Development in Mainland China," *Asian Affairs—An American Review* (New York), Vol. II, No. 5, May–June 1975, pp. 276–94.

China: Science Walks on Two Legs: A Report on Science for the People (New York: Avon Books, 1974).

"China's Price Policy," *China Reconstructs* (Beijing), January 1980, pp. 21–23.

Dean, Genevieve C., (ed.), *Science and Technology in the Development of Modern China: An Annotated Bibliography* (London: Mansell, 1974).

Emerson, John P., *Administrative and Technical Manpower in the People's Republic of China* (Washington, D.C.: U.S. Department of Commerce, International Population Reports Series, No. 72, 1973), p. 95.

Fleron, Frederic (ed.,), *Technology and Communist Culture: The Socio-Cultural Impact of Technology Under Socialism* (New York: Praeger, 1977).

Gelber, H. A., "Economics and Technology in China after Mao," *Asian Survey* (Berkeley), Vol. XVIII, No. 9, September 1978, pp. 439–53.

Goodstadt, L., "China's Wage Crisis," *Insight* (Hong Kong), July 1978, pp. 23–28.

Hoffman, Charles, *Work Incentives and Policies in the People's Republic of China, 1953–1965* (Albany: State University of New York Press, 1967).

———, *The Chinese Worker* (Albany: State University of New York Press, 1974).

Howe, Christopher, *Wage Patterns and Wage Policy in Modern China, 1919–1972* (Cambridge: Cambridge Studies in Chinese History, Literature and Institutions, 1973).

———, "Wages, Prices and the Standard of Living of Urban Workers in the PRC," *China Business Review* (Washington, D.C.), Vol. V, No. 4, 1978, pp. 4–16.

Ishikawa, S., "The Chinese Method of Technological Development," *Developing Economics* (Tokyo), Vol. XIII, No. 4, December 1975, pp. 430–58.

"Labor Insurance and Benefits to the Workers," *China Reconstructs* (Beijing), Vol. XXIII, No. 5, May 1974, p. 35.

"National Conference on Learning from Tachai in Industry," Various reports: *Peking Review* (Beijing), Vol. 20, No. 18, April 29, 1977, pp. 3–6, 15–20.

Nickum, James E., and David C. Schack, "Living Standards and Economic Development in Shanghai and Taiwan," *China Quarterly* (London), No. 77, March 1979, pp. 25–49.

Prybyla, Jan S., "Work Incentives in the People's Republic of China," *Weltwirtschaftliches Archiv* [Review of World Economics] (Kiel), Vol. CXII, No. 4, 1976, pp. 767–91.

"Regulating Role of the Market," *Beijing Review* (Beijing, Vol. XXIII, No. 10, March 10, 1980, pp. 5–6.

Richman, Barry M., *Industrial Society in Communist China* (New York: Vintage Books, 1969).

———, "Maoism and Motivation: Work Incentives in China," *Bulletin of Concerned Asian Scholars* (San Francisco), Vol. V, No. 1, 1973, pp. 10–24.

Riskin, Carl, "Incentive Systems and Work Motivations," *Working Papers for a New Society* (New York), Vol. I, No. 4, 1974, pp. 27–31, 77–89.

———, "Workers' Incentives in Chinese Industry," in *China: A Reassessment,* pp. 199–224.

———, "China's Rural Industries: Self-Reliant Systems or Independent Kingdoms?" *China Quarterly,* No. 73, March 1978, pp. 77–98.

Schran, Peter, "Unity and Diversity of Russian and Chinese Industrial Wage Policies," *Journal of Asian Studies* (Ann Arbor), Vol. XXIII, No. 2, February 1964, pp. 245–51.

———, "Institutional Continuity and Motivational Change: The Chinese Industrial Wages System, 1950–1973," *Asian Survey* (Berkeley), Vol. XIV, No. 11, November 1974, pp. 1014–32.

Science and Technology in China. Two Reports: (1) Annotated Bibliography on Science and Technology in China. (2) Science and Technology in the People's Republic of China, Background Study No. 2 (Washington, D.C.: Subcommittee on Domestic and International

Scientific Planning and Analysis of the Committee on Science and Technology, U.S. House of Representatives, U.S. Government Printing Office, September and November 1976).

"Should There Be Competition in a Socialist Economy?" *Beijing Review,* June 2, 1980, pp. 19–22.

"Wages and Prices in China," *China Reconstructs* (Beijing), Vol. XXIII, No. 4, April 1974, pp. 40–41.

Wheelwright. E. L., and Bruce McFarlane, *The Chinese Road to Socialism: Economics of the Cultural Revolution* (New York: Monthly Review Press, 1967).

SIX

Money and Banking

The monetary system is discussed in a separate chapter because, even though it is important and effective, it has not been explored in depth. Chinese officials have been reticent on the subject, an uncommunicativeness explainable in the past by ideological hostility toward money and all its works.

PROBLEMS

Monetary instability and financial mismanagement have plagued China for centuries. This affliction and the fragmentation of the economy into different monetary areas strengthened the ever-present centrifugal forces in the political sphere. In the last years of the Nationalist regime, hyper-inflation made a significant contribution to the collapse of the government and the disintegration of the economic system. [1] Although blame for galloping inflation can be put on the cumulative effects of years of foreign and civil conflict, poor judgment by Chiang's economic advisers and the ineffectiveness and corruption of the Nationalists' administrative machinery were also involved.

[1]Chou Shun-hsin, *The Chinese Inflation, 1937–1949* (New York: Columbia University Press, 1963).

Once runaway inflation was checked (by 1951–1952), the new monetary system was counted on to act as one of the agents for the implementation and control of the new regime's economic plan. The monetary system was expected to, and did in fact, perform an integrating and unifying function in China's relatively decentralized, centrally planned economy.

POLICIES

Currency

In December 1948 the communist government established the People's Bank, which had the sole right to issue the new "people's currency" or *Renminbi,* known popularly as the *yuan.* The yuan replaced the various currencies circulating in the country at that time and became the sole national legal tender. Gold and silver may be held by individuals in limited quantities in the form of jewelry but may not be sold except to the People's Bank. The Bank is also the only source of gold for industrial, medical, and other uses. The same restriction applies to trading in foreign currencies. Individuals are not permitted to take out of the country any amounts of the national currency. At the end of 1979 the exchange rate of the yuan against the U.S. dollar was roughly 1 yuan = $0.60.

Two basic principles ("cash plan") govern the issue of currency. First, the volume of issue must be closely correlated with the circulation of commodities, which in China's context means essentially consumer goods and services (plus part of the agricultural means of production). This is so because, second, the circulation of notes and coins is severely restricted; all transactions except those involving consumer goods and services and minor agricultural equipment are made through book transfers at the People's Bank. [2] (A significant part of consumer goods, especially food, is distributed in kind.) Perhaps as little as 10 percent of all transactions consist of cash (meaning currency) transfers. More than 90 percent of the currency released is used for paying wages and purchasing farm and sideline products. The velocity of circulation of the yuan (the number of times the yuan is spent per year) is said to be low. In recent years the principal reason has been workers' and others' holding

[2] "Money [meaning currency and unrestricted demand deposits]," said Dostoevski, "is coined freedom."

part of their savings in cash for eventual purchase of relatively expensive consumer durables, such as bicycles, watches, radios, and sewing machines. Currency is issued in small denominations. Before 1964 the denominations were higher, but large notes were withdrawn, presumably to prevent hoarding by corrupt cadres and to forestall any possibility of the Soviets' smuggling large amounts of high denomination notes into the country. According to most accounts, the purchasing power of the yuan has been remarkably stable over the years.

The retail price index (1952 = 100) was 109 in 1957 and 124 in 1974 (the 1974 figure is a Japanese guess). Reports from refugee sources do not, on the whole, bear out the contention of price stability. One reason, no doubt, is that the index includes only the prices of rationed commodities, which are kept at below equilibrium levels and have not been allowed to rise significantly. Prices of many nonrationed goods, however, have increased substantially over the years. Also, some goods and services can be procured only, or at least more expeditiously, by bribing the appropriate officials. This, too, represents a real if concealed price increase for the commodities and services in question, and it applies not just to consumer items but to intermediate goods and raw materials as well. Camouflaged price hikes practiced by state-operated firms and stores include tampering with the scales, the sale of inferior goods at top quality prices, keeping the price unchanged but reducing the quantity, and other manipulations. When imbalances occur between the supply of cash and the availability at state-fixed prices of consumer goods and services (plus some agricultural capital goods), the situation is typically handled in the following ways.[3]

1. Adjustments may be made in the retail prices of the individual goods and services particularly affected by the imbalance. Where sales taxes are present, the adjustment may be made by fiscal means through varying the rate and/or amount of the applicable tax. In either case the measures do not normally affect the producing enterprises, whose output and assortment plans are not supposed to be responsive to changes in the retail prices of their products, but only to the enterprises' plan expressed in physical (tons, meters, or technical coefficients) and financial (yuan) terms.

2. Adjustments may be decreed by the planning authorities in the

[3]A. Donnithorne, "China's Anti-Inflationary Policy," *Three Banks Review,* No. 103, (September 1974), pp. 3–25, and B. Richman, *Industrial Society in Communist China* (New York: Vintage Books, 1969).

volume of output of particular goods originally set for the enterprise in the state plan.

3. The imbalance may be allowed to work itself off through queues at retail outlets (such queues are a manifestation of suppressed inflation).

4. The state may elect to cope with critical goods shortages by releasing a portion of the inventories that it holds in reserve.

5. Rationing of goods in short supply can be, and has been, resorted to; the phenomenon is known in official phraseology as "planned supply" by the state.

6. "Patriotic savings campaigns" and other inducements and pressures on the population to channel their cash balances into the banking system are used.

7. Wages, particularly the higher ones, may be reduced; a measure that can always be justified in terms of equity of income distribution.

All seven ways have been used in the past to correct imbalances, but until recently methods 4 through 7 appear to have been the favorite. Today, adjustments 1 and 2 seem to be most in use. Given the need to improve the incentive mechanism, especially at the level of the experienced specialist, upper-bracket wage reductions are not likely to be used in the foreseeable future to correct inflationary cash-goods imbalances.

It is officially stated that all internal (bond) indebtedness has been eliminated. But, as we shall see, some of the nominally voluntary individual saving is in the nature of forced bond subscription extracted by means of peer-group pressure organized by grassroots branches of the People's Bank and credit cooperatives. Moreover, after the fall of the radicals some of the formerly used procedures to write off the state's indebtedness (for example, putting bond-holders in jail) were disavowed and the debts are back on the books.

The Banking System

Since the early 1950s the banking system in China has been modeled on that of the Soviet Union. The single most important financial institution is the People's Bank, which has over 10,000 major branches in all parts of the country, not counting district and enterprise offices, temporary bureaus, and service groups. The bank operates directly under the State Council, the highest governmental body in China.

In addition to the People's Bank, there are three major banking institutions: the Bank of China, which used to be subordinate to the People's Bank but in recent years was put directly under the State

Council in recognition of its importance in matters of international financing; the Agricultural Bank of China, which was abolished in 1957 when its functions were transferred to the People's Bank and the ministries of Finance, Agriculture, Forestry, and Water Conservancy, but which was resurrected in 1979 and is also directly under the State Council; and the People's Construction Bank of China. [4] The Bank of China handles foreign exchange transactions. The Agricultural Bank of China is in charge of loans to communes, state farms, and individual peasants, presumably including families in dire financial straits. It also supervises rural credit cooperatives. The intention seems to be to make this institution the financial overseer of the ambitious agricultural modernization plan extending to 1985 and beyond. The People's Construction Bank of China is charged with paying out and supervising state budgetary appropriations for investment in all sectors of the economy (except agriculture) and with the supervision of investments from enterprise funds. It also gives short-term credits to construction enterprises working under contract on capital projects. As noted earlier (Chapter 4) the Construction Bank in late 1979 began experimenting with loans for fixed capital construction to state-sector enterprises. These credits were expected eventually to replace nonreturnable state budgetary grants as the source of investment for state enterprises. In short, in 1979 the banking system was administratively and functionally restructured to support the projected modernization effort more effectively. The net result of the restructuring was a decentralization of the functions formerly exercised by the People's Bank, and a partial return to the situation as it existed between 1963 and the outbreak of the Cultural Revolution. A possible explanation for the reform of the banking system in the wake of the radicals' fall was the need for tighter anti-inflation control over the vast sums that would be involved in the four modernizations. The People's Bank found it increasingly difficult to carry out properly the many duties vested in it. Factional troubles within the bank's sprawling bureaucracy were not helpful. Unnamed agents of the gang of four "on the one hand extended more credits, and on the other wrote off debts. In this way, isn't the right of issuing money vested in the central agency nothing but empty words? What safeguards are there to guarantee the stability of the monetary situation and prices?" [5]

[4] Agence France Presse, Hong Kong, May 18, 1979, in *FBIS*, May 21, 1979.

[5] *Guangming Ribao*, January 23, 1978, in *FBIS*, February 2, 1978. "The banks must . . . curb certain leaders who indiscriminately approve loans and violate fiscal discipline." Fujian Provincial Broadcasting Station Fouzhou, May 21, 1979, in *FBIS*, May 25, 1979.

With some adjustments for the respective roles of the other two banks, the People's Bank is the main agency charged with carrying out the planners' cash balance and credit balance.The "credit balance" is the precept that flows from the credit plan; it means balance between state bank loans and the funds earmarked in the economic plan for such loans. Borrowing, lending, sales on credit, and advance payments by enterprises on their own initiative are not permitted.The two functions (cash and credit) can be broken down into the following specific tasks of the bank: currency issuing; holding accounts of state administrative departments; holding accounts of state enterprises and collectives (i.e., in this regard the bank performs the rough equivalent of commercial bank functions in other systems); holding savings accounts of individuals; issuance of short- and medium-term credit to state industrial enterprises and collectives (together with the Agricultural and Construction Banks); issuance of financial regulations governing commercial transactions in conformity with the economic plan; and management consulting. Foreign exchange transactions are handled by the Bank of China under direct supervision of the State Council.

HOLDING ACCOUNTS OF STATE DEPARTMENTS The People's Bank keeps the accounts of all state organs and public institutions (including PLA units) at all levels of the state administration. Financial transactions among government departments have to be made exclusively by bank book transfers. Government revenue accounts at the bank receive income from the agricultural, industrial, sales, and social security taxes and from profits remitted by state industrial and other enterprises. (At the present time, these profits reportedly constitute 50 percent of state budgetary revenues, compared with 34 percent in the early post-1949 years.) [6] The bank is not responsible for the actual collection of taxes, a function that devolves on administrative organs. Credit balances of state organs and public institutions do not earn interest.

HOLDING ACCOUNTS OF ENTERPRISES State budgetary allocations of capital to state sector enterprises are made through entries in the state expenditure accounts at the bank (at the Agricultural Bank for state farms).The bank is responsible for seeing that all revenues and expenditures are made in strict conformity with the state's financial plan.The bank, therefore, performs a control and audit function vis-à-vis the state

[6] In 1979 profits remitted by enterprises constituted 45 percent of total state budgetary revenues and the agricultural tax, 3.7 percent.

administration. It should be noted that state departments at every level must remit all their cash holdings above a certain plateau (reportedly above three days' normal expenditure) to the bank. The state machine is regulated in the superstructure by the Party line and in the base by the yuan.

Every other enterprise (collective, rural people's commune) has an account in the People's Bank.[7] All receipts and payments are handled through the bank accounts and no cash transactions among enterprises, collectives, etc., are permitted. All enterprise funds above a certain modest amount (essentially petty cash) have to be deposited regularly in the enterprise's account with the bank. All enterprise profits are transmitted to state revenue accounts from the enterprise accounts at regular intervals. People's communes and their subdivisions are not required to transmit their profits to the state.

On pay days an enterprise will withdraw from its account cash to the amount of the wages and salaries fund stipulated in the enterprise's plan. Similarly, a production team will withdraw such cash as it needs for the payment of a part of the work points earned by its members during the year or half year. Credit balances of enterprises carry interest at the rate of 0.15 percent per month or 1.8 percent a year. [8] This income is not subject to tax. No enterprise is allowed to overdraw its account. Transactions are scrutinized by the bank, and no book transfers are made unless they are in conformity with the revenues and expenditures laid down in the enterprise's plan. The bank, in other words, together with the Agricultural and the Construction banks, is a nationwide clearinghouse for economic transactions and a control agent in the matter of plan execution.

In practice, every transaction of every enterprise cannot be audited. The bank's control over enterprise accounts tends to focus on fairly aggregated major components of firm financial transactions. The most troublesome problem has apparently been the propensity of enterprises to use investment funds for working capital and vice versa. In the wake of the Cultural Revolution and its antiexpert, antibureaucrat bias, the work of the bank—especially its control activities—was for a while revolutionized, which meant that departures from stringent financial codes not only were overlooked by the "hidden agents of the gang of

[7]Under the reorganized system, commune accounts are likely to be held at the Agricultural Bank.

[8]P. H. Cassou, "The Chinese Monetary System," *China Quarterly*, No. 59, July–September 1974, p. 560. These rates vary over time.

four'' in the bank, but were in fact encouraged in the name of revolutionary redness—false revolutionary redness, one is told now. ''They use the viewpoint of classes and class struggle to criticize the counter-revolutionary revisionist line of 'putting business in command,' controlling money but not ideology, controlling money without distinction of classes. They take the bank as the battleground for class struggle and stand guard for the consolidation of the proletarian dictatorship.''[9]

HOLDING SAVINGS ACCOUNTS OF INDIVIDUALS Individuals in China do not have the right to own checking accounts; neither can individuals obtain loans from the bank. A possible exception to the rule barring private persons from access to credit facilities would be in the case of peasant families in natural disaster areas or loans to individuals for unusually high medical expenses. Such emergency loans are usually given by rural credit cooperatives (since 1979 under the Agricultural Bank) or urban mutual-aid savings associations, supervised by the bank. [10] Before 1949 Chinese peasants borrowed heavily for weddings, funerals, and food during bad harvest years. At the present time seasonal financial difficulties that beset households have to be resolved primarily with the aid of the household's subsidiary production on its private plot.

On the other hand, individuals can, indeed are encouraged to, open personal savings accounts with the People's Bank. Encouragement takes various forms. There is, first of all, a good deal of pressure put on private persons to deposit their savings with the bank. [11] In the absence of consumer credit facilities, individuals find it necessary to save money for the future purchase of relatively expensive consumer durables. As in Japan, personal savings are regarded as evidence of frugal and whole-

[9] ''Financial and Monetary Affairs,'' *Peking Review,* No. 50, December 15, 1972, pp. 16–17.

[10] The credit cooperatives in rural areas act as agents for the bank both in channeling bank loans and collecting deposits. At the commune level the cooperatives are also known as commune financial departments. At the production brigade level they are sometimes referred to as credit stations. Their history has shown wide fluctuations. Introduced in 1951 they disappeared in 1958, reemerged in 1961, were suppressed during the Cultural Revolution, and have reappeared since.

[11] The workers of the People's Bank service group at Fushun ''have launched among the vast masses of residents five-economizing and one-saving activities—economizing on grain, economizing on coal, economizing on water, economizing on electricity, controlling childbirth, and saving money for revolution.'' ''Carry Out the Great Principle of 'Developing the Economy and Ensuring Supplies,' ''*Hongqi,* No. 2, 1971, in *Chinese Economic Studies,* Vol. VI, No. 2, Winter 1972–73, p. 35. These same workers ''would frequently go to the homes where both husband and wife work, to handle deposits and withdrawals.''

some living. The bank has opened numerous cash counters, including many at places where people work, to facilitate deposits. It pays interest on individual savings deposits: 0.45 percent a month or 5.4 percent a year for one-year deposits (up to 6.84 percent a year for five years) and 0.24 percent per month or 2.88 percent a year for current deposits. The interest income is tax free; rates vary over time. Savings deposits are transferrable to heirs.

Withdrawals of any amount are said to be on demand of the depositor, and it is asserted that no obstacles are put in the way of withdrawals. Group pressure and "heart-to-heart chats" however, have frequently been used to prevent the withdrawal of personal savings for what were officially considered to be "trivial," bourgeois-influenced purposes. "One day an old woman happily came to the [People's Bank] service group to make a withdrawal. While collecting her money she murmured: 'My son is taking a wife. The wedding must be well prepared.' The comrades of the service group took the view that extravagance was a way of bourgeois thinking, so they warmly told her about the great significance of industry and frugality. Three days later, this old woman happily redeposited over half the money she had withdrawn saying: 'My neighbors, my son, and my daughter-in-law—all of them like your idea.' "[12]

The total amount of private savings deposits in 1957 was 2.74 billion yuan, rising to 7 billion yuan in 1958. Although the 1958 figure has to be taken with care, the breakdown is of interest as indicating the very wide gap which, at that time, still existed between urban and rural living standards. The urban population contributed 4 billion yuan, while the total savings of peasants (80 percent of the population) came to only 3 billion yuan. In February 1980 it was reported that there were then 100 million depositors and that 80 percent of the deposits were time deposits, with the total value of individual savings reaching 30 billion yuan.

Press reports since the Cultural Revolution convey the impression of an upsurge in savings, especially in the countryside. Cassou[13] questions this and leans toward the hypothesis that total personal savings in 1973 were no higher than in 1957. The average wage earner is said to save 4 to 5 percent of his total wage each year. In 1980 the average per capita savings of city dwellers were said to have amounted to 200 yuan.

The relationship between the rate of increase of individual savings

[12]Ibid., p. 34.

[13]P. H. Cassou, "The Chinese Monetary System," *China Quarterly,* No. 59, July–September 1974, p. 560. In the first half of 1980 rural savings rose by 1.9 billion yuan over the corresponding period of 1979. *Beijing Review,* July 28, 1980, p. 5.

and that of retail sales is not clear. If, as has happened in the Soviet Union, retail sales to the population have risen significantly slower than savings, it would indicate a degree of involuntariness of the savings process, i.e., people save because there is little to buy (or the wrong things are offered for purchase). In the U.S.S.R. this phenomenon is known euphemistically as "deferred demand."

CREDIT [14] The People's Bank is the source of short-term credit for industry and commerce.The Agricultural Bank is in charge of short-term credit for the farms and of medium-term credit for buying agricultural equipment.The Construction Bank handles short-term loans to construction units working on capital projects under contract. Like individuals, government departments and public institutions cannot obtain bank loans. Short-term (maximum term, 12 months) credits are made for working capital purposes only: building up inventories of raw materials, establishing stocks of finished goods and semimanufactures, purchasing seeds, manure, fodder, insecticides, and so on.These credits are known as "loans for production expenses." and as a rule do not cover more than 10 percent of such expenses in the countryside. Short-term loans to industry and commerce carry an interest rate of 0.42 percent a month of 5.04 percent per year. Short-term loans to agriculture carry an interest charge of 0.36 percent per month or 4.32 percent a year. These rates are subject to change.There is no interest on bank credit extended to state agricultural procurement agencies in order to enable them to make advance payments to communes for farm deliveries.

The Agricultural Bank extends medium-term credits (known as "loans for production equipment") to communes for the purchase of farm equipment, water conservation, and the acquisition of livestock. Loans for the purchase of agricultural equipment and water conservation must be repaid within five years at the most.The monthly interest rate in the early 1970s was 0.18 percent a month or 2.16 percent a year. Loans of up to three years are made for the purchase of livestock. In 1973 enterprises reportedly could get loans for up to 70 percent of their short-term credit needs; the rest had to be financed from equity funds supplied by the state budget.This represents a significant expansion from the 1952–1962 period when less than 30 percent of enterprise short-term credit needs were financed by bank loans. Despite recurrent ideological disparagement of credit and the past minimization of its role

[14]Cassou, pp. 562–64. Donnithorne, *China's Economic System,* p. 430, and "China's Anti-Inflationary Policy," *Three Banks Review,* September 1974, pp. 3–25.

in promoting economic growth, the part played by credit in the economy has increased markedly since the early 1960s, as has the importance of the People's Bank within the economic plan. Assuming the continued survival of the post-Mao pragmatic line, financial guidance and control of the plan are likely to assume still greater significance. As we have had occasion to note earlier, the allocative effectiveness of control by the yuan—no matter how many or few the agencies responsible for it and to whom—hinges in the last analysis on the economic rationality of the price and wage system. Much work remains to be done in this crucial area. But at least since 1977 the willingness of China's effective decision-makers to pay heed to scarcity relationships within the economy (the as yet imperfectly articulated "law of value") has been once again in evidence, and this is, after all, the important first step.

In order to obtain a loan from the banking system, an enterprise must have its financial plan approved by the People's Bank. Moreover, the purposes for which the loan is requested must conform to certain specified types of transactions: inventory formation or the distribution of final goods, for example. The banking system is supposed to make sure that the amounts of the loan are spent only for approved purposes. Investment funds are still allocated to industrial and other state firms out of the state budget, free of charge and in accordance with the state investment plan. Collectives, including people's communes and their subdivisions, make fixed investments out of their own capital accumulation funds. [15]

Deposits of enterprises, collectives, government departments, and individuals constitute the bulk of the revenues of the People's Bank. Other resources of the bank include that portion of profit from the bank's operations which the bank is not required to remit to the state, the income from currency issue, and in the case of the Agricultural Bank, state budgetary allocations made to that bank so that it may extend "loans for production equipment" to the commune sector. The banking system's major outlays consist of these credits as well as loans for foreign exchange transactions. The banking system's profit and loss ac-

[15]The principle that governs fiscal policy is the "balance between state revenues and expenditures." Over most years since the early 1950s the state budget at various levels has been balanced or showed a surplus. "We will absolutely not make up financial deficits by issuing bank notes, let alone resorting to the methods used in old China of floating huge domestic and foreign loans and issuing bank notes to balance financial deficits." Wang Ping, "No Inflation in China: Long-term Stability of 'Renminbi,' " *Peking Review*, No. 11, May 23, 1975. This absolute aversion toward deficit financing has been toned down considerably since 1977, especially in regard to foreign transactions.

count includes receipts from interest charges by the banks on loans and, on the expenditure side, interest paid on the deposits of enterprises and collectives and on the savings accounts of individuals. The net receipts from interest are partly remitted to the state in the form of a tax, the remainder being plowed into the system's capital accounts or held in a reserve account.

FINANCIAL REGULATIONS In accordance with general guidelines laid down in the national economic plan, the People's Bank issues instructions and regulations governing commercial operations. The Cultural Revolution with its anti-rules-and-regulations bias probably made the execution of this part of the bank's work more difficult and delicate than it had been in earlier years, although after 1971 the left's hostility to what it called "bureaucratic structures" met with growing resistance. Because the nature of the bank's business makes a high degree of technical competence indispensable, the post-October 1976 decline of the leftists has lessened tensions within the banking community by shifting emphasis away from revolutionization and toward the everyday discharge of technical duties.

MANAGEMENT CONSULTATION An important function of the People's Bank is financial and technical consultation work done for enterprises and collectives. The bank reviews the firms' investments and other projects and advises on ways and means of obtaining the most economical results. After the Cultural Revolution the dominant tendency was to induce enterprises and collectives to use their productive potential fully. "With an eye to promoting the development of production [bank personnel] take the initiative in helping the enterprises tap their internal potentials, practice austerity severely, and solve the problems of funds actively."

FOREIGN EXCHANGE TRANSACTIONS The Bank of China—an organ under the State Council—is in charge of China's external financial transactions. In addition to handling foreign exchange and international settlements arising from trade and aid deals, the Bank of China is heavily involved in remittance business from overseas Chinese. It has offices (including a large and active branch in Hong Kong) in a number of foreign countries in Europe and southeast Asia. Branches have been or are being established in Luxembourg and some other international financial centers. In 1979 the bank had correspondent relationships with over 2,000 branches of some 800 banks in 129 countries and territories.

The importance of the bank has been enhanced by the post-Maoist leadership's more open external policy and emphasis on foreign trade. In addition to its standard functions, the bank has become the agency that takes care of international settlements involved in technology transfers, capital equipment imports, processing of raw materials on foreign account, joint ventures, and compensatory trade. Its research department monitors international financial movements and the utilization of foreign capital in a planned way.

As in the U.S.S.R., the domestic price structure is insulated from the structure of international prices by the state's foreign trade monopoly. International prices serve as benchmarks for China's foreign trade and other external transactions.

Whatever the shifting language of politics, the integrating, plan control, and financial-technical evaluation functions of the People's Bank and its sister institutions have at all times constituted an integral and significant part of the economic process in China.

SUGGESTED READING

"Bank Loans: Problems." Hohhot, Nei Monggol Regional Service, May 28, 1980, in *FBIS*, June 4, 1980.

Bonavia, David, "The Banking Paradox," *China Trade Report* (Hong Kong), May 1980, p. 8.

Cassou, Pierre-Henri, "The Chinese Monetary System," *China Quarterly* (London), No. 59, July–September 1974, pp. 559–66.

Donnithorne, Audrey, *China's Economic System* (New York: Praeger, 1967), Chapter 15.

———, "China's Anti-Inflationary Policy," *Three Banks Review* (Edinburgh), No. 103, September 1974, pp. 3–25.

Ecklund, George N., "Banking and Finance," in Yuan-li Wu (ed.), *China: A Handbook* (New York: Praeger, 1973), pp. 579–94.

"Financial and Monetary Affairs," *Peking Review* (Beijing), No. 50, December 15, 1972, pp. 16–17.

"Higher Interest Rates for Bank Savings," *Beijing Review* (Beijing), No. 15, April 14, 1980, p. 6.

Hsiao, K. Huang, *Money and Monetary Policy in Communist China* (New York: Columbia University Press, 1971).

Hu, Teh-wei, "Dynamics of Hyperinflation in China, 1945–1949," *The Southern Economic Journal* (Chapel Hill, N.C.), Vol. XXXVI, No. 4, April 1970, pp. 453–57.

Peking Review (Beijing). Three articles on inflation and the financial system: (1) Ti, Chi, "No Inflation in China: Stable Prices and the Reasons," No. 9, May 9, 1975, pp. 17–20. (2) Wei, Hsia, "No Inflation in China: Long-Term Balance in Revenue and Expenditure," No. 10, May 16, 1975, pp. 16–17. (3) Wang, Ping, "No Inflation in China: Long-Term Stability of 'Renminbi,' " No. 11, May 23, 1975, pp. 18–21.

Richman, Barry, *Industrial Society in Communist China* (New York: Vintage, 1969), pp. 107–10, 476–90.

Tsiang, S. C., "Money and Banking in Communist China," in *An Economic Profile of Mainland China*. Studies prepared for the Joint Economic Committee, Congress of the United States (Washington, D.C.: U.S. Government Printing Office, 1967), Vol. I, pp. 325–39.

Yang, Pei-hsin, "Why China Has No Inflation," *China Reconstructs* (Beijing), Vol. XXIV, No. 4, April 1975, pp. 4–9.

SEVEN

Transportation and Communication

A good transportation and communications network in a country China's size is essential from political, military, and economic standpoints. Politically, transportation and communications (telephone, telegraph, radio, television, newspapers, and mail) are important means of integration: they aid in the diffusion of the common ideological code—a key means of political integration in China—and make possible an expeditious transmittal of political instructions as well as the enforcement of follow-up checks on performance.

The military significance of an adequate transport and communications system needs little elaboration. Rapid movement of troops and materiel from the industrially more developed and densely populated eastern areas to sensitive border areas and troublesome minority nationality regions is an essential ingredient of any rational defense policy and—as has been the case in Tibet—of the consolidation of power in a rebellious part of the People's Republic. In fact, much of the work on major national highways has been done in the past and continues to be done by the People's Liberation Army and its Production and Construction Corps.

The economic significance of improved transportation and communications in the Chinese context consists of the following:

1. An administratively directed economy would seem to require

reliable and efficient lines of communication between the various administrative-economic decision-making units (loosely, the central planners) and the executors of commands. If market relationships are promoted by good communications media, so are relationships resting on administrative orders, only more so. In China, as in other administratively commanded economies, the telephone is an important tool of economic planning. Since 1958 telephone conferences have been a regular feature of Chinese planning procedures. (It has been suggested that initially, when the nationwide telephone network was first installed in late 1957, the results were counterproductive. One of the reasons cited for the vast confusion of the Great Leap Forward was the excessive use and tying-up of the telephone system by bureaucrats who had found a new toy.)

2. Adequately developed rural transport is an important factor in the intersectoral transformation of agriculture, an objective that figures high on the list of China's priorities. The new strains of rice, wheat, corn, etc., require large quantities of chemical fertilizer, pesticides, improved seeds, and weedkillers. Because in the major grain-producing areas the maturing period is short and because inter-cropping and multiple cropping significantly shorten the slack season time, a heavy responsibility falls on the transportation network to deliver the needed inputs on time and carry off the produce as expeditiously and with as little loss as possible. Also, many rural industries continue to rely on technical information and some prototype capital equipment supplied to them by the modern industrial sector. Such linkages, although they do not imply dependence of semitraditional rural workshops on the modern urban sector of industry, can be rendered more useful and help raise the level of rural industrial development when goods and ideas travel faster. The practice of the modern sector's subcontracting to rural establishments parts of the industrial process, in such fields as electronics, will also be aided by the development of transportation and communications.

3. Given the relatively decentralized nature of the Chinese system of central planning and management, the tendency toward excessive intraregional specialization and other autarkic proclivities will to an extent be counterbalanced by ready access to goods and services produced outside the borders of any given administrative division.

4. From the national standpoint a better developed inland transport network would conceivably lessen China's need to ship in food grains from overseas to feed the coastal cities, and so relieve some of the pressure on relatively limited foreign exchange reserves.

5. Good transportation within a region can contribute toward easing

the problem of distribution of goods—including incentive items for consumers—and thereby stimulate and improve retail trade.

6. Improved transportation facilities make lighter work for the people involved in moving goods, as well as making movement smoother and faster. The development of transport and communications, when coordinated with the state's locational policy, can help promote the dispersion of industry, an enduring if not always consistent objective of China's communist leadership.

PROBLEMS

At the beginning of the communist era in China, and to an extent to this day, the transportation system reflected the dual nature of the economy. Side by side with a relatively small modern sector consisting of railways, roads, steamships operating on inland waterways and coastal waters, and a few air routes, there was a large traditional sector of animal- or man-powered carts, junks, sampans, pushcarts, and human carriers. Both the mechanized and animal or "natural" modes of transportation are still evident on the roads and rivers of China. Intermediate technology, however, is also clearly visible: in the cities bicycles now carry people as well as goods; the man-drawn vehicles for the conveyance of passengers have disappeared and have been replaced by bicycle-drawn rickshaws. Increasingly, heavy loads are pulled by 12-h.p. mini-tractors hitched onto 2- or 4-wheeled platforms. But the sight of people, including elderly women, pulling telephone poles on carts or carrying heavy loads at the dockside is still common. But because roads have been repaired, the potholes filled in, and the mud puddles drained, it has been possible to put rubber tires on the cart wheels and to use bicycles where once one had to make it on foot, tugging at ancient conveyances.

The size of the modern transportation and communications sector in 1949–1950 was extremely modest for a country of China's size. Moreover, at that time the system (such as it was) was disorganized to the point of chaos by decades of international conflict and civil war and by years of neglect. From 1876 through 1949 about 22,600 kilometers of railroads had been built, only 11,000 kilometers of which were operative at the beginning of 1949. This compares with Tsarist Russia's 73,000 kilometers in 1913 and India's 58,000 kilometers in 1950. The total length of highways at the time of the communist takeover was variously reported at 88,000 to 99,000 kilometers, only 75,000 kilometers of which were usable in early 1949. The usable roads were in poor condition;

many of them were impassable much of the year, undrained and undefined. In 1949 the total length of navigable waterways was 73,600 kilometers, and many of them were silted up. There was neither rolling stock production nor much modern shipbuilding. All the steel needed for building ships as well as for repairs had to be imported.

With over 14,000 kilometers of sea coast and 1,600 rivers, and some of the best natural harbors in Asia, China at that time had no merchant fleet under its control and no port facilities it could call its own. The gross tonnage of modern shipping was 200,000 tons at the end of 1949, the total length of scheduled air routes in the precommunist period was 17,000 kilometers and 11,400 kilometers in 1950. Even as late as 1965, the Civil Aviation Administration of China (set up in 1950) had a fleet of only 120 airplanes, most of them Soviet-made craft of advanced age.

At the end of 1949, in all of China there were only about 3,400 railway engines, 44,400 freight cars, and 4,400 passenger cars. There were no pipelines for transporting petroleum or natural gas. The per capita freight capacity of railways at the end of 1949 was 2.5 kilograms, that of highways 0.3 kilograms, and of waterways 0.3 gross tons. The speed of mainline trains in the 1930s ranged from 32 to 45 kilometers per hour, of motor vehicles 40 to 60 kilometers per hour, and of steamships 6 to 25 kilometers per hour. Most goods, however, were moved by human carriers, one-man handcarts, one-animal carts, and junks, at velocities ranging from 1.5 to 4 kilometers per hour. Before 1949 very few rivers were spanned by bridges. In 1949 there were no bridges crossing the Yellow (Huanghe) River. Wu points out that in 1949 more than half the carrying capacity of the traditional transportation sector was available for very short hauls only. [1] Because full mobilization of that sector's theoretical carrying capacity (estimated at 90 billion ton-kilometers in 1949) was not possible for organizational and other reasons, the actual contribution of the traditional sector to China's total transportation capacity fell far short of the theoretical potential.

In addition to the modest dimensions of the modern transportation sector in China at the beginning of the communist period, problems were posed by the system's lopsided geographical distribution. The economically more developed regions of the north, northeast, and east accounted for 77 percent of the total length of operating trunk railroad lines in 1949–1950; six coastal provinces had 42 percent of the total. In terms of railway densities, in 1949 the more developed regions had 5

[1] Yuan-li Wu, *The Spatial Economy of Communist China* (New York: Praeger, 1967), p. 125.

kilometers of track per 1,000 square kilometers, whereas the less developed regions had only about 1 kilometer of track per 1,000 square kilometers. Many of the less developed areas were traversed by only a single, one-track railway. Some areas of the country, for example Sichuan and Tibet, had no truck railway lines at the end of 1949. More surprisingly, the eastern province of Fujian had no trackage at all.The same imbalance, but in reverse, could be observed in the distribution of highways and waterways. In 1949, 42 percent of the national highways and 30 percent of navigable waterways were located in the developed regions of the country. Given the vastness of the underdeveloped regions, highway densities showed a different picture. In east China, for example, the density of natural highways in 1949 was 15 kilometers per 1,000 square kilometers; in the southwest the density was 4 per 1,000 square kilometers.

The pre-1949 distribution of the railway network reflected in large part historical forces at work during China's "semicolonial, semifeudal" period. Most of the trunk railroads were built at the turn of the century by Western financial interests and took little note of China's domestic developmental needs. Chinese railways were built to serve the profit-making activities of foreign investors: they moved in radial lines from the treaty ports inland as far as was needed to bring out raw materials and sell the goods made in the coastal cities.The system lacked important linkages, notably north–south connections (Map 2).

But not all the woes of China's transportation system were due to nineteenth-century and early twentieth-century foreign malevolence and the ravages of war. Some of them were brought about by the communists' post-liberation wrangling, sudden economic leaps that put great strain on transport and communications, and outbursts of factionalism that at times paralyzed key sectors of the transportation network.Transportation and communications became clogged during the Great Leap Forward and again during the Cultural Revolution, when strikes, sabotage, the seizure of trains and trucks, and attacks on transportation facilities were widely reported.

After the Cultural Rvolution trouble on the railroads continued.It was to be ascribed (after October 1976) to the nefarious activities of the radical faction. "Railway transport had been the salient weak link in the national economy due to the serious damage caused by the 'gang of four.' It affected industrial and agricultural production, the interchange of goods between city and countryside, our preparedness against war and the people's livelihood." [2] Slow freight unloading and turnarounds,

[2]*Peking Review*, No. 13, March 25, 1977, p. 5.

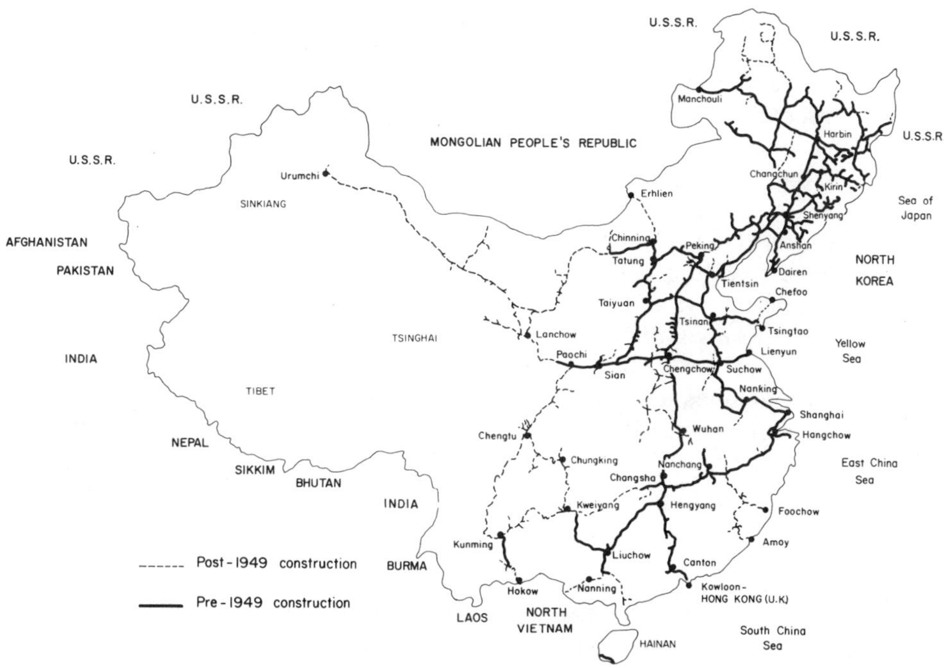

Map 2 Railroads: Trunk Lines, Single and Double Track

the piling up of freight, slowness of trains, near absence of automatic blocking lines, and deficient maintenance work have been identified as specific problems. Also, the longest highway bridge in China across the Yellow River at Loyang was started in 1973 and opened for traffic at the end of 1976: "the work was interrupted time and again for a total of eight months in three years as a result of interference and sabotage by the 'gang of four.' "[3] Geographically, the Wuhan, Zhengzhou, Nanjing, and Taiyuan Railway Bureaus appear to have been the focal points of the troubles. Although the accusations leveled against the fallen radical leaders are no doubt true (railways like coal and oil became prize pawns in the factional struggle), other reasons for labor unrest in the railway sector may also be cited. Railwaymen in China tend to be politically advanced and alert and aware of their strategic value to the economy; some have the opportunity to travel around the country, to see and compare ways of life for themselves. Others come into direct contact with those who have traveled a great deal. Railwaymen in China are among the better paid workers and they benefit from very good health care facilities and programs. It is apparent that in the post-Cultural Revolution years it was the better-off workers who were in the vanguard of labor unrest.

POLICIES

During the early reconstruction period (1949–1952) the major objectives of the communist regime were to reclaim at least some of the rolling stock, trucks, and other vehicles lost to the Soviet occupation troops in Manchuria as part of the 1945 process of liberation, and to salvage, repair, and put in working order the transportation and communications equipment that had been put out of action during the war and the Nationalist retreat. Apparently a good part of the equipment requisitioned by the Soviets was returned to China in 1949, much of it damaged. A third objective was to link the disparate transportation and communications networks into an integrated national system.

The longer-term objectives included the development of the transportation and communications networks in harmony with the country's industrial locational policy; increase in and modernization of plant and equipment; creation of, until then nonexistent, transportation and communications industries; increase in operating efficiency; semi-

[3]*Peking Review,* No. 5, January 28, 1977, p. 31. See also "How the Gang Crippled Railway Transport," *Peking Review,* No. 10, March 4, 1977, pp. 16–17.

mechanization of traditional modes of transportation; and the construction of strategically important military highways linking China proper with the country's border regions, such as Tibet and Xinjiang.

Transportation, Communications, and Locational Policy

The objectives of China's locational policy were not followed consistently during the period from 1949 to 1980 (Chapter 5), but the net movement was in the direction of a geographical dispersal of industry away from the more developed coastal areas. This movement has been accompanied by a similar evolution of transportation and communications policy, aided by increasingly pressing arguments of military strategy and the rapid development, after 1960, of rural industrialization. It should be noted that, at least until 1957, the pattern of transportation development (especially that of railways) was to an extent constrained by projects already begun but not completed under the Nationalist regime. Thus, according to Wu, [4] from 1949 through 1957, 42 percent of the new railways put into service represented lines started under the Nationalists.

Between 1949 and the end of 1963, 80.6 percent of new railway lines were located in the less-developed regions of the country (center, south, northwest, and southwest), and the remaining 19.4 percent were in the industrialized areas of the north, northeast, and east. Out of a total of 29,500 kilometers of new highways built by 1953, 27,000 kilometers were located in the less-developed regions. Out of a total of 39,400 kilometers of highways reconstructed between 1953 and 1960, 20,900 kilometers were to be found in underdeveloped areas.

After 1957 local initiative was emphasized as a supplement to the national effort being expended on construction and maintenance of the transportation network, in line with Mao's behest to "let the localities undertake more work under unified central planning." Between 1949 and 1971, provinces municipalities, and autonomous regions built 4,000 kilometers of local railways. From 1962 through 1971, provinces, cities, special administrative regions, counties, and people's communes surfaced almost 200,000 kilometers of highways. In 1976 alone, the greater part of the 35,000 kilometers of highways added during the year was built "by relying mainly on local resources." [5] In construction work on both local and national projects, it appears that people's militia units are widely employed under commune and production brigade commands.

[4]Yuan-li Wu, op. cit., p. 155 and numerical data.
[5]*Peking Review,* No. 15, April 8, 1977, p. 32.

Table 18 gives data on the change in the locational pattern of China's transportation network between 1949 and 1963. Quantitative data for subsequent years are hard to come by; however, indications are that the distributional trend indicated in Table 18 continued. The importance of railroads as an indicator of the pattern of transportation development is paramount. In 1952, for example, the freight volume carried by railways was 60 billion ton-kilometers, whereas motor vehicles accounted for less than 1 billion and waterways for 10.6 billion ton-kilometers. In 1979 railways carried 559 billion ton-kilometers of freight, trucks 27 billion and waterways 456 billion. To this day, railways are the principal modern means of transport in China, despite the development of the highway and waterway systems. By the end of 1978 the total length of operating railways was estimated at about 50,000 kilometers (20,200 km in 1949–1950). It is thought that there were around 890,000 kilometers of all-weather operating roads (61,800 km in 1949–1950), and 136,000 kilometers of waterways (95,000 km in 1952). [6]

The locational trend is further indicated by data on regional highway distribution in years for which reliable information is available (Table 19). By early 1977, except for Tibet, every province, municipality, and autonomous region had railroads, and 80 percent of the country's rural people's communes were accessible by all-weather roads. The actual political and economic significance of this remarkable development cannot be overestimated. Some statistics on northwestern Shaanxi Province and the Qinghai Plateau illustrate this point. At the end of 1974 highway mileage in Shaanxi was 6 times what it had been before 1949 and 1.5 times that of 1965. In 1949 there were 4,300 kilometers of highways, mostly located on the plains that form about 20 percent of the province's area. At the end of 1974 there were over 25,000 kilometers of highways, and the annual volume of freight carried by motor vehicles was 204 times what it had been immediately after 1949. Since then, over 40 trunk highways have been built by the central and provincial governments, and a number of other roads were built by such local authorities as counties and communes. [7] In Qinghai Province, once almost roadless, there were about 14,000 kilometers of trunk highways, 1,000 road bridges, and over 1,000 culverts at the end of 1971. In addition there was a network of mostly gravel, feeder roads built by counties, communes, and brigades. The whole network was maintained the year round by over 600 roadwork crews. [8]

[6]CIA, *China: A Statistical Compendium* (July 1979), p. 11; *Bejing Review,* July 6, 1979, p. 39; *Beijing Review,* May 19, 1980, p. 20.

[7]*Peking Review,* No. 52, December 27, 1974, p. 20.

[8]*Peking Review,* No. 11, March 17, 1972, p. 15; No. 15, April 8, 1977, p. 32.

TABLE 18 **Route Length and Density of Railways by Regions in 1949–50 and 1963**

	Route Length (km) of Operating Railways			*Density (km/1,000 km) of Route Length of Operating Railways*		
Region	*1949–50*	*1963*	*Net Increase*	*1949–50*	*1963*	*Net Increase*
Developed						
Northeast	9,763	9,977	214	12	13	1
North and Inner Mongolia	3,063	6,699	3,636	2	4	2
East	2,854	3,529	675	6	7	1
Underdeveloped						
Central	3,114	4,108	994	4	6	2
South	978	3,009	2,031	2	5	3
Northwest	441	4,420	3,979	0.1	1.5	1.3
Southwest	—	2,493	2,493	—	1	1
Grand total	20,213	34,235	14,022	2	4	2

SOURCE: Reprinted from *The Spatial Economy of Communist China,* New York: Praeger (For Hoover Institution Press) 1967 by Yuan-li Wu with the permission of the publishers, Hoover Institution Press. Copyright © 1967 by the Board of Trustees of the Leland Stanford Junior University.

TABLE 19 **Regional Distribution of All-Weather Operating Highways**

Areas	*1949–50*	*1960*	*Net Addition 1949–50 to 1960*
Developed regions, km.	25,923	83,247	57,324
Underdeveloped regions, km.	35,902	116,753	80,851
Total, km.	61,825	200,000	138,175

SOURCE: Reprinted from *The Spatial Economy of Communist China,* New York: Praeger (For Hoover Institution Press) 1967 by Yuan-li Wu with the permission of the publishers, Hoover Institution Press. Copyright © 1967 by the Board of Trustees of the Leland Stanford Junior University.

As of late 1979 four major railroad projects were under construction: (1) a 470-kilometer line from Turpan to Korla in southern Xinjiang Province, which when completed will link up with the trunk line from Urumchi to Lanzhou (the Korla-Lanzhou line will connect China's nuclear testing areas with a major nuclear industry center); (2) the Qinghai-Tibet line (Xining to Lhasa), the first stage of which (830 kilometers from Xining to Gomud) has been completed; (3) the 560-kilometer line from Wuhu, Anhui Province, to Guxi, in Jiangxi Province, which will shorten the distance from Nanjing to Jiangxi and Fujian Provinces by 300 kilometers; (4) a line from Beijing to Tongliao in Jilin

Province (870 kilometers). This is the second line linking north China with the northeast.

With Japanese technical assistance, three trunk lines have been selected for transformation into high-speed corridors. These are: (1) Beijing-Tianjin-Shanghai (1,127 kilometers); (2) Beijing-Zhengzhou-Wuchang (1,207 kilometers); and (3) Beijing-Harbin (1,368 kilometers). Runs on these three corridors were to reach a speed of 160 kilometers per hour by 1981, and 220 kilometers per hour as soon as feasible thereafter.

Postal and telecommunications networks have been established in previously undeveloped areas; where systems did exist, they have been improved and vastly expanded. Here again, stress has been put—especially in more recent years—on the underdeveloped regions of the country. For instance, intracounty telephone lines, which totaled 3,500 kilometers in 1952, were increased to roughly 26,000 kilometers by 1958; the total length of telecommunication wires tripled during that period, and the length of postal routes almost tripled. By 1958 practically all of China's towns and townships were linked by both postal and telephone services. In 1952, postal services were available in only 60 percent of these localities, and telephone service was available in only 9 percent. By the end of 1974, Tibet, which remains one of China's less-developed regions, had 90,000 kilometers of mail routes served by 1,300 postmen. Almost all of Tibet's districts and 94 percent of its communes were served by the postal network. The newspaper account reporting this information noted approvingly the resultant phenomenal rise in Tibetan circulation of the Party periodical *Hongqi* and the Tibetan edition of the *People Daily*. [9] In 1979 there were reportedly 2 million kilometers of telephone lines in China's countryside; 680,000 production brigades were equipped with phones. The number of rural post offices was put at 43,000. [10]

Increase in and Modernization of Plant and Equipment

Production of freight, maintenance, and passenger cars began in the 1950s; diesel locomotives were first produced in 1958, and a year later electric locomotives were being turned out in small numbers. Today 2,000-h.p. diesel engines are produced and 3,000–6,000-h.p. engines are being produced on a trial basis at the Beijing Rolling Stock Plant (among

[9] *Peking Review*, No. 11, March 14, 1975, p. 22.
[10] *Beijing Review*, May 18, 1979, p. 30.

others), an establishment employing over 9,000 workers. The Beijing plant formerly concentrated on repair and maintenance work. Steam locomotives have been manufactured since 1952, when 20 units were turned out. By 1978 annual output of steam locomotives was more than 500 units, and the output of freight cars was 17,000 units (compared to less than 6,000 in 1952). In 1964 the first Chinese factory making wheels and wheel rims for locomotives and railroad cars was put into operation. Wooden and, perhaps more commonly, concrete ties are being mass produced. In 1950 China began to train women as engine drivers. In the mid-1970s women were being taught to operate 2,000-h.p. diesel engines. Since 1966 the Chinese have been active in designing and building railroad lines abroad, including the Tan-Zam trunk line in Africa. [11] Passenger train schedules, I have noticed, are scrupulously adhered to, even though the radicals have lately been blamed for putting forward the counterrevolutionary slogan: "Better a socialist train late than a capitalist train on time." This turned things upside down and confused the masses.

Bridge construction has been vastly expanded. In the nineteen years from 1953 through 1971 the total length of new railway bridges was four times the length built in the seventy-three years from 1876 to 1949. Among the more impressive structures is the double-decker (rail and road) bridge, commissioned in January 1969, across the Yangtze River at Nanjing. It has a 6,700-meter double-track railroad on the lower deck, and a 4,500-meter, four-lane road on the upper deck, flanked on both sides by sidewalks. Built entirely by the Chinese from their own designs (after Soviet advisers had precipitously abandoned the project—taking the blueprints with them), the bridge is an engineering achievement of the first order. Reportedly, it has withstood several severe tests including a 1974 typhoon and flood. Traffic across the railway deck of the bridge is, I noticed, almost continuous. It is the third bridge across the Yangtze built since 1949, the other two are near Chongqing and Wuhan.

The Chongdu-Kunming trunk-line railway, opened in 1970, has 653 bridges (there is an average of one large or medium-sized bridge every 1.7 kilometers). The combined length of bridges and 427 tunnels exceeds 400 kilometers. Connecting with the Paochi-Chongdu railroad to the

[11] The designers, engineers, and architects who had worked on the Tan-Zam project were brought together in 1979 in a civil engineering company the purpose of which was to enter into contracts with foreign governments and private interests (including joint ventures with overseas Chinese) for surveying, designing, and constructing railroads, bridges, tunnels, factories, and housing abroad. The company was also to provide consulting service and labor. Beijing Radio, May 19, 1979, in *FBIS*, May 21, 1979.

north, the line forms part of the major northwest to southwest communications artery. Another artery linking Hunan Province in central-south China with Guizhou Province in the southwest and connecting at Guiyang (the capital of Guizhou) with a line to Kunming (capital of Yunnan Province on China's southwestern border) was put into operation in 1974. The whole track-laying job took two years to complete. The work was done mostly by hand labor and involved hundreds of thousands of militiamen from the two provinces, working around the clock in mountainous terrain. Given the advances made by China's electronics industry and the importance attached to the transportation and communications sectors of the economy, [12] the computerization of some major trunk railroad lines appears to be likely in the near future. Electrification, which had been slow to materialize in the past, also appears to be on the agenda. By the end of 1978 China had roughly 1,000 kilometers of electrified track, or 2 percent of total railway track length. It was assumed that the electrification plans would necessitate the purchase abroad of a sizable fleet of rail cars suitable for an electrified system, equipment which at the moment China did not possess in sufficient quantities.

Although railroads remain the principal means of transport, the concurrent development and modernization of road and inland waterways reflect the Chinese regime's balanced approach to economic growth, contrasting sharply with the Soviet experience especially in the matter of highway construction. In addition to the needs of agriculture, a major impetus to road building has always been provided by military considerations, both from the standpoint of defense and of Chinese communist support of insurgency beyond China's borders. An additional consideration was Beijing's determination to control minority nationalities inhabiting China's border provinces.

Among the more impressive military road-building feats are the three major highways across the Qinghai-Tibet Plateau (Sikang-Tibet, Qinghai-Tibet, and Xinjiang-Tibet). At the beginning of 1975 Tibet, China's political problem region, had 91 highways totaling almost 16,000 kilometers. A number of newly built highways in Guangxi and Yunnan connect with roads going into Burma, Laos, and Vietnam. In 1974 alone,

[12] Audrey Donnithorne, *China's Economic System* (New York: Praeger, 1967), p. 270, notes that in 1960 state investment (including investment by localities and state enterprises) in transport, posts, and telecommunications was 21 percent of total state investment, and investment in railways 15 percent. Of a total of 106 billion yuan of central government budget devoted to investment from 1950 to 1958, roughly 15 billion yuan was channeled into transportation. Of this, some 11 billion yuan went to the development of railroads.

roads in Yunnan exceeded the total mileage constructed from 1949 through 1973—reflecting a zeal not unconnected with political and military events in Indochina. Since the outbreak of the Sino-Soviet dispute in the early 1960s, much work has been done to improve and extend the road network in the northeast and northwest. All in all, in 1978 China had reportedly 890,000 kilometers of roads, or nine times what existed in 1950. China's trunk roads are used primarily for the movement of freight by domestically produced trucks. Local road networks are used by traditional and semitraditional modes of transport for relatively short hauls.

The production of trucks began in 1956 in Changchun, Jilin Province (the first auto plant was built there with Soviet assistance). In 1977 the city had 240,000 workers in over 1,000 factories producing not only cars and trucks of all kinds but also tractors, electric motors, chemicals, optical goods, and military hardware. There were also about 500 "neighborhood" factories at Changchun, small establishments doing contract work for the major automobile plants. In 1975, for example, these mini-factories produced about 30 main parts for a type of light truck that went into production that year at the No. 1 Motor Vehicle Plant. The plant turns out many types of trucks as well as limousines for official use. [13]

Inland navigable waterways have been extended and considerably improved through construction of locks, regular dredging, control of banks, and installation of mechanized or semimechanized port facilities and shipbuilding and repair yards. Apart from the improvement of some portions of the Grand Canal, China's only major north-south waterway, little appears to have been done thus far to augment north-south navigable connections. Between one-quarter and one-third of the existing inland waterways can be used by modern motorized vessels.

Significant progress has been made over the years in improving and extending the equipment of inland ports and seaports. Wuhan on the Yangtze has been completely refurbished and equipped with modern wharves, shipbuilding yards, and mechanized loading and unloading facilities. Modernization has also proceeded in such centers as Shanghai, Whampoa, Qinghuangdao, and Tianjin. A large three-year port construction and improvement program was initiated in 1973. By mid-1976, 40 deep-water berths had been built in nine of China's major ports. The berths include deep-water bulk-load berths for coal, ore, and

[13] Li'n Ch'un, "Changchun: Green Auto City," *China Reconstructs*, Vol. XXVI, No. 5, May 1977, pp. 22–26.

mixed cargo, berths for 100,000-ton tankers, and container berths. In 1959 China built its first 10,000-deadweight tons class ocean-going freighter. Domestic production of modern freighters as opposed to the purchase of ships abroad became an issue between the Party's factions. Buying ships abroad was labeled by the radicals as "worshipping things foreign." It implied that Chinese-made navigational instruments were not reliable enough for trans-Pacific crossings. The issue came to a head in 1974 in connection with the completion of a roundtrip to Europe by the Chinese-made freighter "Fengqing." [14] Such squabbling did not prevent China from achieving significant results in ship construction. In 1976 ship production was estimated at 319,000 tons (light ship displacement, that is, the actual ship weight) compared to 61,300 tons in 1958 and a low of 13,500 tons in the recession year 1962. There is no doubt that the major upsurge in ship output came after the Cultural Revolution, beginning in 1970, and that it has been particularly marked in the case of large vessels.

Although the bulk of petroleum continues to be moved by rail, and to a lesser extent by tanker trucks, pipeline construction has become increasingly urgent because of the burgeoning oil extraction and refining industry. The absence of pipeline transport between the main oil-producing and oil-consuming areas is a bottleneck that has inhibited the development of newly found oil deposits. The first two oil pipelines (totaling 300 kilometers in length) were built in 1958–1959 from the Karamai fields (Xinjiang) to a refinery at Tushantzu. In 1974 an 850-kilometer pipeline linking the Daqing field with the modernized loading facilities in the port of Dalian was completed.

Chinese domestic and international airlines use a variety of modern craft of British, Soviet, and American make. More than 100 domestic scheduled routes radiate from Beijing to some 70 cities. There are seven international jet airports equipped with up-to-date traffic-control installations. As of 1980 China had air transportation agreements with more than 40 countries. Nevertheless, air transport in China is still in its infancy, and its contribution to total freight and passenger carrying capacity is very modest. A part of the civilian air fleet is used exclusively to service agriculture and industry. As a rule, scheduled flights are made only in impeccable weather.

Communications equipment (including vacuum-tube and transistorized portable radios, shortwave transmitters, black-and-white tele-

[14] "The Farce Concerning the Freighter 'Fengqing,' " *Peking Review,* No. 10, March 4, 1977, pp. 18–19. Also "The 'Yacht' Incident," ibid., p. 19.

vision transmitters, microwave equipment, automatic crossbar switchboards, electronic teleprinters, telegraphic facsimile equipment, and specialized military communications hardware) is produced in more than 60 large plants that appear to do considerable subcontracting of specialized components. By far the best part of the output and the more advanced levels of technology are reserved, it would seem, for military uses. Not counting subcontracted labor in neighborhood and village industries, the work force employed on these tasks was about 100,000 in 1971, while the output value of the whole electronics industry (including manufacture of computers) was then estimated at $1 billion, or about 0.5 percent of the gross national product.

Production of consumer entertainment equipment includes transistorized radios, vacuum-tube radios, and monochrome television receivers. Although radio and television receivers for home use continue to be made in relatively small numbers and are priced accordingly, in recent years there seems to have been a significant increase in the availability of transistorized radios, and their prices were lowered in 1975. In several locations, including trains, some public parks and squares, and at commune headquarters, I have encountered the hallowed communist institution of the wired radio, broadcasting the Party line in the form of news bulletins, talks, exhortations, slogans, and plays on appropriately uplifting themes. In 1950 there were 51 wire broadcasting stations and 2,200 loudspeakers in China. In 1958 the respective figures were 6,772 and nearly 3 million.

Despite the many problems that remain concerning both the quantity and efficiency of modern transportation and communications, the advances made since 1949 are nothing short of spectacular. Together with work now in progress, the existing transportation and communications network, while overloaded at present, provides China with an infrastructure capable of supporting ambitious projects in the coming years.

The Press

As is the case in other communist countries the controlled press plays an important role in transmitting the latest nuances of the political line and parallel economic intelligence to cadres and the population at large. A veritable explosion has taken place in the dissemination of the printed word. In 1950 the circulation of newspapers was almost 800 million copies; in 1972 it was almost 11 billion copies, including 30 million copies daily of national and provincial papers. The daily circulation of the *People's Daily* (*Renmin Ribao*) was 3.4 million in 1972, including 1.5

million copies in Beijing.These circulation figures do not include journals. In 1950, 1957, and 1958, the annual output of journals was respectively (in millions of copies): 35.3, 315.0, and 532.4. No data are available for the circulation of journals since 1958. Most newspapers and journals suspended publication during a part of the Cultural Revolution, being replaced at that time by wall posters. Most of them resumed publication in the 1970s.

The effective circulation of newspapers is several times the statistical circulation for at least two reasons. First, about 90 percent of the newspapers go to institutional subscribers—factories, schools, libraries, and production teams in the countryside. Group newspaper reading sessions are held regularly, so that a single copy of a paper disseminates its message many times over. Second, the message is reproduced in factory, school, office, commune, production brigade and production team wall newspapers, pamphlets, brochures, and handouts. Copies of the major national and provincial papers are posted in glass display cases on city and town streets. I have seen sizable crowds in Shanghai, Beijing, Nanjing, and other cities reading the latest edition of the national and local product. Major editorials are broadcast every day. Workers, employees, peasants, soldiers, and students write reports based on current newspaper articles, and are sometimes even involved in writing such articles; lectures and speeches at mass meetings draw on newspaper material. The message is hammered home through loudspeakers, plays, books, and motion pictures. It is not an exaggeration to say that 30 million copies of newspapers distributed each day reach 970 million people. Moreover, the readership's understanding of the content is constantly monitored by the cadres. Incorrect comprehension is promptly rectified. In a sense, the whole country is one vast newspaper. Still, as the record shows, the message is sometimes garbled in subtle ways, with or without premeditation. Frequently it seems to fall on unreceptive, incredulous, or even deaf ears.

Because the masses were bored with what they read in the officially controlled press and heard on the officially controlled radio, because they widely disbelieved and discounted what was fed them by the media and turned to alternative channels of information (including the rumor network), and because the post-Mao regime insisted on "seeking truth from facts," even as the new agencies of control over the media saw these facts, the press and radio underwent a rare session of self-criticism aimed at restoring a measure of their shattered credibility. In an article published on July 29, 1979, *Renmin Ribao* pointed out that "news reports must be completely true." False and partially false reports that still "occasionally" appeared in newspapers were "like weeds in green rice paddies" ("poisonous weeds" was once the left-inspired expression). It cited instances of gross deception drawn from its own now-emancipated (post-Mao) columns, including false economic construction reporting and erroneous news stories about miracle acupuncture cures of the deaf-mute by PLA barefoots.The "evil practice of cheating" was criticized. Journalists still could not "distinguish between news reporting and literary creation.They even made up for shortages of material by fabricating events by a 'reasonable imagination.' " The trouble with seeking truth from facts, it appeared, was that "the facts are like a piece of clay which can be shaped as they wish." The "bad habit of writing articles according to changes in the direction of the [political] wind" was still much in evidence.

In order to popularize newspaper reading and comprehension, the number of characters used in paper publishing has been reduced to fit the average level of literacy, and some characters have been simplified.The *People's Daily* uses 6,000 characters; often only 2,000 (2,000 characters are regarded as roughly fitting the peasant level of literacy; 3,000 to 4,000 characters are presumed to reach the level of literacy of industrial workers). By slowly pronouncing the characters in local dialect, the problem of "letter blindness" can be reduced considerably. Subsequent explanation by the cadre-reader and peer-group pressure will do what is necessary toward ensuring correct comprehension. Undesirable interpretation is kept at bay by (a) restricting newstand distribution of newspapers, (b) concentrating over-the-counter sales of daily papers in post offices where (especially in the smaller towns) the buyer is easily identified, and (c) banning foreigners from subscribing to provincial and lower level papers in which, presumably, highly aggregated central instructions are translated into bread-and-butter issues.

To lend credibility and grassroots excitement to the line promulgated by the central Party and government organs and to keep elitist professionalism in its place, "barefoot reporting" was introduced after the Cultural Revolution, especially in the radicalized Shanghai-based press. "Barefoot reporters"—the journalistic equivalent of the "barefoot doctors" (Chapter 9)—were workers and poor and lower-middle peasants who after a brief period of training became part-time worker/peasant correspondents for major national and provincial papers. In the greater Shanghai area in 1975 there were some 2,000 such correspondents. "Whatever happens anywhere in Shanghai," said the deputy director of the Shanghai daily *Wenhui Bao*, "we soon know." [15] After the radicals' fall a year later, the barefoot reporting practice was quietly dropped. To prevent the press from sliding back into its accustomed dullness, promote "freedom of speech," "help strengthen popular supervision over the work of the government and leading cadres, and combat malpractices in society" the *People's Daily* and other papers began publishing (after 1978) readers' columns carrying "suggestions and opinions from the masses." [16] These suggestions and opinions were screened by special editorial departments in charge of masses' work, and echoed fairly faithfully the current line.

While deploring the "book famine" and "spiritual hunger" of the decade following the outbreak of the Cultural Revolution, the same *People's Daily* (January 10, 1978) noted that the gang of four, at whose door the hunger and famine have been laid, "wasted a total of 40,000 tons of paper" on publishing "reactionary" material (i.e., the gang's version of the line).

According to Western reports special places exist, closed to the public at large and accessible only to selected cadres bearing special permits, where other literature may be borrowed. The books available there are usually stamped "internal reading materials" and cover a wide range of contemporary foreign works—Soviet and American for the most part—in Chinese translation. Circulating through this back door are books such as *Krushchev Remembers* (stamped "absolutely confidential"), Marshal G.K. Zhukov's *Reminiscences and Reflections* and *The General Staff during the War Years*, Z.A.B. Zeman's 1969 *Prague Spring*, John Barron's *KGB*, Winston Churchill's *The Second World War*, Richard Nixon's *Six Crises*, the memoirs of Gerald Ford and Henry Kissinger, Kissinger's *Nuclear Weapons and Foreign Policy*, William Shirer's *Rise and Fall of the Third Reich*, and various Western best-sellers (*Love Story, Jonathan Livingston Seagull*). Circulating from hand to hand among adolescents in *samizdat* form are some less exalted materials produced locally, notably *A Maiden's Heart*. [17]

A more serious purpose was served by various underground periodicals published in mimeographed form by a number of dissident groups in 1978–79. Among the better known was *Explorations* (*Tansuo*),

[15] *New York Times*, June 8, 1975, p. 5.

[16] *Beijing Review*, September 28, 1979, pp. 5–6.

[17] Miriam London and Mu Yang-jin, "What Are They Reading in China?" *Saturday Review*, September 30, 1978, pp. 42–43. See also Miriam London and Ivan D. London, "China's 'Byroad' News Leaks: A New People's Channel," *Freedom at Issue*, September–October 1978, pp. 9–12.

circulated even after the arrest in spring 1979 and subsequent incommunicado imprisonment of the two original editors. One of them, Wei Jingsheng, the son of a Party official, became widely known through his big character poster calling for an indispensable fifth modernization—democracy—to complement the four officially sponsored modernizations of agriculture, industry, science-technology, and national defense. [18]

SUGGESTED READING

"Aviation," *China Trade Report* (Hong Kong), Vol. XV, February 1977, p. 3; Vol. XVI, July 1978, pp. 6–8.

"Building Up China's Rail Transport," *China Reconstructs* (Beijing), October 1979, pp. 74–77.

Chen, Nai-Ruenn, *Chinese Economic Statistics: A Handbook for Mainland China* (Chicago: Aldine, 1967), pp. 372–84.

Chu, Godwin C., *Popular Media in China: Shaping New Cultural Patterns* (Honolulu: University Press of Hawaii, 1978).

Chung, Tai, "Railways for the Rugged Southwest," *China Reconstructs* (Beijing), Vol. XXV, No. 4, April 1976, pp. 15–19.

Craig, J., "Domestic and International Telecommunications," in *China: A Reassessment*, pp. 289–310.

Donnithorne, Audrey, *China's Economic System* (New York: Praeger, 1967), Chapter 10, pp. 251–72.

Hsiang, Jung, "Ports of China," *Peking Review* (Beijing), No. 11, March 11, 1977, pp. 14–17.

Hunter, Holland, *Chinese and Soviet Transport for Agriculture* (Pittsburgh, Pa.: University Center for International Studies, 1974).

MacFarquhar, Roderick, "A Visit to the Chinese Press," *China Quarterly* (London), No. 53, January–March 1973, pp. 144–52.

"New Microwave Communications System," *China Reconstructs* (Beijing), Vol. XXVI, No. 6, June 1977, p. 43.

Petrov, Victor P., *China: Emerging World Power* (Princeton: D. Van Nostrand, 1967), Chapter 5, pp. 70–94.

Powell, Ralph L., "The Role of the Military in China's Transportation and Communications System," *Current Scene* (Hong Kong), Vol. X, No. 2, February 7, 1972, pp. 5–12.

[18] *New York Times*, October 7, 1979, p. 3.

Reichers, Philip D., "The Electronics Industry of China," in *China: A Reassessment*, pp. 86–111.

Smith, F., "A Glimpse of China's Shipping and Shipbuilding Effort," *Shipping World and Shipbuilder* (London), June 1976, p. 463.

"Transportation," *Peking Review* (Beijing), No. 48, December 1, 1972, pp. 16–17.

Vetterling, Philip W., and James J. Wagy, "China: The Transportation Sector, 1950–71," in *People's Republic of China: An Economic Assessment* (Washington, D.C.: U.S. Government Printing Office, 1972), pp. 147–81.

Wu, Yuan-li, *The Spatial Economy of Communist China*. (Published for the Hoover Institution on War, Revolution and Peace by Frederick A. Praeger, New York, 1967), Chapters 6, 7, 8, pp. 103–207.

EIGHT

Domestic and Foreign Trade

Domestic trade and internal prices are insulated from external transactions and international prices by the state's foreign trade monopoly, exercised on the financial side by the Bank of China and on the goods side by other state agencies.

DOMESTIC TRADE PROBLEMS

Three sets of problems confronted the communist government in the post-1949 decade: the first two were connected with the changeover from war to peace and from capitalism to socialism; the third, which became prominent around 1957, had to do with China's modification of the socialist system, which until then had been patterned, not too accurately, after the Soviet-Stalinist blueprint. A fourth set of problems, which emerged in the 1960s and 1970s, lay in the expansion and diversification of trade.

Reactivation of Commodity Markets

The first problem to be faced was the reactivation of commodity markets disrupted by war and inflation. In 1950 total retail sales amounted to only

17 billion yuan or about 33 yuan per capita; by 1957 retail sales had climbed to 47.4 billion yuan or roughly 74 yuan per capita. A contributory cause of the revival of domestic commerce was the goverment's success in containing inflation and restricting speculation in deficit commodities.

Change in Ownership Structure

The second postwar problem consisted in the need, as the communists perceived it, to change the ownership structure of domestic commerce. The problem was overcome by 1955–1957 through several means, which included (a) the takeover by the government of property belonging to the national and class enemies: the Japanese (and by 1955 the Russians), Western corporations, the Nationalist government ("bureaucrat capital"), Chinese big ("comprador") capitalists—including the "four families" related to Chiang Kai-shek and his wife—as well as the assets of other categories decreed undesirable; (b) the elimination of "national capitalists" (the ideological equivalent in commerce and industry of rich and upper-middle peasants) through a series of mass terror campaigns, which included the "Three-Anti" and "Five-Anti" suppression drives of 1951–1952 and various antirightist campaigns; (c) discriminatory, not to say confiscatory, taxation; (d) discrimination in supplying the private sector with essential inputs and price and credit restrictions placed on the marketing of private output; (e) audit harassment; and (f) all sorts of threats and pressures put on small traders and peddlers to induce them to join cooperative arrangements. The fear of danger was, and still is, more terrifying than the danger itself—bad as it may be—when it materializes. Where those threatened have no room for the exercise of individual choice, fear becomes a powerful weapon of social policy. The results of the socialization measures may be seen in Tables 20 and 21.

TABLE 20 **Socialist Transformation of Retail Commerce**

	Percentage Distribution of Retail Sales				
Year	*Socialist Commerce*	*State-Capitalist and Cooperative Commerce*	*Private*	*Sales Handled by Socialist Commerce (million yuan)*	*Index (1950 = 100)*
1950	14.9	0.1	85.0	1,780	100
1957	65.7	31.6	2.7	26,220	1,470

SOURCE: *Ten Great Years* (Beijing: 1960), pp. 39, 40.

TABLE 21 **Socialist Transformation of Wholesale Commerce**

	Percentage Distribution of Wholesale Sales	
Year	*State and Cooperative*	*Private*
1950	23.9	76.1
1955	95.6	4.4
1957	100.0	0

SOURCE : Kuan Ta-tung, *The Socialist Transformation of Capitalist Industry and Commerce in China* (Beijing: 1960), p. 66.

It should be noted that state-capitalist commerce (Table 20) amounted in practice to nationalization. The private partner in a joint state-capitalist undertaking was, in terms of decision-making, a figurehead. He was kept in place—*used* was the official term—because he possessed the needed technical expertise and business experience which, at that time, the cadres lacked. Once that particular deficiency of the cadres had been overcome, and assuming correct behavior on the part of the former owner, the private partner was relegated to the ranks of the laboring masses. Incorrect behavior, flexibly defined, earned consignment to a labor reeducation (concentration) camp or a residence "under the supervision of the masses," which often amounted to the same thing.

The problems connected with the change in ownership structure were greater and more intractable in industry than commerce: commercial assets could be, and to an extent were, easily removed by foreigners, bureaucrat capitalists, and others before the communist takeover.

Capitalist Tendencies and Revisionism

Long after the formal socialization of the economy, Mao and the leadership's left wing, sensitive as they were to the essence rather than the form of phenomena (especially superstructural phenomena), continued to detect serious flaws and incipient dangers in the new socialist relations of production and trade. Two kinds of problems were seen as endangering the "newly born things": the spontaneous tendency of the masses, especially the peasants, for capitalist restoration and the propensity of the bureaucratic apparatus toward capitalist-roading or revisionism. The first tendency, according to Leninist dogma, is ever-present, that is, until the advent and final consolidation of full communism. The tendency allegedly feeds on the existence during the socialist stage of neocapitalist institutions, particularly the residual free (although supervised) peasant markets and household subsidiary plots. After the socialization of commerce, a significant portion of rural trade consisting of the produce of the plots continued to be transacted on such markets.

The cash value of this trade has not been revealed, and during my 1974 stay in China officials were reluctant to discuss the subject. [1] Sporadic attempts—as during the early months of the Great Leap Forward and the Cultural Revolution—to suppress peasant markets proved ineffective, if not downright destructive of a good part of rural trade and of peasant morale.The continued existence of such trading arrangements and their importance in supplementing the income of the peasantry were seen by the regime during Mao's lifetime as a blot on the ideological landscape and a threat to the socialist transformation of China. But the problem of capitalist tendencies among the masses is not only one of residual marketing institutions, it is also one of political consciousness.This more ingrained and elusive aspect of the problem has been dealt with by the two methods of economic policy that were discussed in Chapter 1: mass mobilization and intense group pressure or ideological remolding, both designed to bring about the required superstructural heightening of the masses' political awareness.

In March 1975 the Party's theoretical organ *Hongqi* (Red Flag) published an article by a leading exponent of the left-wing view, Yao Wenyuan (one of the gang of four). Entitled "On the Social Basis of the Lin Biao Anti-Party Clique," this essay signaled the launching of yet another mass rectification campaign; this one intended to consolidate the dictatorship of the proletariat and eradicate old and new "bourgeois rights" in China's society.The article said in part: "The remnant forces of small production still remain and a section of the peasantry still clings to the habits of small production in varying degrees. Spontaneous capitalist tendencies have often cropped up in the countryside and the struggle between the socialist road and the capitalist road is still very fierce." Such tendencies have apparently also cropped up in the cities among industrial workers and cadres.

Zhang Chungqiao, another left-wing spokesman (and since October 1976 counted among the gang) warned in his report to the Fourth National People's Congress (January 13–17, 1975) that "in some enterprises, the form is that of socialist ownership but the reality is that their

[1]Since then, the subject has been discussed widely in the press.

leadership is not in the hands of Marxists and the masses of workers." Both statements attacked not only spontaneous capitalist tendencies among the masses but the emergence of revisionist propensities among the leaders.The latter's institutional base, according to the left, was in the revisionist economic and social model peddled by the Soviet Union, but the crux of the problem resided in the still low level of political consciousness of a section of the cadres, including most of the post-October 1976 national leaders. "Two henchmen of the gang [of four], with Goebbels' fascist fanaticism, slanderously averred that the older generation of proletarian revolutionaries had 'turned into their opposite' and become persons who 'failed to keep up with the revolution.' "[2] The gang's "talk about eliminating bourgeois right and realizing communism was just so much nonsense designed to deceive people."[3]

Expansion and Diversification of Trade

A fourth problem encountered by domestic trade in the 1960s and 1970s was the need to expand and diversify commercial transactions so as to cater more fully to the needs of the population.The left's hankering after barter, however ideologically respectable in terms of the Marxist prescription, was not realistic.The seeds of capitalism embedded in the expansion and diversification of trade relations can be effectively controlled, the post-1976 leaders argue, by the existing proletarian institutions, including legal ones.This does not really answer the left wing's contention that social institutions are only as good as the political consciousness of those who operate them. But for the time being the left, if not altogether silenced, is reduced to using Aesopian communication skills, and so the dialogue is muted.

DOMESTIC TRADE POLICIES

Organization

Paralleling the decentralization of other sectors of the economy in 1957, the domestic trade system moved away from the top-heavy organization

[2]*Peking Review,* No. 16, April 15, 1977, p. 28.
[3]*Peking Review,* No. 11, March 11, 1977, p.7.

that (in imitation of the Soviet model) characterized it in the early years. Figure 3 shows in general outline the present organization of domestic commerce. The decentralization is not merely organizational; lower level trading authorities, both state and cooperative, possess operational latitude in matters of market research, creation of retail outlets, and (at least at the provincial/municipal level) direct contracting with producers.

MINISTRY OF TRADE The Ministry of Trade is the overseer of the whole domestic trade sector and the coordinator of trade with other segments of the national plan. Once the plan has been prepared in consultation with the various hierarchical levels of authority, however, operational details are devolved onto provincial/municipal and lower level trading bodies. Again, as elsewhere, it is the spirit of decentralization rather than its formal structure that makes the difference. The Ministry of Trade, under Party guidance and with help from the fiscal and monetary system, remains the guardian of unified planning. But within this exacting but broad constraint the difference with the previous arrangement (and Soviet experience) resides in the importance attached to domestic commerce.

Commodity circulation, though decried in some (for the time being discredited) left wing ideological quarters as a potential superstructural danger because of the profit-making possibilities inherent in it, is in practice regarded as an activity to be nurtured under proper safeguards, and not treated as a poor relation. Consumer interest, provided it avoids "excess," is not seen as something to be neglected or stamped out, especially so since the fall of the ultraleft. In the regime's estimation, quality and quantity control over domestic commerce can best be exercised by operational latitude at the grassroots points of contact between the correctly inspired producer, state and cooperative trader, and the user.

PROVINCIAL AND MUNICIPAL TRADE BUREAUS A step in the desired direction is the ongoing consultation and the granting of broad plan enforcement powers to provincial and municipal level trading authorities. Once the plan is initially agreed upon, these organs (together with the trading corporations and cooperatives closely linked with them) hold meetings with enterprise managements to thrash out details of the plan

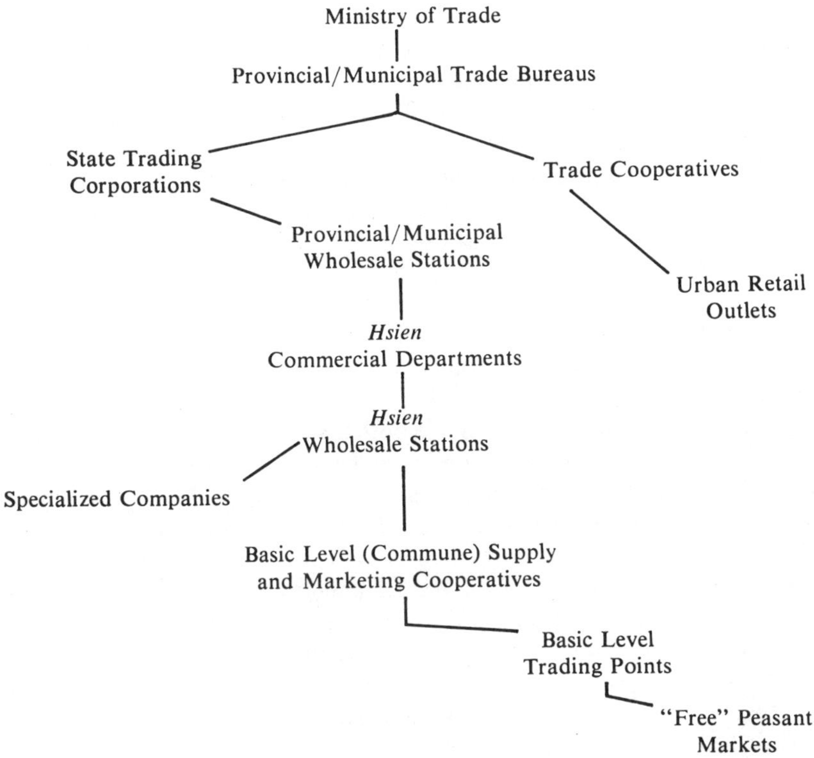

FIGURE 3. *Organization of domestic trade.*

as it applies to the province/municipality, to reconcile any differences that arise, and to work out contracts between producers and the appropriate provincial/municipal trading bodies. I suspect that the conferences are marked by a give-and-take and pliability that cannot be reproduced on an organizational chart. It is not an exaggeration to say that the provincial and municipal commercial departments and their subordinate units are an influential component of the planning matrix and a clearinghouse for economic information.

STATE TRADING CORPORATIONS AND TRADE COOPERATIVES State trading corporations handle the bulk (about 80 percent) of wholesale trade and more than a third of retail business. They are organized along commodity group lines and depending on the group of goods, are closely meshed with provincial municipal trade bureaus, or in some cases ministry. Trade cooperatives handle the bulk of retail trade, especially consumer perishables, and a small part of wholesale trade. Both the state trading corporations and trade cooperatives remit their profits to the state organs under whose jurisdiction they operate. Similar remittances are made to the appropriate state authorities by lower level trade organs.

XIEN AND LOWER LEVEL STATE ORGANS An important characteristic of the Chinese system of domestic trade is the proliferation of lower level commercial organs, including a comparatively large number of retail outlets and purchase points in both urban and rural areas. This is in sharp contrast to the Soviet experience. There are two major advantages to this: (a) it reduces crowding in stores, a perennial feature of Soviet and East European commerce, and (b) it enables the state traders to keep a tab on consumer preferences and the changing pattern of tastes. The same remarks apply to wholesale agencies that handle supplies for and receive the products of state and cooperative producing enterprises, including rural communes and their subdivisions. The value of the government-sponsored consumer opinion polls is somewhat lessened by the fact that many consumer and user wants are suppressed by political education and will not be revealed to the pollsters. If such wants are revealed, they are declared illegitimate and derogated. The subject of such excessive desires is rectified and sooner or later conforms to the official norm of expectations. In the same way, there is a mass norm that applies to the rate and direction of change in consumer/user tastes.

An attempt is made to minimize (ideologically legitimate) user frustrations by a variety of market-testing arrangements. [4] For example: (a) trade organizations engage periodically in consumer surveys and report their findings to higher bodies; (b) all retail points must keep customer complaint and suggestion books, which are regularly examined by higher-up trading authorities and Party organs as much for their business material as their political content—customers are urged to make use of this opportunity to express themselves; (c) large department stores periodically hold public forums at which suggestions and customer grievances are aired; (d) when new product lines are introduced, de-

[4] H. V. Henle, op. cit., p. 59.

partment stores and the larger retailers are obliged to reserve a special counter for these products and to solicit customer reactions (in the case of goods destined for rural markets, trial sales at commune and lower level trading points are mandatory, and representatives from higher level wholesale organizations and trade bureaus are required to make trips to the villages to record customer responses and to communicate them to the appropriate authorities and producing enterprises); (e) monthly meetings between wholesalers and their retailers are held to discuss problems of marketing, volume, quality, and appropriateness of the commodities handled; (f) mobile teams are sent out regularly to make "on-the-spot investigations" of user needs and responses; and (g) wholesalers keep representatives at the plants of their major suppliers to act as liaison agents for user interests.

It is, of course, difficult to say how effective such administrative arrangements and sociological experiments in customer opinion really are. In the final analysis the decision to alter the volume, quality, and assortment of products, speed up their delivery, and discontinue obsolete or misallocated lines of goods remains with the provincial/municipal and higher-up planning authorities, and ultimately with the Party and governmental policy on these matters. Moreover, in the context of a quasi-permanent sellers' market, customer preferences are likely to receive short shrift, whatever the regulations drawn up to protect the user may say and no matter what the arrangements designed to implement these rules. Combined with the system of the trader's upward responsibility (i.e., given the success indicators, his rewards and punishment come from up on high) rather than accountability downward to the mass of customers, the realized quality of service to the consumer will tend to be less than the planned quality. In China retail commerce seems to serve the customer better than elsewhere in the socialist world, partly perhaps because of a long tradition of such trading in Chinese culture. But there have been and continue to be problems. [5]

Like the rest of the economic-governmental-Party apparatus, the commercial system has been kept in a permanent state of tension designed to make it conform to the current Party line on trade. User complaints, actively encouraged (often, one is inclined to suspect, man-

[5]E.g.: "In the heyday of the gang of four, loving and growing flowers was stigmatized as decadently bourgeois and the sale of flowers was banned because it was 'one form of peddling revisionism.' " Now that the gang is down, "even the flowers seem to smell sweeter and bloom better" *Beijing Review,* March 23, 1979, p. 31. In Nanjing there are 1.7 million people but only 170 barbershops. Almost half the 1,700 hairdressers are over 50 years old. Before the

dated) were used before October 1976 to ferret out unapproved behavior on the part of trade network officials and stamp out "bureaucratic airs." There was probably a good deal of resentment and resistance by trade officials to the constant, as these officials saw it, interference by the masses on behalf of upper-echelon ideologists in what they considered to have been their arduous and specialized business. But until Mao's death there was not much they could do about it.

The trading network at the basic levels has also initiated a number of procedures that may be described as "customer services." I had the impression in the various stores I visited, that the store clerks were actually interested in what they were doing, in sharp contrast with what goes on in the Soviet Union, for example. Customer service features include the late closing (around 1:00 A.M.) of some retail stores in the cities to serve workers on late factory shifts, home delivery to older or physically incapacitated people, bicycle repair shops open day and night, delivery of food to peasants working far away from their home or village stores, and the availability of completely prepared dishes that need only be heated to be served (the Chinese version of TV dinners). Although there are exceptions, the system seems to be pervaded by pride in the work done. To Western eyes the appearance of most retail stores is drab, lightened only by the variety of the simple goods displayed. [6]

Special note should be taken of *commune level supply and marketing cooperatives*. These agencies act on behalf of the state for the procurement of second-category agricultural produce (Chapter 3) as well as for purchases of part of the household subsidiary produce. A designated portion of such purchases is marketed by the cooperatives acting as agents of *xien* wholesale stations, for which service the cooperatives earn a commission. Some of this activity is handled through basic-level trading points (or branch stores), usually at the production brigade level. The cooperatives also channel into the communes and their sub-

---

introduction of barber examinations in 1979, school leavers were assigned to barbershops by the city's labor department. "Neither the school leavers nor the shops could choose, so some people unwilling or not suited for the job were given the job and those who would like to become hairdressers missed out. That did not make for good service" *Beijing Review,* June 29, 1979, p. 30. In Liaoning Province "the food and vegetable supply was indeed scanty in those days when the gang of four and their provincial followers waved the baton to oppose capitalist tendencies" Beijing Radio, August 2, 1979, in *FBIS,* August 3, 1979.

[6]On several occasions I found that having purchased one item of a particular good, the store was unable to furnish another identical item. I suspect that for some goods, what you see is what you get.

divisions all inputs they buy from their respective *xien* wholesale stations. Insofar as they have pricing rights in respect of local produce, these are strictly supervised by the state trading corporations and trade cooperatives in accordance with guidelines laid down by the provincial and higher-up trade bureaus. Profits of the commune-level supply and marketing cooperatives are transferred in part to the commune budget and are held in part by the cooperatives for disposal by higher-up state organs.The cooperatives act as a conduit for the banking system's production expenses and production equipment loans disbursed by commune credit cooperatives.

After the fall of the leftists much ink was spilled in defense of cooperative sector enterprises in the countryside as well as in towns. Apparently for years such undertakings were restricted as to personnel, scope of operations, supply of merchandise, taxes, welfare benefits, and tariff wages on the grounds that they were only "semisocialist" and of "transitional form." One of the results had been the rapid exodus of former store owners, small traders, and vendors from the cooperative retail sector. In 1979 there were only 200,000 of them left in the sector, that is, less than one-third of the total number of employees in the cooperative stores. [7] One of the effects of this attrition was a deterioration in the quality of retail service, bringing China almost into line with other socialist countries in this regard.The problem, which in fact has its roots in the "Anti" campaigns of the 1950s, was aggravated by the policies pursued during the Great Leap and the Cultural Revolution. By 1979 the collectively owned consumer-serving enterprises were said to be "politically half dead and economically discriminated against." [8]

Agricultural Procurements and Profit Margins

The state through its basic-level commercial organs obtains from the commune sector (a) the agricultural tax, which, as we saw in Chapter 3, is fixed percentage of the "set yield," and is mostly collected in kind; (b) the industrial and commercial tax levied on commune industries and commercial activities; (c) a fixed percentage of grain and some other products that the communes are obliged to hand over at state-fixed procurement prices (these are known as *cheng-ku liang* or "tax-and-purchase grain," and *kung liang*, "public grain"); and (d) above-quota produce, mainly grain (known as *yü-liang* or "surplus grain"). Grain

[7] Beijing Radio, August 1, 1979, in *FBIS*, August 2, 1979.
[8] *Renmin Ribao*, editorial, July 21, 1979, in *FBIS*, August 1, 1979.

distribution to the cities (*shang p'in liang*, "commercial grain") is handled exclusively by the state in a planned (i.e., rationed) manner through trading corporations and trade cooperatives.

Peasant households used to be encouraged to sell any surplus from their sideline activity to the supply and marketing cooperatives for disposal through state channels rather than on private markets. Pressure was reinforced by a procurement price policy which, unlike its Soviet predecessor, was designed to be competitive with prices ruling on the free market. In this way, it was hoped, the peasants would save themselves the time and bother involved in private marketings by the simple procedure of selling their sideline surplus to the cooperatives.

Profit margins of wholesale and retail trade organizations have been curtailed since the early 1960s, especially where commodities officially defined as "necessary" are concerned. Sales and turnover taxes, which figured prominently in the Soviet capital accumulation process, are much less important in China.They appear to have reached their peak around the time of the Leap and have been on the decline since, in terms of their relative contribution to state budgetary revenues.They were seen as having an inhibiting effect on domestic commerce.

Domestic trade is seen by those presently in charge of policy decisions as important to the proper functioning of the economy.To use a metaphor, it is the grease that enables the wheels of production forces to turn smoothly, without the jarring noises and breakdowns that occur where trade is neglected. At the same time, some argue, domestic trade has to be watched carefully.Trade is business, and business is full of capitalist dangers. Socialist trade, while structurally liberated from its capitalist antecedents, nevertheless retains some characteristics of the old system. It is a commodity-dealing profit-oriented, money-tainted activity, which, according to doctrine, produces no tangibles. It breeds unhealthy attitudes. In the wake of the radicals' demise this line of reasoning was put aside.The liveliness of business and legitimate profit-making were again granted official favor. For the time being, trade (at which the Chinese are very good) was to be used to further the objectives of socialism. Commercial advertising reemerged from a long slumber; it had been banned for over twenty years as bourgeois and capitalist. In 1979 Shanghai television began to show commercials for medicines, while the city's paper *Wenhui Bao* ran ads for a local brand of soft drinks called "Lucky Cola," which, it was claimed, had "a taste that revives the spirits and a lightness pleasing to the palate." Ads were also run for "Butterfly" hair oil, "Phoenix" antiwrinkle cream, and

"Peony" face cream. *Wenhui Bao* explained the rationale behind the ads: "We should use advertisements to convey knowledge and help people, as well as to establish and cement the ties between the people and the departments responsible for the production and sale of commodities." For a time, under the gang, even window displays and showcases were banned. Following the retirement of the gang, "attention was again given to designing shop window displays." [9]

The difference between the factions on the subject of domestic commerce has always been, I believe, one of degree only. The left, with Mao's tacit approval, insisted that trade should serve politics and deemphasize profit. [10] The trade workers' role was to serve the people unstintingly by going deep into the masses, educating the masses, and in turn being educated by them. The left, too, strove to educate the consumer in the image of ascetic selflessness and total commitment to the common good defined along class lines. It tried to shape wants, discarding some and promoting others, before they emerged in the form of demand. A politically correct demand obviates the necessity for institutional control and avoids the spawning of revision-prone bureaucracy. The right, on the other hand, is inclined to handle wants as they come in the form of revealed preferences; to adapt demand to the available supply by price and wage manipulation, physical rationing, credit controls, and through other institutional instruments available to the state planners. While not neglecting the remolding of man's consumption habits and impulses, the right sees the reeducation as a very lengthy process that cannot be relied on to solve the problems of the here and now. Notwithstanding the high-flown rhetoric, both sides in the debate shared an underlying commitment to the promotion of domestic commerce.

FOREIGN TRADE PROBLEMS

The problems that faced the Chinese in the field of domestic commerce in the post-1949 decades were paralleled by those the regime set out to solve in the area of foreign exchanges.

[9] *Beijing Review,* March 9, 1979, p. 31; Agence France Presse, Beijing, February 6, 1979, in *FBIS,* February 6, 1979.

[10] "Socialist commerce is an important tool for exercising dictatorship over the bourgeoisie and is not an enterprise which simply deals with business transactions." Hunan County Handles Commerce Problems: Kunming, Hunan Provincial Radio Service, June 30, 1975, *FBIS,* July 1, 1975.

The first two sets of problems consisted in the reactivation of foreign trade volume and the change in the ownership structure of foreign trade enterprises.The third, which emerged in the late 1950s and early 1960s, had to do with China's socialist reorientation, a movement away from the Soviet trade prototype. A fourth set of problems consisted in the expansion of China's foreign exchanges, continuing adjustment in the commodity structure of trade, and the provision of aid to countries that the Chinese considered friendly and useful to the realization of their vision of socialist revolution. As with population policy, sectoral priorities, planning machinery, and technological options, foreign trade policy went through not always consistent phases, reflecting in part the continuing debate and differing perceptions of the national and class interest among contending leadership factions.

Reactivation of Foreign Trade Volume

In 1950 the total value of imports and exports was 4.2 billion yuan, rising to 10.5 billion yuan in 1957. In 1950 capital goods (including military hardware) were 87 percent of total imports, rising to 93 percent in 1957. The bulk of exports in 1950 (almost 91 percent) consisted of processed and unprocessed agricultural products, especially the latter; by 1957 this proportion had dropped to 73 percent, a small but significant shift toward the exportation of industrial products. Basically, however, China remained throughout the 1950s an exporter of raw materials and unprocessed agricultural produce and a buyer of capital goods, mainly for heavy industry.

Change in Ownership Structure

Residual foreign equity participation in China's foreign trade as well as all traces of private and former Nationalist property were quickly done away with and replaced by the government's foreign trade monopoly exercised through the Ministry of Foreign Trade, state foreign trade corporations organized on commodity lines, and—on the financial side—by the Bank of China.

Geopolitical Pattern

China's departure from the Soviet model in the late 1950s and early 1960s entailed a significant change in the geographical pattern of foreign trade, the ending and repayment of Soviet credits, and an adjustment in the

TABLE 22 **Geographical Pattern of Foreign Trade**

Year	Total Trade	Trade with Non-Communist Countries (%)	Trade with Communist Countries (%)	
			Total[a]	USSR
1950	100	71.0	29.0	26.4
1957	100	36.0	64.0	42.8
1964	100	63.0	37.0	4.0
1973	100	83.0	17.0	2.7
1978	100	85.0	15.0	2.0

SOURCE: Percentage distribution derived from Robert L. Price, "International Trade of Communist China," in *An Economic Profile of Mainland China* (Washington, D.C.: U.S. Government Printing Office, 1967), Vol. 2, p. 584, Table 1, and "Communist China's Balance of Payments, 1950–65," ibid., p. 644, Table 10; *China: A Reassessment of the Economy* (Washington, D.C.: U.S. Government Printing Office, 1975), pp. 23, 631; CIA, *China: A Statistical Compendium* (July 1979), p. 13.

[a]Including Yugoslavia, Albania, North Korea, North Vietnam, and Outer Mongolia.

commodity composition of trade, especially that of imports. Until 1959 the principle guiding China's foreign exchanges was reliance on socialist countries, especially the U.S.S.R., for both imports and exports, a pattern indicated by Table 22.

The close involvement with the Soviet Union in the 1950s (a policy of "leaning to one side") can be readily comprehended: relations with the U.S.S.R. were friendly if not warm; the Soviets appeared to have a viable economic model that had served them well; they were willing to trade and offer aid in respectable if not generous amounts; and the trade embargo placed on China by Western industrial countries in the wake of the Korean War, left the Chinese no acceptable alternative but to lean to Stalin's, and later—less enthusiastically—his successors' side. The Soviets' willingness, indeed eagerness, to conduct foreign trade on the basis of bilateral barter deals suited the Chinese, whose reserves of Western currencies were at that time minimal. In 1957 China's net international financial resources were estimated by Western observers at 285 million U.S. dollars, including 35 million dollars in gold holdings. In that year China's total trade turnover was 3 billion dollars.

In terms of trade balance, the period of "leaning to one side" may be divided into two subperiods. From 1950 through 1955 Chinese imports from the U.S.S.R. exceeded exports to that country by an estimated 900 million dollars.The situation was reversed from 1956 through 1964, when Chinese sales to the U.S.S.R. exceeded purchases by more than 1 billion dollars, reflecting the accelerated repayment by China of credits obtained from the Soviets in the first subperiod. After 1964 the picture was mixed. A sharply curtailed volume of trade between the two countries revealed occasional surpluses and deficits on both sides. Although exchanges with Eastern Europe were affected by the deteriorating climate of political relations with the U.S.S.R., the decline in that trade was less than in Sino-Soviet exchanges, particularly if China's trade with Albania and Rumania is included in the calculation.

"Leaning to all sides," characteristic of the 1960s and 1970s, was China's foreign trade equivalent of the domestic policy of "walking on two legs." With careful safeguards for China's sovereignty and international class perspective, trade deals with capitalist countries could be made to offset the danger of excessive reliance on the Soviet Union. While going along with the policy and acquiescing (albeit reluctantly) in its underlying dialectical principle, the Chinese leadership's left wing continued to issue warnings against the dangers of capitalist restoration and revisionism inherent in the situation. The focal point of the danger, as the left saw it, was too much admiration of things foreign (including technology) and a waning of the spirit of self-reliance and mass inventiveness. In the mid-1970s, following the seminormalization of relations with the United States, the left's warnings were extended to cover the increase in tourist trade and other "cultural" contacts with the West. The influx into China of delegations, camera teams, orchestras, and so on, was thought to involve an undesirable importation of the demonstration effect and a possible undermining of the masses' ascetic devotion to the revolutionary cause.

Shortly after the forced retirement of the radicals, the attitude toward outside contacts changed drastically. The fear of things foreign was replaced by an enthusiasm, at times excessive, about almost anything that came from abroad, especially, engineering and managerial technology. The initial euphoria (1977–1978) gradually yielded to a more sober and cautious appraisal of the possibilities and limits of external economic, scientific, and cultural relations, particularly economic relations. In a rather "left" editorial published on June 1, 1979, the *People's Daily* reminded its readers (perhaps also the majority of policymakers) that in bringing about socialist modernization China must look mainly to "self-reliance, hard work, and what we have now. Importing technology, that is, making use of the latest technologies from abroad, is aimed at improving our ability to do things by ourselves. . . . The Four Modernizations should be brought about through self-reliance and hard work, not through purchase and borrowing. It is imperative to keep to the revolutionary spirit of working hard and bring this spirit into fuller play, and spend our limited foreign exchange on what is needed most." Such sentiments, however, became the exception as the doors to the outside world opened wider than they had in twenty years. "We should emancipate our minds and pay attention to learning from foreign advanced experience in enterprise management." [11]

Expansion and Adjustment

The reorientation of trade consequent to the ebb in Sino-Soviet relations and the restructuring of China's domestic economy had to be accompanied by adjustments in the commodity composition of imports and exports. Marginal adjustments continue to be made as the pattern and level of domestic economy evolve over time. To meet the Soviet challenge in the developing world, both communist and noncommunist, China began to offer loans, render technical assistance in areas such as water conservation, transportation, and public health, and give military aid in the form of small arms, training, and strategy advice. The volume of foreign exchanges has been and still is carefully tailored to China's current ability to pay, which hinges on the sale of Chinese goods abroad. Notwithstanding the progress made in science and technology by the Chinese with only limited foreign assistance, China needs foreign goods of advanced technological content, and it has to buy scientific and technical information if only to save on laborious and costly research and development at home of things that have already been researched and developed elsewhere. Even after the sharp increase in external commerce after the radicals' fall, China's total yearly foreign-trade turnover in 1979 was around $27 billion, or roughly $27 per head. Whereas China has just under one-quarter of the world's population its foreign trade represents a little better than 1 percent of annual world trade. The picture could change dramatically if the promise of important petroleum finds on the mainland and in offshore areas materializes and transforms China into a major exporter of oil at the currently high and rising prices, and if the ambitious post-Mao modernization plans (implying a heavy burden of imports) are actually carried out. Chinese foreign trade representatives are astute bargainers and quick learners, and the country's settlement record in foreign transactions so far has been im-

[11] Tianjin City Radio, August 12, 1979, in *FBIS*, August 14, 1979.

peccable. Inexperience, lack of business acumen, and shoddy business ethics are not obstacles, on the Chinese side, to the expansion of China's external exchanges.

FOREIGN TRADE POLICIES

The principles governing China's foreign trade policy in the 1970s and the means used to enforce them are summarized in the following sections.

"Leaning to All Sides"

The diversification of markets and supply sources in the wake of the Sino-Soviet dispute has already been mentioned. The general guideline is that trade may be carried on with almost all countries, irrespective of their political coloration, provided such trade is deemed by the Party and governmental authorities to be in the interests of China's socialist construction and is not contrary to national sovereignty. The desired ideal is to preserve a geopolitical balance in external economic relations and avoid, insofar as possible, too heavy a reliance on any one seller or buyer—whether it be the Soviet Union or Japan. China's foreign trade in the mid-1970s was geographically distributed as shown in Table 23.

With the announcement of the plan to modernize China's agriculture, industry, science-technology, and national defense ("four modernizations"), the whole notion of the role of foreign trade in national economic construction was reappraised. Foreign economic relations were no longer seen as a residual, something to be resorted to, reluctantly, after all the ways of self-reliance, native ingenuity, and hard work have been exhausted. The need for massive infusions of up-to-date foreign technology—both know-how and equipment—was now stressed, although not always with a single voice. Nearly all the former restrictions

TABLE 23 **Approximate Geographical Distribution of China's External Trade about 1976**

Area	*Percent*
East Asia	33.3
Western Europe	25.0
Communist countries	20.0
Other	21.7

SOURCE: Foreign trade statistics of China's trading partners.

on the volume and scope of foreign trade were reexamined, and most of them were declared invalid.The only serious limitations, it was now said, were China's ability to pay and the system's capacity to absorb the influx of sophisticated capital and techniques. [12] While the rule of leaning to all sides was to be observed, China began to bend more markedly toward the advanced countries of the West and Japan, especially the latter.

Balance of Payments

The traumatic experience with Soviet credits, on which payment was exacted from China even during the bad years following the Great Leap Forward, made the Chinese wary of falling into indebtedness on their foreign exchange accounts and careful in accepting long- and medium-term foreign loans. Like its internal budget, China tried to balance imports and exports every year, or preferably to have a surplus on the commodity trade account. From 1968 until 1972 China's external trade consistently showed a surplus, although there were deficit transactions with a number of individual countries and areas (especially Western Europe, North America, Australia, and Japan). Deficits in some areas were made up by surpluses in others (e.g., Hong Kong and Malaysia) and remittances from overseas Chinese. China claimed that it had no external indebtedness, a claim that could not be fully substantiated because of discreet "informal" debts to capitalist business firms in the guise of seller-arranged credits and other inconspicuous borrowings. In 1976 and again in 1977 China's payment obligations on foreign accounts came to an estimated $1.3 billion, which represented a 23 percent debt-service ratio based on hard-currency exports.

After Mao's death and the elimination of the gang of four the former conservatism in matters of foreign trade and payments was considerably moderated. Foreign trade became the key link in the chain of modernization. If the plans—even in their scaled down version—are adhered to, imports of complete plant and equipment would exceed $20 billion in

[12] It should be noted, however, that a good deal of buying of sophisticated foreign plant and equipment took place when the gang was around. Between 1973 and 1977 China imported enough sets of equipment from Western Europe and Japan to fully furnish some 200 projects, including Beijing's 300,000-ton capacity ethylene plant, Wuhan's rolling mill for 1.7 meter sheets, and Shanghai's large petrochemical works.Thirteen huge chemical fertilizer installations were also purchased. By comparison in the "Liuist" period (1962–65) only 80 projects benefited from equipment imports from Japan and Western Europe. *Beijing Review*, July 27, 1979, p. 9.

1985 alone, compared with under $3 billion over the 1973–1977 period. Under existing agreements, by 1985 China is committed to export 40–50 million tons of crude oil to Japan. In February 1978 the two countries signed an eight-year trade pact amounting to $20 billion. In 1978 China signed contracts worth $7 billion with foreign firms, including over $2 billion with Japanese businesses. That year Japanese exports to China rose by 60 percent over the preceding year (to around $3 billion), while total two-way Japan-China trade rose by 46 percent (to over $5 billion), or roughly one-quarter of China's total trade turnover in 1978. Even when the gang was alive and well (1966–1976), foreign trade grew at an average annual rate of 12 percent (18 percent a year from 1970 through 1976); from 1976 through 1978 the average annual growth rate was 29 percent.

Exports China's foreign exchange reserves in 1979 were estimated at only about $2 billion. To support the projected massive volume and rising cost of imports, a heroic export effort will be needed. There are three types of commodities that can be used for export in the foreseeable future: oil, materials from agriculture (e.g., rice, processed foods), and manufactures.

Four problems arise in connection with oil exports. First, the quality of Daqing oil (which accounts for about half of all oil exported) leaves much to be desired; the oil has a heavy wax content and calls for the installation of expensive dewaxing facilities in the importing countries. Japanese refiners have done this with the help of sizeable government subsidies. Second, the output of the Daqing field reportedly has peaked (in part due to the use of wasteful recovery methods over the years). From 1970 through 1975 oil production grew at an annual average rate of 20–25 percent; the yearly growth rate between 1978 and 1985 is expected to be not more than 13 percent. There is, of course, the possibility of new finds, especially offshore. However—and third—to get at the offshore deposits, very large initial investment in exploration and production equipment is needed, in addition to know-how. Fourth, modernization of the type and on the scale envisioned by the plans will inevitably lead to a substantial increase in China's domestic oil consumption. This has to be factored in when estimating China's future oil exporting capacity, and by implication, the country's ability to pay for massive equipment and technology imports.

The main obstacle to expanding exports of agricultural materials is likely to be the problem of raising farm output at rates substantially above the rates of natural population increase.

Exports of manufactures will have to negotiate three major obstacles. First, over one-third of such exports consists of textiles, which are import sensitive in most Western countries and Japan; that is, they compete directly with important domestic industries and quickly evoke protectionist responses. Second, there are problems of marketing Chinese products in highly sophisticated and fickle Western markets; both the quality of the goods and the quality of marketing techniques are at issue. Third, there is the competition from other low-cost producers such as Taiwan, Hong Kong, and Singapore.

To promote exports, Chinese foreign trade corporations were given greater latitude in accepting foreign export orders. Specifically, beginning in 1978, these corporations were authorized to (1) accept export orders made according to buyers' designs and trademarks; (2) accept export orders made with buyers' own materials; (3) accept export orders packed or packaged with buyers' own materials; (4) accept export orders under which the components, spare parts, or complete sets of tools were made according to the specifications of the buyer's own machines; (5) adopt different forms of payment according to concrete conditions; (6) sell goods at Chinese trade exhibitions abroad; undertake consignment sales in other countries; and (7) reasonably adjust the prices of export commodities in accordance with prevailing prices on international markets.

In 1979 China joined the International Standards Organization, which formulates recommendations regarding international manufacturing standards.

It is recognized that commodity exports alone are unlikely to carry the burden of imports in the short to medium run. To ease pressure on exports China has taken steps to increase service sales, especially tourism. Chinese investments in booming Hong Kong real estate and hotel business rose sharply in 1978. China has also announced that it is ready to accept contracts for construction work abroad to be done by Chinese construction organizations.

Chinese negotiators are, by all accounts, slow, methodical, highly skillful, and tough. They try lowering the price, no matter what the cost in time. In their search for loans in Japan and elsewhere, they have held out for credits quoted in depreciating U.S. dollars and have bargained hard to obtain the lowest interest rates possible.

CREDITS There are no longer any serious inhibitions about accepting long-term loans from foreign banks and loans or loan guarantees from foreign government-related agencies such as Export-Import Banks (Japan, U.S.A.). The progression was in seven steps consisting of acceptance of seller-arranged deferred payments, progress payments, foreign bank deposits in branches of the Bank of China, project-related foreign bank loans, syndicated international credits, bank loans unrelated to specific projects (straight commercial borrowing), and lines of credit secured from governmental export credit agencies. In yet another break with the past, China has approached a number of United Nations agencies (e.g., the U.N. Development Program, World Health Organization, UNESCO) regarding the possibility of loans to help finance, among other things, foreign language training in China. Membership in the International Monetary Fund and the World Bank was obtained in 1980.

Seller-arranged deferred payments, the main credit-financing method used by China between 1972 and 1978, were used in connection with purchases of complete plants, sets of industrial equipment, and modern technology. Complete plant contracts usually specified a 20 percent downpayment, the balance being paid over a five-year period beginning upon completion of the plant and subject to an interest rate of 6 percent. In the case of most Western European countries and Japan, such credits were guaranteed by government export assistance programs up to 85 percent of the annual payment due on the debt.

Progress payments, still widely used in trade for the purchase of complete plant and equipment sets, typically involve the following: (a) payment in two stages, of 20–30 percent of the price before the first shipment; (b) payment of a percentage of the value of each subsequent shipment; and (c) last two payments made on acceptance and expiration of the guarantee period for the plant or equipment.

By mid-1979 China had arranged for about $20 billion in long-term standby buyer credits with French, British, Italian, and Canadian banks. Direct commercial borrowing amounted at the time to another $8 billion. Consortium-arranged loans were a prominent feature of China's credit relations with Japan and Western Europe. The same applied to loans guaranteed (for up to 85 percent of total value) by government-sponsored export-import agencies. This type of financing began only in March 1979 with a British credit line of $5 billion; by May of that year, foreign government-secured credits for China had risen threefold, France, Italy, Britain, and Japan being the major participants. The loan periods varied from five to fifteen years, with annual interest rates ranging from 6.26 to 8 percent.

INVESTMENT After 1976, measures were taken to stimulate foreign investments in China and to encourage the import of advanced technology.

Perhaps the most startling measure has been the Chinese willingness to enter into joint ventures with foreign companies within China. A Law on Joint Ventures was adopted on July 1, 1979. [13] It required a minimum foreign capital contribution of 25 percent, but set no upper limits on the foreign share of total investment in any given joint venture. While typically in the past, foreign participation in joint undertakings was held down to below 50 percent, statements made by Deng Xiaoping suggested that 100 percent foreign equity share in some ventures would be acceptable to China. It was presumed, however, that ownership of such a venture would revert to China by stages after a period of ten to twenty years. The foreign contribution was expected to consist in most instances of machinery and equipment, technology, and working capital; the Chinese share would comprise land, buildings, infrastructural facilities, and labor. Raw materials were to be provided by one or both of the partners, as convenient. The chairman of the board of directors was to be appointed by the Chinese, while the vice-chairman would be nominated by the foreign participant. Profits earned by the foreign partner (fixed in proportion to the share invested) were subject to PRC income tax on joint ventures, deductions for various enterprise funds (e.g., welfare, reserve, expansion), and deductions for bonuses. Income tax could be reduced or eliminated for two to three years in certain circumstances (e.g., where the joint venture introduced technology that was up-to-date by world standards). Personal earnings by foreign employees of joint ventures could be remitted abroad after payment of personal income tax.

The law on joint ventures remains vague, and numerous potential obstacles will have to be removed. For example, it was not clear at the time of the law's promulgation what value the Chinese side would want to attach to labor input. Profitability would be considerably reduced if the Chinese insisted on paying workers Hong Kong or Taiwan level wages, which in 1979 were five to six times higher than comparable PRC wages. The implied threat of an eventual return of ownership to China may also be a deterrent to foreign investment, unless the issue is clearly spelled out and the terms of the ownership transfer are hammered out at the outset.

In order to expedite foreign investment and the importation of advanced technology, the China International Trust and Investment Corporation was set up in October 1979. [14] The corporation was placed directly under the State Council, and its main function was to enter into

[13] The text of the law may be found in *Beijing Review*, July 20, 1979, pp. 24–26.
[14] *Beijing Review*, October 19, 1979, pp. 4–5.

short-term and long-term joint venture agreements with competent Chinese authorities under commission from foreign firms. The corporation was entitled to accept funds from foreign businesses or individuals or raise funds abroad by issuing bonds. It was to act as agent under contract for foreign manufacturers and merchants in relation to advanced technology and equipment, and engage in joint ventures inside and outside China, or make investments itself.

Another means of attracting foreign investment is by compensation or buy-back trade: the foreign investor supplies machinery and equipment and receives payment (or part payment) in the goods turned out by this machinery and equipment. Usually the arrangement provides for payment to be completed within 5–10 years. The foreign investor normally is entitled to a discount on the goods that he takes for his own use. It is also usual for the investor to be granted, if he wishes, exclusive right to acquire the whole output earmarked for export and produced with the machinery and equipment supplied by the foreign investor. Until early 1980 compensation trade was most important in the area of light industrial products, and the bulk of the trade was conducted with Hong Kong and Japanese firms. Eventually, however, this method of conducting business is to be extended to offshore oil exploration and mining.

China has also indicated a readiness to process raw materials brought in by foreign entrepreneurs. The resulting goods would be owned by the foreigner and would be marketed by him abroad. The Chinese would receive a commission for the processing work done. By the end of 1979 some 200 processing agreements had been concluded, mainly with Hong Kong firms. An export processing zone—a device long used by Taiwan—was established in the county of Bao An, just north of Hong Kong's New Territories. Two other zones were to be set up in Shanghai and Tianjin.

Remittances from overseas Chinese have been used for years as a source of hard currency income, and a number of ingenious arrangements have been worked out in the past to facilitate such payments. Some of these arrangements suffered badly during the Cultural Revolution, but have been rebuilt and enlarged since. In May 1979 the Fujian Provincial Investment Company was founded. Its purpose was to encourage investments in China by overseas Chinese and by others through the offer of shares in Chinese and foreign denominations carrying a guaranteed dividend of 8 percent per annum over a twelve-year period at the expiration of which the original capital sum would be repaid. The company is also entitled to enter into compensation trade contracts, conclude joint venture agreements, and set up processing enterprises in a designated export processing zone.

China is ready to engage in barter deals involving unrelated goods; for example, Chinese oil for grain. As a rule barter is easier between two socialized centrally planned economies than when one of the partners is a private business concern not equipped to market the goods it receives in settlement of its exports. In fact, a good portion of China's trade with other socialist countries is handled in this way through the agency of trade and technical cooperation agreements concluded with each partner and by annual trade protocols deriving from these agreements. The treaties and protocols specify the goods to be exchanged, their prices, assortments, delivery schedules, and other factors.

Anywhere from a quarter to a third of China's trade with Western industrialized and noncommunist developing countries is generated at the Canton (Guangzhou) Export Commodities Fair held every spring and fall. The role of the fair in overall trade appears to be gradually diminishing with the proliferation of mini fairs, exhibitions, and special technical seminars, and the rising practice of foreign business representatives' negotiating directly in Beijing with the appropriate foreign trade corporations or, in some cases, with end users at the users' place of business. Still, the fair attracts annually some 30,000 visitors from more than 100 countries. At the fall 1979 session the volume of business transacted was $1.6 billion.

Foreign Trade Organization

The principal means used to correlate external trade with the Party's mass line and the government's foreign policy is the monopolization of external transactions by the state. The chief agents of this monopoly were the Ministry of Foreign Trade, the thirteen export-import corporations subordinated to it, a foreign trade transportation corporation, three shipping enterprises, the People's Insurance Company of China (marine insurance), the China Insurance Company, the Shanghai Advertising Corporation, Guozi Shudian publications center, and the Bank of China subordinated to the State Council.

The relatively simple foreign trade organization that existed until 1979 grew more complex and less clear that year. To promote trade, a variety of new agencies were spontaneously added to the existing trade corporations. Among these new (or restored) creations were industrial corporations that negotiated with foreign buyers and sellers on behalf of their ministries independently of the foreign trade corporations. In addition, provincial level governments have been known to engage in negotiations with foreign businesses, and, in a radical departure from previous practice, end users themselves (factories under provincial or central state authorities) frequently conducted trade talks and concluded contracts without prior approval of their provincial or central state supervisory agencies. Central allocations of foreign exchange to local production units for the purchase of foreign equipment were sharply increased. New foreign trade companies were set up to coordinate the work of existing state trading corporations with the needs of production units involved in the export-import business, and provinces (e.g., Quangdong, Fujian) were granted powers to enter directly in negotiations with foreign buyers and sellers. An early result of the rapidly growing number of units engaged in foreign trade transactions was duplication and overcommitment and a subsequent downward readjustment of orders placed with foreign firms.To coordinate what was threatening to become a huge bureaucratic muddle, yet another agency was set up in 1979: the General Administration for Exchange Control, which with the Bank of China was charged with supervising, and approving or disallowing all foreign exchange deals.

Reorientation in the Commodity Pattern of Trade

Two kinds of shifts in the commodity composition of Chinese trade have been and continue to be made. First, as a result of the Sino-Soviet dispute and the adoption around 1961 of a fresh approach to domestic economic development, the structure of imports and, to a lesser extent, exports had to be adjusted.The second involves a longer-term shift reflecting the changing structure and income level of the domestic economy.

On the import side the most spectacular change was the massive importation of grains (especially wheat) beginning in 1961. Such imports have continued at an annual volume of about 6 million tons (9.4 million tons in 1978).The importation of wheat from Canada, Australia, France, and lately the United States is explained in terms of (a) logistics—it is cheaper for China to bring in wheat by sea to feed the coastal cities than to haul it in by rail from inland wheat-growing areas; (b) change in dietary habits—bread consumption has been spreading into what were formerly predominantly rice-consuming areas; (c) international price considerations—by and large it paid to purchase wheat and sell rice, which is what the Chinese have been doing; and (d) international solidarity—China sent quantities of food, including wheat purchased abroad, to North Vietnam, the communist insurgents in Laos, Cambodia, and Thailand, as well as to friends and allies in Africa and other parts of Asia. Some Western economists have also suggested that the wheat import program is necessitated quite simply by an insufficiency of domestic production. A large-scale inventory-building program may also be a cause.

A second major change in the post-1960 pattern of imports has been the importance assumed by chemicals and chemical fertilizers. The rapid growth in the domestic production of chemical fertilizers since 1966 has resulted in a stabilization of these imports by 1973 and a reduction in their share of total imports. Among the capital goods imported (roughly one-fifth of total imports in 1977) have been complete, large-scale chemical fertilizer plants, as well as machinery and equipment, especially equipment for the petroleum and petrochemical industries, power generation (including atomic power), transport and telecommunications, and metal-working (including transfer machines and numerically controlled machine tools). These imports will assume added importance as the modernization plans progress. In addition to grains, basic materials imported include raw cotton and synthetic yarns and fibers that are processed and exported as fabrics or clothing. Iron and steel scrap, steel structurals, seamless steel tube and pipe, nonferrous metals (aluminum, nickel, and copper), and semi-manufactures are also imported. A significant change in the commodity pattern of imports has been the disappearance of mineral fuels from the list of purchases. In the 1950s petroleum imports accounted for roughly 10 percent of total imports; by 1964 they had fallen to 4 percent. In 1974 China emerged for the first time as a net exporter of oil, a development to be closely watched for its revenue-earning potential.

In 1977, 216,000 barrels per day of petroleum and petroleum products were exported (almost twice the 1974 volume), 134,000 of them to Japan. A slower but equally significant change has been the growing share of manufactured and semimanufactured industrial goods in the export trade. While in 1957 this group of commodities accounted for 25 percent of China's exports, manufactures and semimanufactures now represent about 50 percent of the annual volume of exports.

Chinese consumer goods—including processed foods (meat and fish preparations), bicycles, clothing, cigarettes, sewing machines, musical instruments, arts and handicrafts, glassware and pottery, silk screens and garments, as well as machinery and equipment used in pharmacy, perfumery, and the manufacture of insecticide, plus cement and some other items—find a ready market in Asia and to a lesser extent in Africa. In future years these items will no doubt be joined by products of the electronics and automotive industries (radios, television sets, trucks, ships, railroad cars and engines). Although unprocessed food and drink (live animals, meat, rice, fish, fruit, vegetables, and tea) and raw agricultural produce (e.g., silk, undressed hides and furs, and hog bristles) are still important in the total export trade (roughly one-third), particularly in trade with industrialized Western countries, the emphasis is on increasing the share of processed foods and agricultural materials in total sales.

Foreign Market Research

Sensing the need to move away from treating foreign trade as a residual, an appendage to domestic self-reliance, and striking out boldy, the Chinese have been actively exploring the demand patterns in a number of their more difficult export markets, especially Western Europe, Canada, and the United States. Since 1972 they have striven to make their export goods more appealing to Western tastes, to be more competitive with similar products produced locally or imported, and to conform to regulations such as those of the U.S. Food and Drug Administration. Conversely, some of China's new trading partners, the United States, for one, have adopted a more flexible attitude toward the remaining impediments to the flow of trade. In March 1979 the "frozen assets" issue dating back to the early 1950s was resolved. It had been a major stumbling block in the way of normalization of trade relations between the United States and China.The United States agreed to deblock $80.5 million worth of Chinese assets in the United States in return for China's payment of $80.5 million to American claimants over a period of five years. Since total claims by American businesses, religious organizations, and individuals against China came to $196.9 million, the settlement meant that the Chinese would pay 41 cents on the dollar. In July 1979 China and the United States concluded a three-year (renewable) trade agreement.The conclusion of this agreement was an important first step in granting China "most favored nation" status.

On the Chinese side, since the fall of the radicals, the learning process has been relatively uninhibited by ideological preconceptions. If ideological explanations are needed, the argument would normally be formulated as follows. Like domestic capitalists in the early stages of the domestic proletarian revolution, foreign capitalist powers can be used in the early stages of the international proletarian revolution. Lenin himself had at one time legitimized such procedure.The use of foreign capitalists to further socialist objectives, it is said, will tend to be less politically perilous in future years, as China gains economic muscle and consolidates its internal political controls.

Foreign Aid

China provides substantial amounts of aid in the form of both developmental loans and grants to Third World countries.[15] In the 1960s Chinese economic aid was frequently and rather obviously, tied to China's political aims, and included assistance to dissident political movements in African and Asian countries that were being aided by Beijing. There was naturally much resentment on the part of the governments of the recipient countries and friction that at times (e.g., Burma and Indonesia) led to cessation of diplomatic relations.

In the 1970s the earlier somewhat crude tying-in of economic aid to political-subversive aims was considerably toned down. By 1977 the reputation of Chinese aid projects among most recipient countries was excellent.

The amount of aid in 1970–1974 was more than double the amount extended in the previous 14 years (1956–1969): $2.4 billion compared to $1.1 billion. The $2.4 billion figure represented offers of which roughly half had actually been cashed in by 1974. An additional sum (estimated at about $1 billion from 1956 to 1974) must be added to include technical project services provided by China, but not counted in the officially published aid figures. About two-thirds of Chinese aid goes to Africa, the rest to Asia.

In Africa the two most important beneficiaries have been Tanzania and Zambia, which received more than one-third of China's total aid to Africa between 1970 and 1974. In Asia, Pakistan is the most important recipient. Very little aid has been channeled into the Middle East and even less into Latin America. The most significant Chinese aid project has been the railway linking the Zambian copper fields with the Tanzanian port of Dar es Salaam. Almost $100 million a year (not counting technical services) was spent by China on this project which was completed in 1974. In addition to materials and technical expertise, China supplied unskilled labor for the construction of the line.

The Tan-Zam railway project points to the type of aid the Chinese prefer. The bulk of Chinese loans and grants goes for infrastructural investment, especially transport and communications, the development of energy and raw material sources, and agriculture. Industrial projects financed by China are of the light variety, mostly labor intensive, moderate in size, and employing local labor, local materials, and intermediate technology. Less than 5 percent of China's aid expenditures have gone to

[15]The description of China's foreign aid draws on C. H. Fogarty's "China's Economic Relations with the Third World," in *China: A Reassessment*, pp. 730–37.

heavy industry, almost the exact reverse of the proportion of Soviet aid devoted to heavy industry. In sum, the Chinese concentrate on the aid projects that are most familiar to them and at which they are very good.

To avoid the problem of the recipient countries' inability to absorb the aid because of a shortage of local funds to pay for local costs, China has made it a practice to include in the aid package light industrial goods for sale in the recipient country's market; the proceeds are used to pay for local costs of the aid projects. The quality of Chinese-aided projects is high, delivery schedules are adhered to, and projects are completed on time. [16]

Loans are granted on liberal terms. No interest is charged, and the credits are repayable over 10, 20, or 30 years following 10 years of grace. Repayment is normally made in goods produced by the recipient country. Total Chinese grants since 1956 come to about one-half billion dollars.

In contrast to earlier years when Chinese technicians and others appeared to have engaged in disruptive political activity in the host countries, the behavior of Chinese aid personnel in the 1970s has been on the whole exemplary.

Military assistance to legitimate governments of Third World countries as well as to insurgent movements had been given in the past and continues to be given—particularly to the former. [17] From 1958 through 1969 China's military aid to Third World governments was about $250 million, mostly in the form of straight gifts of small arms, ammunition, communications equipment, light and medium tanks, and various items of logistical support, including training. From 1970 through 1974 military aid rose to $300 million, two-thirds of it destined for Pakistan and another 10 percent to Tanzania. In all, about eighteen countries of Asia and Africa were receiving Chinese military aid in the mid to late 1970s.

SUGGESTED READING

Domestic Trade

"Domestic Trade in Communist China." Selected translations from the P.R.C. press, January–October 1961, Nos. 1–41. Published by the *Joint Publications Research Service (JPRS)*, (Springfield, Va.).

[16]Ibid., p. 733.
[17]Ibid., p. 735.

Donnithorne, Audrey, *China's Economic System* (New York: Praeger, 1967), Chapter 11.

Henle, H. V., *Report on China's Agriculture* (Rome: Food and Agriculture Organization of the United Nations, 1974, pp. 57–61.

"Szechwan Daily Comments on Finance, Trade Roles." Chengtu Szechwan Provincial Service in Mandarin, July 8, 1975, in *Foreign Broadcast Information Service (FBIS),* July 9, 1975, pp. J1–J3.

Foreign Trade

Bennett, Gordon (ed.), *China's Finance and Trade: A Policy Reader* (White Plains, N.Y.: M. E. Sharpe, 1979).

Chen, Nai-Ruenn, "China's Foreign Trade, 1950–74," in *China: A Reassessment,* pp. 617–52.

China Business Review (Washington, D.C.: National Council for U.S.–China Trade).

China Trade and Economic Newsletter (London: Monitor Consultants). Monthly.

China Trader (Hong Kong: Sino Communication Co.). Quarterly.

China Trade Report (Hong Kong: Far Eastern Economic Review). Monthly.

China's Foreign Trade (Beijing). Monthly.

China's Foreign Trade Corporations and Organizations (Beijing: China Council for the Promotion of International Trade, 1978).

Chiu, Hungdah (ed.), *The Chinese Connection and Normalization* (Baltimore: University of Maryland School of Law, 1979).

Cooper, J. F., *China's Foreign Aid: An Instrument of Peking's Foreign Policy* (Lexington, Mass.: Heath, 1976).

Denny, David L., "International Finance in the People's Republic of China," in *China: A Reassessment,* pp. 653–77.

Fogarty, Carol H., "China's Economic Relations with the Third World," in *China: A Reassessment,* pp. 730–37.

Hardy, R. W., *China's Oil Future: A Case of Modest Expectations* (Boulder, Colo.: Westview Press, 1978).

Hsiao, Gene T., *The Foreign Trade of China: Policy, Law, and Practice* (Berkeley, Los Angeles: University of California Press, 1977).

Kaplan, Frederic M., and Mary Lou Teel (eds.), *JAL Executive Business Guide to China* (Fair Lawn, N. J.: Eurasia Press, 1979).

Li, Victor H., *Law and Politics in China's Foreign Trade* (Seattle: University of Washington Press, 1977).

Neilan, Edward, and Charles R. Smith, *The Future of the China Market: Prospects for Sino-American Trade* (Washington, D.C.: American

Enterprise Institute for Public Policy Research and the Hoover Institution, Stanford, California, August, 1974).

Prybyla, Jan S., "United States Trade with China," *Current History* (Philadelphia), May/June 1979, pp. 209–13, 222–23.

"Reforming Trade Practices," *China Trade Report* (Hong Kong), May 1980, p. 12.

Szuprowicz, Bohdan, and Maria Szuprowicz, *Doing Business with the People's Republic of China: Industries and Markets* (New York: Wiley, 1978).

U.S. Department of Commerce, *U.S. Trade Status with Communist Countries* (Washington, D.C.). Monthly.

Wilson, D., "Another Good Year for the Bank of China," *U.S.–China Business Review* (Washington, D.C.), Vol. III, No. 3, May–June 1976, pp. 8–9.

Zhang Zehyu, "China's Growing Tourist Industry," *Beijing Review,* July 7, 1980, pp. 14–26.

NINE

Public Health and Education

We saw in Chapter 1 that an important component of China's basic problem is how to keep a large and growing population in good physical and mental health; in other words, how to provide quality medical care and education. It is, of course, easier to define good physical health than to agree on what constitutes good education. The two converge at various points: public health presupposes an educational effort to promote principles of hygiene, for example, and medical delivery systems cannot function without medical training programs and research. In this chapter we shall deal first with the problem of public health and the policy responses to it. In a second part we shall examine educational problems and policies.

PUBLIC HEALTH PROBLEMS

The economic benefits of a healthy citizenry and a well-developed public health system include higher productivity of the work force, reduction in the number of workdays lost to illness, longer participation in the labor force resulting from a decrease in mortality rates, and, where health delivery points are rationally distributed, reduction in working time lost by traveling to medical centers and waiting for treatment. In addition, there are important psychological benefits flowing from the availability of medical help when it is needed.

In underdeveloped countries, perhaps the major cause of widespread poor health is malnutrition. Malnutrition has deleterious effects on intelligence, resistance to disease, and physical size. It also reduces labor productivity. In short, malnutrition breeds an inherently inferior work force. [1] The problem of public health is, therefore, more than simply a question of supplying medical care to the multitudes; it has ramifications in many areas of economic policy, especially agricultural policy. Here, however, we shall be concerned only with initial problems and the organization, operation, costs, and benefits of the medical-public health system.

China's medical-public health system in the 1950s and early 1960s was not very different from those of other developing economies: there was not enough medical care, and the services that did exist were poorly distributed. Specifically, the problem may be broken down into three components: a shortage of physicians, maldistribution of medical-public health personnel, and a shortage of resources to finance the medical-public health system.

Shortage of Physicians

Hu [2] estimates that before the Cultural Revolution the doctor (strictly defined) to population ratio in China was 1:5000. In the rural areas it was 1:8000. Out of some half million medical personnel in 1965, only 100,000 held the title of doctor. While this represented an improvement over 1955, when there were 370,000 medical workers, 8 percent of whom held a medical doctor's degree, it was clearly an unsatisfactory situation. Statistics for the number of doctors per 100,000 inhabitants for 35 countries in 1965 show that China ranked twelfth, behind Mexico, India, and the Philippines, among others. At that time the number of doctors per 100,000 people in China was roughly one-third of what it had been in Japan at the end of the nineteenth century. The paucity of medical care was, around 1965, to an extent offset by the progress that had been made

[1] Pedro Belli, "The Economic Implications of Malnutrition: The Dismal Science Revisited," *Economic Development and Cultural Change,* Vol. XX, October 1971, pp. 1–23, and comments by W. T. Wilford, R. H. Franke, G. V. Barret, and F. M. Peterson, and reply by Pedro Belli, ibid., Vol. XXIII January 1975, pp. 337–57.

[2] Teh-wei Hu, "An Economic Analysis of the Cooperative Medical Services in the People's Republic of China," Paper presented at the Allied Social Science Association Meetings, San Francisco, December 1974, p. 10.

since 1949 in basic public hygiene (achieved mainly through mass mobilization campaigns against the "Four-Evils"—rats, flies, mosquitoes, and grain-eating sparrows) and the improvement in nutritional standards. In these respects China was better off than many other countries with comparable per capita income. Most endemic diseases, such as cholera, bubonic plague, and smallpox, had been eliminated, and a number of parasitic diseases (e.g., schistosomiasis) had been brought under control. Nevertheless, the situation remained precarious. [3]

During the Cultural Revolution three reasons were given for the slow increase in medical personnel in the first fifteen years of the regime. First to be cited was "overtraining" of physicians in medical schools modeled after the Soviets, particularly the time it took to complete formal medical studies (from three years for middle-level doctors to eight years at the China Medical University).The second reason given was the concentration of medical personnel on "exotic" research into rare diseases, requiring elaborate and costly treatment, at the expense of "mass" research and direct service to the community. An attempt to reverse this trend had been made during the Great Leap Forward, but apparently without significant results.The criticism voiced during the Cultural Revolution was part of the general antielitist, serve-the-masses Maoist line, which we have come across earlier.The third reason cited was the disparaging attitude of the "Liu Shaoqi-Lin Biao clique" toward traditional Chinese medicine and toward the quarter million (mainly rural-based) practitioners of that medicine, and the clique's excessive preoccupation with foreign (i.e., Western) medical training and procedures. Many such procedures, some argued, were highly capital-intensive and were a financial burden on the state. Besides, they insisted, some of these methods and procedures were unsuited to China's clinical needs. A dose of national pride was thus added to an argument cast primarily in class proletarian and economic terms. After 1976 this argument was seldom heard.

Maldistribution of Medical and Public Health Personnel

Hu's investigations reveal that before 1966 about 80 percent of the physicians were located in urban areas where less than 20 percent of the

[3]A broadcast from Wuhan, Hubei Province (May 23, 1979), spoke of areas in the province "plagued" by schistosomiasis and noted the need to raise the standards of medical teams engaged in fighting the disease.

population lived. In terms of capital construction, the emphasis was on city and specialized hospitals, and health stations, clinics, dispensaries, and hospitals in the countryside were neglected. Most of the doctors and medical facilities were found in the developed areas of the east and northeast, especially in the coastal provinces.

Financial Problems

The cost implications of the public health system as it existed before 1966 have already been mentioned in the discussion of medical training, research, and concentration on Western medical practices. A system of this kind relied heavily upon state financial contributions and, despite the decentralizations of 1957 and the communization of the following year, tended to be top heavy. Before 1966, roughly 80 percent of the state's expenditure on national health went to urban areas—most in the east. [4] At the end of 1957 only 6.6 million state sector workers (out of roughly 40 million) benefited from free medical care. Rural producers' cooperatives at that time set aside about 10 percent of their annual gross income for their members' welfare (including medical care). In many cases this was mere tokenism, as it had been earlier in Soviet collective farm experience.

Reciting of the problems that faced China's public health services in the 1950s and early 1960s should not obscure the accomplishments.The mass mobilization campaigns of the 1950s against schistosomiasis, the eradication or control of other parasitic and endemic diseases, the improved hygiene and sanitation, the greater availability and awareness of proper nutrition, the suppression of drug addiction, and other measures, represented significant contributions (and relatively inexpensive) toward the betterment of the people's health.The three problems just examined were largely ones of medical training and research, distribution, and sharing of financial burdens.The excessive language used during the Cultural Revolution, and for some time after, to saddle this or that faction with blame for the remaining shortcomings must be, to a degree, discounted.To paint one's defeated enemies and all their works in black colors is standard communist procedure; it is used as a dialectical means to bring out the brightness of the present. By the Maoists' own admission in 1969, 95 percent of all physical disabilities in China fell under the category of "common illnesses," certainly a vast improvement over the situation in the early 1950s. Precisely because the tradi-

[4] Teh-wei Hu, op. cit.

tional killers had been checked by repeated massive assults known as "patriotic health campaigns," backed by the skill of small numbers of qualified experts in the fields of medicine and public health, it was possible to elaborate certain organizational forms and approaches that looked promising. In this area, as in others, the contradiction between past and present was not as sharp as it was often made out to be. [5]

PUBLIC HEALTH POLICIES

In this section we shall review the public health policies pursued by the Chinese since the Cultural Revolution.Three areas of concern will be examined: solving the manpower shortage, redistributing medical and public health personnel, and minimizing costs.

Solving the Manpower Shortage

The economic objective of increasing the number of medical and public health personnel was combined for a time (i.e., until the fall of the radicals in October 1976) with the left ideological goal of antielitism and anticredentialism. As noted earlier (Chapter 2), the public health function was linked to the drive for family planning.

Three interrelated measures were strategic to the attempt to solve the manpower problem: (a) a reform of the medical training system; (b) the reintroduction and expansion of paramedical and allied public health personnel; and (c) an emphasis on the use of practitioners of traditional Chinese medicine.The resolution of the medical manpower shortage in the countryside, especially in the less-developed regions, was tackled by these three means and by measures to be discussed under the heading of manpower redistribution.

REFORM OF THE MEDICAL TRAINING SYSTEM The left-sponsored reform of medical schools from 1966 until 1976 was part of a more general restructuring of China's educational system, the broad outlines of which will be discussed later in this chapter. Here we need only note the essentials particular to the medical profession:

1. Admission to medical schools was popularized. Preference was

[5] After October 1976 the fallen radical leaders were, of course, blamed for drawing such dark pictures of pre–Cultural Revolution reality. "They magnified the interference by Liu Shaoqi's revisionist line after liberation and painted a totally dark picture of the first 17 years (1949–66) after liberation." *Peking Review,* No. 13, March 25, 1977, p. 14.

given to poor and lower-middle peasants, workers, and soldiers. Candidates were to be unmarried and were expected to possess at least two years' practical experience in production. The reformed admissions policy worked against a rapid increase in enrollments. Most Chinese medical schools in 1974–1975 had enrollments substantially below 1965. Part of the difficulty was to find the right combination of correct class background and ability to handle the medical learning process. In addition, a portion of the shortened study time had to be devoted to what was euphemistically described as "make-up study," i.e., tutoring.

2. The average period of formal medical training was reduced from six to three and a half years (of which one-half year was devoted to make-up study). Among the reasons cited (at the Canton Medical College) for this telescoping of study period at the time of my visit (1974) was the "tremendous motivation" of the new student body which enabled the students to learn better, faster, and more economically, and the fact that large portions of the curriculum could be shortened and simplified (e.g., legal medicine) or drastically pruned (e.g., dermatology and the study of venereal diseases) because the social and clinical conditions in new China allegedly made such topics less urgent and relevant than before. It was claimed that a good deal of earlier duplication and overlapping of subject matter had been eliminated.

3. Beginning with the first year, students spent a portion of their formal training in practical medical and public health work outside the school, especially in rural areas.

4. Formal graduate instruction was abolished. After completing the three and a half years of general training, graduates went out into the field. Following five years of practical experience, some returned to school to deepen their specialty acquired through practice.

5. Highly theoretical, pure ("exotic") research was drastically cut back in favor of applied research by the faculty. Much of this was carried out in the field.

In short, the left-sponsored reform tried to accelerate the training process and make semiskilled medical services available to the population during the shortened study period.

After October 1976 (cautiously and quietly even before that time) the bulk of the left-sponsored reform of medical training was rolled back. Most of the changes made during 1966–1976 were declared to have been motivated by an ultraleft obscurantist philosphy: "The educational front," commented *Renmin Ribao* (May 17, 1979), "is a heavily damaged area." Admission to medical schools was depopularized; it became contingent on the successful negotiation of tough entrance examinations in which mastery of technical subject matter dominated.The two-year production experience requirement was not officially repealed, but neither was it considered central to the admissions process.The average period of formal medical training was lengthened to about six years—what it had been before the Cultural Revolution.The shortened version of medical study introduced during that troubled period was dismissed after 1976 as "haste makes waste." The existence of some diseases formerly denied (e.g., mental illness, especially schizophrenia; venereal diseases) has been admitted and the need for training physicians to deal with these disabilities was again recognized. Courses in legal medicine were reinstituted as part of a general restoration of "socialist legality" and denunciation of the reign of subjectivism and arbitrariness under the gang of four. Practical medical and public health work by students during their period of formal medical training was not abandoned; however, such practical experience was approached more from the standpoint of its value to the students' professional training than from that of political consciousness ("immersing the intellectuals in the broad masses"). Formal graduate instruction was restored in 1978, the normal progression being from undergraduate to graduate school without a mandatory period of practical work in the field. Theoretical, even "exotic," research was again put in the regime's good graces.

The impression given by the post-gang reform of medical education was of a return to the condition that existed before the Cultural Revolution, especially during the "Liuist" period 1961–1965. Of course, here as in other fields things will never be quite the same, not only because of the passage of time but because of the cataclysmic impact of the events of 1966–1969 on the very substance of China's society. In the rush to serve the people, much expertise and special training was lost. The Cultural Revolution overcorrected what had been a debatable system of medical training, given China's level of development and urgent public health needs. Perhaps in the desire to correct this overcorrection, the post-Mao leadership of Deng-Hua has again overcorrected, this time in the direction of professional elitism with an urban bias. By 1979, for medical school aspirants as for others, IQ was what counted, plus a solid preparation in the natural sciences and good examination grades. No doubt, a well-connected relative was also helpful. But, for the time being, the days of walking into the operating theater straight from work in the rice paddies on the recommendation of one's fellow poor peasants and with the approval of populist-minded (or at least populist-posturing) Party brass are all but gone. It is possible that under the new system (the system of "restoration," as the leftists used to call it), "barefoot doctors" who have had some medical and public health training will tend to have an edge in medical admissions competition over other applicants. [6]

PARAMEDICAL PERSONNEL Since 1966 China has trained 1,600,000 paramedics and well over 3 million part-time health workers, most of whom serve in the rural areas. In the countryside the paramedics are known as "barefoot doctors"; [7] in urban areas they are called "red worker doctors" when attached to a factory, or "street doctors" in residential neighborhoods (streets and alleys). Barefoot, street, and red worker doctors are trained in the elements of medicine over a period of from three to six months. Barefoot doctors are given such instruction either in the nearby town hospital or by a visiting mobile medical team in the rural locality. Sometimes, particularly in the more remote areas of the country, new barefoot doctors are trained by experienced barefoot doctors. Paramedics supervise and instruct the health workers assigned to them.

Both barefoot doctors and health workers spend part of their time in production work on farms or industrial tasks in the brigade or team to which they belong. Barefoot doctors, for example, are required to devote at least 100 working days a year to such employment. Red worker and street doctors are also part-time workers. From conversations in Shanghai, I assume that frequently red worker doctors (many of them women) when not performing their medical duties are assigned to the factory nursery, kindergarten, or school, or perform other socially oriented, nonmanual tasks. In the countryside, significant numbers of barefoot doctors are recruited from among rusticated urban youths. Most street doctors are housewives who tend to the health needs of workers' dependents in the street or alley to which they are assigned and on which they live, while the working members of families are normally taken care of by red worker or other doctors at the enterprise in which they work. Under the supervision of the street and red worker doctors in towns and barefoot doctors in the countryside, public health workers make sure that the place is clean and that twice a year (in the spring and fall) the patriotic health campaign—a vast cleaning-up operation—is properly carried out.

[6]This is implied by a *Beijing Review* article of June 1, 1979, p. 6.

[7]The first barefoot doctors emerged in the suburbs of Shanghai during the Great Leap Forward years. The system, after lapsing for a while, was revived in response to Mao's June 26, 1965 call: "In medical and health work, put stress on the rural areas." In 1965 (as compared with 1958), it received a more pronounced rural orientation.

Paramedics, in both town and country, diagnose illnesses, refer the more serious cases up the medical-organizational ladder, treat the simpler cases, and instruct health workers under their supervision to carry out vaccinations, distribute birth control pills and information, check on the cleanliness of homes, restaurants, and retail stores, and perform other public health duties. Hu [8] estimated the ratio of paramedical personnel (barefoot, street, red worker doctors) to population in 1970–1973 as 1:760 and that of health workers to population as 1:265, which was much better than the pre-1966 physician: population ratio of 1:5000 (1:8000 in the countryside). In terms of formal medical qualifications the two sets of figures are, strictly speaking, not comparable. On the basis of official Chinese figures, the ratio of (formally qualified) physicians to population in 1978 was 1:939. If only senior physicians of Western medicine are considered (i.e., not the products of Cultural Revolution-type medical training) the ratio was 1:2,737.

There are a number of actual and potential costs involved in the paramedical system. One is the possibility of faulty diagnosis and wrong treatment. Such cases surely happen, and when they do, loss of confidence in the system occurs and rapidly spreads through the neighborhood or village. One may counter by saying that this is no worse than the loss of confidence in fully trained, neighborhood medical doctors that most of us have experienced in our lifetime.The second problem concerns the operation of the referral system. Assuming correct diagnosis, serious cases are referred to more qualified medical personnel and better-equipped facilities at the commune, county, urban, district, or municipal levels, or to specialized hospitals. A strict yet flexible control of referrals is needed in order not to overburden the county, district, municipal, and specialized hospital system, and at the same time not leave the paramedics with cases they are not competent to treat. One means used to reduce the flow of patients to higher-level facilities is the registration fee required for each visit and the charging of some hospitalization costs to certain categories of patients.There is also the question of the competence of post-Cultural Revolution doctors trained under simplified and hurried curriculums. Cynics suggest that given the state of medical schools, it would be the better part of wisdom not to be referred at all, but to take one's chances with the medics.

Questions have also been raised about the opportunity cost of training large numbers of paramedics. Although difficult to quantify, there appears to be a consensus among Western students of the Chinese

[8]Teh-wei Hu, op. cit., pp. 12, 14.

paramedical system that the system is rational in China's present conditions and that substantial net benefits accrue to the community from its operation. One analysis concludes that the benefit: cost ratio ranges from 5 to 14, with an average of 10. [9] The quantification of the problem reinforces visual impressions of notable achievement. It should be added that the paramedics are an integral part of the alley, street, production team, or brigade community; they are part-time workers, many of them raised where they are now employed. They know everybody and everybody knows them, not just professionally but personally. In this sense, and abstracting from the political control potentials of this situation, the paramedics bridge the gap between the purely professional and personal sides of doctor-patient relationship. The system, although it has many characteristics imbued with specifically Chinese cultural mores, is worthy of study by other developing countries.

TRADITIONAL CHINESE MEDICINE Supplementing the 770,000 doctors of Western medicine are 250,000 physicians practicing traditional Chinese medicine based on the use of herbs and acupuncture, but comprising wider interests. Traditional methods of diagnosis and cure have always been important. Since the Cultural Revolution this branch of medicine has been accorded official legitimacy and is, in fact, extensively used. Many, probably most, commune-level, neighborhood, and factory medical facilities are staffed by doctors of traditional Chinese medicine. The art is taught to students of Western medicine during a part of their formal college training.

At the Canton Medical College I was told that veteran practitioners of traditional medicine were invited to give lectures at the college for periods of up to six months. Surgical operations using Western medical knowledge are sometimes performed with the aid of acupuncture anesthesia. In place of aspirin, I have swallowed evil-smelling but effective pills made of crushed antelope and rhinoceros horns. Research is being conducted into the scientific principles and theories underlying the traditional art of healing. Provincial colleges of traditional Chinese medicine, some of which operate branches within their province, also exist. Doctors of traditional medicine make a significant contribution to the availability of medical and public health personnel at the intermediate level, i.e., the level just above the production team/brigade, alley, and street, which, as we have seen, are staffed by paramedics and health workers. Use of herbs and allied preparations, procured locally

[9] Ibid., p. 33.

for the most part, reduces the cost of medicines and increases the supply of drugs. Collection and preparation of such medicines under the supervision of practitioners of traditional medicine becomes a neighborhood or commune project, part of the collective, self-help activities that constitute an important aspect of China's social policy.

The disappearance of the radical leadership in 1976 appears to have had no profound repercussions in the field of traditional Chinese medicine. There seemed to be less enthusiasm about acupuncture and herbal medications prepared by politically conscious practitioners of the art than there had been in the ideologically broiling, xenophobic, miracle-cure days of the Cultural Revolution. But this was by and large a matter of shifting emphasis. The relationship between the Chinese and Western schools of medicine was the subject of a nationwide conference on health work held in 1977. The conference devoted a good deal of thought to "speeding up" the integration of the two schools in a planned manner. An All-China Association for Traditional Chinese Medicine was established in Beijing in 1979 and an Acupuncture Society was concurrently affiliated with it. As in other areas of endeavor, the post-gang approach to traditional Chinese medicine stressed rebuilding formal (one is almost tempted to say "Leninist") organizational structures under Party and government supervision. Judgment as to the usefulness and future position of traditional Chinese medicine tended to be based on criteria that were ideologically more centrist and directly relevant to the modernization program.

Redistributing Personnel

The Cultural Revolution gave impetus to the idea of relocating large numbers of medical and public health personnel from urban to rural areas. This relocation, a part of the more general policy of "downward transfer," involved both temporary and permanent transfer. Temporary transfer was of various kinds. The most common was the mobile team, which made its rounds in the countryside for a period of six months to a year. It was estimated in the mid-1970s that roughly one-third of the medical personnel of urban hospitals were normally on the road. Mobile teams on their rounds provided diagnosis and treatment for rural patients, inspected the work of paramedics, especially the record of referrals, and trained new barefoot doctors. Some mobile medical teams were attached to the People's Liberation Army. Faculty members of medical schools made trips to the countryside (or factories) with their students for varying periods of time. "They go down to the rural areas, make investigations, and learn by practice; they combine practical experience with book knowledge." In 1968, 700,000 medical workers from the cities went to the countryside for temporary duty.

Many doctors settled permanently in the countryside after the Cultural Revolution. Between 1971 and 1973 about 300,000 medical workers of all kinds (including newly graduated doctors and pharmacologists) were moved to rural areas.

The emphasis in medical manpower distribution was on the poor and rural rather than the rich and urban. Insofar as the benefits and costs of shifting manpower from city to country can be quantified, the marginal benefits accruing to the poor and rural areas exceeded the marginal loss of benefits to the rich and urban areas. The shifting about and the moving, combined with the openly anti-intellectual temper that prevailed from the time of the Cultural Revolution till the death of Mao, however, did entail long-term costs for China's medical science. Medical research that could not be directly connected with current needs of the rural poor and that could not be applied in short order was deemphasized and considered ideologically incorrect and harmful. Some of it surely went on at various institutes of the Academy of Sciences, but not in the medical schools and affiliated hospitals. Already cancer is emerging as China's second most frequent killer, and other "modern" diseases are not far behind. The Chinese are acutely aware of this new problem. The left argument that "intellectuals without exception are working to dig up the foundation of socialism" and that they "constitute the social basis of the capitalist-roaders" was resolutely refuted immediately following the arrest of the four leading radicals. [10]

Rustication of medical doctors, dispersal of urban-based medical research teams, and the disruption of orderly process by constant ideological reeducation and rotation of researchers and laboratory workers were subjected to critical examination after the fall of the gang as part of a more general reappraisal of China's skilled manpower needs in the context of the proposed economic, scientific, and military modernization program. Like the *xia xiang* movement, the legacy of the Cultural Revolution as regards the redistribution of personnel between town and country was being rather hastily dismantled in 1979. This, perhaps more than any other social readjustment of the post-Mao

[10] "A Serious Struggle in Scientific and Technical Circles," by the Theoretical Group of the Chinese Academy of Sciences, *Peking Review*, No. 16, April 15, 1977, pp. 24–27. According to this article, the gang of four classified 70 percent of the members of the Chinese Academy of Sciences Party nucleus group as "bourgeois inside the Party" and described the Academy's Party organization as "bourgeois in nature."

Deng-Hua period, carried with it the risk of political backfiring. The provision of rudimentary medical and public-health care to 800,000,000 rural Chinese has become since 1966 a reality that can be undermined by the new urban-and-expert temper only at the risk of serious penalties for those who do the undermining. Under a liberalized policy, medical workers trained in Western medicine are likely to resist even temporary downward transfer, while those already rusticated may be expected to try to make their way back to the cities. That is perhaps why so much attention is being given to the role of practitioners of Chinese medical science and the relationship between the two schools. That is also possibly why there is talk of "putting shoes on the barefoot doctors" (a phrase that would have been blasphemous while Mao was alive), which means upgrading their skills in anticipation of greater responsibilities that may have to be assumed as others with more advanced training return to the cities.

Minimizing Costs

Since 1966 two main solutions have been offered to the problem of financing a nationwide medical-public health service that would, in fact and not just on paper, serve the people. The first solution was organizational, and consisted of the introduction in the countryside of a Cooperative Medical Service as an addition to (a) the already existing free or quasi-free medical service for workers and employees in the state sector (this system continues to operate under the labor insurance and social security laws adopted in the 1950s), and (b) the system of full payments for medical services by certain classes of individuals. The second solution to the financing problem was, as has already been mentioned, greater resort to herbal medicines and acupuncture.

COOPERATIVE MEDICAL SERVICE The principal objective of the Cooperative Medical Service is to supply medical and health care to 80 percent of China's people on a continuing basis. This objective is in sharp contrast with the classical Stalinist policy of neglecting the physical welfare of the rural population, a policy that held sway in the Soviet Union until the late 1950s. The main pillars supporting the system are self-financing, accompanied by considerable operational discretion at the local level, and the million-and-a-half-strong army of paramedics. The system at the production-team, production-brigade, and commune levels is expected to pay its own way without significant outside (state) subsidies. It is fair to say that whereas the Soviet medical-public health service in the countryside under Stalin existed mainly on paper and, where it did operate, consisted as a rule of a Red Cross box in the outhouse, the Chinese Cooperative Medical Service is an effective reality. Table 24 summarizes its main characteristics.

Given the condition of Chinese economic science from 1966 to at least 1976, [11] and the heavy input of practical politics and ideology into economic decision-making, it is doubtful that before launching a major project, the Cooperative Medical Service for example, the dominant Chinese leadership faction of the time resorted to careful and refined cost-benefit studies. On the contrary, evidence points to an impetuous and instinctive breaking down of obstacles in the way of what was believed to have been the right thing; an irreconcilable one-divides-into-two shock therapy that subsequently had to be corrected in a succession of two-legged revisionist compromises. Nevertheless, as in rural industries, location, and choice of technologies, the short- and medium-range benefits seemed to outweigh the economic costs. Perhaps the more lasting benefit of this approach was the close involvement of the public in their own affairs. This involvement was by and large involuntary, despite the rhetoric used to explain it, but over time it was built into the behavior pattern of the community, and in the case of the Cooperative Medical Service was beneficial to the physical health of those who had been neglected and deprived. The community was pushed and goaded out of apathy and the beggar-thy-neighbor mentality; it was prodded into self-reliance in what was perhaps the world's largest bootstraps operation. This is as much as to say that the post-gang portrayal of the radicals' line as capricious and economically illiterate is not the whole truth, but that it contains large elements of scapegoatism and score settling. While many of the things born of the Cultural Revolution and the earlier Great Leap Forward were undoubtedly abusive and prejudicial to some sections of the community (notably the intellectuals, large chunks of the Party and government apparat, those arbitrarily branded as being of the incorrect social lineage and their descendants, and more generally the urbanites), there were portions of the left's policies that benefited others (especially the poorer sections of the rural community). While Western Marxists sympathetic to the Chinese left's cause are predictably upset by the post-gang revisions of Mao's message, [12] the casting of stones on the Deng-Hua line is not limited to

[11]George Braybrooke, "Recent Developments in Chinese Social Science," *China Quarterly,* No. 79, September 1979, pp. 593–607.

[12]Charles Bettelheim and Neil Burton, *China since Mao* (New York: Monthly Review Press, 1978).

them. There appears to be much nervousness in the ranks of the left, as yet not totally silenced, especially in the poorer rural areas, about a possible readjustment of the Cooperative Medical Service as part of the four modernizations drive. The modernizers may be touching a potentially worrisome raw nerve of the new China.

Admittedly, the main longer-range drawbacks of left-inspired policies have been the excessive anti-intellectualism that pervaded their mass-involvement campaigns, the class antagonism generated, and the damage done to the constructive and creative remnants of individualism which could have been harnessed to the public good. The organization of the rural and urban health-care system in China is outlined in Figures 4 and 5.

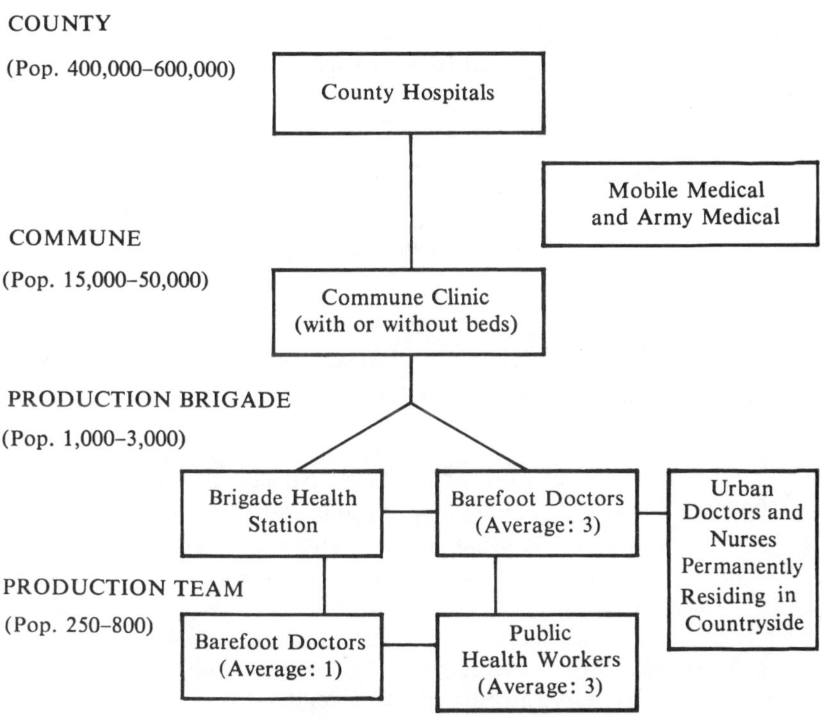

SOURCE: Teh-wei Hu, op. cit., p. 6.

FIGURE 4. *Rural health care system.*

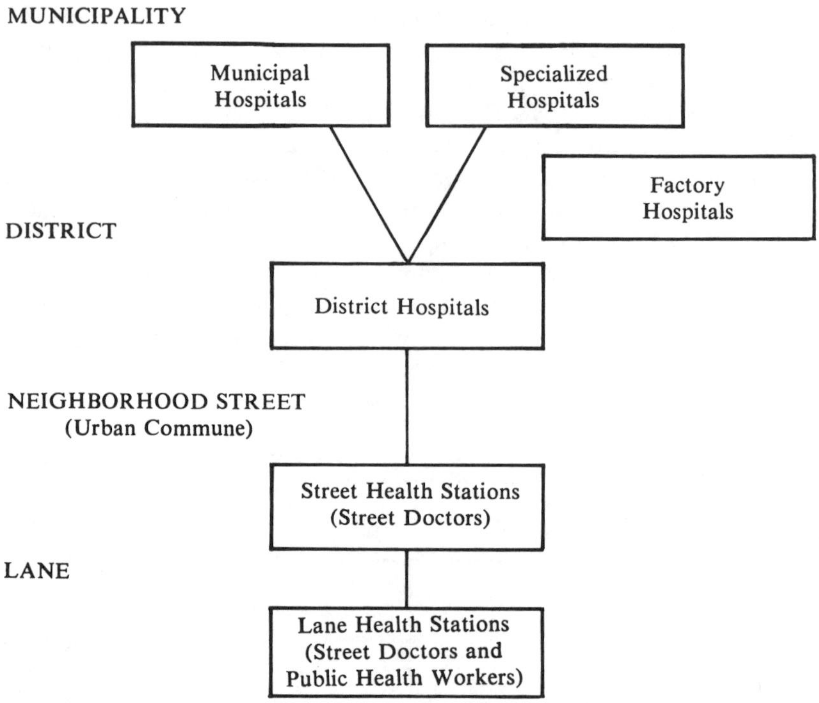

SOURCE: Teh-wei Hu, op. cit., p. 7.

FIGURE 5. *Urban health care.*

A few words must be said about the urban health-care system. Workers in state sector industrial, mining, and transport-communications enterprises as well as the employees of such enterprises and of trade, cultural, educational,[13] construction, governmental, and Party organs and mass organizations are treated for the most part in enterprise-related hospitals and clinics, or, if the problem cannot be handled at that level, are referred to district, municipal, or special hospitals. Two kinds of payments are made by the patient: (a) a registration fee amounting to about 0.10 yuan per visit, and (b) the full cost of meals during hospitalization. If the illness is work related, the patient pays for only 20 percent

[13]Students of higher educational institutions are included. Also included are teachers in secondary schools, except those under commune management.

TABLE 24 **The Cooperative Medical Service**

Item	*Description*
Membership	Membership is open to all members of rural people's communes, irrespective of age. Until 1977 the "Five Black Classes" were excluded, in some cases even the children of the branded. By 1974, 70 percent of production brigades had joined the system. This would mean close to 500 million people. Participation is voluntary.
Personnel	250,000 practitioners of traditional Chinese medicine; medical doctors trained in both Western and traditional Chinese medicine who visit the countryside in mobile teams; city medical personnel resettled permanently in the countryside; 1.6 million barefoot doctors; and over 3 million health workers. Army medical teams lend assistance to the system.
Financing	
Income	The system is self-supporting "in the main." The following are the major sources of income. (1) *Annual membership fee*. This varies from place to place and in the same place over time, depending on the balance of costs and expenditures. The fee range per person per year is from 0.35 yuan to 3.60 yuan. The average is about 1.50 yuan per person per year. For a family of five, this would represent an annual expenditure on medical insurance of 7.50 yuan. Based on data presented in Chapter 3, such expenditure would represent 0.5 percent of the gross income from communal work of an exceptionally well-off family of five with three working members and 8.3 percent of the gross income from communal work of a family of five (three working members) in a very poor production team. The membership fee burden for poor and middle income rural families is therefore quite significant. (2) For each consultation at the production-brigade health station *a consulting fee* of between 0.03 and 0.05 yuan is paid. The measure appears to be intended primarily to discourage indiscriminate use of the brigades' medical facilities by members. (3) For each subscribing member in a production team, *the production team pays a contribution* of between 0.10 and 1 yuan a year out of the team's welfare fund. The exact size of the contribution depends on the costs of operating the system and the team's income from farm production in a given year. (4) At the *production brigade level,* monies are earmarked for the CMS from both the welfare and construction funds. (5) *The commune contributes funds* to the system from two sources: (a) the welfare fund—to cover current operational costs, and (b) the reserve fund—for capital expenditures. (6) Commune-level resources for capital construction are supplemented on occasion by (central and/or provincial) *state funds*. Such funds are normally allotted to commune and county authorities for the construction of hospitals, dispensaries, and clinics. The state also supplies the system with medicines not procurable locally, as well as surgical and other equipment. Some of these supplies have to be paid for; some are given as grants. (7) *Subsidiary sources* of income.
Expenditure	Cost reductions are sought through the preparation of herbal drugs, use of acupuncture, and the part-time employment of medical-public health

TABLE 24 **The Cooperative Medical Service (Continued)**

Item	Description
	personnel in production. Barefoot doctors are paid regular wages for the medical work they do by the production team to which they belong or the production brigade at the health station of which they work. They are remunerated in work points for their farm production activities. An average production team will have one barefoot doctor and three health workers. An average production brigade has 3 barefoot doctors and 9 health workers. Health workers are paid in work points for all their work (health and other), like ordinary peasants, by the production team or brigade to which they belong or for which they perform public health services. Hu estimates that the cost to a production brigade of training one barefoot doctor over a six months' period is in the neighborhood of 150 yuan.
	Although coverage varies considerably from place to place, it is fair to generalize that CMS covers on the average about half the costs of hospitalization if the patient cannot be treated at the production brigade health station or the commune clinic. At least at the brigade health station and the commune clinic, prescription drugs are given free of charge. How much does hospitalization cost at a county or municipal hospital?

Medical Service	Cost (yuan)
Physiotherapy, 1 session	0.50
Chest X-ray	0.30
Chest or brain surgery	30.00
Ordinary operation	10.00-15.00
Tonsillectomy (5 days in the hospital)	15.00
Childbirth	5.00
Complicated childbirth (including postnatal care)	16.00
Penicillin, 200,000 units	0.14
Streptomycin, 1 gm.	0.24
Terramycin, 0.25 gm.	0.35
Tetracycline, 0.25 gm.	0.05

Assume a peasant of middle income, earning 20 yuan a month from communal work in his production team. His annual CMS membership fee is 1.50 yuan. He checks in at the brigade health station (0.05 yuan). Appendicitis is diagnosed. Patient is referred to county hospital where appendix is removed (15.00 yuan). Assuming no further illnesses the cost to the patient is 1.50 + 0.05 + 7.50 = 9.05 yuan or 3.8 percent of his annual income of 240 yuan. (The remaining 7.50 yuan of hospital costs are paid to the hospital by the production brigade out of the portion of its welfare fund earmarked for the CMS.) The point to note is that both the membership fee ("insurance premium") and treatment costs for more serious cases represent a sizable charge on individual and family budgets. The system is far from being a minor burden on personal and household budgets, as some travelers' reports imply.

of the cost of meals. All other costs (laboratory tests, treatment, drugs) are paid for by the worker's or employee's enterprise out of the enterprise's insurance fund. This fund is fed by deductions from the enterprise's total monthly wage and salary payroll, the rate of deductions being about 3 percent. During the period of hospitalization and recovery the worker or employee retains his job. He receives a portion of his normal wage/salary, the ratio depending on length of employment and the duration of the sick leave. In the event of work-related illness he receives his full wage/salary. Where the patient's dependents are adjudged to be in financial difficulties due to the worker's or employee's illness, the enterprise pays the family an "appropriate" subsidy.

Dependents of workers and employees in state sector industrial, mining, and transport-communications enterprises make the following payments: (a) registration fee for each consulting visit, (b) full cost of meals during hospitalization, and (c) 50 percent of the cost of treatment, drugs, and special laboratory tests (normal laboratory tests are free).

Dependents of all other employees in state sector agencies (trade, mass organizations, educational and cultural institutions, construction enterprises, governmental and Party administration, etc.) pay the full cost of registration, food, treatment, laboratory tests, and drugs.

Retired workers and employees of state enterprises and organs are treated in the same way as active workers and employees. They retain their pensions during the period of illness. The same rule applies to war invalids.

Special benefits accrue to working expectant mothers. For example, periodic prenatal examinations are free, as is confinement. Such costs are paid out of the enterprise labor insurance fund (for workers) and from state social security funds (for employees). The length of the working day, normally eight hours, is reduced to seven hours for expectant mothers, beginning with the seventh month of pregnancy. Maternity leave is set at 56 days with full pay (plus two more weeks in the case of the birth of twins or difficult labor). Women workers are entitled to retire at 50, compared with the normal retirement age of 55.

HERBAL MEDICINES AND ACUPUNCTURE Little need be added to what has already been said about the second cost minimization measure: greater resort to locally procured and processed herbal medicines and to various traditional methods of treatment, including acupuncture. Western medical opinion agrees that such means are medically sound as a complement to Western medicine and in some cases superior. Their contribution toward reducing the cost of health delivery services is thought to be significant.

EDUCATION: PROBLEMS AND POLICIES

Education, from preschool to postschool, is more than the "formation of human capital," as the economists choose to call it, but it is that too. The dynamic efficiency of any economic system is measured by the increase over time of total factor productivity, especially the productivity of labor and capital. Both depend to a crucial degree on the quanitity and quality of education—manpower training and research. From the economic standpoint the volume and quality of education will be judged by their appropriateness to the economic problems facing society now and in the foreseeable future. Given the uncertainties attaching to this and the nature of the educational process, such judgment will be marked by controversy. As may be expected, in China this controversy—at first muted—assumed, around the time of the Great Leap Forward and in subsequent years, a virulent one-divides-into-two genre.

Quantity

LITERACY Before 1949 illiteracy was widespread. Perhaps as much as three-quarters of the population could neither read nor write. What is sometimes forgotten is that "letter blindness," as the Chinese call it, is normally accompanied by arithmetical illiteracy—the inability to perform any but the most rudimentary mathematical operations. This deficiency, together with poverty, has traditionally been at the root of the illiterate peasant's exploitation by the literate and arithmetically proficient moneylender and tax collector. Illiteracy rates were higher in the countryside than in the cities, higher in agriculture than in industry. Even so, according to one account, [14] in 1949, 80 percent of the workers at the Tianjin Shoe Factory were illiterate. The consequences of this on labor productivity and intraenterprise labor-management relations may easily be imagined. The case for raising the degree of literacy of the work force would seem to be well established on economic grounds alone.

PRESCHOOL EDUCATION The great majority of preschool children before 1949 were taken care of within the home. Nursery and kindergarten facilities were few and far between, even if one could afford them. Given the communists' desire to see as many people as possible work

[14]Barry Richman, *Industrial Society in Communist China* (New York: Vintage Books, 1966), p. 135.

full time and the tenor of their collectivist philosophy, the establishment of preschool facilities must surely have ranked high among the planners' priorities. According to Chinese communist sources, before 1949 (best year) there were only 1,300 kindergartens with 130,000 children and 2,000 teachers.[15]

ELEMENTARY EDUCATION In a peak pre-1949 year, fewer than 24 million children were enrolled in primary schools, that is, roughly 20 percent of the eligible age group; 4.6 million children were graduated from elementary schools. Expansion of formal elementary schooling was seen by the new regime as an important component of the fight against letter blindness.

MIDDLE SCHOOL EDUCATION Before 1949, in a good year, about 1.5 million pupils were enrolled in junior and senior divisions of academically oriented, middle (secondary) schools, and the graduating class numbered about 326,000 in a country of approximately 400 million people.

Enrollment in full-time technical (vocationally oriented) middle schools in a peak pre-1949 year was, according to the communists, 383,000, with a graduating class of 73,000.

HIGHER EDUCATION In a pre-1949 peak year institutions of higher learning had a total enrollment of 155,000. Fewer than 5,000 engineering students were graduated in such a year, and there were over 3,000 teachers and roughly 3,000 liberal arts graduates. Medical schools turned out about 1,200 graduates and departments of natural sciences, 1,700. Roughly 2,000 students were graduated from agricultural colleges and 3,000 from schools of economics and finance.

FEMALE STUDENTS The education of girls and women was particularly neglected before 1949. In a peak pre-1949 year girls represented only one-quarter of primary school enrollments, one-fifth of the middle school population, about the same proportion of enrollments in technical middle schools, and 18 percent of the student population in institutions of higher learning—or 28,000 university women.

THE SITUATION IN 1957 At the end of the First Five-Year Plan (1957)

[15]These and subsequent figures are taken from *Ten Great Years: Statistics of the Economic and Cultural Achievements of the People's Republic of China* (Beijing, 1960), pp. 187ff.

TABLE 25 **Full-Time Students Enrolled in Schools**

	Students (thousands)					
Educational Level	*1949*	*1957*	*1958*	*1965*	*1971*	*1978*
Kindergartens[a]	140	1,090	29,500			7,870
Elementary Schools	24,391	64,279	86,400	110,000	120,000	146,240
Middle Schools[b]	1,268	7,059	11,990	10,300	30,000	65,480
Institutions of higher learning (enrollment)	117	441	660	670	200	850
(Graduates)	21	56	72	200	40	165

SOURCES: 1949, 1957, 1958, *Ten Great Years* (Beijing, 1960), pp. 133ff. 1965–1971 Western estimates; 1978 Communique of the State Statistical Bureau, June 27, 1979, *Beijing Review,* July 6, 1979, pp. 40–41.
[a]1950.
[b]Includes technical middle schools.

significant quantitative improvement had been registered at all educational levels. Table 25 summarizes the situation compared with 1949. In addition to the educational effort and partly overlapping it, there was the training in Party dogma and discipline given to large numbers of future cadres and the "reeducation" of intellectuals in mass study groups and in "revolutionary universities," the curricula of which consisted almost exclusively of ideological and political indoctrination. This remolding of the intellectuals became linked in 1951–1952 with the "Three-Anti" and "Five-Anti" *(San-fan, Wu-fan)* terror campaigns. Students were encouraged to criticize and "struggle" against teachers at student-teacher meetings and "drag out" the teachers' bourgeois backgrounds and education.[16] Table 25 does not indicate the fact that class attendance during the period was strictly enforced, in contrast to the situation that prevailed during the turbulent decade before 1949.

Despite the dramatic improvement in the quantitative situation up to 1957, quantity problems of a different kind began to emerge just before the launching of the Great Leap Forward in 1958. Two major kinds of problems can be identified: (a) bottlenecks began to appear within the educational pipeline, and (b) troublesome job-placement problems occurred at the various outlets of the educational system. It was reported early in 1957 that about 4 million school children leaving elementary school that year (or roughly one-third of the graduating class) would not be able to go on to junior middle school in spite of acceptable creden-

[16]David M. Raddock, "Between Generations: Activist Chinese Youths in Pursuit of a Political Role in the *San-fan* and in the Cultural Revolution," *China Quarterly*, No. 79, September 1979, pp. 511–28.

tials, and some 800,000 students leaving junior middle schools would find themselves blocked from entering senior grades because of a shortage of space and teachers, despite the fact that most schools worked in two shifts around the year. About 90,000 senior-school graduates could not find places in the universities.

Those unable to continue their education at whatever level, but especially above junior middle school, were discovering that jobs were often unavailable. As we saw in Chapter 2, under the Soviet-based strategy of economic development emphasizing capital-intensive heavy industry, only 2 million new positions were created in modern urban industry between 1953 and 1957. Urban unemployment among the young became worrisome. Moreover, many school graduates who did find jobs discovered that these were only marginally, if at all, related to the training they had acquired in school. As in other developing countries, a pool of unemployed, underemployed, and misemployed educated labor began to emerge with all the attendant disillusionment and frustrations. At about that time, the downward-transfer movement gathered momentum. In the setting of the type of education dispensed at that time—its qualitative aspect—the movement was at best a palliative that did not touch the problem of shattered career expectations.

THE SITUATION IN 1958 At this juncture the leadership debate on the nature of the educational process, an acrimonious dialogue that had been muted until then, burst into the open in actions rather than words. It was part of the general reappraisal of developmental strategy and of the ethical framework within which that strategy unfolded. From the standpoint of absorbing educated manpower, the Great Leap Forward was the leadership left's answer to both the quantitative and qualitative problems of education. We shall defer discussion of the qualitative side to deal briefly here with the solution offered to the quantity problem.

The Leap sharply raised output targets for practically everything from nuts and bolts to grade school graduates. Total industrial employment (i.e., in both urban modern and rural semitraditional industry) rose by 16.6 million in 1958 alone, in response to strong upward pressures on production targets. The massive water conservation campaigns absorbed any remaining unemployed or underemployed manpower in the countryside and the cities. [17] Simultaneously the output of schools was augmented as shown in Table 25.

[17]There must have been considerable overstaffing and consequent new underemployment as enterprises hoarded labor in expectation of further upward revisions in their planned output targets.

Although the figures for 1958 have to be read with caution, they do point to a substantial increase in educational intake and output. Particularly striking are the data for enrollment in kindergartens, reflecting the establishment of numerous day-care centers in the newly formed rural people's communes to take care of young children while the parents and grandparents worked on water conservation and other projects. Many of these kindergartens were simple babysitting arrangements. Also notable were the expansion of elementary spare-time education and the liquidation of separate part-time middle technical schools. The rice paddies and backyard furnaces became spare-time outdoor schools during the Leap.

THE SITUATION IN 1965 The unemployment, underemployment and misemployment of 1957 returned in more acute form in the wake of the post-Leap recession beginning in 1959. From then until 1963, when the Socialist Education Campaign marked a revival of leftist influence on culture and education, there was retrenchment in the schools and in other areas of activity and a partial return to the pre-1958 educational system. From a high of 955,000 university and college students in 1960, enrollments dropped to 670,000 in 1965, the last year before the Cultural Revolution. Primary school enrollments, which reached a high of over 90 million in 1960, dropped sharply during the depression years (1961–1962) and then began an upward climb. Middle school enrollments before the Cultural Revolution peaked in 1961 at 13.5 million and then followed an erratic path to reach 10.3 million in 1965. (It should be noted that the enrollment figures refer only to full-time students.) Large numbers of people received training outside the formal educational network, especially in a multitude of spare-time courses at the primary, secondary, and advanced levels.

Quality

Quantity was only one of the problems in education—one, moreover, on which disagreement among leadership factions was comparatively mild. The eradication of illiteracy and the provision of basic education for as many people as possible were not really disputed by anyone. A significantly more serious question on which opinions presumably differed since the days of Yanan and which became the subject of bitter confrontation at the time of the Great Leap, again in 1963–1964, and which finally erupted in the great purge of the Cultural Revolution (1966–1969), concerned the qualitative substance of pedagogy and the appropriate form to be given to the educational system.

We shall pass lightly here over what one could call the Western democratic approach to the problem, since that was not at issue in China after 1949. This position, as I read it, is that while illiteracy and the paucity of educational opportunity should rightly be regarded as absolute evils, literacy and educational opportunity can be harmful too, if used for the political ends of a ruling autocracy. The ability to read and write, indeed, the whole learning experience should be accompanied, according to this point of view, by a wide choice of reading material and by the right to set down and propagate, in competition with others, one's own interpretation of what are loosely called "facts." The Soviet peasant's and his worker or technician son's vulnerability to exploitation had not been significantly lessened by their newly acquired letter and numbers vision. They were permitted to read only that which was served up to them, and all the counting that mattered was done for them by the nonelected representatives of the dictatorship of the proletariat. Literacy, runs the argument, can be used as easily, or perhaps more easily than its opposite, to oppress, exploit, and intellectually enslave.

To Lenin and to his Chinese followers, literacy is a class weapon of the victorious proletariat, embodied in and represented by the mass line of the Party. Literacy and the educational process have to be class-correct. To the Head of the Educational Department of the (1947) Communist Border Government at Shaanxi, education was "not a way of life in itself: it is only an instrument" in the hands of the workers and the poor and lower-middle peasants. All opinions at odds with the mass line of the moment have to be extinguished in conformity with the dialectical dictate of one divides into two. [18] The superstructure of ideas has to be cleansed of all impurities. The inconvenience of this monolithic interpretation of knowledge is that agreement on what constitutes class correctness is sometimes difficult to reach. There is the danger that erroneous ideas will persist, indeed multiply, by the simple expedient of "waving the Red flag while opposing the Red flag." This is what Mao thought had occurred in China between 1961 and 1965. To stop the rot, he and his allies unleashed a vast mental cleaning-up operation known as the Great Proletarian Cultural Revolution.

The controversy among leaders about the substance of correct education is by no means settled. But for the time being the Left solution—experimented with fleetingly during the Great Leap Forward, propagated during the Socialist Education Campaign of 1963–1964, and pushed to its limits during the Cultural Revolution—has been replaced,

[18]Things are not always what they seem. As noted earlier, there exists in China a large trade in used books. People read nonpolitical literature quite openly.

again, by a more orthodox neo-Stalinist system. The problem may be analyzed at two interrelated levels defined by Marx: the level of the economic base and that of the superstructure.

ECONOMIC BASE The Soviet-type prescription for economic development, which the Chinese adopted with some modifications from 1953 to 1957 and to which (with many modifications) they returned after 1976, is capital and skill intensive, focusing on modern producer-goods industries in the cities. It demands an influx of highly trained and specialized technical, engineering, and scientific manpower. The Soviet-Stalinist system of economic planning and management, with its high degree of concentration and relatively elaborate methodology, requires roughly the same thing. Scientific, engineering, technical, and economic-administrative expertise acquired through structured full-time education and a rising degree of difficulty and selectivity attested to by one's ability to negotiate examinations is at the core of the system of human capital formation. The system relies on formal certification of skills by academic authorities and Party organs. Its absorptive capacity at the higher echelons, especially at the level of university-trained people, is comparatively limited. Despite important exceptions (having a well-connected relative in the right place does help), the system rewards the achiever.

From a social perspective it is essentially elitist and meritocratic, always bearing in mind the requirement of correct redness (which, in practice, often simply means pliability) and the possibility of upward mobility for the less gifted but scripturally well versed. The obverse of all this is that despite protestations the system overlooks and leaves in relative ignorance the peasant masses. Even within the urban community, the intellectual gap between the managerial-technical elite and the rank-and-file working men and women is significant. In short, the Soviet educational system as it has operated in recent decades, in tune with the economic system's assumptions and priorities, creates a new upper class based on a combination of technical expertise and monoparty privilege. In actuality, if not in the doctrinal description of it, the Soviet economic base gives rise to a class-ridden superstructure: political, social, and cultural. It is state capitalism pure and simple. The remaining question is whether with rising general income levels the social tensions inherent in such a situation will be attenuated or, on the contrary, worsened as expectation horizons at the lower echelons broaden.

It was natural that with the change of China's strategy of economic development in 1958 and the emergence of the system described in

Chapters 3, 4, and 5, a reorientation of educational philosophy and policy should follow suit. Since the way the economic base was progressing until that time was seen as incompatible with China's specific conditions and factor endowments, it was not surprising that the rejection of the Soviet economic model should have been followed in short order by the discarding of the Soviet educational system. Because of the failure of the Leap and the subsequent abandonment of the Leap's wilder schemes, and also because of stubborn resistance to the new pedagogy by an influential segment of the Party, governmental, and academic establishments, it took a decade to sort things out to the approximate satisfaction of the left reformers. It took nothing less than a wholesale shutting down of the schools, the purge of professional journals and publications, and the rectification of teachers and administrators in "May 7th" schools (thought rectification camps) for the newborn thing hesitantly to emerge.

The system of education modeled on Soviet experience, the Chinese left reformers maintained, not only failed to remove the vestiges of China's pre-1949 educational philosophy and method, it in fact strengthened the age-old propensity toward Mandarinism, atrophy, and irrelevance when compared with the needs of the country's economic base. It created experts for nonexisting industries, raised expectations well above what the economy could (or should) satisfy, spawned obfuscations and "academic airs," and ended up in unemployment, underemployment, and misemployment. What the economy needed in large numbers were moderately trained peasants and laborers, not delightfully sophisticated annotators of Confucian analects or experts in brain surgery and heart transplants. Under the Soviet-inspired system of education, the quality of manpower supply outrun the quality of demand. Too many people were overtrained, too few were trained to perform in a more efficient manner the existing tasks.

The "struggle between the two lines on the educational front," as the controversy is officially known, simmered through the early 1960s, occasionally boiling over, as during the Socialist Education Campaign. The Cultural Revolution sought to eliminate the contradiction by an assult on the educational superstructure and its trustees.

SUPERSTRUCTURE In his essay "On Contradiction" (1937) Mao had written: "When the superstructure (politics, culture, etc.) obstructs the development of the economic base, political and cultural changes become principal and decisive." In 1964, during an interview granted a delegation from Nepal, he outlined what he considered to be the main obstacles to the development of the economic base presented by the educational component of the superstructure: "The school years are too long, courses too many, and various methods of teaching unsatisfactory. The children learn textbooks and concepts which remain merely textbooks and concepts: they know nothing else. . . . The method of examination is to treat candidates as enemies and ambush them."

On May 7, 1966, Mao issued an instruction that elaborated on a 1958 Party statement that "Education must be combined with productive labor." The instruction said: "While their main task is to study, they [the students] should, in addition, learn other things, that is, industrial work, farming and military affairs. They should also criticize the bourgeoisie. The period of schooling should be shortened, education should be revolutionized, and the domination of our schools by bourgeois intellectuals should by no means be allowed to continue." On August 27, 1968, he added that "in the countryside schools are to be run by the most reliable allies of the working class—the poor and lower-middle peasants." Finally, on December 22, 1968, Mao gave formal approval to the downward transfer of urban educated young people: "It is absolutely necessary," he wrote, "for educated young people to go to the countryside to be reeducated by the poor and lower-middle peasants." Together these statements constitute the foundations of the educational reform instituted on a nationwide scale during the Cultural Revolution. These foundations rested on a groundwork of experience gained during the days of Yanan in the late 1930s and early 1940s.

The reform could be summed up as a leveling down and a speeding up. Its major components were the following.

ENROLLMENTS After dismissal of the student body in 1966, recruitment of students began again in 1967 for the middle schools and in 1970 for the universities. As late as 1977, when the reform had already been repudiated, university enrollments were still substantially below 1965 levels and activity on most campuses was slight. From 1970 through 1976 recruitment of students was based on the following principles: (a) candidates had to have had at least two years' working experience in agriculture or industry; (b) they should have been, as a rule, less than 20-years old and unmarried; (c) they were to be recommended by their fellow workers, approved by the Party and government authorities at their place of work (such approval would normally take into account the candidates' class background [19] and work record), and their application

[19]Preference was given to candidates of worker, soldier, and poor and lower-middle peasant origin.

had to be approved by the university or high school authorities, which meant essentially by the Party and revolutionary committees of the schools; (d) all candidates had to have demonstrated a revolutionary spirit of struggle and self-denial—they had to show that they were motivated not by a desire to become officials but that they intended to work unselfishly in employments and locations to which they would be assigned.There had been some "slipping into the universities through the back door," i.e., through influence and, as far as I could determine, the children of cadres still constituted (1974) a sizable contingent in some universities. [20]

The important point to note, however, is that the completion of senior high school was not in itself a valid credential for entry into institutions of higher learning. In fact, many of the worker-peasant-soldier students I encountered in the universities during the reform period were graduates of junior middle schools. Similar observations apply to progression of students from elementary to middle schools and from junior to senior levels, although there was less class discrimination as one moved down the education ladder. All schools became coeducational (before 1966 there were a number of single-sex schools). Schools for particularly talented pupils were abolished. At the No. 9 Middle School in Suzhou, Jiangsu Province, I asked whether there were any students of landlord, rich peasant, and capitalist backgrounds.The answer was: "There are in the school some such special categories of students." Question: "How are they treated? Can they join the Red Guards and the Communist Youth League?" Answer: "Students with different class backgrounds can be educated [in a political sense].When they qualify, they can join the Red Guards and the Communist Youth League.There have been such cases in this school."

Almost all the practices and procedures introduced during the Cultural Revolution were eliminated after the ouster of the radical leaders (1977–1979). Even as late as 1979, however, the educational system was described as a "heavily damaged" area that was still at a stage of restoration and adjustment, "like a person recovering from serious illness." The four modernizations, with their emphasis on advanced science and technology, their essentially urban temper, and their united-front perspective, required (it was now argued) a different approach to enrollments from that adopted by the radical reformers: "To enroll students for institutes of higher learning is to select talented people for the four modernizations." "Talent" was now the operative

[20]After October 1976 the fallen radical leaders were accused, among other things of making a big thing out of the "back door" problem.

criterion, and talent could be spotted only by professionally oriented examinations and a spotless record of formal studies. The post-gang university and college admissions policy was to return, by and large, to guidelines followed during the 1961–1965 period.

The general line in this matter came to be known as "One Red Heart and Two Preparations." The one red heart was interpreted as the candidate's determination to make contributions to the four modernizations, in itself a significant reinterpretation of the meaning attached to redness not long before. The two preparations meant that if the applicant succeeded in passing the prescribed entrance examinations, he would determinedly pursue his studies at the university; if he failed in the examinations, he would subordinate himself to the interest of the state and work wherever he was assigned while widening his knowledge through spare-time studies.

Because of the shortage of classrooms (many school buildings were occupied by army and government units that refused to vacate the premises despite orders from on-high and public protests by students), teachers, books, library facilities, and funds, entrance examinations administered to the better (as judged by school grades) upper-middle school graduates became, after 1977, the main means of tailoring the demand for higher education to the available supply of teaching personnel, materials, and facilities. The supply was being augmented by the reopening of institutions of higher learning closed during the Cultural Revolution, the establishment of new schools and institutes, the launching of correspondence schools, spare-time schools, radio and television courses, and the sending abroad of students who, upon their return, were expected to take up teaching and research positions. Of the roughly 7 million upper-middle-school graduates in 1979, 4.6 million (or 65.7 percent) took university entrance examinations, and of these, 270,000 were actually admitted (i.e., 5.9 percent of those examined). In Beijing, 128,000 candidates took the entrance examinations in July 1979; of these, 5,000 were admitted to "key" universities and colleges, 5,000 to the ordinary ones, and 1,000 who had passed the examinations were not admitted. [21] Examination questions were standardized, as were

[21]*Beijing Review*, October 12, 1979, p. 6. "An official on the municipal committee in charge of enrolling college students patiently explained to these [rejected] students why they were not admitted. He said: 'There were more applicants this year for such specialities as automation, computer science, and medicine than for agronomy, geology, and mining. So there was the possibility that candidates of the former category were not admitted even though they got better marks, while those of the latter category were admitted in spite of their lower marks. Some were not admitted because their marks for subjects related to the

schedules and criteria for assessing answers. Annual quotas for university enrollment were no longer communicated to basic level units (e.g., factories, farms, secondary schools, offices) but were to be controlled by provincial authorities.The importance attached to examinations (not only for entering the educational pipeline, but for the more desirable job assignments) raised the specter of cheating and corruption. Reports of cheating on examinations began to appear in July 1979, and instances of privileged bureaucrats' using their muscle in behalf of their offspring were cited with disapproval.The examination fervor which gripped China after 1976 was decried in both dissident democratic and leftist circles. An essay by a young leader of the democratic movement (circulated among foreign correspondents in Beijing in May 1979) explained the failure of the movement in China by citing the lack of activists among young intellectuals—students and teachers.The tepid support received by the democratic movement (led, for the most part, by young workers who had not been to universities and who were between 20 and 30 years old) was due, the essay argued, to "favoritism" shown by the post-Mao regime toward the intellectuals, and to obsessive preoccupation with examinations. "There's nothing but exams, exams, exams, as if their lives depended on them. Everyone's afraid of not getting into the university, not becoming a research worker, and not being promoted to the position of technician." [22] The left opposition to the stress on professional examinations was, of course, the same that earlier (under Mao and the gang), gave birth to educational reforms that put correct class background and political consciousness before "book learning."

The "key" universities (and middle and primary schools) mentioned in connection with the Beijing exams were reintroduced after 1976; they had existed during the "Liuist" interlude of the early to mid-1960s. About 100 universities (out of a 1979 total of 600) were designated "key" institutions.This meant—and the same applied to middle and primary schools—that they were provided with better teachers, students, equipment, and funding than other schools. In 1979 such favored universities enrolled 67,000 students. Moreover, a growing number of schools adopted a multiple-tracking system: they divided students in the same school year into quick and slow learners. Some schools set up special classes for the intellectually exceptional. Extra tutoring was provided for those who had fallen behind academically as a result of the

specialty they wished to study were too low although they got the required total marks. Some candidates were not physically fit for the specialities they had chosen, such as geology, mining, and navigation.' "

[22]Agence France Press, Beijing, May 28, 1979, in *FBIS*, May 29, 1979.

educational practices of the Cultural Revolution and the years immediately following. The pendulum for a while seemed to have swung too far. The tendency in some schools and places to pay attention only to key classes and schools to the neglect of others was decried as a "deviation"—a serious charge. [23]

The former left insistence that those who enter the universities should have at least two years' practical experience in manual work was modified in the post-Mao years. Bright high school graduates could go straight to the university if they successfully negotiated the entrance examinations. In 1979 those admitted to the universities directly from upper middle schools represented 20 to 30 percent of all those admitted. Moreover, all school graduates above a certain grade-point average were given the opportunity (beginning in 1978) to take entrance examinations and to state their choice of two or three colleges and subjects, the latter divided into liberal arts and natural science categories. Those opting for liberal arts schools were examined in a variety of subjects, which included political science (presumably the correct understanding of the current line), Chinese and foreign languages, mathematics, history, and geography. Those opting for science were examined in, among others, political science, Chinese and foreign languages, mathematics, physics, and chemistry. In all cases the results of foreign language tests in the entrance examinations were to be included in the student's permanent transcript for future reference. In 1977–1978 the upper age limit for applicants to universities and colleges was extended to 30 so as to give a chance to at least some of the victims of the Cultural Revolution's educational holocaust. In 1979 this limit was lowered to 25, "in general." Unmarried applicants under 28 years of age, however, could still apply to take entrance exams provided their parent basic units certified that they had a satisfactory academic record. In future years the age limit for college applicants will be lowered. While married applicants were not to be rejected offhand, single applicants had a distinct edge over married ones. First-year students who had worked in production for five years or more were to receive scholarship grants rather than (as previously) regular wages from their parent production units.

The "pernicious influence of the reactionary theory of 'family lineage' " was to be eliminated. An applicant's incorrect social category was to be evaluated in the light of his own past service to the socialist community and on the basis of his academic qualifications.

[23]E.g., *Beijing Review*, May 18, 1979, p. 6.

What constituted minimum passing grades was to be determined for key universities and colleges by the Ministry of Education on the basis of all the applicants' records. In the case of other colleges and universities, this determination was to be made by the appropriate provincial and municipal educational authorities.

In 1979 secondary vocational schools were allowed to enroll graduates of both upper and lower middle schools. Later, vocational middle schools are to enroll only graduates of lower middle schools. [24]

LENGTH OF STUDY The educational reforms that issued from the Cultural Revolution shortened the period of undergraduate study at the university level from four to five years (longer in medical schools) to between two and a half and three and a half years. After the fall of the radicals the period of university study began to be lengthened again. By 1977 it had reached four years, and was later to be extended to four and a half years. The radicals had compressed the period of secondary schooling from six years to five years in the cities (three years' junior and two years' senior school) and four years in the countryside (two years' junior and two years' senior education). Primary education before the Cultural Revolution lasted six years. The Cultural Revolution reforms shortened this to five years. While these reformed periods of study at both the middle school levels remained substantially unchanged as late as 1977, the general thrust of the educational debate was in favor of returning to the pre–Cultural Revolution 6 years' primary—6 years' secondary schooling system. Graduate studies at institutions of higher learning were abolished during the Cultural Revolution. They were reestablished after 1976. Research work at universities, by and large halted during the Cultural upheaval, was slowly resumed around 1977.

Roughly 95 percent of children in the eligible age group (7–12) attend primary schools. About 40 percent of young people in the eligible age bracket (12–17) attend secondary schools. The proportion of those eligible who actually attend junior middle school is much higher than the proportion of those eligible who attend senior middle school, especially in the countryside. An American educational study group reported in 1978 that at the San Lin commune on the outskirts of Shanghai (an obviously superior commune), the middle school had an enrollment of 1,280 at the junior level and only 120 at the senior level. Not more than 2 percent of all middle school students are enrolled in vocational or

[24]Beijing Radio, Xinhua, May 17, 1979, in *FBIS*, May 18, 1979.

technical middle schools.This proportion is to be increased in future years. Vocational schools are usually operated by factories or transportation enterprises and provide training intended to form semiskilled workers.Technical middle schools concentrate on teaching service and clerical skills (e.g., bookkeeping).

CURRICULUM The Cultural Revolution reforms combined theoretical knowledge at all levels with industrial or farm labor. Even in the kindergartens children were taught simple manual tasks, such as putting together ballpoint pens. School time (at all levels) was devoted roughly one-third each to "book knowledge," practical work in school-run or regular factories and farms, and political education in Marxism-Leninism-Mao Zedong Thought.The number of courses offered after 1969 and before 1977 (especially in the universities) had been drastically cut compared with the situation before the Cultural Revolution.The content of courses was simplified for the benefit of the less intellectually gifted (but politically correct left-alert) students, and given a more applied emphasis.The same was true of textbooks—the few, that is, that were actually in use. During my 1974 visit, most school texts were in pageproof form, being revised and rewritten by constantly shifting committees of teachers, students, workers, poor and lower middle peasants, and cadres. All teaching materials, whether in mathematics or foreign languages, contained a heavy dose of politics (most of it of ultraleft persuasion). Instructional materials frequently included editorials from the *People's Daily*. But the main emphasis under the radical educational reforms was on learning by doing, that is, working in the fields or workshops and making on-the-spot investigations and summarizing them in reports.

After 1976, practical (manual) work and study were not divorced, but within the school system emphasis clearly shifted in favor of study. Instead of one-third of the school time being devoted to learning by doing, only 15 percent was mandated, and even this "work" was interpreted to include mental labor and, in fact, could be performed during school vacations. Only in technical and agricultural schools was the manual work requirement of one-third (in some cases half) of instructional time retained, and that only because by its very nature theoretical instruction in these areas has a highly applied bias. An American educational delegation noted in 1978 that it was not impressed with the work projects it saw in schools, except for technical and agricultural schools. "They seemed to be more 'for show' than of basic importance. . . .We got the impression that neither students nor teachers took it very seriously.'' [25] Those symptoms were detectible as early as 1974. Also, after 1977, many courses that had been dropped were reinstituted, and new courses were added. The preparation of textbooks was speeded up. The new books and other teaching materials were still loaded with politics, albeit of the latest correct kind. But the ballast was lighter than it had been in the heyday of the radicals.

TEACHER-STUDENT RELATIONS What the reformers described as the ''absolute authority of teachers'' was reportedly done away with, at least for a while. Students were encouraged to question and to criticize—even to ''struggle'' against—their mentors in the classroom and in wider forums. I sensed, however, that even in 1974, when the radicals were very much in charge of culture and education, a discernible distance still separated teacher from student, although without doubt the older teachers had been cowed by the rough remolding they received during the Cultural Revolution and after. The ''bourgeois academic authorities'' (for the most part professors and others who had been held over from pre-1949 days, some of them educated abroad) were, for the most part, kept at their posts, but their influence was minimal. They gave the appearance of broken reeds. The younger teachers I met were alert, dedicated to the propagation of the mass line, and in my estimation, closed minded. The old method of teaching and learning by rote was said to have been done away with, although I came across instances of it, especially at the middle school level and lower. There was emphasis on self-study using collectively written draft books. Formal examinations were said to be on the decline in 1974, but the trend was apparently being resisted already at that time. Examinations, it was argued, used to stress memorization and their object was to entrap the worker-peasant-soldier students. Such examinations as were retained tended to stress the student's ability to solve practical problems. A variety of tests were tried. The impression given, however, was that the results of formal examinations were secondary to the student's overall record, which included primarily devotion to the revolution and readiness to serve the people. Physical education was and continues to be stressed at all levels.

There was, no doubt, something to be said for some of the reforms—especially those pertaining to student-teacher relations,

[25] *Observations on the Relations between Education and Work in the People's Republic of China*, Report of a Study Group, 1978, Clark Kerr, Chairman (Berkeley, Calif.: The Carnegie Council on Policy Studies in Higher Education, 1978), p. 7.

memorization, entrapment-type examinations, divorce of subject matter from practical reality—introduced during the Cultural Revolution and in force for some years thereafter. As with other changes in socialist China, however, the educational reform pendulum swang too far and too rapidly, and it became enmeshed in baroque doctrinal and factional disputes. The professors were toppled from their pedestals in a manner not conducive to classroom discipline and for reasons largely irrelevant to the strictly functional educational process (i.e., they were "dragged out" for the most part not because of professional incompetence, but because of wrong class background and the political opprobrium of having been educated abroad). Alternative classroom procedures had not been carefully worked out in advance, and the resulting void encouraged truancy, anarchy, and the reign of ignorance. "This was the time when our schools were adversely affected. Then our students were dissuaded from studying under the pretext of guarding against the emergence of 'intellectual aristocrats.' Opposition to 'the teachers' dignity' was used as an excuse, and our teachers were often criticized and not allowed to run schools and give guidance to the students as they should. So a growing number of teenagers were led astray, which was not at all surprising." [26]

Discipline in the classroom and the authority of teachers were reintroduced, with difficulty, after 1976. [27] The deep humiliation to which many teachers had been subjected for years and the cockiness actively encouraged in students during and for some years after the Cultural Revolution, are not readily reversible. A large number of teachers left their profession, either on their own (to escape the stress of the job and to find safer employment in factories) or under orders from left-wing authorities. This thinning out of the professorial ranks—and the same

[26]Zhou Zheng, "Save the Teenage Delinquents," *Beijing Review*, November 2, 1979, p. 22. The article describes the reopening of reformatories in Beijing in 1978–79 after they had been closed since 1966. The article paints a somewhat idealized picture of these schools for delinquent youths (the "contaminated blossoms"). In the 1950s and early 1960s these institutions were apparently inhabited for the most part by orphaned children of incorrect class background, whose parents had been executed or jailed by the communists. At present, most of the inmate population seems to be composed of disoriented class-correct products of the Cultural Revolution.

[27]Teachers "deserve respect from people in all walks of life." "Outstanding teachers loyal to the Party's educational work should be commended and rewarded." Students, while in school, should make "an earnest study of basic scientific knowledge." Xinhua, Beijing, August 29, 1977, in *Survey of People's Republic of China Press* (*SPRCP*), No. 6419, September 9, 1977, pp. 182–84.

applies to research personnel—cannot be remedied overnight. A broadcast from Urumqi, Xinjiang, in early 1979 pointed to what was surely a more widespread phenomenon: "Surveys show that while our region has over 100,000 scientific and technical personnel, 15,000 of them no longer hold scientific and technical posts. Although over 80,000 still work in scientific and technical jobs, it is not clear if they are working in their fields of specialty or are otherwise properly employed." [28]

While discipline, teacher authority, and professional examinations are again in vogue, the situation is not quite one of status quo ante. An event of the depth and all-embracing scope of the Cultural Revolution does not vanish without a trace. While students today are encouraged to study hard, listen to their teachers, and pass academically exacting tests, there is to be no more "formalism," i.e., no trick questions, "pop quizzes," and similar exercises in ensnarement, and teachers are not to puff themselves up and wrap themselves in academic robes, as apparently they were wont to do in the past, before they were deflated and stripped of their gowns by the Cultural Revolution. This may be a case of easier said than done. Educational Mandarinism has deep roots in China and the adoption of the Soviet school model in the 1950s did little to change things. In addition, there are bitter intrafaculty scores to be settled. Already a rift has developed between those who had obtained their academic preferments during the 1950s or early 1960s and those who were "helicoptered" into college positions by the Cultural Revolution. These *arrivistes* are seen by the surviving members of the older faculty as so many ignoramuses, who when it comes to hard knowledge don't know what they are talking about. They are also tainted in the eyes of the survivors by their political association with the gang. Those graduates of the Cultural Revolution who have so far managed to survive the post-gang purges of the universities, reciprocate by charging the old timers with "egoism."

GRADUATION AND PLACEMENT Upon graduation students are assigned to places of work, as needed by the state. Until 1977, in the matter of his future employment, the student, formally, had no choice. There

[28]Xinjiang Regional Broadcasting Station, Urumqi, February 2, 1979, in *FBIS*, February 5, 1979. "Over 100,000 actors and folk artists throughout the country had been forced to switch to new professions or had been transferred to work in other fields. In Shanghai [during the reign of the gang of four] more than 40 district and county theatrical troupes, representing 13 different kinds of operas and more than 2,000 actors were disbanded." Beijing Radio, January 18, 1979, in *FBIS*, January 22, 1979.

were, however, and still are, informal ways of lessening the severity of one's job placement and discreetly obtaining a relatively "soft" assignment.[29]

Beginning in 1977 assignment of junior and senior school graduates to jobs or higher (often simply other) schools became partly a matter of further examinations. A graduate of a junior or senior middle school would no longer automatically, and with minimum consultation, be assigned to a job decided on by the relevant labor bureau. He was to be given at least a marginal opportunity to express his preferences with regard to the type and location of employment or further education. This expression of preference usually took the form of examinations both with regard to job placement and continued schooling. Given the number of school graduates involved, one may question whether the concept could, in fact, be applied even if only the better applicants were considered. To cushion the transition from school to employment (or avoid immediate unemployment) much emphasis was placed after 1976 on "nontraditional" educational programs, including evening schooling, three-day schools (under this system students attend classes three days in the week, and work the other three days), correspondence courses, radio and television instruction, part-time schools, factory-related training programs, and so on.

ADMINISTRATION While the Cultural Revolution reforms put down a number of mandatory guidelines concerning the content and mechanics of education, the implementation of such guidelines and the administration of the schools were left to local authorities. Here as elsewhere there was considerable operational decentralization and contextual unity. Rural schools at the primary level were and continue to be managed by production brigades for the most part, while junior and frequently senior middle schools are run by the communes. Urban schools are administered by municipalities or towns and their subdivisions. There are also (as we have noted) many elementary and middle schools run by industrial enterprises, as well as some technically oriented colleges. The emulation model for the technically oriented colleges had for some time been the Shanghai Machine Tools Plant's "July 21 College," which recruits students from among the plant's workers. Upon completion of their studies the students return to the plant's workshops, presumably at

[29]As soon as the new post-gang educational reform measures became known, high cadres began to pressure various authorities into assigning their children graduating in 1979 to jobs or colleges in Beijing, Shanghai, and other big cities. *Renmin Ribao*, May 6, 1979, in *Beijing Review*, June 1, 1979, p. 8.

higher job grades. The American educational delegation that visited the plant and its "college" in 1978 was not very impressed. Doctrinal purity before 1976 was assured by the school's Party committees and by worker or peasants' propaganda teams permanently residing in each school. The teams have since been disbanded.

Regular administration of the system within each school (which under the Cultural Revolution reforms was vested in the school revolutionary committee composed of cadres, teachers, worker-peasant soldiers, staff members, and student representatives) is again in the hands of the school director (whatever title he may have) and his Party-government appointed staff. The influence over the school system of central (provincial and national) authorities and the Party has been strengthened. After 1976, "unified" criteria and direction were the order of the day.

FINANCING Western readers are sometime surprised to learn that elementary and secondary public education in China is not provided "free" to the users. It is, however, heavily subsidized. In Jiangsu Province the school fee per child per six months is about 3 yuan for elementary school and 5 yuan for middle school. In addition, the cost of books and stationery over a six-month period comes to about 2.50 yuan per child. Nurseries and kindergartens are not free either. In central-south China the weekly (six days) fee for keeping one child in a nursery is reportedly 7 yuan—a sizable drain on the family purse.

The provision of public health care and of education from the Cultural Revolution until 1977 had a number of traits in common. The emphasis was on supplying moderate quality services (drawing on something that could broadly be called intermediate technology) to as many people as possible, especially the rural poor. The expansion under commune management of middle-school education in the countryside was comparable to the establishment of the Cooperative Medical Service. The changed teacher-student relationship, the training of teachers by shortened courses, and the vocational orientation given to study, could be compared with the introduction of paramedical and public health personnel and the establishment of a changed doctor-patient relationship. In both health and education, pure research was deemphasized and applied research was politicized. Formal credentials did not carry much weight; practical experience, especially industrial and farm work, did. The long-term danger was, of course, that the sacrifice of top-grade quality and the dogmatic aversion to distinguishing intellectual from manual labor could have become endemic.The reform of the public health care and educational systems had many commendable features, but it was imbued with an anti-intellectualism so virtulent and a comprehension of multifaceted knowledge so narrow and pedestrian as to cast serious doubt about its future.

After October 1976 the educational reform went overboard almost at once.The four modernizations called for precisely those intellectual qualities the reform had spurned as elitist.Those intellectuals who had not been irreperably maimed by the Cultural upheaval were brought back into the fold; they were to be used once again for socialist economic construction under the banner of a united front of all those who could be united. For the time being, the definition of those who could be so united was comparatively broad. On past record, however, the specter of yet another leftist turn looming ahead could not be overlooked.The Party's latest alliance with the intellectuals is a marriage of convenience; it is a temporary and tactical relationship subject to dissolution without notice. By now the Chinese intellectuals know this, but, one may presume, they live day to day and reap what benefits the united front interlude brings.The health service part of the Cultural Revolution reforms was less affected by the post-gang changes. However, changes in the educational system and, more generally, in the Party's attitude toward professionals did spill over into the realm of medical and health care, which also became less egalitarian.

SUGGESTED READING

Public Health

Akhtar, Shahid, *Health Care in the People's Republic of China: A Bibliography with Abstracts* (Ottawa: International Development Research Centre, 1975).

Ascher, Isaac, *China's Social Policy* (London: Anglo-Chinese Educational Institute, Modern China Series, No. 3, 1976).

A Barefoot Doctor's Manual.The American translation of the official Chinese paramedical manual. (Philadelphia: Running Press, 1977).

Dimond, E. G., *More Than Herbs and Acupuncture* (New York: W. W. Norton, 1975).

Health Care in China. (1) "The Mass Line," by Joshua Horn. (2) Annotated Bibliography. (London: Anglo-Chinese Educational Institute, Modern China Series, No. 8, 1976).

Hu, Teh-wei, *An Economic Analysis of Cooperative Medical Services in the People's Republic of China* (Washington, D.C.: U.S. Department of Health, Education, and Welfare, Public Health Service, National Health Service, 1975).

———, "The Financing and the Economic Efficiency of Rural Health Services in the People's Republic of China," *International Journal of Health Services* (Farmingdale, N.Y.), Vol. VI, No. 2, 1976, pp. 239–49.

Hua Sheng, and Hsiang Jung, "Kwangsi: Revolution in Health Work." Two articles: (1) "Put the Stress on the Rural Areas," *Peking Review* (Beijing), No. 8, February 18, 1977, pp. 20–23. (2) "Barefoot Doctors and Cooperative Medical System," *Peking Review* (Beijing), No. 9, February 25, 1977, pp. 19–23.

Kao, F. F., and J. J. Kao, "Traditional and Modern Medicine in China," *Impact of Science on Society* (Paris), Vol. XXV, No. 3, 1975, pp. 259–66.

Lampton, M., "Health Policy during the Great Leap Forward," *China Quarterly* (London), No. 60, December 1974, pp. 668–69.

Lin Yang, "Medical and Health Service, " *Beijing Review,* June 23, 1980, pp. 17–27.

"Mother and Child Care in Rural China," New China News Agency (NCNA) (Beijing), March 7, 1977 in *Survey of People's Republic of China Press* (SPRCP), (Hong Kong), No. 6299, March 15, 1977, pp. 61–62.

Orleans, Leo A., *Health Policies and Services in China, 1974* (Washington, D.C.: U.S. Congress Committee on Labor and Public Welfare, U.S. Government Printing Office, 1974).

Prybyla, Jan S., "Growing Old in China," *Current History* (Philadelphia), Vol. LXXI, No. 419, September 1976, pp. 56–59, 80.

Quinn, J. R. (ed.), *Medicine and Public Health in the People's Republic of China* (Bethesda, Md.: National Institute of Health, H.E.W. Publication 72–67, 1973).

Sidel, Victor W., and Ruth Sidel, *Serve the People: Observations on Medicine in the People's Republic of China* (New York: Beacon Books, 1974).

Taber, George M., "Chinese Social Policy Today," *Journal of the Institute of Socioeconomic Studies* (White Plains, N.Y.), Vol. IV, No. 2, Summer 1979, pp. 1–11.

United States Department of Health, Education and Welfare, Public Health Service, National Institute of Health, *A Bibliography of Chinese Sources on Medicine and Public Health in the People's Republic of China: 1960–1970.* A publication of the John E. Fogarty

International Center for Advanced Study in the Health Sciences (Washington, D.C.: H.E.W., 1973).

Wegman, Myron (ed.), *Public Health in the People's Republic of China* (New York: Josiah Macy Foundation, 1973).

Yang, Hsiao, "The Making of a Peasant Doctor" (Peking: Foreign Languages Press, 1976).

Education

Cheng, Chu-yuan, *Scientific and Engineering Manpower in Communist China, 1949–63* (Washington, D.C.: U.S. Government Printing Office, National Science Foundation, 1965).

Fraser, Stewart E., and K. L. Hsu, *Chinese Education and Society: A Bibliographical Guide, The Cultural Revolution and Its Aftermath* (White Plains, N.Y.: International Arts and Sciences Press, 1972).

He, Zhuo, "China's Education: The Type of People It Brings Up," *Beijing Review*, January 7, 1980, pp. 17–27.

McCormick, Robert, "Revolution in Education Committees," *China Quarterly* (London), No. 57, January–March 1974, pp. 133–39.

Mauger, Peter, et al., *Education in China* (London: Anglo-Chinese Educational Institute, January 1974).

"New College Enrollment System," *Peking Review*, No. 46, November 11, 1977, pp. 16–18.

Observations on the Relations between Education and Work in the People's Republic of China. Report of a Study Group, 1978. Clark Kerr, Chairman (Berkeley, Calif.: Carnegie Council on Policy Studies in Higher Education, 1978). Summary and extended versions.

Pepper, Suzanne, "An Interview on Changes in Chinese Education After the 'Gang of Four,' " *China Quarterly* (London), No. 72, December 1977, pp. 815–24.

Prybyla, Jan S., "The Life of a Chinese Professor," *Journal of General Education* (University Park, Pa.), Vol. XXVI, No. 3, Fall 1974, pp. 195–204.

———, "Notes on Chinese Higher Education: 1974," *China Quarterly* (London), No. 62, June 1975, pp. 271–96.

"Reform of Higher Education," *Beijing Review*, July 28, 1980, pp. 19–24.

Scalapino, Robert A., "The Struggle over Higher Education: Revolution versus Development," in *Proceedings of the Fifth Sino-American Conference on Mainland China* (Taipei, Taiwan: Institute of International Relations, National Chengchi University, 1976), pp. 435–45.

TEN

Summary and Prospects

The preceding pages reviewed the major problems, both past and current, which Chinese economic policy seeks to resolve. This concluding chapter summarizes the findings and speculates briefly on some of the problems and possible responses that may emerge in the future. The last part of the exercise is, of course, tentative and perilous. The future of China's economic model depends on many economic and noneconomic variables, some of which are latent in the present situation and related to past performance, while others are not perceptible as yet, or are quite simply unimaginable. The economic record to date, however, can be of help in forming an educated guess about future options and trends.

Ideology, Organizational Forms, and Methods of Struggle

In the past quarter of a century, China's economic policy has alternatively followed two principles: (a) massive storming of major obstacles and the consequent elimination or suppression of the inhibiting contradiction, followed by (b) prolonged periods of compromise and consolidation of gains. These latter periods have also been marked by occasional resurgence of the breakthrough principle. We have labeled the two principles: "one divides into two," and "two combine into one" (Chapter 1). In Marxist doctrinal terms the first principle is intended to lift society to a higher stage (or socialist substage) through brute uprooting of such vestiges of the previous and existing stages as are deemed incompatible with the desired new situation. For example, the leap from new democracy (1949–1955) to socialism necessitated, in the view of the Maoist leadership, the destruction of the remaining capitalist relations of production. Seen through the same prism, the upgrading of newly implanted socialist institutions required, in that same perspective, the communization of social relations, a task formally accomplished by the Great Leap Forward (1958–1960) and the earlier (1957) decentralization of the planning and managerial apparatus on the basis of self-reliance.The purification of these higher relations demanded a clean sweep of the superstructure, which was tentatively accomplished by the Great Proletarian Cultural Revolution (1966–1969). The Revolution and its lead-in, the Socialist Education Campaign of 1963–1964, were intended to eliminate revisionist tendencies that, in the estimation of the Maoist leadership and allied factions, has spread within the body of socialism and contaminated socialist institutions.

Equally important have been those periods of relative calm during which the down-to-earth work of feeding, clothing, housing, and ministering to the mental and physical health of the people was being accomplished. It was during these times of comparative stability that the Chinese economic model was worked out in operational detail, with compromises and not a little doctrinal backsliding.The two most clearly defined periods during which the principle of two combine into one predominated were from 1961 through November 1965, and the years since the death of Mao and the toppling of the radical faction (1977–present).The alternative leaping on one leg and walking on two legs lends to the model a wavelike progression.

Since the founding of the People's Republic of China (earlier in the "liberated areas") three methods had been used to implement the two principles: the method of orthodox administration, mass movements, and peer-group pressure.These methods were employed concurrently but with differing emphasis, depending on which dialectical principle dominated at a given moment. In times of uprooting, tearing apart, and head-on confrontation the stress was on mass movements and intense peer-group pressure.When the principle of reconciliation dominated, orthodox administration, bureaucratic structures, and the link-by-link approach were emphasized.While mass movements and peer group pressure are integral parts of China's formal economic and political institutions (the planning, managerial, and control machinery of the Party and state), in times of dominance by the two-combine-into-one principle, these movements and pressures are strictly controlled, guided through approved bureaucratic channels, and spelled out in laws and regulations. Thus, the mass movement for the attainment of the four modernizations launched after the fall of the radicals in October 1976 was a comparatively structured and controlled campaign that made use of incentive wages, bonuses, professional examinations, well-defined hierarchies, laws, regulations, procuratorial and judicial procedures, and the public security apparatus. Its predecessor, the Cultural Revolution (1966–1969) was, by contrast, an almost volcanic eruption that smashed existing institutions, dissolved established relationships, and replaced them with a network of shifting arrangements, volatile and unpredictable even in their short-term outcomes. Their focal point, in Marxist terminology, was the superstructure or political consciousness, while their legitimacy and survival depended critically on Mao's support. With Mao gone, this gossamerlike newborn thing was struck down by the resurgent apparat. From stressing the transformation of the base through radical alteration of political consciousness, attention shifted to a more orthodox and longer-term remolding of consciousness by means of technical-scientific changes in the economic base of society (the four modernizations).

For those, and they are legion, who had made their careers in the days of the gang's supremacy, the adjustment to the post-Mao two-combine-into-one principle and the methodology of highly structured bureaucratic administration was not easy. "Although the situation has changed, their thinking remains at the old stage. We often describe this as 'thinking unable to keep up' or 'thinking lagging behind the situation.' "[1] There was also bitter rear-guard resistance to the new conception and implementation of the line. "The pernicious influence of the ultra-leftist line will not become a street mouse without any place to hide just because leading comrades have stepped out to say a few words, or because the press has published a few articles. Instead, it will take shelter in some people's minds, and when the right time comes, it will pop up in disguise and continue with its menace."[2] These unrepentant leftists kept popping up in disguise even at the height of the pragmatic "seeking truth from facts" post-Mao era. "Pragmatists have only one standard—anything goes so long as it serves their nefarious schemes. If it fits their requirements, it is the 'truth.' " The correct dialectical line,

[1]Wang Da, Second Secretary, Hunan Provincial CCP Committee, Hunan Provincial Broadcasting Service, Changsha, August 12, 1979, in *FBIS*, August 14, 1979. Half of the present Party members were admitted into the Party during the leftist years 1966–76.

[2]*Renmin Ribao* commentary, Beijing Radio, July 31, 1979, in *FBIS*, August 14, 1979.

all seemed to agree, is the line of those who are "in the position to make life a hell for anyone who [does] not agree with them." [3]

Population

Indications are that after periods of uncertainty about the policy to be adopted regarding population growth, China has fairly consistently opted for birth control. The obstacles to the policy remain formidable, rooted as they are in tradition and to a lesser extent in Party wavering. The sheer logistics of the operation defy the imagination. The impression one gains from incomplete and scattered information, however, is that the objective of reducing annual population growth to 1 percent or less is being pursued with determination and the help of a large public health force (Chapter 2).

In contrast to most other developing countries, for more than a decade China has pursued a policy of limiting the growth of urban populations. Large numbers of urban-educated young people were sent down to the countryside, a measure that has been imitated only by the Khmer Rouge, but with greater brutality in Cambodia. The Chinese sending-down movement was part of an economic strategy that aimed to form capital in the countryside, raise the technical-educational level there, and prevent urban unemployment, but it was also a political measure designed to expose young intellectuals to manual work and the presumed class benefits flowing from such exposure. The downward transfer movement had been resented all along by those subject to it: the young people from the cities and their families. This resentment translated itself into apathy and passive resistance, which put to question the realization of one of the two major practical objectives of the measure: the formation at low cost of capital in the countryside, including human capital (through the educational activities of the urban youths). The other practical objective of downward transfer was to prevent the emergence of teenage unemployment in the cities. This was not achieved because large numbers of the sent-down youths filtered back into the cities despite admonitions and prohibitions. Since there were no urban jobs for them, and (because of their illegal residence status) no ration cards, they lived by crime. In 1978–1979 the whole concept of downward transfer began to be reexamined at the highest level. There were indications that the program would be phased out. Yet the original question of what to do with millions of urban primary and middle school graduates that annually enter the job market, remained starkly posed. By 1979, reflecting the temper of the times, the previously vaunted

[3] *Beijing Review*, February 2, 1979, pp. 17, 19.

ideological benefits of rustication—the cross fertilization of urban professional knowledge and peasant revolutionary consciousness—were no longer mentioned.

The policy with respect to minority nationalities is a blend of force and longterm cultural assimilation. Despite the designation, "national" aspirations—especially when they express themselves in a demand for autonomy or independence—are promptly stamped out by the application of the one-divides-into-two principle, the agents of which, in this case, are the People's Liberation Army and the public security apparatus. Strivings for national identity are seen as bourgeois manifestations, and nationality is legitimate only when it conforms to the proletarian class mold and expresses itself in relatively harmless folkloric manifestations. An important variable in the long-range solution of the minority nationalities problem is the overwhelming numerical strength of the Hans.This quantitative superiority is translated into large-scale settlements of Han populations into minority nationality regions. Over the years, the Mongols and others have become strangers in their own lands.

Agriculture

In agriculture as in other sectors, a careful distinction must be made between what the institutional charts say is done and what actually happens. In theory, agriculture since 1961 has been accorded high priority on the planners' scale of sectoral preferences, modified only by considerations of national defense and the perceived need to develop other activities simultaneously. Agriculture has been declared the "foundation" of economic development, and industry the "leading factor." The idea was that Stalinist-type exploitation of one sector for the benefit of others should be carefully avoided (Chapter 3).

After the fall of the gang of four, it was alleged that agriculture had been seriously neglected since 1966 for at least five reasons: (1) political and social instability; (2) wrongheaded (egalitarian) incentive systems that were "unfavorable to arousing the peasants' production enthusiasm"; (3) inadequate and ineffective state aid (i.e., too much stress on the need for commune self-reliance); [4] (4) neglect of technical innovation and agricultural research and education (i.e., too much reliance

[4]Beijing Radio, July 29, 1979, in *FBIS*, August 3, 1979. From 1966 through 1975 state (provincial) investment in agriculture, a sector theoretically at the top of planners' priorities, represented only 31 percent of Guangdong Province's total investment. On the other hand, investment in heavy industry was 61.6 percent; in light industry, 7 percent. Guangdong Provincial Broadcasting Service, Guangzhou, August 12, 1979, in *FBIS*, August 14, 1979.

on the inventive potential of the masses of poor and lower-middle peasants, and too little attention to scientific research and professional formation);[5] (5) inefficient implementation of the principle of all-round development of farming, forestry, animal husbandry, sideline occupations, and fishery (i.e., too much stress on the cultivation of grain at the expense of other farming and allied pursuits).[6] The last resulted, among other things, in widespread ecological damage.[7] For example, more than one-fourth of China's grasslands have deteriorated into sand or have been alkalized.

Since 1961 the choice of techniques of production reveals on the whole a balanced approach between modern industry-based inputs and traditional and semitraditional ones. The use of traditional and intermediate technology to the fullest extent was and continues to be encouraged at the local level, while modern industry is urged to supply the farming sector with the capital and current inputs needed to break out of the traditional production trap. There are contradictory indications of whether China's agriculture has succeeded in the last objective and whether the race between population and food supplies is being won. The situation remains precarious and there is much apprehension within leadership ranks lest new political leaps upset the delicate bal-

[5]In Anhui Province (1979) there were 10,000 agricultural technicians out of an agricultural population of 42 million. Of these, only 23 were certified agricultural technicians. Not a single forestry technician title had been conferred in the province since 1949. There were "many" agricultural scientists and technicians over fifty years old. "However, they are given the same political treatment and the same living and working conditions as those just graduated from school. Agricultural and scientific personnel are given much worse political treatment and working conditions than such personnel in other departments. . . . There have been many false charges against and frameups of [agricultural technicians and scientists in the past]." Beijing Radio, July 27, 1979, in *FBIS*, August 8, 1979.

[6]In Hunan Province (1978) out of a total of 400,000 hectares of ponds and lakes suitable for fish breeding, 255,000 hectares (63.8 percent) were used for that purpose. Only 7 percent of the province's farmland was sown in industrial crops. Average per capita income of peasants from communal activity was 6.77 yuan a month (0.22 yuan, or roughly 14 U.S. cents a day). Beijing Radio, August 13, 1979, in *FBIS*, August 14, 1979.

[7]"The denudation of forests and grasslands and the practice in many localities of filling in lakes to expand farmland acreage were carried out in the past because of undue emphasis placed on grain production. . . . This undermined our ecological environment, and the consequences are so serious that they will harm the younger generation. Some localities have not learned the lesson from this undesirable practice and are still denuding the forests to expand farmland." Beijing Radio reporting on a meeting of agro-scientists, August 13, 1979, in *FBIS*, August 14, 1979. Cf., "Chen Pixian [First Secretary of Hubei Provincial CCP Committee and head of the provincial government] pointed out in an important speech . . .: 'To promote agriculture it is first necessary to get a tight grasp on grain production.' " Hubei Provincial Broadcasting Service, Wuhan, July 28, 1979, in *FBIS*, July 31, 1979.

ance and narrow the thin margin between barely adequate food supplies and starvation. So far increases in farm output have been achieved, by and large, through extensive means, mostly, that is, by the addition of factors, especially labor. The post-Mao leadership claims, rightly, that future increases must come from improvements in factor productivity. To this end a large program of agricultural investment in mechanization, irrigation and drainage, chemicalization, education, research, and infrastructure has been initiated. At one point mechanization was seen as the answer to China's farm problems. This simplistic view was subsequently discarded and by late 1979 intensive mechanization of basic and ancillary farm operations was to be carried out selectively with priority being given to "areas with the necessary conditions, so that they would achieve modernization first, and be models in helping promote mechanization in other parts of the country." The importation, manufacture, and popularization of farm machinery were seen as parts of a broader general technical equilibrium system that, in addition, was to include infrastructural facilities (roads, railroads, telecommunications), scientific research, technical education, extension work, and so on.

The seriousness of the food-population balance and the dangers inherent in it do not, however, detract from the accomplishments registered to date. There is much room for increases in yields per acre and per man, the food potential of the rivers and seas has hardly been tapped. The elements—while curbed—are yet to be tamed. Even in a comparatively advanced province such as Guangdong, "the ability to fight natural disasters is low." [8] Under all these headings, however, steady work has been done despite political difficulties and errors of economic judgment. The unusually frank and critical examination of the agricultural record after the death of Mao should not detract from the overall effectiveness of the effort expended to date. Agricultural technology and

[8]In the agriculturally prosperous Guangdong Province (1979) 11 million *mou* (734,000 hectares) of fields were without any water-conservation facilities. "The standard of the 28 million *mou* (1,868,000 hectares) of fields with guaranteed good harvest despite drought and waterlogging is not high." "Nearly half the dams and embankments along rivers and seas which are defending 17 million *mou* (1,134,000 hectares) of farmland have not reached a sufficient standard for the prevention of floods." "There are still some 15 million *mou* (1,000,500 hectares) of low yield fields with annual per *mou* yield below 800 *jin* (6,600 kilograms per hectare)." Between 1976 and 1978 (after the gang had already fallen), oil supplied to Guangdong's agriculture satisfied less than half the needs. Every year Guangdong loses between 50,000 and 100,000 tons of grain because of insect pests and plant diseases. To make a dent in the problem "most of the local financial revenue at the provincial level and 80 percent of the financial revenue at the prefectural and county levels should be spent on agriculture." Guangdong Provincial Broadcasting Service, August 12, 1979, in *FBIS*, August 14, 1979.

its embodiment in capital are serious but not insuperable problems for China. The priorities are right and the will and organizational capacity to break out of the Malthusian circle are there—so is the ability.

The social organization of agriculture hinging on the rural people's commune seems to be in theory appropriate in its present form to the variegated tasks that it is called upon to discharge. Here, again, theory has in the past significantly departed from practice. Conceptually the three levels of social ownership (commune, production brigade, and production team) and the division of functions within the commune organization should lend to the system a flexibility that the collective farm-type organization did not have. The commune, according to the concept, is to be mainly in charge of public administration and water conservation work at the local level, whereas farm production and income distribution are to be done by production teams and, more rarely, production brigades. The blueprint provides for consultation among the various levels of the planning and managerial hierarchy and for attentive hearing to be given to the opinions of those who actually do the farming.

Unfortunately practice did not conform to the ideal, apparently not even remotely. Violations of the theoretical prescriptions were especially blatant, we are now told, during the gang-dominated period 1966–1976. Specifically mentioned are transgressions against the three-tier ownership model (commune, brigade, team) with the team getting the roughest treatment; violations of the teams' quite slender right of self-determination; egalitarian exercises in income distribution which "sapped the peasants' enthusiasm" for collective production (i.e., made them stay home); and the denial to peasants of the right to cultivate private plots and trade in rural fairs. All these so-called deviations are, in fact, inherent in the socialist (Soviet-type) economic system and are not limited to China. In a hierarchical monoparty social organization lateral links among participants are tenuous or nonexistent. Consultation among different levels of the power pyramid tends in practice to turn into monologue and order giving. As a necessary outcome of the system's inner logic, the smallest and lowest unit—whether producer or consumer—gets the worst deal.

The rebureaucratization of China's agriculture following the casting out of the gang is not likely to change matters drastically in respect to the propensity of higher planning and Party authorities to meddle in the business of the basic producing units and to push these units around. That is perhaps why the very concept of the people's commune as the social core of China's agriculture seems presently to be undergoing close scrutiny. The reappearance of work groups within the commune organization may not be symptomatic only of a production crisis; it may in some way symbolize a deeper process of change in the regime's conception of the appropriate agricultural organization. It is conceivable that together with other Maoist creations the rural people's commune will one day be revised beyond recognition. A new set of Regulations Concerning Work in Rural People's Communes was to be submitted to the Third Session of the Fifth National People's Congress in 1980. The commune form of organization was intended by its now discredited creator—Mao—to promote production and farmland capital construction in the spirit of the foolish old man who removed the mountain, that is, in the spirit of struggle, self-reliance, self-denial, and hard work. These Maoist virtues are now under critical scrutiny in terms of their contribution to modernization. The accent is on science and technology, on specialization rather than self-sufficiency and all-aroundness, on getting rich instead of staying nobly poor, and on making work easier rather than on work as struggle. The commune concept just might fall victim one day to this shift in perceptions.

Incentives to farms and farm households combine material and moral inducements. Since the arrest of the radicals, experiments with egalitarian methods of income distribution have been terminated and the work-point system has been given more weight. Peasants are again allowed (as they had been before the Cultural Revolution, particularly in 1961–1963) to cultivate household plots and are permitted to trade any surpluses from private plot production on rural fairs. As during the Liuist period, households are encouraged to grow rich through productive labor, and there is less official fear about interhousehold income differences and the possible implications of such differences for the rural social class structure. To improve agriculture's terms of trade with industry, procurement prices for grain, cotton, oils and fats, pork, beef, mutton, and some other commodities (eighteen in all) have been raised while the prices of essential agricultural inputs have been kept steady. The new regime has made it clear that it wants no interference from higher authorities with the production teams' right to program their production within the parameters of the state plan as expressed in the teams' delivery obligations. The formerly widespread practice of brigades', communes' and counties' commandeering team labor without compensation and requisitioning private homes for their bureaucratic needs is to be stopped. The production team is to remain the unit of income distribution. In fact, in a number of instances the income distribution unit appears to be the small work group below the team, and the authorities have typically tended to look the other way so long as the system whipped up the elusive "production enthusiasm" among the peasants. There are influential forces within the present leadership that argue against the administrative, physical, and command approach to agricultural planning and for greater resort to indirect, financial ("law of value") inducements.

Although living standards have improved, life in the village remains hard. Shi Shan, a member of the Chinese Academy of Social Sciences, in an article published by *Guangming Ribao* (July 27, 1979) argues that structural and organizational reforms are urgently needed in agriculture in order to reach the following modest annual per capita consumption standards in the countryside: 500 kilograms of grain (the net foodgrain supply at present is in the neighborhood of 200 kilograms per head per year), 40 kilograms of meat, 6 kilograms of eggs, and 150 kilograms of vegetables. He also stresses the need to raise rural incomes to narrow the large urban-rural income gap. There is a distinct possibility that the policies of the four modernizations, given their essentially urban temper, might widen rather than narrow the spread between rural and urban incomes.

Industry

The single most important feature of China's industrialization from 1961 till 1977 has been the stress on the development of rural, small- and medium-scale industry using intermediate technology. Such industry was brought into being largely from indigenous resources, using locally conscripted labor; and it was managed by local authorities from the production brigade on up. Rural industrialization had several benefits. Among these was the flow of current agricultural inputs, such as chemical fertilizer, the distribution of which would prove more problematical if local plants were not scattered over the countryside. Local industry also turned out and repaired producer goods needed by the farms and supplied a significant portion of rural power requirements and consumer items.

In line with the policy of walking on two legs, the development of large-scale, capital- and skill-intensive industry was pursued simultaneously, and the rate of expansion correlated with the ability of agriculture to supply the needed raw materials and food (Chapters 4 and 5). With the formal adoption of the plan for the four modernizations, emphasis shifted to more orthodox methods of industrialization: the promotion of large-scale, capital-, skill-, and technology-intensive industries in the established urban industrial centers, improvement of existing facilities (e.g., the Anshan and Wuhan iron and steel complexes), and the importation of advanced factories and equipment. The village-industry concept (bringing industry to the peasants rather than peasants to urban industry) was not, after 1976, shunted aside; but it began to be given less weight in the new regime's overall strategy of industrialization. For the first time, the drawbacks and costs of rural industrialization were openly discussed. Local industries were not always formed from local resources, nor did they limit themselves to locally procured labor, power, and raw materials. They often competed for capital and current inputs with provincial level and sometimes national state enterprises. Even very small-scale, technologically backward operations tried to assure their sources of input supply by vertical integration, so that China's industrial landscape became littered with countless mini-empires, each trying to be self-sufficient while sacrificing economies of scale and the benefits of specialization. [9] The product of small industries, it is now said, was often inferior, amounting to so much wasted time, effort, and material. The whole theory of rural industrialization and intermediate technology is under review and the criteria employed in the review appear to be less saturated with ideology than they had been in the past. The reexamination is not without precedent; something similar was carried out in the years following the Great Leap Forward when many Maoist mini-industries (including most of the backyard furnaces) were closed down.

Under the Maoist extensive strategy of economic development, insofar as questions of equity of income distribution, governance, and political consciousness permitted, attention was paid to output performance. The input side of the production process was taken care of by simple addition of factors: more labor, more land (through, for example, drying up of lakes or plowing up of grasslands), and more of the same kind of machines. After the death of Mao and the political death of his gang, there was a new preoccupation with the input side of the production process: with labor performance per man-hour, capital input-output ratios, the proper combination of chemicals, labor, improved seeds, drainage, irrigation, and machinery to obtain rising yields per acre—in short, with intensive development.

In this perspective, the material- and labor-intensive rural industries

[9]In mid-1979 the State Council issued regulations on industrial standardization, which were expected to pave the way for the reorganization of industry according to the principles of specialization and coordination. Beijing Radio, August 14, 1979, in *FBIS*, August 14, 1979.

were bound to come up for critical reappraisal. They were seen increasingly as supplements to intensive industrialization, absorbers of some of the surplus labor and obsolete capital discarded by technically advanced, large-scale urban industry.[10] Some inefficient unfinished large enterprises could also fall, it was suggested, to the rationalization axe. "The scale of our national construction must be compatible with our financial and material resources. This determines whether the economy can remain stable. We must admit the basic fact that our current fuel, power, and raw material resources cannot 'support' the existing 350,000 industrial enterprises. If we continue the practice of having 'five people eat rice enough for three people' we will find that 'nobody will have enough to eat and nothing can be accomplished well.' " To this end it was essential to liquidate some existing enterprises as well as to write off many half finished or unfinishable "political factories." But this was not easy given the system of free budgetary grant allocations for investment. Some comrades criticized the proposed retrenchment as "stirring up the wind of dismounting a horse." Others refused "to look actual conditions of disproportion squarely in the face and held that it was very hard to curtail the capital construction front."[11] The complaint is familiar to students of the Soviet-type centrally planned administrative economy.

There is a fair measure of flexibility to the structure of industrial management at the macro- and micro-levels. The bulk of industry, both large-scale modern and semitraditional local, is under the authority of

[10]"We have been talking about readjusting the '5-small' industries for several years. We must deal with each case on its own merits and in the light of local resources and production conditions. Decisive measures must be adopted to readjust the 'coal consuming tigers' and 'electric power consuming tigers'—enterprises that were developed blindly, are nonessential to production, and consume an alarming amount of coal and electricity; duplicating factories and processing industries the products of which exceed demand; enterprises without raw material sources that were developed without plans and compete with large industries for raw materials; and enterprises that turn out poor quality and unmarketable products and sustain losses over a long period of time." *Renmin Ribao* editorial, July 26, 1979, in *FBIS*, July 31, 1979. "The situation of the supply of coal, petroleum, electric power, and certain raw materials is tense, and the situation of large consumption and immense waste is still very common." Guangdong Provincial Broadcasting Service, Guangzhou, July 31, 1979, in *FBIS*, August 1, 1979. In Shanghai, it was pointed out, 1 million workers were employed in several thousand collectively owned (small) enterprises developed from handicraft cooperatives or production teams of the 1950s. These enterprises produced consumer goods for both domestic and foreign markets and filled orders from large state-owned firms. They were helpful in providing employment for urban educated youths. Beijing Radio, August 1, 1979, in *FBIS*, August 2, 1979. A spirited defense of small and medium-sized collective enterprises was contained in a *Renmin Ribao* editorial of July 21, 1979 (in *FBIS*, August 1, 1979).

[11]*Renmin Ribao* editorial, July 26, 1979, in *FBIS*, July 31, 1979.

provincial, municipal, and lower-order state or cooperative organs. Enterprises move in and out of the various managerial and supervisory structures with comparative ease, the criteria for such reassignments being for the most part economic and technical.

After 1976 the structure of industrial management was subjected to contradictory pulls. At the macro level there seemed to be on the one hand a fairly strong trend in favor of administrative recentralization. The size and complexity of the factories and mills that were to be imported under the modernization plans and the renewed concern given to integrated planning seemed to augur a tightening up of reins in the planning process, a reassertion of central control that had been loosened by years of factional bickering. This gradual slide into structured, centralized, hierarchical, administrative planning, which over time was to cover more than just a few hundred key commodities, appeared to be supported by the essentially bureaucratic, veterans-of-the-apparat personal history of the post-Mao leadership.

But, at least at the turn of the 1970s, there were pulls in the opposite direction as well. The "seeking truth from facts" approach to the economy and the repeated calls for cadres and others to "emancipate their minds" and explore hitherto forbidden conceptual nooks and corners, suggested that a certain flexibility would be observed in selecting organizational and structural alternatives to the Maoist way of conducting the nation's economic business. Calls for greater resort to the "law of value" way of signaling economic information and coordinating resource allocating decisions, and the willingness to free some prices testified to an antiadministrative centralization undercurrent within the leadership. "The gang of four said that if we allow the exchange of commodities on the market, we will generate capitalism. This is simply nonsense, but it had a real effect. In the countryside it stopped farmers planting some things because these things were labelled as commodities. . . . For many years we have not discussed management, not any kind of management. This is a big problem. . . . In the West this is a speciality, but here in China we do not have any managers, or to put it another way, we do not have anybody who manages well!" [12] Management in the widest sense was at issue: management of the economy (the systemic structure of the system) as well as enterprise management. In a 1979 book on China's economic system, the noted economist Xue Muqiao called for a restructuring of the country's

[12]George Braybrooke, "Recent Developments in Chinese Social Science, 1977–79," *China Quarterly*, No. 79, September 1979, p. 599.

economy in the direction of greater enterprise autonomy vis-a-vis central planners, greater resort by the planners to markets, prices, and indirect monetary and fiscal means of ensuring concordance between planners' intent and enterprise and consumer preferences, and emphasis on indicative rather than mandatory planning. "Sales on the market," Xue argued, "must not be determined by production plans but the other way round." [13] In Sichuan an experiment in enterprise self-management covering some 100 enterprises in 11 trades and occupations was carried out, beginning in 1979.The experiment had some features in common with the Bolshevichka and Mayak experiments in enterprise autonomy carried out in the U.S.S.R. in the early 1960s. For one thing, the enterprises selected were among the best in the province "with strong leading groups and internally unified." The experiment was much more conservative than the proposals for reform advanced by Xue Muqiao, but its very existence was of historic significance. [14] The results, as of end 1979, were said to have been relatively encouraging, but there was much passivity and outright opposition.The calls for greater enterprise autonomy within a reformed planning system were described by some as "only thunder but no rain." "In some places support had not been given by all circles to help the selected enterprises work out a detailed experimental plan and official papers traveled for months without result." [15] The passivity, opposition, and complaints were almost identical with those voiced almost twenty years earlier in the Soviet Union. Piecemeal

[13]A chapter from this book can be found in *Beijing Review*, October 26, 1979, pp. 14–20. Another economist who advocates advanced marketization of the administrative command economy is Sun Yefang, whose book *Several Questions Concerning Socialist Economy* was published by the People's Publishing House in July 1979.The book consists of twenty articles and reports, most of them written before the Cultural Revolution. "The author emphasizes the objectivity of economic laws and advocates respect for and action on the objective economic laws. He stresses the importance of the circulation of commodities in a socialist economy. He is opposed to the practice of setting the law of value against the basic economic laws of socialism and against the laws for the development of the national economy in a planned and rational manner. He advocates that planning and statistics be based on the law of value. He holds that when price fundamentally conforms to value or production cost and other conditions, profits are the major criterion to determine whether an enterprise is well managed. He advocates expansion of an enterprise's power of decision and favors giving an enterprise the power to make decisions on the depreciation of its assets and replacement of its equipment, as well as an independent accounting system for the enterprise. He advocates establishing a contract system among enterprises for the sale and procurement of commodities, and calls for a reform of the pricing system so that prices are set according to production costs." Beijing Radio, August 2, 1979, in *FBIS*, August 3, 1979.

[14]*Renmin Ribao*, July 14, 1979, in *FBIS*, July 31, 1979.

[15]*Renmin Riabo* editorial, op. cit., July 26, 1979.

reform of the administrative command system from the bottom up was not likely to improve matters a great deal. In 1979 the newly semiautonomous enterprises were still operating under the old physical planning constraints and in an environment that was generally hostile to market and price relationships, lateral contracts, and decentralized investment initiative. [16]

After the dissolution of enterprise revolutionary committees and other three-in-one combinations (faction-prone products, it was alleged, of the Cultural Revolution) and the reestablishment of the directorial principle, questions of worker representation in management did not automatically vanish. While order and discipline had to be brought back to the factories, the need for some form of managerial copartnership or, at a minimum, worker check on possible managerial autocracy was not denied. Years of intra-Party factionalism, which spilled over onto the factory floor and produced an anarchical form of democracy by default, and of hammering home the Maoist message that workers are masters of their workshops, could not be undone overnight. Improved incentives in the form of a larger supply and greater variety of consumer goods at affordable prices (which might reduce worker irritation with managers and planners) would take time to materialize. In the meantime some sort of arrangement had to be found to prevent enterprise managements from riding roughshod over the workers, as they used to do in the days of the First Five-Year Plan (1953–1957). The resurrected trade unions were to be used to represent worker interests, but their track record on this score was far from exemplary and no one seemed to put much faith in them. The Yugoslav model of workers' councils was looked into cautiously. At the end of the 1970s the picture was blurred. All kinds of experiments were being carried out in different enterprises and parts of the country. Three major developments were discernible, but it was

[16] "*After* [the experimental] enterprises have completely fulfilled the state plan, they can organize increases in production and receive materials for processing as well as unsold products from independent marketing and trade departments, from commodity departments, and from supply and distribution departments. To improve the enterprise funding system and to differentiate the various situations, enterprise funding is drawn on the basis of total annual wages and planned targets for profits. The proportion of depreciation funds for fixed assets has been increased in favor of the factories for their use in technical improvements and newer equipment. . . . Working capital has been reevaluated; interest free loans, low interest loans, or high interest loans have been accordingly issued." The Sichuan reform of 1979 clearly did not go far beyond the Soviet Liberman-type reforms of the 1960s. *Renmin Ribao*, July 14, 1979, in *FBIS*, July 31, 1979. Enterprise autonomy, such as it was, was contingent on the prior fulfillment of the state plan. By then "free" inputs were no doubt few and the enterprises' freedom of decision-making quite illusory.

impossible to predict which, if any, would ultimately survive. First, there were experiments with electing heads of workshops and shifts in factories by workers from lists prepared by the enterprise Party committee. Secondly, and ideally, such lists would be based on opinion polls carried out by the committee among the workers. In some places the opinion poll was final; it guided the Party committee in its middle- and lower-level cadre appointments. Third, there were to be regularly held conferences of representatives of workers and staff. These could "discuss major issues in the enterprises and work out and put into practice resolutions relating to production plans, management regulations, labor organizations, financial expenditures, welfare, and labor protection." The system existed around 1956 and was "now being restored in many places." [17] In essence, the coparticipation discussions in the later 1970s centered on the workers' right to elect (from Party-prepared lists) and remove leading cadres at the grassroots level, not enterprise directors and their staffs. In other words, the drift was more noticeably toward the pre-1957 system rather than in some spectacularly innovative and liberalized direction. But the issue at that time and the outcome were, so to speak, up for grabs.

The system of remuneration in industry employs intraplant wage differentials intended to encourage the upgrading of skills by workers and to act as a spur to productivity. There are also interindustry earnings differences for comparable wage grades, but (as of 1979) labor was allocated to different industries, plants, and regions primarily by administrative order, supplemented in some instances by examinations. [18] Although time-rate wages remain the principal incentive mechanism, the current system of industrial remuneration contains also elements of non-material incentives. Piecework wages, which had been on the decline, were reestablished in certain industries after 1976. Bonus and overtime payments, abolished during the Cultural Revolution, were also brought back. As the 1970s came to a close, there were numerous complaints about the way in which the bonus wage was being handled. The criticism centered on the loss of incentive due to an egalitarian tendency in the distribution of bonuses. What seemed to have happened

[17] *Beijing Review*, November 9, 1979, pp. 6–7.

[18] Beginning in August 1979, Beijing planned to recruit 40,000 new industrial workers (in both the state and cooperative sectors) by examination. Some 70,000 youths applied in six days (84 percent of those qualified to apply). It was explained that "formerly jobs were assigned to applicants by labor departments only. The method was too rigid and handicapped the initiative of the enterprises in matters of employment. The applicants could not choose plants or trades to suit their own merits." Beijing Radio, July 28, 1979, in *FBIS*, July 31, 1979.

was that managements simply divided up the bonus fund equally among all workers in the enterprise, viewing the bonus as a supplement to the low basic wage. Between 1977 and 1979 three rounds of basic wage increases had been carried out, accompanied by promotions of workers and employees to higher job grades. Wages in the cooperative sector of industry continued to be below those in the state sector. The "four checks" on collective enterprises (checks on average wages, manpower, materials supply, and finance) were decried after 1976 as a distortion brought about by the gang of four, but the distortion apparently persisted. Not only were average wages lower in collective than state enterprises (irrespective of efficiency), but no college graduates or graduates of technical schools had been assigned to those enterprises for years, and there were explicit stipulations that such collectives could employ only housewives, unemployed persons, the sick, and the disabled. Collective enterprises were not guaranteed a regular supply of materials and equipment. In many instances the collectives' rights of independent economic accounting had been rescinded: all profits earned had to be surrendered to the state. Moreover, "according to some leading departments in Beijing, enterprises under collective ownership should make up for one another's deficiencies. In other words, the enterprises gaining profits must pay the debts of the ones with losses."[19] This arrangement was unlikely to promote or encourage efficiency.

The wage hikes of 1977–1979 together with the reintroduction of bonuses and overtime pay began to exert open inflationary pressures in the economy, the more so since the output of consumer goods had been sluggish for some years. "A relatively big gap exists between the social purchasing power and the available quantity of commodities. . . . [Especially] light industrial and textile items." [20] There was an acute short-

[19]*Renmin Ribao* editorial, July 21, 1979, in *FBIS*, August 1, 1979. Handicraft output, which in 1978 represented more than 10 percent of China's industrial output value and 40 percent of the value of light industrial and textile output, was in bad shape. Foreign exchange earnings derived from handicraft exports represented 14 percent of China's total foreign-exchange earnings and nearly 80 percent of such earnings from light industrial exports. Retail sales of handicraft products accounted for 17 percent of the total value of sales of manufactured goods. "In the last dozen years handicraft products had been in short supply with variety decreasing and output down." Some localities were apparently still imposing restrictions on handicraft units in matters of production, supply, and marketing. Included was "political and economic discrimination against [the 6.8 million] handicraft workers" who were viewed in some hard-core leftist quarters as "appendages of capitalism." *Renmin Ribao*, editorial, July 19, 1979, in *FBIS*, August 1, 1979.

[20]*Renmin Ribao*, July 26, 1979, in *FBIS*, July 31, 1979. Black markets and graft followed in short order.

age of residential housing, which together with the scarcity and modest quality of industrial consumer goods and the stiff increases in the prices of many nonstaple foods, had an adverse effect on the regime's effort to strengthen the incentive system and put an end to "chaos in the enterprises." [21]

Improvement in the motivational system is certainly needed in China, judging by widespread complaints about absenteeism, slackness on the job, underemployment of labor, low labor productivity, capital hoarding by enterprises, and so on. Ad hoc wage increases and price adjustments and a loosening up of the administrative labor allocation system will not, however, do the job alone. The wage and price system has to be thoroughly reformed to reflect more accurately the relative costs and utilities within the system. Soviet experience with wage and price reform shows that the venture, while monumental, is only marginally successful in improving the incentive system so long as the revised prices and wages continue to be based only on average branch cost and to be rigidly controlled by the planners rather than by contractual market relationships and so long as key inputs are physically rationed by the authorities through special material-technical supply channels. [22]

The social wage in the form of disability, retirement, and other benefits represents a significant portion of the total wage for workers and

[21]Guangdong Provincial Broadcasting Service, Guangzhou, August 11, 1979, in *FBIS*, August 14, 1979. Speech by Xi Zhongxun, First Secretary Guangdong Provincial Party Committee. In industry, said Xi, "problems are piled up, tasks are heavy. . . . The light and textile industries are unable to increase their output." To help ease the situation many military factories were "tapping their potential to produce a variety of civilian goods, after fulfilling their own production plans." Among the consumer goods produced by these enterprises were sewing machines, cameras and lenses for wide-screen movies, and lenses for color television. Beijing Radio, July 30, 1979, in *FIBS*, August 1, 1979. In 1979 the government began encouraging individuals to build houses with government subsidies. In that year the state had earmarked 3 billion yuan for housing construction. This would provide 30 million square meters of floor space, "far short of demand." *Renmin Ribao*, July 25, 1979, in *FBIS*, August 1, 1979.

[22]*Renmin Ribao's* (July 26, 1979) catalogue of woes regarding materials supply sounds as if it came straight out of *Izvestia*. "On the one hand there are serious strains in material supply; on the other there is serious overstocking and waste." The (systemic) reasons include: gaps in the materials plan which lacks an overall balance; production and demand are not properly linked—goods produced are not suited to needs; exclusive reliance on administrative measures which results in rigid control and low efficiency; existence of "hidden reserves" (a perennial problem of taut, centrally planned, administrative command economies): "They [enterprise managers] grab anything they can and put it in the warehouse;" some enterprises order materials not for their own use but for exchange with other enterprises. "We should study some economic methods to link the success of materials supply work with the personal interests of workers and staff members of enterprises."

employees in the state sector. In contrast to the left wing's (and Mao's) longer-term preference for the elimination of individual, competitive, material incentives and their replacement by collective, cooperative, moral incentives—and eventually by endogenous work enthusiasm—the post-Mao policy has been to apply the socialist distributive principle of "from each according to his ability, to each according to his work" and its corollary "more pay for more work, less pay for less work, no pay for no work." Pay has been interpreted to mean individual material recompense in the form of basic and bonus wages and various prizes for innovation and invention. If not in so many words, the existing wage differentials were considered to have been too narrow from the standpoint of encouraging vertical labor mobility (skill improvement).

Thus far (1979–1980) prices are not expected to play an autonomous guiding function in the economy. They are determined outside the enterprises by the competent state authorities. For the enterprise managers, prices are value expressions of the physical input and output plan, hopefully consistent with that plan. The experience of other socialist economies suggests that the allocative neutrality of state-set prices is a myth and that the presence of prices gives rise to significant allocative responses (some of them at odds with the physical plan) on the part of management. China is not an exception to this rule. Retail prices do play an equilibrating role between supply and demand; where physical rationing does not apply, prices together with the state's wages policy adapt consumer demand to the goods available. For pricing purposes consumer goods are classified by the planners as essential, everyday necessities, and secondary, the price level rising as one proceeds from the first to the third category. Wide profit margins exist between the retail price and production costs of goods classified as secondary. Selective price adjustments, mostly benefiting lower income groups, are carried out from time to time, well behind increases in labor productivity. The consumer price index has reportedly been stable over the twenty years before 1976 but this stability might have been to a degree "statistical." It edged upward after 1978 in the wake of sharp increases in the prices of a number of nonstaple foods and some other consumer items. These increases were ordered to help lessen the burden on the state of sizeable subsidies represented by the difference between state farm produce procurement prices and state retail prices for the same produce. Suppressed inflation manifests itself in occasional shortages of particular goods, lines outside stores, and black markets. An indirect measure of this inflation consists of free market (rural fair) prices for identical foodstuffs.

If the advocates of bold reform have their way, prices will play a much more important role in the economy than they have in the past, and for most goods they will be formed in the market through the interplay of supply and demand. At the end of the 1970s it was not possible to predict how far down the road of systemic reform post-Mao China was prepared to go. At the most conservative the rehabilitation of the "law of value" would not go beyond the contemporary Soviet stage. Prices, in other words, would remain accounting devices, established, changed, and controlled by the planners, and only vaguely—if at all—reflective of relative scarcities in the system. The economy would remain basically administrative with the physical plan predominant. The tools of physical planning (input-output tables, material balances, linear programming) might be refined, but systemic frontiers would not be crossed. At their boldest the reforms might go beyond the Hungarian experience, which combines central planning with limited markets, and plunge into basic systemic changes of the Yugoslav type. [23]

Industrial location policy has on the whole stressed diffusion of industry and its establishment in the country's less-developed regions. Although a gradual shift in industrial capacity toward those regions is evident, the coastal provinces were so far ahead at the outset that the catching-up process is likely to be prolonged. The launching of the four modernizations augurs a marginal shift in favor of the established industrial centers if only because of the comparative availability in such centers of the skilled labor, technical expertise, and infrastructural facilities needed to operate the sophisticated plant, equipment, and processes that are being imported. Future industrial location policy, however, is unlikely to neglect the industrialization needs of the less-developed provinces if only for political reasons.

China has made significant strides in industrialization. With occasional interruptions the industrialization process since 1961 has been geared toward the development of other sectors, especially agriculture. The overall impression is one of steady and fairly balanced growth. Serious problems remain on the input side. Overall planning methodology has been neglected, enterprise management is weak, the incentive system (to both managers and workers) remains in serious disrepair, static efficiency is wanting, materials intensity is far too great for comfort, industrial accidents are common, and the technical level of even the most advanced enterprises is low by the industrialized world's stan-

[23] Jan S. Prybyla, *Issues in Socialist Economic Modernization* (New York: Praeger, 1980), Chapters 1, 3, 4.

dards. Some of these defects are correctly attributable to political instability (the "sabotage and interference of the gang of four," as the official phrase has it) and to Mao's preoccupation with equity of income distribution at the expense of the rate of income growth. The most troublesome problems, however, are inherent in the administrative command system that the Chinese have adopted from the Soviets and with which they have been tinkering ever since. The "gaps" [24] and sectoral disproportions, the "hidden reserves" and unusable goods, the unfinished and unfinishable investment projects, the lack of competition and resulting high costs and low quality of products, the quasi-permanent sellers' market and suppressed inflation, the activity cycles ("slackening off during the first ten days of the month, making changes during the next ten days, and working desperately during the last ten days"), all these and many more are built-in systemic defects with which the Soviets have wrestled without much effect ever since Stalin introduced the administrative command system into Russia in the late 1920s. The post-Mao Chinese leadership and some of the economists who serve that leadership seem to know this. As of the end of 1979 they had gone a long way toward readjusting the institutions of the economy, but they shied away from crossing the borders of the system. At that time information flows in the economy were still predominantly vertical, input and output instructions were issued by the planners not by intermediate and final users, and the orders were given primarily in physical terms backed by nonscarcity prices. The planning bureaucracy was being rebuilt, pointing perhaps to a drift in the general direction of a Chinese version of contemporary Soviet-type economies. But the signs were contradictory and the situation extremely fluid.

Money and Banking

Monetary and credit management is carried out by the People's Bank (and associated institutions) in accordance with the economic plan (Chapter 6). In this sense monetary and credit operations, while important, are essentially passive; their principal function is to ensure that "value" transactions conform to the dimensions and directions prescribed by the physical plan. This is achieved primarily by reducing to

[24] The weak links as of 1979 were electricity, coal, steel, and transportation. Because of shortages of electricity many industrial and mining enterprises in Guangdong Province were operating only three days a week, and only about half the irrigation and drainage equipment in the Pearl River delta could be put into operation. *Nanfang Ribao* (Guangzhou), August 3, 1979, in *FBIS*, August 14, 1978.

the minimum managerial extraplan options that liquidity would give them. All interenterprise transactions are handled by transfers in the bank's books and almost all profits have to be transmitted to the competent state authorities' accounts held by the bank. The bank and its sister institutions (the Agricultural Bank and the Construction Bank) are the only sources of short- and medium-term credit for enterprises (including people's communes). With very rare exceptions, bank credit is not extended to individuals. In all these respects the bank plays a unifying and centralizing role. The only point of contact between the banking system and an individual is the personal savings account; citizens are urged to deposit their unspent cash in such accounts. Here, too, the intent seems to be to limit the individual's range of choice and prevent suppressed inflation and black marketeering. The bank also performs a variety of general service functions, including managerial consultancy and, through the Bank of China, foreign exchange control.

The role of the bank in the overall management of the economy increased sharply after 1976. One school of thought argued, as we have seen, for a much enlarged function of money and credit in planning. This school appeared to be gaining ground as the decade of the 1970s moved to its close. Experiments in various places (e.g., Sichuan) with enlarged enterprise decision-making rights involved the utilization by enterprise managements of enterprise funds formed from the portion of profits not remitted to the state, depreciation allowances, and bank borrowing for both working and fixed capital purposes. (By June 1980 about 16 percent of state-owned industrial enterprises had been granted—experimentally—greater powers of self-management. Their output value and profits represented respectively 60 and 70 percent of the total.) The Bank of China, too, gained in importance as one of the major institutions in charge of the vastly expanded volume of foreign exchange transactions.

Transportation and Communications

The progress made in improving and extending the transportation and communication networks has been notable (Chapter 7). Like the People's Bank, the Party and public security apparats, transportation and communications perform an integrating function within the economy. Railway and road building, the improvement of inland navigation, the beginnings of shipbuilding and ocean transportation, and the gradual expansion of civil airlines are geared to the industrial location policy and to the defense needs of the country. Construction of intercontinental highways and railroads is financed from central or provincial budgets with labor participation by localities and a significant input by the People's Liberation Army. Much work of local significance is done by production brigades, communes, and counties.

The result has been that many rural people's communes are today linked by roads to nearby county towns and to provincial highways and railroads. Maintenance of the road, rail, and inland waterways system is the responsibility of local authorities with provincial and central state assistance in the case of the major arteries.The importance of an adequate transportation system to economic growth appears to be understood, as is the contribution of telecommunications to the management of a centrally planned, operationally decentralized economy.

Domestic and Foreign Trade

China also understands the importance to economic growth of domestic and, increasingly so, foreign trade (Chapter 8). Domestic commerce is carried on by state trading corporations and trade cooperatives at state-fixed prices. Among the peculiarities of the system, compared with other socialist countries, is the large number of basic level (retail) trading points, a fact that to a degree reduces user frustrations in what is still a sellers' market. Flanking the state commercial network are some 33,000 comparatively free peasant markets on which the produce of household subsidiary activity is exchanged, and a rising number of individually owned retail stores (10,000 in Shanghai in mid-1980). Since 1977 the authorities have been increasingly responsive to customer needs.The officially encouraged asceticism of the Mao era was after 1976 attributed to the hypocritical machinations of the gang of four, and the late chairman's own mistakes. The workers' desire to acquire not just the basics of survival but some "secondary" goods as well, and to live in less cramped conditions were recognized as fully socialist and legitimate provided the means of acquisition were earned through honest labor. Honesty, too, came to be defined in laws and regulations that were to be enforced not by the whim of the masses, but by duly constituted public security, procuratorial, and judicial organs under Party supervision.The official post-Mao (Hua-Deng) recognition of the consumers' right to consume was prompted, at least in part, by the concurrent recognition that the incentive system was inadequate and that individual material incentives had to be strengthened if production and productivity were to pick up and the four modernizations were to be successful. Provision of consumer goods in quantities and qualities consonant with the money demand for them was seen as a key link in the reform of the motivational system. To improve retail distribution and the availability of consumer services, individuals were granted permission to engage in peddler-type trade, and groups of individuals were encouraged to form (fairly loose) cooperative undertakings in the cities: paintshops, furniture-manufacturing workshops, barbershops, repair centers for bicycles and handcars, child-care centers, kindergartens, and so on. [25] In addition to filling a service need, such activities, it was hoped, would help absorb urban teenage unemployment.

Until the mid-1970s foreign trade was viewed as a residual activity. External exchanges were insulated from the domestic market by the state's foreign trade monopoly, a situation that was altered marginally in 1978–1979 by the proliferation of agencies (including enterprises) that began to deal directly with foreign buyers and sellers. This development was to be brought under central control, however, since it contributed to the inflation of Chinese orders for foreign plant and equipment, an inflation that put a great strain on China's ability to meet its financial obligations. The principle that governed foreign trade transactions before 1977 was rooted in the perceived need to maintain equilibrium between imports and exports and to avoid medium- and long-term foreign indebtedness. Moreover, until the mid-1970s foreign offers of credits were few and the terms were not liberal. Another basic rule, practiced since 1961, was to deal with any party willing to trade on the condition that such transactions did not in any way infringe on national sovereignty, domestic socialist construction, and the leadership's (somewhat divided) perception of international socialist solidarity and revolutionary purpose. In this perspective, even South Africa and Rhodesia could at times be used to further international proletarian objectives, a viewpoint not shared by all sections of the leadership.

Although the conduct of foreign trade is harmonized with the domestic political mass line of the moment, in practice external commercial transactions were at all times carried out scrupulously in accordance with the code of internationally acceptable business conduct. Chinese foreign trade officials have shown themselves to be sharp negotiators and quick learners. Increasingly they have displayed a willingness to research foreign demand patterns, however exotic these may appear in their eyes. Such adaptability is necessary because exports have been and remain, with the exception of remittances from overseas Chinese,

[25] "More Licenses for Individual Laborers," *Beijing Review*, December 7, 1979, pp. 5–6.

the most important source of revenue to pay for required imports. If the promise of oil finds on the mainland and in offshore areas materializes, in the coming decades China may emerge as one of the world's major earners of foreign currency from the sale of petroleum, a development that would be welcome in view of China's ambitious post-Mao import program.

The structure of Chinese imports has been altered since 1960, the most notable change being the importation of significant quantities of grain, especially wheat, from the West. There has also been stress, especially after 1976, on the import of advanced technology embodied in capital goods and of complete sets of industrial plant and equipment, particularly in the areas of petrochemicals, steel, nonferrous metal industries, mining, farm machinery and equipment, and transportation-telecommunications. The structure of exports underwent a slower secular transformation in the direction of processed foods and manufactured consumer goods. China, however, is still primarily an exporter of raw and semiprocessed agricultural materials.

Aid in the form of loans and some outright gifts has been given to selected friends and actual or potential allies in Africa and Asia. In addition to military assistance (hardware and strategic-tactical information), the Chinese have helped in railroad and highway construction, tea and cotton cultivation, water conservation, and public health work.

There is no doubt that the great significance attached to external economic transactions and the many flexible, pragmatic arrangements introduced in China to facilitate the flow of foreign trade, investment, and payments are among the more spectacular policy reorientations of the post-Mao, post-gang era. The four modernizations depend to a crucial extent on the massive importation of advanced foreign technology and equipment. The virtues of self-help and of turning inward upon one's own resources and peasant capabilities propagated during Mao's lifetime have been brutally shunted aside and given at best a grudging ritual bow. But unease persisted in many quarters about the rush to buy and learn from abroad. In 1979 there was still a palpable fear of future retribution by a resurgent left, a possibility that conceivably could materialize if the modernization drive ground to a halt and the high expectations of the late seventies turned out to have been a mirage. At a forum on the world economy held in Beijing in the summer of 1979 the participants huddled together and tried to reassure one another: "as this subject was trampled on by Lin Biao and the gang of four for years, many people still have a lingering fear about studying foreign things and there are still many forbidden zones that they dare not enter." [26] There was occasional thunder from an unrepentant left: "With bread in your mouths you complain loudly: 'We are too backward'!" [27]

Public Health and Education

The task of providing for the physical and mental well-being of the population has been tackled through vast public health and educational offensives (Chapter 9). The results of the public health program are less controversial than those of the educational program.

After 1965 in public health the problem of qualified manpower was attacked by enlisting the services of rapidly trained paramedics and by recruiting practitioners of traditional Chinese medicine. This entailed simplification and shortening of medical education and the transfer of large numbers of doctors and nurses to the countryside on both permanent and temporary (rotating) assignments. To correct the geographical maldistribution of medical and public health workers, significant numbers of those sent down to the country were settled in the less developed, inland, rural areas. The problem of financing a nationwide medical-public health system was approached through the establishment of the Cooperative Medical Service and its urban equivalent (both largely self-supporting), the use of herbal medicines and acupuncture, and the simplification and telescoping of medical training. Public health personnel not only take care of the medical and hygienic needs of the population; they also act as agents of the state for family planning.

After the death of Mao and the removal of the leftists, parts of the public health reform dating from the Cultural Revolution (some, like the barefoot doctors, going back to the Great Leap Forward) were subjected to critical professional scrutiny. The Maoists claimed, among other things, that certain subjects on the medical schools' curriculum could be removed since they were no longer relevant to the social conditions of new China.

The "description of utopia without thieves and gangsters is at best exaggerated. If what [was said was] true, then the public security procuratorial, and judicial personnel might fluff up their pillows and go to sleep. . . . Even a primary school pupil knows the falsehood of such a statement. . . . Seamy aspects of the proletariat and its allies, of Party

[26] Beijing Radio, July 28, 1979, in *FBIS*, August 1, 1979.

[27] Li Jian, " 'Praise Virtue' or 'Lack Virtue,' " *Hebei Wenxue*, No. 6 (1979), reprinted by *Renmin Ribao*, July 31, 1979, in *FBIS*, August 14, 1979.

and government cadres, and of socialist society and the tragedies that have occurred should be exposed and satirized if they are real and typical.'' [28] In the post-Mao climate of seeking truth from facts, the Maoist picture of China as a land and people without rape and prostitution, almost free of violent crime, with healthy skins, and no psychiatric disorders was laid to rest together with other fantasies.The medical curriculum was lengthened, entrance requirements for medical schools were stiffened, professional requirements for graduation and certification were raised, laboratories were reopened, and graduate study was taken up again.The compulsory settlement of medical personnel in the countryside was reexamined together with the broader concept and policy of rustication.The need to upgrade the quality of paramedics and public health workers so as to reduce the incidence of faulty diagnosis and incompetent treatment was urged.The precise place (scientific and economic) of traditional Chinese medicine in the overall provision of medical and public health care became the subject of professional discussions at national and specialized forums.The xenophobic assumption that because it was Chinese it was ipso facto good was no longer accepted. [29] It is possible that the professionalization and a certain reurbanization of China's medical and public-health services might result in the neglect of the vast countryside where most of China's population lives and where most physical ills occur.There has been anxiety over this among sections of the post-Mao leadership and there have been the usual dire warnings from the defeated but still breathing left. In this as in other fields, the danger exists that the scientific, technological, and economic imperatives of modernization will assert themselves through short-term neglect of social welfare and equity considerations, especially in rural areas. At some point this could produce a politically explosive situation.The rural medical cooperative service, one of the ''new socialist things'' born of the Cultural Revolution, had not been disbanded by the end of the 1970s, but—together with other newborn socialist things—it was being critically evaluated, ''rationalized,'' and professionally upgraded.

More than other endeavors, education in China has been synonymous with the stimulation of proletarian political consciousness. Its precise modalities and the principles that should guide learning have

[28] *Guangming Ribao*, July 20, 1979, in *FBIS*, August 14, 1979.

[29] ''During the days of their ascendancy, Lin Biao and the gang of four pursued an obscurantist policy, always frantically proclaiming that 'the old man is No. 1 in the world' and that everything Chinese is good.'' *Guangming Ribao*, July 20, 1979 (refutation of article by Li Jian published in *Hebei Wenxue*, No. 6, 1976), in *FBIS*, August 14, 1979.

been the subject of bitter controversy in high places. After the reorganization of the educational system in 1952 along Soviet lines, the most important events have been the Cultural Revolution (1966–1969) and its predecessor the Socialist Education Campaign (1963–1964). Both were intended to promote the Maoist, Yanan line on education, and both—but especially the Cultural Revolution—shook the school system to its foundations. The Yanan way abhors elitism, structures, credentialism, and the functional distinction between professional competence and political awareness (the "red versus expert" dilemma). It puts a premium on knowledge grounded in practice, especially manual practice, correctly inspired self-study based on case-by-case investigations, applied science, and the presumed creativity of poor and lower-middle peasants. It opposes the pursuit of knowledge for its own sake or for the sake of personal material and status advancement, and spurns—at least on the rhetorical plane—pure ("exotic") research. It is torn between its subjective opposition to the absolute authority of the teacher and the objective need for everyone to think and act alike.

After the fall of the gang of four and the death of the gang's protector, large parts of the Yanan educational philosophy and of that philosophy's Cultural Revolutionary extensions were thrown out. The major change consisted in a reduction in the purely ideological content of education; not the removal of ideology from the curriculum, but a readjustment of the proportions devoted to the acquisition of scientific and professional knowledge *sensu stricto* and of political consciousness. The content of political consciousness was recast in a rightward mold, to make it serve, or at least not obstruct, the four modernizations. The stress thenceforth was to be on brains rather than ideological mouthing. Ability was to be tested and confirmed by examinations administered by the educational establishment and containing primarily questions on "book knowledge." The pervasive anti-intellectualism of the Maoist era was replaced by an almost frenetic official adoration of intellectual accomplishment that at the policy level was translated into yet another united front. "Key" elite schools catering to exceptionally talented students—especially in mathematics and the natural sciences—reemerged from twenty years in limbo. Curricula at all levels were beefed up, students (most of them in their thirties) were sent abroad, foreign instructors were invited to come to China, and plays, operas, films, literature, and music not seen or heard for years were again allowed. On the literary front—as on others—opposition continued to this relative blossoming of the hundred flowers (relative because of the still existing, rather arbitrary prohibition against "bad," "corrupting," and "counterrevolutionary" literary and artistic productions). [30] As late as June 1979 a provincial literary magazine, *Hebei Literature (Hebei Wenxue)* published a virulent attack on the liberalized new course. As later commentators put it, it used "disgusting language" and "wielded a stick randomly." [31] After ritually conceding that "of course, a 'shameless dog's' literature and art singing the praises of the gang of four should be repudiated," the article went on to ask: "is it not good to praise Chairman Mao . . . and his brilliant thought?"—a delicate question. It then expounded the left doctrine on literature and art and berated literary elitism.

> In a class society every writer must have a class character; there are no superclass so-called "pastoral poets." Revolutionary writers must be the eyes of the class and the hands and feet of the people.They must share weal and woe with the Party. . . . Those who advocate that literature and art are without class or Party character are no better than worms in the decomposed bodies of the revisionist mentors buried in the rubbish heap of history. . . . Sunflowers always lend a fantastic beauty to the golden sun, whereas beasts which hide in dark corners and are fond of smelling the stink of blood and sludge, can only curse the red sun. . . . Some people refuse to go deep into the masses, saying that they suffer a lot while immersing themselves with the laboring people whose feet are smeared with cowdung and whose hands are soiled. . . .They claim to be high and lofty and detach themselves from the workers and peasants. How can they create excellent works by simply wracking their brains under green willow trees? . . . We must annoint our works with the peasant fragrance of soil and grease so they will shine with the brilliance of youthful vigor.

Little wonder that the post-gang line on education, literature, and art, like the post-Mao line on almost everything else, suffered from an acute case of nerves acquired during the Cultural Revolution, the Great Leap Forward, the anti-rightist witch hunts of 1957, and other Maoist and ultraleft periods. [32] Also, education, art, and literature had been un-

[30]On July 24, 1979, *Renmin Ribao* explained for the benefit of anyone who still might not have been clear on the subject, that "a counterrevolutionary crime is a crime against the revolution." It also noted that during the reign of the gang "the number of wrong and false counterrevolutionary cases handled . . . accounted for about 40 percent as a whole, as high as 60 or 70 percent in some areas." "We must pay attention to the criteria and suppress the genuine counterrevolutionaries, not the phoney ones." All of which is, of course, a matter of the interpretation of the line, or Lenin's old "who whom?."

[31]*Hebei Ribao*, July 22, 1979, reprinted in *Renmin Ribao*, July 31, 1979, in *FBIS*, August 14, 1979.The original article was titled " 'Praise Virtue' or 'Lack Virtue,' " by Li Jian, *Hebei Wenxue*, No. 6 (1979), reprinted in *Renmin Ribao*, July 31, 1979, in *FBIS*, August 14, 1979.

[32]The press tried to give practical examples of the criterion of truth. "For example, the machines of the [Mihe, Yidu County, Shandong Province] pumping station had been seriously sabotaged. It was first suspected that this might have been done by class enemies. A final investigation, however, clearly showed that the sabotage was caused by some ten-

shackled in a quite limited way. They still had to share weal and woe with the Party. The Party had changed only its leading personnel, and sharing weal and woe with it now meant promoting the four modernizations. After mid-1980 the process of de-Maoization was accelerated and made more explicit. Mao's precept that "we should not fear heaven, we should not fear ghosts, we should not fear the dead," was turned against him. "If a leader's wisdom were boundless, his theory absolutely correct, his plan absolutely effective and his role all-decisive, then, he would no longer be a man of this world: he would be a 'god.'. . . Fundamentally, isn't this just modern supersition and personality cult?" [33] "[Mao] was a man, not a god, and he was not immune to mistakes." [34]

The Chinese economy is at a crossroads, the search is on for new methods and structures that will help raise factor productivity and promote the modernization of the country. The search is marked by an unprecedented willingness to learn from foreign experience and a realism that had long been absent. It would be fruitless to make firm predictions about the direction the economic system might take, the extent and durability of reforms, and final outcomes. But one cannot help but remain cautiously optimistic. The optimism rests on an analysis of the record, which for all its blotches remains impressive, and on a recognition of the enormous store of talent, application, and organizational ability that is China's. The greatest question is the same as in 1919: "The most important problem confronting the Chinese people is to have enough to eat." [35]

SUGGESTED READING

Barnett, A. Doak, *Uncertain Passage: China's Transition to the Post-Mao Era* (Washington, D.C.: Brookings Institution, 1974).

year-old children who removed electric wires and spare parts." "A pile of fagots in the home of a production team leader was burned down. Final investigation showed that the pile of fagots was burned down by an unconvinced and angry commune member who had been criticized by the team leader in an oversimplified and crude way." i.e., it had "nothing to do with landlords, rich peasants, counterrevolutionaries, and other evil elements." The problems were "all caused by daily trifles among the people." *Renmin Ribao*, August 8, 1979, in *FBIS*, August 14, 1979.

[33] "On the Role of the Individual in History," *Renmin Ribao,* July 4, 1980, in *Beijing Review,* August 11, 1980, p. 20.

[34] Hua Guofeng interview with Yugoslav correspondent D. Janekovic, July 26, 1980, in *Bejing Review,* August 18, 1980, p. 14.

[35] Deng Xiaoping, October 15, 1979, in *Beijing Review*, January 14, 1980, p. 21.

Baum, Richard (ed.), *China's Four Modernizations: The New Technological Revolution* (Boulder, Colo.: Westview Press, 1980).

Bucknall, Kevin B., "Some Evidence on Managerial Behavior in Chinese Industry," *Bulletin of the Association for Comparative Economic Studies* (Bloomington, Ind.), Vol. XXI, No. 2, Summer 1979, pp. 53–69.

"China's Perception of the World in the 1970's." Twenty-two articles from P.R.C. sources. *Chinese Law and Government* (White Plains, N.Y.), Vol. IX, Nos. 1–2, Spring–Summer 1976.

Dernberger, Robert F., "Prospects for the Chinese Economy," *Problems of Communism* (Washington, D.C.), Vol. XXVIII, Nos. 5–6, September–December 1979, pp. 1–15.

Dittmer, Lowell, "The Legacy of Mao Zedong," *Asian Survey* (Berkeley, Calif.), Vol. 20, no. 5, May 1980, pp. 552–73.

Domes, Jürgen (ed.), *Chinese Politics after Mao* (Cardiff: University College Cardiff Press, 1979), Chapters by J. S. Prybyla, E. B. Vermeer, M. C. Bergère, D. Duncanson, C. W. Wu, and H. W. Wang.

Eckstein, Alexander, *China's Economic Revolution* (New York: Cambridge University Press, 1977).

Kraus, Willy, *Wirtschaftliche Entwicklung und sozialer Wandel in der Volksrepublik China* (Berlin, Heidelberg, New York: Springer-Verlag, 1979).

Matthews, Jay, "China after Mao." Three reports. *Washington Post* (Washington, D.C.), May 15, 16, and 17, 1977.

Michael, Franz, "In Search of a Chinese Future," *Asian Affairs: An American Review* (New York), Vol. II, No. 3, January–February 1975, pp. 129–44.

Prybyla, Jan S., "Changes in the Chinese Economy: An Interpretation," *Asian Survey* (Berkeley), Vol. XIX, No. 5, May 1979, pp. 409–35.

———, "China in the 1980s," *Challenge* (White Plains, N.Y.) May–June 1980, pp. 4–20.

Schram, Stuart R., "Chairman Hua Edits Mao's Literary Heritage: 'On the Ten Great Relationships,' " *China Quarterly* (London), No. 69, March 1977, pp. 126–35.

Index